REIMAGINING SHAKESPEARE FOR CHILDREN AND YOUNG ADULTS

Children's Literature and Culture
Jack Zipes, *Series Editor*

WHITE SUPREMACY IN CHILDREN'S
LITERATURE
*Characterizations of African Americans,
1830–1900*
by Donnarae MacCann

RETELLING STORIES, FRAMING CULTURE
*Traditional Story and Metanarratives in
Children's Literature*
by John Stephens and Robyn McCallum

THE CASE OF PETER RABBIT
*Changing Conditions of Literature for
Children*
by Margaret Mackey

VOICES OF THE OTHER
*Children's Literature and the
Postcolonial Context*
edited by Roderick McGillis

EMPIRE'S CHILDREN
*Empire and Imperialism in Classic
British Children's Books*
by M. Daphne Kutzer

A NECESSARY FANTASY?
*The Heroic Figure in Children's Popular
Culture*
edited by Dudley Jones and Tony Watkins

LITTLE WOMEN AND THE FEMINIST
IMAGINATION
Criticism, Controversy, Personal Essays
edited by Janice M. Alberghene and
Beverly Lyon Clark

IDEOLOGIES OF IDENTITY IN ADOLESCENT
FICTION
by Robyn McCallum

NARRATING AFRICA
George Henty and the Fiction of Empire
by Mawuena Kossi Logan

TRANSCENDING BOUNDARIES
*Writing for a Dual Audience of Children
and Adults*
edited by Sandra L. Beckett

CHILDREN'S FILMS
History, Ideology, Pedagogy, Theory
by Ian Wojcik-Andrews

RUSSELL HOBAN/FORTY YEARS
Essays on His Writings for Children
by Alida Allison

TRANSLATING FOR CHILDREN
by Riitta Oittinen

THE PRESENCE OF THE PAST
*Memory, Heritage, and Childhood in
Postwar Britain*
by Valerie Krips

INVENTING THE CHILD
*Culture, Ideology, and the Story of
Childhood*
by Joseph L. Zornado

PINOCCHIO GOES POSTMODERN
Perils of a Puppet in the United States
by Richard Wunderlich and
Thomas J. Morrissey

WAYS OF BEING MALE
*Representing Masculinities in
Children's Literature and Film*
by John Stephens

THE FEMININE SUBJECT IN CHILDREN'S
LITERATURE
by Christine Wilkie-Stibbs

RECYCLING RED RIDING HOOD
by Sandra Beckett

THE POETICS OF CHILDHOOD
by Roni Natov

REIMAGINING SHAKESPEARE FOR
CHILDREN AND YOUNG ADULTS
edited by Naomi J. Miller

REPRESENTING THE HOLOCAUST IN YOUTH
LITERATURE
by Lydia Kokkola

REIMAGINING SHAKESPEARE FOR CHILDREN AND YOUNG ADULTS

EDITED BY
NAOMI J. MILLER

ROUTLEDGE
NEW YORK AND LONDON

Published in 2003 by
Routledge
270 Madison Ave,
New York NY 10016

Published in Great Britain by
Routledge
2 Park Square, Milton Park,
Abingdon, Oxon, OX14 4RN

Transferred to Digital Printing 2009

Library of Congress Cataloging-in-Publication Data

Reimagining Shakespeare for children and young adults / edited by Naomi
J. Miller.
     p. cm.—(Children's literature and culture; 25)
   Includes bibliographical references and index.
   ISBN 0-415-93856-2
     1. Shakespeare, William, 1564–1616—Adaptations—History and criti-
cism. 2. Shakespeare, William, 1564–1616—Film and video adaptations. 3.
Shakespeare, William, 1564–1616—Dramatic production. 4. Shakespeare,
William, 1564–1616—Study and teaching. 5. Young adult drama—Study
and teaching. 6. Children's plays—Study and teaching. 7. Children's
plays—Presentation, etc. 8. Drama in education. I. Miller, Naomi J., 1960-
II. Children's literature and culture (Routledge (Firm)); 25.

PR2880.A1 R45 2002
822.3'3—dc21   2002007397

ISBN10: 0-415-93856-2 (hbk)
ISBN10: 0-415-80360-8 (pbk)

ISBN13: 978-0-415-93856-3 (hbk)
ISBN13: 978-0-415-80360-1 (pbk)

For Bruce

Contents

Series Editor's Foreword   xi

     Jack Zipes

Acknowledgments   xii

**"What's in a Name?": Collaborating with
Shakespeare at the Millennium**

     Naomi J. Miller   1

I. Biography, Adaptation, and Fictionalization   11

1. In Love with Shakespeare

     Aliki   13

2. The Story Behind the Man Behind the Plays

     Diane Stanley   22

3. Bravo, Mr. William Shakespeare!

     Marcia Williams   29

**4. "This is Young William": Shakespeare and
the Cumulative Tale**

     Rebecca Piatt Davidson   39

5. "All the Colours of the Wind":
Shakespeare and the Primary Student

    Lois Burdett   44

6. Nutshells and Infinite Space:
Stages of Adaptation

    Bruce Coville   56

7. Puck's Gift

    Sophie Masson   67

8. Shakespeare Speaks: Getting the
Language Right

    Gary Blackwood   74

9. The Players, the Playmaker, and Us

    J. B. Cheaney   81

II. Interpretation and Critique   87

10. Staging Shakespeare's Children

    Mark H. Lawhorn   89

11. Canning the Classic: Race and Ethnicity in the
Lambs' *Tales from Shakespeare*

    James Andreas   98

12. Alice Reads Shakespeare: Charles Dodgson and
the Girl's Shakespeare Project

    Georgianna Ziegler   107

13. Strutting and Fretting on the Page: Representing
Shakespeare'sTheater in Illustrated Books

    Megan Lynn Isaac   120

14. Mediating the Supernatural in Adaptations of
Shakespeare for Children: Three Unique
Productions through Text and Illustration

    Douglas King   129

15. **"The Play's the Thing": Genre and Adaptations of Shakespeare for Children**

Alison H. Prindle 138

16. **Promoting the Original: Perspectives on Balancing Authenticity and Creativity in Adaptations of *The Tempest***

Amy E. Mathur 147

17. **First One I and Then the Other: Identity and Intertexuality in Shakespeare's Caliban and Covington's Lizard**

Cynthia Perantoni 153

18. **Harry Potter and the Shakespearean Allusion**

Miranda Johnson-Haddad 162

19. **Playing with Shakespeare: Making Worlds from Words**

Jennifer Lee Carrell 171

20. **Descending Shakespeare: Toward a Theory of Adaptation for Children**

Howard Marchitello 180

III. Pedagogy and Performance 191

21. **The Bard for Babies: Shakespeare, Bettelheim, and the Reggio Emilia Model of Early Childhood Education**

Sheila Cavanagh 193

22. **Visions of Shakespeare in a Montessori Classroom**

Regine Ebner 201

23. **Shakespeare Steps Out: The Primacy of Language in Inner-City Classrooms**

Janet Field-Pickering 207

24. "Your Play Needs No Excuse": Shakespeare and
    Language Development in Children

    Kristen L. Olson   217

25. Players, Playgrounds, and Grounds for Play:
    Play v. Theater v. Realism in a Touring Children's
    Version of *King Lear*

    John Barnes   231

26. Presenting Shakespeare's Life and Times for Young
    People: An Outline Using *Midsummer Night's Dream*
    and Susan Cooper's *King of Shadows*

    Tiffany A. Conroy   239

27. Understanding Texts and Contexts: Teaching
    Shakespeare to Future High School Teachers

    Pamela J. Benson   252

28. Redistributing the Riches: Shakespearean
    Adaptation in *Moss Gown* and *Mama Day*

    Caroline McManus   260

29. Learning by Playing: Performance Games and
    the Teaching of Shakespeare

    Greg Maillet   269

30. Reimagining Shakespeare through Film

    Gregory Colón Semenza   279

31. Performing Pedagogy

    Edward L. Rocklin   289

Bibliography   298

Contributors   305

Permissions   311

Index   312

Series Editor's Foreword

Dedicated to furthering original research in children's literature and culture, the Children's Literature and Culture series includes monographs on individual authors and illustrators, historical examinations of different periods, literary analyses of genres, and comparative studies on literature and the mass media. The series is international in scope and is intended to encourage innovative research in children's literature with a focus on interdisciplinary methodology.

Children's literature and culture are understood in the broadest sense of the term children to encompass the period of childhood up through adolescence. Owing to the fact that the notion of childhood has changed so much since the origination of children's literature, this Routledge series is particularly concerned with transformations in children's culture and how they have affected the representation and socialization of children. While the emphasis of the series is on children's literature, all types of studies that deal with children's radio, film, television, and art are included in an endeavor to grasp the aesthetics and values of children's culture. Not only have there been momentous changes in children's culture in the last fifty years, but there have been radical shifts in the scholarship that deals with these changes. In this regard, the goal of the Children's Literature and Culture series is to enhance research in this field and, at the same time, point to new directions that bring together the best scholarly work throughout the world.

Jack Zipes

Acknowledgments

My first thanks go to Anne Davidson, the Routledge Senior Editor who recognized the potential in a volume of essays addressing the topic of reimagining Shakespeare for children, and saw the volume through a gestational period that included the gestation and birth of her own child. Emily Vail assisted in the multiple particulars of the production process with patience and good humor. I would like to express my appreciation as well to Jack Zipes, the Editor of the Routledge Children's Literature and Culture Series, who granted the manuscript its first reading and offered it a place in the series.

This volume of essays originated in a seminar on "Playing with the Bard: Shakespeare for Children at the Millennium," at the Shakespeare Association of America (SAA) Conference that took place in Montreal on April 8, 2000. The seminar was particularly noteworthy for involving not only Shakespeare scholars and teachers, as is traditional at SAA conferences, but also children's book authors who had adapted Shakespeare's plays for younger audiences. The two children's book authors, Lois Burdett and Bruce Coville, who participated in that seminar also spoke in a larger SAA panel on "Writing, Publishing, and Performing Shakespeare for Children Today." Their essays from that conference appear in this volume, along with essays by all the other members of that seminar, which included Pamela Benson, Janet Field-Pickering, Megan Isaac, Douglas King, Gregory Maillet, Howard Marchitello, Amy Mathur, Kristen Olson, Alison Prindle, and Tiffany Conroy. I believe it would not be an exaggeration to observe that the 2000 SAA seminar offered a "sea change" for many of the participants, who shared their passionate delight at bringing Shakespeare to children of all levels, in the intellectually rigorous and professionally liberating context of the seminar setting. I would like to thank each member of that SAA seminar for the playful and probing attention to the topic that resulted in many of the essays in this volume, and to extend my thanks as well to other SAA colleagues, such as Sheila Cavanagh and Miranda Johnson-Haddad, whose observations helped to extend the parameters of this volume. I particularly want to thank SAA Executive Director Lena Cowen Orlin, for her unremitting encouragement and support.

The next conference occasion that supported the emergence of this volume was a panel of children's book authors on "Reimagining Shakespeare for Children and Young Adults," at the International Reading Association Conference in New Orleans on May 29, 2001. The participants in that panel, all of whom have essays in this volume, included Marcia Williams, Aliki, Bruce Coville, Sophie Masson, Gary Blackwood, and J. B. Cheaney. Speaking to an audience of educators, these children's book authors electrified their listeners with their accounts of their journeys through and with Shakespeare. I was privileged to work with these authors on that panel, and I want to express my gratitude to each of them for their love of Shakespeare and their dedication to bringing Shakespeare alive to a range of audiences.

The realization of the concept for this volume would not have been complete without the continuing motivation of my students at the University of Arizona, whose participation in my "Adapting Literary Classics for Children" seminars, at both the undergraduate and graduate levels, challenge me daily to rethink the parameters of my own engagement with the topic, and bring me the greatest joys as a teacher of Shakespeare that I have ever experienced in the classroom. Working with my students, many of whom are current schoolteachers or aspiring schoolteachers, and working with my own children's classroom teachers as a parent volunteer, observing their work with children in primary and secondary school classrooms over the course of several years, I have come to understand that anything is possible where Shakespeare is concerned: no audience is too young, no students too unprepared, to appreciate the magic of Shakespeare's words and worlds. For that, and for so much else, I thank all of my students in those classes, and all of the children and teachers with whom my students have worked in so many classroom settings. The deep delight of engaging with Shakespeare at such a multiplicity of levels has brought me the closest to feeling that I have begun to realize my own potential as a teacher and lover of Shakespeare in twenty years in the classroom so far.

I must thank, as well, my close friends and Shakespeare colleagues around the country, most particularly Mary Thomas Crane and Howard Marchitello, who have shared with me the sometimes bemusing yet always invigorating experience of being, simultaneously, parents and Shakespeare professors. Through many shared conversations, and much laughter as well as some groans, we are realizing the profound pleasures and continuing challenges of bringing Shakespeare to our own children, inextricably intertwining our work and life perspectives on this "brave new world." Speaking of which, my next heartfelt thanks go to my four children, Fiona, Isaiah, Damaris, and Elias, who have been audience and actors of Shakespeare in their own right, reading, reciting and reimagining passages and poems over the many years that we have shared Shakespeare. Their presence in my life inspired me to begin to explore the connections that led to my classroom seminars, my conference panels, and ultimately to the compilation of the essays for this volume. And their varying degrees of patience with the piles of manuscripts adorning my study floor instructed me in the necessity of securing "a local habitation and a name" for my work, in order to enlist their support, if not always consciously, for this project.

I want to give special thanks to Bruce Coville, with whom I am collaborating on a novel, called *Sea Changes*, that reimagines Shakespeare's *The Tempest* for a young adult audience. My final appreciation goes to my husband, Hugh, whose tolerance for my enthusiastic book-purchasing practices during the course of my work on this volume has been complemented by his willingness to support my venture into the field of reimagining Shakespeare in my own writing. My work on the novel as well as on this volume of essays has taught me that sea changes are not only possible, but essential.

"What's in a Name?"

Collaborating with Shakespeare at the Millennium

NAOMI J. MILLER

"What's in a name?" asks Juliet, observing: "That which we call a rose / By any other word would smell as sweet."[1] What *is* in a name? The name of William Shakespeare has exerted a powerful force in the development of Western culture for over four hundred years now. Shakespeare's plays have been produced and transformed in many media over the centuries, enabling not only countless dramatic performances and film productions in the twentieth century alone, but also numerous other "reimaginings," from poems and novels, paintings and operas, to video games and Web sites.[2] Confronted with this plethora of imaginative engagements with Shakespeare's plays, one might be tempted to ask, "Will the real William Shakespeare please stand up?"

But of course that is the point: to a contemporary audience the *real* William Shakespeare is as much, or indeed even more, a product of our millennial culture as he is a representative voice of Renaissance England. What's in a name? Immense marketing potential for one thing, with the resounding success of Marc Norman and Tom Stoppard's screenplay for *Shakespeare in Love* indicating only the tip of the popular-culture iceberg,[3] not to mention the triumphant debuts of such other contemporary film versions of Shakespeare's plays as Baz Luhrmann's *Romeo + Juliet* and Michael Almereyda's *Hamlet*. It might be argued, of course, that the issue is not simply the name of Shakespeare, but rather the endlessly versatile appeal of the plays themselves, and perhaps the brilliant ingenuity evidenced by such individual productions as those mentioned above. At the same time, the name of Shakespeare does prove on many occasions to be more than the sum of his plays.

To return to Shakespeare's own words for a moment, when Juliet asks "What's in a name?" she is apparently attempting to convince herself that only Romeo's name of Montague, and not his beloved self, is her enemy. She wishes aloud that he would "be some other name / Belonging to a man," just as "a rose / By any other word would smell as sweet."[4] And yet the aria of

1

Juliet's outpouring of passion rings musical changes upon the repeated use of the very name that she seemingly wishes to discount, so that her twice-repeated invocation of the name "Montague" in two lines, followed by her thrice-repeated verbal caress of the name "Romeo" in three lines conveys her aural delight in the very name itself.

Overhearing her reflections, Romeo's impulse is to offer to doff his name and be "new baptized," so that were his name to be written, he would "tear the word."[5] And yet Juliet's immediate response after having "drunk a hundred words" of his voice is to exclaim: "I know the sound. Art thou not Romeo and a Montague?"[6] Everything, it turns out, must be understood in relation to the name after all, from the unmistakably sensory, and sensual, "sound" of Romeo's voice to the function of his name as a harbor for Juliet's passion. What's in a name? Only all the world—for that which we name, we believe we can know.

Shakespeare's worlds of words cannot be separated from the almost incantatory power of his name in contemporary Western culture any more than Romeo's name can be separated in Juliet's ears from the sound of his voice. The consequences of this synergy of name and voice in the example of Shakespeare must not be underestimated, for whenever another writer or composer or artist dares to reimagine one of Shakespeare's plays in a new form, the name of Shakespeare can be and has been invoked as the ultimate weapon in ratifying the literary status quo, however variously that status quo might be defined. Thus, more often than one might think, the attitude of "how dare one meddle with the Bard?" surfaces in the face of imaginative transformations of "the source" of Shakespeare.

And yet, as not only any scholar but also many popular audiences for Shakespeare's plays are well aware, "the Bard" himself was notoriously adept at manipulating *his* sources, changing plot lines, adding characters, often shifting the entire dramatic logic of a story in order to achieve the emotional resonance of a brave new world about which, could his sources have complained, he might have observed " 'Tis new to thee."[7] Which brings me to the subject of this present volume of essays: reimagining Shakespeare for children and young adults.

Of all the new audiences for Shakespeare, children and young adults are at once the most open and enthusiastic as well as potentially the most likely to be misdirected or even disappointed by their initial encounters with the Bard. At the same time, children and young adults represent an enormous potential market for Shakespearean material, both through the school systems of Great Britain and the United States in particular as well as through such mass market adaptations as the popular film version of *The Taming of the Shrew* known as *Ten Things I Hate About You*, and such video versions of the plays as the Wishbone *Hamlet*. And yet we have not come too far from Baz Luhrmann and Michael Almereyda even now.

The point of all these reimaginings is really best summed up, once again, in Shakespeare's own words, when Duke Theseus muses in *A Midsummer Night's Dream* that "as imagination bodies forth / The forms of things unknown, the poet's pen / Turns them to shapes, and gives to airy nothing / A local habitation and a name."[8] What's in a name? Not less than everything, for the poet's pen succeeds in making the unknown knoweable by giving to airy nothing "a local habitation and a name." And that is precisely how, at this moment, we can reunderstand the potentially elusive four-hundred-year-old airy nothings of a playwright named William Shakespeare when they are bodied forth in such reimaginings as Baz Luhrmann's *Romeo + Juliet* or Michael Almereyda's *Hamlet*, Jane Smiley's *A Thousand Acres* or John Updike's *Gertrude and Claudius*.[9]

With each such reimagining, we are given, quite literally, "a local habitation and a name" within which to understand Shakespeare anew, whether in the local habitation of one thousand acres of Iowa farmland in the 1950s through which Jane Smiley reimagines *King Lear*, or in the unfamiliar names of Gerutha and Horwendil that John Updike takes from the late twelfth-century Latin text of the *Historia Danica* in order to reimagine the story of *Hamlet*.[10] These local habitations and names give new shapes to long-familiar plays, even as they serve as collaborative engagements with "the source" of Shakespeare that teach us to recognize Shakespeare's voice through the variations themselves. In the end, we might exclaim, with Juliet, "I know the sound."

And that is, finally, the heart of the issue in reimagining Shakespeare for children and young adults. Whether this audience comes to Shakespeare first through videos or Web sites, through picture books or young adult novels, through classroom performances or Royal Shakespeare Company productions, the shared aim of those authors and educators who work to reimagine Shakespeare with the immense range of ages and perspectives represented by this audience is to "know the sound." In other words, by exploring many of the different "local habitations and names" through which it is possible for young people to meet Shakespeare, both within the classroom and without, the goal is at once to communicate and experience together the synergy of name and voice that composes the words, and worlds, of William Shakespeare.

The present collection of essays focuses attention upon William Shakespeare not simply as a canonical, literary figure in college curriculums, or as a launching point for new critical trends in scholarly forums, but as a playing field for literacy and language arts as well as for creativity and dramatic learning, in education extending from elementary to graduate school levels, both inside and outside the classroom. The essays in the volume address reimaginings of Shakespeare that range from picture books and young adult novels to board games and films, and consider what this explosion of interest suggests regarding notions of literature and literacy, pedagogy and performance, and indeed notions of Shakespeare himself at the millennium. The first portion of the volume, "Biography, Adaptation, and Fictionalization," includes essays by a striking array of well-known children's book authors who are writing biographies of Shakespeare, adaptations of Shakespeare's plays, historical treatments of Shakespeare's theater, or fictionalizations of Shakespeare's period and characters, in genres extending from picture books to young adult novels. From Aliki and Marcia Williams to Bruce Coville and Gary Blackwood, the authors who work with Shakespeare for children and young adults offer their unique insights into the creative process.

The second portion of the volume, "Interpretation and Critique," includes essays by Shakespeare scholars and critics who explore adaptations and fictionalizations of Shakespeare's life and plays in written, pictorial, audio, and film genres, as well as in hands-on materials such as games. Whether considering the performative roles of children in productions of the plays, analyzing the implications of adapting Shakespeare as a source who himself adapted his sources, or exploring the relevance of Shakespearean allusions in J. K. Rowling's *Harry Potter* novels, these scholars investigate multiple strategies that link Shakespeare and young audiences.

The final section of the volume, "Pedagogy and Performance," includes essays by teachers of Shakespeare at all levels—from elementary school and high school to college and graduate school—sharing strategies for bringing Shakespeare into the classroom or onto the stage with children and young adults. The approaches extend from enacting Shakespeare scenes on a preschool playground in Atlanta, Georgia; in a Montessori classroom in Tucson, Arizona; and in inner-city schools in Washington, D.C.; to using performance pedagogy in college classrooms across the country to educate the next generation of high school teachers.

The volume as a whole aims to consider the effects of reimagining Shakespeare and his plays through different "local habitations and names," so that each new audience can experience for themselves the "rough magic" of the name of Shakespeare.[11]

The first section of the volume, "Biography, Adaptation, and Fictionalization," opens with an essay, entitled "In Love with Shakespeare," by the noted author-illustrator Aliki, who shares the transformative experience of living with the Bard when she constructed her picture book biography of Shakespeare, which combines biography and history in a "five-act" structure, and links the original Globe Theatre from the 1590s with the creation of the new Globe Theatre in the 1990s. Next, author-illustrator Diane Stanley offers "The Story Behind the Man Behind the Plays," illuminating her picture book narrative of Shakespeare's life and times. Bringing the trio of author-illustrators to a close, Marcia Williams discusses the evolution of her illustrated picture book versions of Shakespeare's plays, which utilize comic-strip style panels of texts and images surrounded by interactive border images of audience members commenting on the plays. In her essay titled "Shakespeare and the Cumulative Tale," new picture book author Rebecca Piatt Davidson reflects upon "the machinery of language, of imagination, of intimacy," in her cumulative verse lineup of the composition of Shakespeare's plays. Next, award-winning teacher and author Lois Burdett offers a narrative of her hands-on experience bringing Shakespeare into the elementary classroom in Stratford, Ontario, using her own *Shakespeare for Kids* adaptations of the plays.

In "Nutshells and Infinite Space: Stages of Adaptation," the immensely popular children's book author Bruce Coville writes with humor and ingenuity about the "terrifying privilege" of adapting five of Shakespeare's plays for publication in storybook format, moving from one "stage" to the next in order to capture the infinite space of each play within the nutshell-sized bounds of a picture book text. Coville also reflects on his strategic interweaving of Shakespearean story elements into one of his middle grade and one of his young adult novels. Then Australian author Sophie Masson explores the significance of "Puck's gift," or the way of the trickster, in enabling her fluid reimaginings of the magical worlds of Shakespeare, which combine fable with individual Shakespeare plays within the framework of young adult novels.

Gary Blackwood opens his essay on his middle grade novel *The Shakespeare Stealer* and its sequel, *Shakespeare's Scribe*, by confessing that he has never been to England, but suggesting that the point of "getting the language right" is that we come to know Shakespeare through the world of words. Finally, J. B. Cheaney offers a bird's-eye view of the journey across space and time that brought her to the creation of her young adult novel set in Shakespeare's space and time, and considers the freedom that Shakespeare's writings afford all who follow in his footsteps.

In the second section of the volume "Interpretation and Critique," Mark Lawhorn opens the critical consideration of how Shakespeare has been reimagined for young people across the centuries by focusing on the actual staging conditions and choices for child actors in Shakespearean productions, from the boy page in *Richard III*, to the lengthy child role of Moth in *Love's Labour's Lost*, and the crucial emotional part of Mamillius in *The Winter's Tale*. James Andreas takes up the matter of one of the first and still best-known reimaginings of Shakespeare for children, Charles and Mary Lamb's *Tales from Shakespeare* from the early nineteenth century, and scrutinizes the racial and ethnic implications of the Lambs' portrayal of Shakespeare's aliens—principally Shylock, Othello, and Caliban—in the narrative versions of their respective plays. Moving to the later nineteenth century, Georgianna Ziegler examines the provenance of the never-completed "Girls' Shakespeare Project" of Charles Dodgson (a.k.a. Lewis Carroll), and draws connections between the several *Alice in Wonderland* books and Dodgson's interest in Shakespeare's girl characters.

Subsequent essays in this second portion of the volume focus on twentieth-century adaptations of Shakespeare's plays for young people of all ages. Megan Isaac explores the ways in which the Globe Theatre and the world of Renaissance acting companies are represented both in non-fiction children's picture books, such as those by Aliki and Stuart Ross, Diane Stanley, and Peter Vennema, and in specific play adaptations, such as those by Margaret Early, and Bruce Coville and Dennis Nolan. Douglas King argues that one of the key attractions of Shakespeare's works for children is the presence of supernatural elements, and investigates how various authors and illustrators depict the witchy, the magical, and the fairy in their treatments of Shakespeare, negotiating the challenging issue of making supernatural elements vivid enough to be compelling and yet not so vivid as to be terrifying.

Alison Prindle addresses the implications of the genre transformation from playscript into narrative, focusing specifically on transformations of *The Tempest* in the hands of Ann Beneduce, Lois Burdett, Bruce Coville, Leon Garfield, Bernard Miles, and Marcia Williams, as well as the classic adaptations by Charles and Mary Lamb, E. Nesbit, and Marchette Chute. Along related lines, Amy Mathur analyzes the literary and pictorial devices employed in picture book reimaginings of *The Tempest* which enable the authors and illustrators to balance the demands of authenticity and creativity. Taking the consideration of *The Tempest* from the realm of picture books to the quite different world of young adult novels, Cynthia Perantoni explores the shifting and ambiguous parallels between Dennis Covington's *Lizard* and Shakespeare's *The Tempest*, making a case for the genuinely heuristic experiences in reading, writing, and discussing offered by a comparison of the two texts.

Turning to the stupendous phenomenon of the *Harry Potter* novels, Miranda Johnson-Haddad offers an examination of "the secret of J. K. Rowling's success," which she suggests depends upon a "rock-solid foundation of archetype, myth, and fairy tale," including an allusive engagement with—surprise!—the plays of William Shakespeare. Meanwhile, Jennifer Lee Carrell employs her expertise as a director, performing arts critic, and writer in considering the role of both stage and silver screen in establishing Shakespeare's lifeline to survival as a great storyteller for all ages. Carrell contends convincingly that Shakespeare's words have the greatest effect when they are treated not as ends in themselves, but as blueprints for the imaginative process of world-making by actors and audiences alike.

Finally, Howard Marchitello concludes the section with an essay that moves "toward a theory of adaptation for children," arguing that adapting Shakespeare for children is not only far more complex than is generally granted (by typical adult readers, at least), but is at the same time "an intensive labor that hides its own traces." Pointing out that "the politics of adaptation" have remained undertheorized, Marchitello queries what part of "Shakespeare" is abstracted and transmitted in adaptations of the plays, and suggests that we might consider Shakespeare not as pedagogical object but rather as pedagogical site for the stories we would like to help others to tell, so that every "point of entry" in the multiple reimaginings of Shakespeare becomes also a "point of departure."

The final section of the volume, "Pedagogy and Performance," offers an immense range of essays by educators and performers who are often one and the same at once. Sheila Cavanagh opens the section with a narrative of her son Davis's journey to Shakespeare, extending from the womb to his stagings of *Romeo and Juliet* on the preschool playground at the age of three. Drawing on the theories of Bruno Bettelheim as well as the educational philosophy of the Reggio Emilia model of early childhood education, Cavanagh demonstrates unexpected ways in which reimagining Shakespeare can facilitate key educational aims even for the youngest of children. Regine Ebner provides another angle on unique educational experiences with her analysis of the transformative effects of Shakespeare on a Montessori classroom of seven- to ten-year-olds, beginning with a hands-on timeline of the Renaissance and three-part story cards of Shakespeare plays and culminating in a dramatic classroom production of key scenes from *Macbeth*.

Introducing yet another educational setting, Janet Field-Pickering's essay documents the evolution of the Folger Shakespeare Library outreach project, *Shakespeare Steps Out*, in several inner-city District of Columbia public elementary schools. Explaining that *Shakespeare Steps Out* strives to reach schools that are located in underserved and economically disadvantaged areas of the city, Field-Pickering describes a successful multidisciplinary approach for teaching Shakespeare in grades three through six that involves history and social studies, music and dancing, language, visual arts, and performance, and concludes by raising some questions about the political implications of teaching Shakespeare or Shakespeare adaptations in inner-city elementary schools.

Kristen Olson approaches the issue of Shakespeare and language development in children through the lens of the English Nanny and Governess School in Chagrin Falls, Ohio, which trains its students to view their work as education rather than child care, and incorporates Shakespeare into the Language Arts curriculum in order to enable educational caregivers to tap into and develop the innate affinity children have for language and its possibilities. John Barnes opens the issue of Shakespeare and young audiences to a consideration of "players, playgrounds, and grounds for play" by sharing the example of a touring children's version of *King Lear* in Colorado that required an immersion experience of play as work and work as play, and in the process illuminated some of the challenges of bringing plays to the theater that confront every performative engagement with Shakespeare.

The educational setting of high school offers a frame for the next several essays, beginning with Tiffany Conroy's syllabus outline for presenting

Shakespeare's life and times for young people, which offers a carefully modulated combination of primary texts ranging from *A Midsummer Night's Dream* to Susan Cooper's *King of Shadows*, as well as a number of secondary texts for children and a list of films and the New Globe Web site. Pamela Benson's essay on teaching Shakespeare to future high school teachers goes one step further up the ladder of the educational system, presenting some crucial texts and exercises that college teachers can use in preparing the future high school teachers who are their students to develop their facility for thinking on their feet as they reimagine Shakespeare in the classroom, rather than falling back on predetermined questions and answers.

Caroline McManus considers the implications of what happens when Shakespeare begins to function as the "property" or "possession" of the educational system, and proposes that teachers might create units that read one of the plays intertextually with its own sources as well as with later adaptations, particularly recent American ones. McManus suggests ways in which *King Lear*, for example, might be read in relation to a range of texts, including the twelfth-century source material from Geoffrey of Monmouth's *History*, the unexpected eighteenth-century adaptation by Nahum Tate (in which Lear lives and Cordelia is not hanged but survives to marry Edgar), and Jane Smiley's 1992 novel *A Thousand Acres*. Focusing more specifically on young adult readers, McManus offers an illuminating exploration of a potential classroom comparison between *King Lear*, William Hooks's 1987 novel *Moss Gown*, and Gloria Naylor's 1988 novel *Mama Day*, the last two of which incorporate Southern settings and matchmaking conjure women.

Gregory Maillet addresses the dynamic effects of performance games in the teaching of Shakespeare, using the example of his own amateur acting troop, ACTIO, that is dedicated to exploring how performance enhances, affects, and effects the meaning of literary texts, and addressing as well the usefulness of a new Shakespeare board game by Aristoplay (aptly titled "The Play's the Thing"), that illustrates further avenues for exploring how performance-based games might serve as valuable aids in the teaching of Shakespearean drama. Meanwhile, Gregory Colón Semenza invites instructors of high school and college students to use film to teach the complexities of Shakespearean drama, as opposed to the "meanings" of the individual plays, and illustrates his genre-based approach to the use of film for the purpose of teaching such challenging concepts as textual indeterminacy, metatheatricality, and intertexuality.

In the final essay in the volume, "Performing Pedagogy," Edward Rocklin focuses on the challenge of conducting courses that invite teachers and teachers-to-be to adopt a performance approach to teaching the plays, whether they are teaching in K-12 or in colleges and universities. Explaining his performance-based pedagogy for dramatic literature, Rocklin moves from examples of different performative moments to a reflection on the elusive vitality of the art of teaching, which enables teacher-students to teach themselves by reimagining their own relation to Shakespeare both inside and outside the classroom.

It was T. S. Eliot who wrote at the conclusion of his *Four Quartets:*

> *We shall not cease from exploration*
> *And the end of all our exploring*
> *Will be to arrive where we started*
> *And know the place for the first time.*[12]

The miracle of reimagining William Shakespeare, whether as authors, critics, teachers, students, parents, children, or simply individuals, is that we might find that the end of all our exploring will be to arrive where we started and know the place for the first time.

Notes

1. William Shakespeare, *Romeo and Juliet*, 2.2.42–43. All Shakespeare quotations in this essay will be drawn from *The Norton Shakespeare*, ed. Stephen Greenblatt, Walter Cohen, Jena E. Howard, and Katharine Eisaman Maus (New York: W. W. Norton, 1997).
2. See the bibliography of the current volume for a comprehensive list of reimaginings of Shakespeare for children and young adults in different media.
3. Marc Norman and Tom Stoppard, *Shakespeare in Love: A Screenplay* (New York: Miramax Books, 1998).
4. *Romeo and Juliet*, 2.2.41–44.
5. *Ibid.*, 2.2.50, 57.
6. *Ibid.*, 2.2.58–60.
7. *The Tempest*, 5.1.187.
8. *A Midsummer Night's Dream*, 5.1.14–17.
9. Two superb essay collections that explore a range of Shakespeare reimaginings for adult audiences are *Shakespeare and Appropriation*, ed. Christy Desmet and Robert Sawyer (New York: Routledge, 1999) and *Shakespeare, the Movie: Popularizing the plays on film, TV, and video*, ed. Lynda E. Boose and Richard Burt (New York: Routledge, 1997). A marvelous sourcebook for bringing the issue of adaptation into the classroom is *Adaptations of Shakespeare: A Critical Anthology of Plays from the Seventeenth Century to the Present*, ed. Daniel Fischlin and Mark Fortier (New York: Routledge, 2000).
10. Jane Smiley, *A Thousand Acres* (New York: Alfred A. Knopf, 1992); John Updike, *Gertrude and Claudius* (New York: Alfred A. Knopf, 2000).
11. *The Tempest*, 5.1.50.
12. T. S. Eliot, "Little Gidding V," *Four Quartets*, in *The Complete Poems and Plays, 1909–1950* (New York: Harcourt, Brace & World, 1971), 145.

I. Biography, Adaptation, and Fictionalization

1. In Love with Shakespeare

ALIKI

The Unexpected

I was stunned when I decided to attempt a book involving Shakespeare. I had
no thought to write a biography of him. It had been done. But I don't choose
my subjects. They choose me. And it is never the whole subject that grabs
me, but a tiny facet of one. A thread. A hook. This one chose me with a stran-
glehold.

An Undercurrent

A related interest began years before. When we moved from New York to
London in the late '70s, I became aware of Sam Wanamaker and his story. I
knew and respected him, this American Shakespearean actor/director who
had been blacklisted in the '50s. I knew that—in a life that paralleled Shakespeare's—he had come to London to begin a new theatrical career. I learned
how his shock and disappointment (on his first day!) in finding no trace of
the Globe, except for a forgotten plaque, urged him to a "dream"—the reconstruction of the Globe as it had been. It may sound romantic in retrospect that
it would take thirty years to achieve this goal, but those lonely years of zeal-
ous determination to raise funds (in which his pleas fell on largely deaf ears)
drew me in. I am a child of immigrants. I understand commitment, sacrifice,
and belief in a worthy cause. I was also proud that it was American passion
which drove him. My husband and I became Friends of the Globe, attended
events, celebrated successes, followed his daughter Zoe's acting career. I felt
part of Sam's family.

The Hook

Then, a few years ago, I was on yet another tour of the new Globe Theatre—
this time with my visiting sister-in-law. We were looking at exhibition photos

of the recent excavations of the Rose Theatre, which had been discovered nearby. She turned to me and said, "Why don't you write a book about this? It's archaeology." I suppose she was thinking I could add this to my other excavated subjects—dinosaurs, fossils, mammoths. I, of course, laughed and said, "No thanks." But something had snapped. "Archaeology" became the hook to an idea.

The Challenge

I thought of IFs. IF I can write a story that comes full circle, IF I can fit in all that I wish to include—a biography of two men (Will Shakespeare and Sam Wanamaker), a history of Elizabethan London and the Queen herself, the growth of theater, two Globes, then fast-forward four hundred years to Sam's story and the rebuilding of the new Globe so that the book ends up alive, not dead—all in thirty-two pages (whew!), I would do it. Much later, I was thrilled when I thought of "The End" being "The Beginning." That is the unexplainable magic that occurs in creating. It happened many lucky times while I worked on *William Shakespeare & the Globe*.

Fig. 1: The Globe

Words, Words, Words

Words come first. There were about twenty-five active books in my studio. Shakespeare biographies, plays, documents, quotations, histories of sixteenth- and seventeenth-century England, Elizabeth I, music, theater, Sam Wanamaker, the building of the Globe. I read, organized, listed, wrote, reread, rewrote, rethought, found more, and started again. I traveled to Shakespeare's haunts, too.

I guess the hardest page to write was that convoluted story on page 25 explaining leases, property rights, landowners, and dismantling of the Globe. So long and complicated. But it couldn't be left out. For months I went back to rewrite it. Later I made the drawing of the team working by the light of the full moon. It seemed right, but sources were hazy.

That summer I was on the beach in Greece, talking to my brother (then president of Temple University). He happened to say his secretary could find anything on the computer. I said, "Oh, really? Well, ask her to try this. What was the phase of the moon on 28 December 1598?" (Ha Ha.) Soon after I received a whole month of moons! And on that night it was FULL!

The Moment of Truth

My diary notes for November 19, 1997:

> Started the Globe dummy! And what does that mean?
> Fear, anxiety, doubt, inability to proceed, sure to fail,
> Impossible to fit into 32 pages. Overcome by depression
> Waaa. I want my Mama!

An accurate premonition. It took three months.

A Light

Dividing up the subjects was major. My diary tells me I spent five days turning blank pages, not drawing a single line. How would it all fit? There would have to be chapters to help the organization. Then a theater friend mentioned by chance that all of Shakespeare's plays have five acts. BOOM! Not chapters. ACTS! Then there could be scenes, a prologue, and (I eventually realized) an aside that would solve my necessary introduction which fit nowhere else. It was a huge breakthrough.

Stuck

The first three spreads took a month and a half of redrawing and replanning all those houses. I was riddled with houses. And doubts. Who in the world would be interested in a bunch of houses? It looked like publicity for an

Estate Agency. Yet they are our rare, tangible evidence of Shakespeare. They can be visited. (Hmmm, I could list them in the back . . .)

I can't go further until I have solved a troubling word, paragraph, or page. So I remained stuck until I saw the light, reduced the houses, and moved out of Stratford as quickly as William had done. Once in London, it finally began to take shape. The London Bridge spread would take weeks and a magnifying glass. Then Queen Elizabeth gave me a break. I love Hilliard's portrait, and used it. Later, when some copyeditor noticed the ferret had only three legs, I said, "If three legs are good enough for Hilliard, they are good enough for me."

Choices

In illustrating a book like this one, the script changes. I am always researching, always finding and adding. Which part should be the story line? Which should fit into captions? Which should be told in words? Which in the illustrations? Which of all this new information I am gathering should I use? Or leave out?

It is in my sharing nature to want to squeeze it all in. When my criminologist friend from Philadelphia saw the published book, he thanked me for the heads on stakes (on page 15). I had seen them in a sixteenth-century etching. How could I leave them out? Or anything else that fascinates me? I was glad I had overcome a short-lived fear that they might be too graphic. In fact—

Fig. 2: Portrait of Elizabeth I

perhaps hoping for more Untapped Gore—Norman later sent me a portfolio of medieval torture methods for further inspiration.

Then, how does one fit in all the information? (Indeed. Where do I store empty jars, bottles, plastic bags, corks, and toilet paper rolls that I save?) One could write an entire book describing London Bridge alone. How could I squeeze all that into two two-line captions? By hundreds of rewrites, that's how.

Expanding

It was about then that I knew I needed more pages. I begged for them. Thirty-two became forty-eight. Now there would be space to list the plays, a chronology, and his invented words. I knew about the words, but so many? And how to introduce them?

I spent weeks inventing a story in which every word was used and underlined, but that was too confusing. Eventually, what started as one paragraph grew to a page, then a double-page spread of words and expressions that took more long weeks to conceive. But what a revelation they were.

Backs and Forths

A dummy is very organic. It is the creative part of doing a picture book, where passion fights with reality, pictures nudge out unnecessary words, and revelations surprise even the creator. Pages and ideas are twisted and manipulated like clay. It ends up a collage of drawings on tracing paper cut, stuck, and rearranged with the type until it is finally solved.

In a complicated book like this, choosing the typeface and setting type is very difficult for the designer (with me huffing down his neck. Did I mention I'm a perfectionist?). It took many tries. But a successful picture book is to me a seamless marriage between the picture and the word, and this is where that happens. Only when I am working, moving things around, can I see what is important and what isn't. The trouble is, I think everything is important. Hence the challenge. If the headings made reading easier, so would a table of contents. So back to the front again. Then each act and heading needed a decoration, no? It took constant redoing to design the right, unobtrusive one. And so it goes.

The Quotes

I knew early on that I wanted to bring in some quotes. Not only for a taste of Shakespeare's incredible words (sometimes I had to read a quote fifty times to understand it), but also for his presence. We know very little about Shakespeare the man. It is his words that make him come alive.

I started with one quote ("o wonderful, wonderful . . .") then scattered other familiar ones where they fit. Then I thought: Why not one for every scene? I love Ophelia's sad "There's Rosemary, that's for remembrance . . ." but I couldn't connect it to any scene. Then, ah. There is the place, back there by the Plays. And Chronology ". . . that's for thoughts." And oh, why not quotes on the endpapers, too? With a little vignette? The book is so dense with information, why not a quiet start? As it turned out, I didn't want them stuck down. So more pleas, this time for separate ends, to open like a rich curtain onto the pages. When I found Ben Jonson's "Reader, looke not on his Picture, but on his Booke," I nearly wept. Ben Jonson, *The First Folio*, in S. Schoenbaum, *A Documentary Life* (London: Oxford Univ. Press, 1975), p. 258. It was perfect for the Aside. He had said in ten words what I had labored into a whole paragraph.

Each quote became a gift. A game of seek and find, with Will smiling over my shoulder. It took all the time I worked on the book to find and choose them. William gave me one for every need. How could I not be in love with him? (Though I "fell" years ago.)

The Jacket

And the jacket? That comes last. The jacket has to project what the book is about. I think I made twenty versions. I knew I needed Shakespeare, and I wanted Sam's Globe somewhere.

Fig. 3: Jacket Art

I drew William standing (odd to see him with legs, like William Penn standing on City Hall in Philadelphia), writing (we need to see his eyes), front face (well . . .), side view (a coin), three quarter view (a bit indirect), back view (desperation), every view. But we are so used to seeing him in the Flower Portrait, we don't recognize him from another angle.

I wanted to give him an earring, as in the romantic Chandos portrait, which was my favorite. But that is the only time we see him with one. I usually don't make a move unless I see/read something in at least three sources, so I backed down. Eventually I grew used to the Droeshout etching, could never believe the disillusioning bust at Holy Trinity, and used them all in the finished portrait. Try as I might, he still looks to me the only Greek Shakespeare in circulation. So much for roots.

But—still on the dummy—the jacket was too stiff and dreary until I brought in the play-vignettes from page 28. They enlivened it, and reflected more about the book.

(Are you really interested in all this?)

Getting There

After the dummy comes the artwork. My dummies are very thought out. The finished art is perfecting them. It is measuring. Measuring paper, margins, gutters, captions, maps, space for type, and spaces in between. I always think of my patient math teacher. She assured me that even an artist would need math every day. Yet she would excuse me from class to paint murals for the Christmas Concert as if she knew a secret.

So I measured. And painted. I used pencil to sketch in the drawings, ink to outline, watercolor, gouache, and pencil crayons to paint, working for the camera, digging into all those books again to recheck every little line, coping with details and that magnifying glass.

This is also when final choices are made. The question of one peaked roof or two on the Globe followed me 'til the end, with the experts getting the final vote.

When he was little, my son Jason used to cut out and put together all kinds of toy theaters, including the Globe. So he inspired the title page. In the finishes, I straightened his hair and turned him into Sam.

London Bridge and the bloody markets (sorry) were probably the most difficult, along with the crowded Globes on pages 27 and 43. In the last one, I squeezed in the Queen, my family, and friends in a final hurrah. (Shall I name-drop?)

And the two spreads of rebuilding the Globe? I see by drawing, and learn by seeing. I always say that if math had been taught to me tangibly, I would have understood it better. (I still see a pie when I divide up or add.) Perhaps that is why I believe in active pictures that explain. Part of the reason that

Fig. 4: Title page art

drew me to illustrating in the first place. So it was fun to find that way to illustrate the step by step process, both for clarity and movement.

Numbers

The finished art took about six months of double-days, the whole book nearly three years. I had spent long months unwilling to leave my desk, unable to sleep. My normal days are eighteen hours long. The last month was a record twenty-one hours as my deadline loomed. We were hoping to publish on the Globe's 400th anniversary.

I had my nightly rendezvous with BBC Radio 3 (classical music) presenters who work through dark to daybreak, whom nobody else knows because they're asleep. Cozy. Concerts just for me.

Saviors

My patient husband, Franz, shopped, cleaned up my kitchen messes and waited. My awesome editor, Phoebe Yeh, charged through every tidal wave like Poseidon. I had a dream-expert in the U.K. (from Shakespeare's Globe), one in the

With their paint, they made the Heavens glow with stars, planets, and signs of the Zodiac. They covered the walls with gods and muses, and turned wooden columns into marble. Exquisite tapestries, woven by 500 New Zealand artists, were donated.

Fig. 5: "The Heavens"

U.S. (from Folger Library). At HarperCollins, everyone bent over backwards granting wishes. My gallant designer, Al Cetta, never blinked when I lastly went to New York for eight days and did the unheard of. I sat by his side—next to his computer—getting the type right. ("Enlarge this, reduce that, pull down, move over, push up, leave a gap, space out . . .") I am sure he was spaced out all right.

Aftermath

I was a wreck. There is always a withdrawal period after intense work on a book, but this one was something else. Yes, Shakespeare had become Will. But I didn't know how deep my involvement until it was all over. The aftermath brought long months of missing him. Will had been by my side, offering inspiration, guidance, clues, and a depth previously unknown. I was bereft. I am sure everyone who works with Shakespeare feels the same. Life changes forever.

A kind of salvation came with perfect timing. *Shakespeare in Love* opened at our local cinema around the corner. I found out that the first showing was at noon. I figured no one would see me sneak in at that time. They'd all be having lunch. And no one did, except for one or two other crazies who chose to spend midday sitting in the dark. I saw it seven times. Those daily clandestine meetings with my buddies saved me.

A Gift

When the book was finally published, I gave a first copy to a friend's seven-year-old, a precocious reader. We were on a car trip, and she—alone in the back seat—didn't lift her head once. She read it cover to cover. I was shocked. Then thrilled. It was one of my best gifts to know first-hand that no one is too young for William Shakespeare. May he change her life, too.

2. The Story Behind the Man Behind the Plays

DIANE STANLEY

Some years ago Dr. William Hunter, a retired English professor living in Houston, led a study group at our church on *The Merchant of Venice*. Before we began reading and discussing the play, Dr. Hunter devoted an hour to filling us in on the background against which Shakespeare lived his life and produced his great works. He explained about the acting companies—men and boys only—and how the parts were written for the actors, rather than casting the actors for the parts as we do today.

He described what it was like to go to the theater in Elizabethan times—the groundlings drinking beer and shouting ribald comments, the vendors wandering through the crowd selling food and drink as at a baseball game, sudden showers getting everybody wet. And he discussed the question of whether Shakespeare actually wrote those plays at all (some theorize that the son of a small-town glover with a grammar school education could not possibly have written them and that the true author must have been someone important and educated, such as the Earl of Oxford). And then he told us why scholars don't take such theories seriously at all.

He spoke at some length about the lack of copyright protection and the tendency of one acting company to rip off the property of another if they could just get their hands on the script. Consequently, there was usually only one complete script; the copies given to the actors consisted of only their scenes and the preceding cue lines, if necessary. This was not only to avoid needless labor in copying but also to protect the work.

Dr. Hunter read us an unauthorized version of Hamlet's soliloquy, clearly written by someone who had gotten hold of a copy of some *other* character's script (presumably he had also seen the play and knew the general drift of the plot). The writer didn't get much past "To be or not to be" before he descended into a laughable and chaotic attempt to recall just how those lines were supposed to go.

Fig. 6

I left Dr. Hunter's lecture enchanted and inspired—determined that the subject of my next book for children would be William Shakespeare. The idea was greeted with polite skepticism from the publisher. Children who read picture books are too young for Shakespeare, so why write a picture book about him? My answer was that my book would not be about Shakespeare's work; it would be about Shakespeare the man, in keeping with my earlier biographies of Peter the Great, Shaka, and Queen Elizabeth.

But, it was pointed out, there was a problem there, too—almost nothing is known about Shakespeare the man. This was true, as I would later acknowledge in an author's note at the beginning of my book: "William Shakespeare is one of the most famous men who ever lived. Yet much of his life is a mystery to us. He did not keep a diary, and none of his personal letters has survived. We do not even know exactly when he was born—only the date on which his baptism was registered. We know a little about his parents, his wife, and his children. Besides his plays and poems, the only other documents we have are business transactions, court papers, and his will."[1]

I was still convinced a picture book about Shakespeare could work, because my book would be the story *behind* the man behind the plays. Painting

in the background has always been an important part of my approach to biography. If my readers don't understand the context, they will not understand
the significance of the actions and accomplishments of the great men and
women I write about. And considering the age of my readers, it can be
assumed they probably will not understand the context. I will have to provide
it. I relish this, actually, because the background material is often the most
interesting and colorful part of the book. In this case, it would take center
stage.

Naturally there would be gaps in the narrative of Shakespeare's life. No
problem there, either. First, it would give me a chance to show my readers
how one approaches history—that some "facts" are mere speculation, others
are conclusions derived from hard evidence, and many are probably false. I
freely admit to my young readers that we don't have a clue what Shakespeare
was up to between the time he left school and his subsequent reappearance as
an actor in London (besides fathering children and getting married, that is). I
provide a few theories and label them as such.

It would also not be a problem because the story behind the man is sufficiently rich and fascinating to carry the reader along until Shakespeare pops
back up again. Meanwhile, I have the chance to present a colorful picture of
life in the sixteenth century—not among the high and mighty who were making laws and waging war—but among ordinary people who were just trying
to make a living and pay the rent.

One of my favorite such anecdotes involves James Burbage, the first
man to design a building solely intended for the performance of plays since
the days of ancient Rome, and who was also Shakespeare's boss. When the
landlord of the theater property kept raising the rent, James and his brother
Cuthbert (presumably accompanied by young Will and the rest of the men in
the company) secretly dismantled the building one night, board by board.
Then, as the landlord later attested in his lawsuit, they "did . . . in most
forcible and riotous manner take and carry away from there all the wood and
timbers." They dragged the lumber across the frozen Thames River to a new
site, where they would use it to build the famous Globe Theatre. (The
Burbages won the suit, by the way, on the grounds that the landlord owned
the land, but not the building.)

It is interesting for my readers to learn how tenuous the life of an actor
could be, his livelihood often threatened by disapproving Puritans (who tried
to close down the theaters) or the plague (which actually did close them
down for several years). We see Shakespeare trying to make ends meet by
writing poems and dedicating them to a wealthy nobleman in hopes of a gift
in return. When the Earl reciprocated generously, Shakespeare invested the
money in Burbage's acting company, thus becoming a partner, and so entitled
to a share in the company's profits. Saving and investing wisely, he was soon
able to retire to the country with a nice, new house.

Fig. 7

Writing about the great William Shakespeare in terms of lawsuits and money transactions has a demystifying effect. I choose this approach intentionally, not to "bring him down to size" but to take an icon and put flesh on him so my readers can understand him better.

Almost every child has seen some kind of stage play, even if only in the school cafeteria. The very idea of a special building designed for the performance of plays is so familiar that children are amazed to learn that it was a new concept in Shakespeare's time. And like so many new things, it was based on what had gone before. In this case it was the courtyards of inns where traveling players often set up their makeshift stages—offering an open space where the audience could stand, surrounded by covered galleries, several stories high, which were undoubtedly the prime spot from which to enjoy the play. This was the model James Burbage used when he built his first theater, an open courtyard surrounded by galleries and a stage built against one side.

Today, children have certain expectations about what a theater ought to look like—a raised platform with a curtain across it, stage lights, and probably some kind of set or backdrop. They wouldn't think to mention that the theater should have a roof overhead and seats for the audience to sit in. They would

Fig. 8

take such things completely for granted. Thus, they find it quite amusing and indeed fascinating to learn that Shakespeare's theaters were open to the weather, had no curtain and virtually no sets, no lights, and no seats for at least half of the customers. And how they giggle when they learn that Juliet and Cleopatra—and all of Shakespeare's other heroines—were played by boys!

The special effects of the Elizabethan theater come as a surprise—and a delight—to young readers. They can imagine a grandly dressed actor portraying a god descending out of the "heavens," lowered through a trapdoor on ropes. They can hear the sound of thunder made by the cannonball being rolled around on the wooden floor over the stage or the blast of a cannon (firing blanks) adding excitement to the battle scenes. A bag of pig's blood, hidden under an actor's tunic, made for a very dramatic death scene when punctured by a knife. Young readers, like the groundlings before them, are always impressed.

The kinds of plays popular in the Elizabethan age and the conventions that went along with them were common to all playwrights of the time: "The main characters in the tragedies, for example, were always doomed to die in the end. The comedies were full of mistaken identities, women disguised as

Fig. 9

men, miscarried letters, and all sorts of silly complications that were resolved in the end, with everyone planning weddings. The histories told the stories of kings and great noblemen in exciting situations, such as war or rebellion."[2] When children learn that Shakespeare followed the same standard conventions as everybody else and that even his *plots* were not original, then they are led to ask the *big question*: what was it, then, that made his plays so great?

I offer them a clue—"he wove humor into his tragedies, put serious problems into his comedies, and brought the issues of the common people into his histories. His characters and the words they spoke were amazing and highly original."[3] But someday, the children who read *Bard of Avon* will actually read or see a play by Shakespeare. They will bring with them an understanding of what Shakespeare set out to do. They will know that he wrote his plays to be acted on a stage, not to be studied in a classroom. And they will be able to picture that stage and the actors on it. They will understand that Shakespeare intended his play to be exciting and funny and that he threw in enough bawdy humor among the fine speeches to keep the groundlings entertained so they wouldn't get raucous and disturb the play. He would have created roles appropriate for the actors who would play them, and he hoped to

Fig. 10

provide a good afternoon's entertainment for people with a penny to spend and a need for a little something to brighten their lives. But it will also be clear to those children, as they approach their first real experience with Shakespeare, that he was doing a good deal more. He was delving into the human spirit, flexing his sense of humor, and playing brilliantly with words. And then they will understand, truly and for themselves, what made Shakespeare great.

Notes

1. *Bard of Avon.*
2. *Bard of Avon*, p. 26.
3. *Bard of Avon*, p. 26.

Work Cited

Stanley, Diane, and Peter Vennema. *Bard of Avon: The Story of William Shakespeare.* Illus. Diane Stanley. New York: Morrow Junior Books, 1992.

3.   Bravo, Mr. William Shakespeare!

MARCIA WILLIAMS

"You don't mess with the great Bard, Marcia." This was the response of my editor when I first proposed a Shakespeare retelling. But children's authors have been messing with "the great Bard" since 1807 when Charles and Mary Lamb published *Tales from Shakespeare Designed for the Use of Young Persons*. Remarkably, this book is still in print as *Tales from Shakespeare*. It is the book that drove me to beg my editor to allow me to do my own retelling. The fact that I was finally given the go-ahead to "try it, Marcia," showed great courage on the part of the publisher and, as I soon came to realize, blind optimism on mine.

Tales from Shakespeare had been my introduction to Shakespeare, and I had yawned and fidgeted through every page. The few times I went to a Shakespeare play as a child, I failed to see the connection between the book's text and the play. As a child I found a Shakespeare performance hard going, but I found the book truly boring. It is not that one would expect a book to live up to the plays, but they are meant to encourage—not discourage—children from seeking out the Bard himself. For one thing, although many artists have illustrated it, I never had an edition that included illustrations. Like Lewis Carroll's Alice, I thought, "what is the point of a book without pictures or conversations?"[1] What is a play if not a visual and verbal experience? For me the Lambs' *Tales* was neither of these things. The few quotations that are included are hidden in dense paragraphs of descriptive text. Even my present edition, bought just a couple of years ago, has no illustrations. Yet how can you, particularly in this day and age, introduce children to plays without giving them a foretaste of the visual experience?

It is interesting to discover that the first edition of *Tales from Shakespeare* published by Godwin, was illustrated. The choice of illustrations was left to Godwin's wife; Charles Lamb thought them "damn'd beastly."[2] But, at a time when illustrations were not a publisher's prime concern, there they were. They are generally attributed to an artist called Mulready, but only

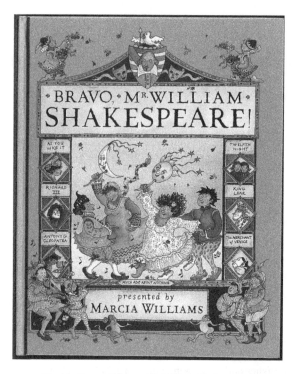

Fig. 11: Cover of *Bravo, Mr. William Shakespeare!*

because he had worked for the Godwins before. The illustrations honored the classical Greek tradition in pose and by today's standards are static, contrived, and ill-suited to children. But at a time when books were scarce, illustrations scarcer, and artwork actually produced for an existing text scarcer still, they must have been pleasing to the eye.

Allowing for the moral norms of the time, Charles and Mary Lamb told the stories with loving care. They must have brought Shakespeare to many children and adults of the nineteenth century, creating a new audience for his work. One could argue that they had invented a new genre, the retelling of the classics for children. It was an exciting new concept born of a desire to share their enthusiasm. In her introduction, Mary Lamb calls them "imperfect abridgements."[3] She said that they were written mainly for "young ladies" as "young gentlemen" had the use of their fathers' libraries.[4] She encouraged the "young gentlemen" to choose passages from Shakespeare, naturally "selecting what is proper for a young sister's ear," and to read these passages to their sisters.[5] Of course, these would be "better relished and understood" after reading her book.[6] The hope of many a reteller today. Looking at them now, it is tempting to say that the diligent care with which they are told strips the plays of their life. But in that same year (1807), another retelling was published, *The Family Shakespeare* by Henrietta Bowdler. Her approach makes one realize just how innovative and lively the Lambs' *Tales* must have appeared when first published. Bowdler explains in the 1807 Preface that her book is for those "who wish to make the young reader acquainted with the various beauties of this writer, unmixed with any thing that can raise a blush on the cheek of modesty."[7] Shakespeare without the naughty bits! The Lambs' retellings certainly raises no blushes, but, as Charles wrote to Coleridge, they were written for the pleasure of children that he felt only had access to the religious and moral tracts so common during this period. The Lambs loved Shakespeare and wanted to share their passion. As any author knows, your own enthusiasm is the best starting point, your own moral fervor, the worst.

So I must heap praise upon the book that did more to put me off Shakespeare as a child than anything else. The Lambs' *Tales* was very well written and it was an immediate success. By 1900 it had been reprinted 74 times and translated into several languages. It had found its audience. But why is it still being sold today? Is it what I should have been given to read in the mid-twentieth century? Should we expect a book, published in 1807, that is a retelling, not an original work of literature, still to talk to the twentieth-century child? At a time when televisions entered almost every home, when comics were regular reading, when color, illustration, and talent filled children's books as never before?

Does there not come a time when books such as the Lambs' *Tales* should take their place in academic libraries and make way for new images of Shakespeare that speak directly to the modern child? For me in the 1950s—and I am sure that I am not unique—the Lambs' *Tales* were out of date, probably less accessible than the rhythmic language of Shakespeare himself! Unless we keep reimagining Shakespeare for a new audience, his works will be inaccessible to vast numbers of every new generation, and they will become the property of an academic elite. Of course there have been many other published retellings of Shakespeare between 1870 and today, but none have stuck like the Lambs' *Tales*. There were retellings like that of G. B. Harrison illustrated by C. Walter Hodges who, as Hodges told me (2001), were mainly aiming for the schools market. Or there was the whimsy of E. Nesbit, who wrote a retelling of Shakespeare during what *The Oxford Companion to Children's Literature* calls her "more or less hack-writing" period. Today this book would probably be seen as patronizing. The illustrations for the early editions of the book sum up the general approach: angelic-looking children take the parts of Shakespeare's great heroes and heroines. The child King Lear, for instance, seems to be stuffed up with a cushion and is wearing a fluffy white beard, looking more like Father Christmas than the tragic father of Shakespeare's play.

The British Shakespearean actress Judi Dench said in a recent television interview, "You can mess around with Shakespeare."[8] I would argue that not only can we, but that if we believe in the Bard, we must. It is worthwhile to do, because he was such a great teller of human tales. In the same television program, the director Richard Eyre said that Shakespeare is a "measure and template of our humanity." Many scholars, many theater-goers, many adults, and young people would, I think, agree with him. For this reason alone I believe that it is worth "Reimagining Shakespeare for children and young adults," as the title to the present volume of essays celebrates. Indeed for anyone who is interested, as for whoever the intended audience of a retelling might be, a book will usually come with its own dynamic and find its own audience. Each generation deserves the best from the Bard. They should be looking to contemporary actors, directors, writers, animators, film makers, teachers, and parents to find a new "reimagining" in order to fire their own imaginations and to inspire them to explore Shakespeare. There is much to be lost by not continuing to mess with the Bard and we would have lost much if the Lambs had not set us on the path. But the timelessness of the Bard is lost if he is not continuously reimagined, just as a play is written to be.

We now live in a fast-moving, visual world and work for children and young people should reflect this. The theater engages all our senses, and reimaginings of Shakespeare should reflect this. Good examples are the recent film versions of *Hamlet* directed by Michael Almereyda, and *Romeo & Juliet* directed by Baz Luhrmann. A new generation of hearts throbbed for Romeo acted by Leonardo di Caprio and likewise for Juliet, acted by Claire Danes. Luhrmann's film was tight, fast-moving, fun, emotional, and most of all relevant to a young audience. It was an original Shakespeare play, but it was a modern film, catering to a modern audience. One could even speculate that it is how Shakespeare might write today. Although, when I think about it, Luhrmann had it easy, for he did not have to fit the whole of *Romeo and Juliet* into four spreads. For writers who reimagine Shakespeare for a younger audience, space will always be a problem. Shakespeare's plays are often long, sometimes too long. Children's books are usually short and sometimes too short! The illustrator Michael Foreman told me that the author Leon Garfield said of their two volumes of Shakespeare retellings, which are longer than most, "it was like trying to paint the ceiling of the Sistine Chapel onto a postage stamp."[9] It could be argued that this works to the advantage of both the child reader and Shakespeare, as the limited space calls for ruthless editing and puts a severe limit on self-indulgent waffle. It would be possible to argue that Leon Garfield's *Shakespeare's Stories*, illustrated by Michael Foreman, has succeeded in becoming the first classic retelling since Charles and Mary Lamb's. A review by Dr. Stanley Wells in the *Times Literary Supplement*, cited on the flyleaf of the 1994 edition of the book, says that they are "Narrated with a vivid sense of their theatrical impact . . . not pale reflections of the plays, but fresh creations with a life of their own." This would seem to me to be very important in retelling any great literature. A retelling that does not take on a life of its own has not succeeded. Leon Garfield was a master craftsman and according to Michael Foreman had a "deep knowledge and understanding of Shakepseare's plays." He brought this, plus his own creative imagination, to the project. He was also supported by the illustrations, which have originality, wit, emotion, and depth, plus Foreman's undoubted ability as a draftsman.

You may wonder, since the second of these two volumes was only published in 1994, why I wanted to set out along a similar path. Garfield's book inspired me to create a book for another audience, those children who might not get hooked into Shakespeare through him. His is an outstanding and scholarly book, a book for children who have ample access to books and are already avid readers. Garfield was a creative academic; I am a creative student. My place is still at the back of the class, doodling and wondering what is for supper. I need to write and illustrate for that student within me, because another bit of me says, someone, somewhere, somehow failed to make literature more interesting than doodle and supper. No one told me that life and literature are all one and that Shakespeare was writing about you and me and the old grump next door. "Shakespeare," I thought, "what a load of old tosh, nothing to do with my burning preoccupations!" On the flyleaf of the 1994 edition of Garfield's book is written: "For All Ages," which is very suitable since it could refer to either epochs or the ages of the readers. But children are various and individual beings, "All Ages" does not mean "all people." Books should be as diverse as the children themselves. Just as continually reimagining Shakespeare so that he remains relevant to any particular generation is important, so is a choice of these reimaginings. After all, there is no perfect method, we must all fail in one aspect or another, only Shakespeare himself can be said to have got it entirely right.

An author/illustrator has the ability to integrate words and pictures in a way that no separate authors and illustrators have. In recreating something like a play, which is so visual, this seemed to me a great advantage at the time. I wonder now whether it did not indulge my megalomaniac tendencies, in which I was author, actor, director, set designer, and even the audience. In fact I have to admit to having had writer's block ever since, as I can find no other way of creating so many roles for myself! But in truth, when I first started the project, it took me a long time to find a way "in." I realized that there had been some truth in my editor's cautionary words, but it was not that you "don't mess with the great Bard," but that you do not mess with him lightly. I followed the same lines of research that I had for other retellings, but nothing quite gelled. What I had always felt lacking in other retellings was the feeling that these were plays to be performed, not stories for silent reading. They were public proclamations on the state of man, they were open to many interpretations and many renditions according to the actor or director, but there was nothing silent or private in Shakespeare's playwriting—I wanted to do him *noisy* justice.

The breakthrough came when I visited the reconstructed Globe Theatre in London. I went whilst it was still being built and was given a tour by an actor. He made me realize that Shakespeare's theater was a bawdy, riotous affair.

Joint rehearsals were few, usually the actors only came together and a play only fully took its shape before an audience. This must have led to a certain frisson and apprehension that is rarely repeated in the theater today. Even a perfectly rehearsed actor would have to compete with heckling from the audience, with vendors and prostitutes selling their wares, the stink of the unwashed bodies, members of the audience wandering on and off the stage, missiles, and garbage. No audience hush followed by polite clapping. But this was the theater that Shakespeare wrote for and I wanted to get some sense of it into my reimagining. There was no curtain between Shakespeare and his audience. The line between stage and life blurred as the audience partook of the performance, some from the stage itself. As Shakespeare wrote, "All the world's a stage." That is what I wanted to capture a sense of, between the covers of my book.

From the point of view of retelling complicated and period stories, adding an audience to your page, as I have done, has many advantages. They not only lend atmosphere, but they can also inform and support the text and the actor's words. They can bring modern humor, anarchy, and idioms that might seem out of place in the main body text. While the rest of the book may be considered my retelling of Shakespeare's conversation with his reader, the audiences' speech bubbles are my conversation with my reader, our personal interaction, gossip, and backchat.

Fig. 12: Illustration from *As You Like It*

But do not be fooled, comic strip is not an easy option. Comic strips require skilled reading and it is my experience that children, particularly of primary school age, are far better at this than adults. In a comic strip it is not enough to be literate, you must also be visually literate, an important ability in this multimedia society and a vital skill when watching a play on stage. You have to have the adeptness to dive in and out of the various levels. In my Shakespeare books there is the narrative text, the visual text, Shakespeare's text, and the audience text. The jokes that develop through the book, and even from book to book, the recurring characters and historic asides. Not to mention the hidden clues that the pictures contain, mirroring the "meaningful gesture" found in stage performance. In fact you could liken comic strips to Shakespeare's own multilayered texts!

I was once asked what I would say to people who might criticize me for retelling "great literature" in comic strip form. This was during the conception of the first Shakespeare book; even the question made me feel defensive. But now that the books exist I feel that Shakespeare's plays continue to exist because they touch a chord with so many people, they should not be treated as rarefied or the domain of academics. Over time all literature becomes a little less accessible as language—society and ideas change, but still it belongs to all of us. Many adults and children will find no voice that speaks to them in my books and that is fine, but we must try to accommodate every taste. We

Fig. 13: Illustration from *Much Ado About Nothing*

all need to find our way into Shakespeare, whether it is through watching the plays themselves, retellings such as Lamb or Garfield, animation, film, or comic strips. We need them all in order to share our enthusiasm for the great Bard, with the widest possible audience.

In Shakespeare's time an eyewitness at the Globe Theatre reported in attendance "tailors, tinkers, cordwainers, sailors, old men, young men, women, boys, girls and such like."[10] The Mayor and Alderman of the City of London tried to limit the number of performances so that there was less absenteeism from work. How many workers today would leave a building site to see a Shakespeare play? But, even though Mr. William Shakespeare was not the most popular playwright of his time, his plays were as popular in Britain as football is today. I do not think that this means we should popularize Shakespeare by dumbing him down or loosening our integrity towards the original text, but I do believe that we should create many doorways. The artist Gerald Scarfe, when asked how far you can stretch a caricature and still maintain a likeness, says that he imagines the face as a piece of chewing gum, you can stretch it and stretch it, but you must not let it snap.[11] I see integrity to the original in the same light, let's have a tug here and there at the great Bard's chewing gum, but let's remember to whom it belongs!

Fig. 14: Illustration from *Hamlet*

When Titania awoke, the first creature she saw was Bottom with an ass's head! Instantly, she fell in love with him. Bottom was not displeased by the attention, especially when Titania ordered her fairies to attend his every whim.

Fig. 15: Illustration from *A Midsummer Night's Dream*

I have had a huge amount of enjoyment working on both my books, *Mr. William Shakespeare's Plays* and *Bravo, Mr. William Shakespeare!* and I hope that if nothing else, this pleasure will be shared with a few of my fellows at the back of the class. They were never meant to be "worthy" books and they were certainly never meant to be textbooks. They are my way of sharing my enthusiasm and hopefully somebody will find them a "good read." My intention is to be nothing more than a stepping stone to the Bard himself and as such I hope the tide of time will wash over my imperfections before they become too glaring. I believe we should only be holding onto the original and unique bits of the past. This means Shakespeare, not Charles and Mary Lamb, Williams or even Garfield. If I, and others like me, have done their job well, today's youth will become the Garfield and Williams of tomorrow, creating their vision of the Bard that is relevant to them and the generation that follows them. Bravo, Mr. William Shakespeare, we are still messing with you. And I would like to encourage as much messing as possible, for us, for our children and for our children's children!

Notes

1. Lewis Carroll, *Alice's Adventures in Wonderland* [1865] (London: Julia Macrae Books, 1988), 1.
2. *Letters of Charles and Mary Anne Lamb*, Vol. II (1801–1809), ed. Edwin W. Marrs (Ithaca: Cornell Univ. Press, 1976).
3. Charles and Mary Lamb, *Tales from Shakespeare* (London: Puffin, 1988), 9.
4. *Ibid.*, 8.
5. *Ibid.*, 8.
6. *Ibid.*, 9.
7. Henrietta Bowdler, *The Family Shakespeare*, 4 vols. (London: Hatchard, 1807).
8. BBC 2, November 5, 2000.
9. Personal interview with Michael Foreman, September 28, 2000.
10. J. R. Brown, *Shakespeare and His Theatre* (London: Viking, 1982), 32.
11. Personal interview with Gerald Scarfe, December 10, 2000.

4. "This Is Young William"

Shakespeare and the Cumulative Tale

REBECCA PIATT DAVIDSON

I am interested in the story of how we come to love stories. For many of us, this story began in the moments we were read to as young children. After all, being immersed in a book is itself a kind of story, since the experience writes itself as a memory that is both distinct from and yet always folding into the story on the page. Residing within us, this story-in-a-story is more a collage than a narrative. This story, it turns out, is about machinery—the machinery of language, of imagination, of intimacy. Moreover, as we grow, we understand it to be the story of how we came to operate these different forms of machinery with success. Enhanced sometimes by pictures and always by the rhythms of the reader's voice and his comfortably close self, this metamoment becomes a particularly nostalgic one for lovers of stories.

As I considered doing a picture book about Shakespeare, I kept returning to my own story of being read to each night by a father who should have taken up acting instead of practicing law. I thought of the way he could put on and take off accents, of the way he came to inhabit the people on the page. These nightly dramas featured a large cast of characters with whom I became familiar and friendly. The story of a listening girl in an attic bedroom in Mt. Baldy, California, is nestled within those stories, or perhaps they are nestled in hers.

Wanting to summon a memorable group of characters for my story, I turned of course to Shakespeare, where memorable characters abound! I decided to introduce my young readers not just to one or two of Shakespeare's characters but to many of them. In so doing, I hoped to create a story that would give children a delicious taste of Shakespeare while adding to their taste for stories. Most of all, I hoped this taste would be habit-forming!

My choice of the cumulative tale as the form for my Shakespeare book (entitled *All The World's A Stage*, illustrated by Anita Lobel and due out in spring of 2003 from Greenwillow Books) turned out to be a happy coincidence. First, I simply loved the form and had wanted for some time to use it. Naturally it allowed me to work in rhyme, an opportunity I relished. Second—and more important—it gave me the opportunity to include my favorite characters from a variety of plays. Because of the tale's format, I now could throw characters from Shakespeare together and have them meet up in ways they otherwise never would. I loved the idea of characters from different plays colliding not only with each other but also with the young Will Shakespeare who is understood to be dreaming up the text of the story in the very moment that readers are encountering it. Moreover, the act of pulling characters from their own plays in order to juxtapose them with characters from other plays intrigued me. On the one hand, Hamlet can leave his play and still immediately be identifiable as Hamlet. For example, when my narrator describes him as the Prince who "stops and . . . goes, and [is] cold and then hot," those who know the play instantly will recognize this Prince as the same brooding, indecisive Prince of Denmark. On the other hand, Hamlet also inspires new story possibilities once he is positioned outside his own play next to the spirited, untamable Kate. We wonder: what would happen if they ran into each other? What would happen if he were to be confronted by someone other than Ophelia? Likewise, what newly exaggerated gestures of love will the heartsick Malvolio enact when the fairies from everyone's favorite midsummer dream feed his fancies? What might our cross-gartered friend do then? And of course there is Prospero, whose magic now is imagined to function beyond the boundaries of his own play, reaching into the lives of Romeo and Juliet and even beyond. This of course resonates with one of Shakespeare's recurring themes—that the plays themselves work the magic and cast the spells. And so I was led by my urge to pair characters that would never otherwise be introduced. The what-might-happen-*then* part is actually beyond the scope of my book, but the just-what-*if* part nevertheless hangs there invitingly at the moment each unlikely pairing occurs.

In addition, cumulative tales tend to be circular, to come back to where they began, though often with a twist. My book both begins and ends with a young Will Shakespeare ablaze with ideas; however, the story twists when Will is given inspiration from the very characters he then creates. They both fuel his creative life and are the product of it, bodied forth almost in the moment they touch him. The irony twists again with the example of the Muse, who inspires young Will even as she watches the amusements in *The Comedy of Errors*, thus ironically giving Will inspiration even as she takes it from him. This recursive quality to the story seemed especially fitting considering the many ways in which Shakespeare's plays explore the nature of poetic inspiration.

I found as I worked on this very simple story that there were layers of implications to the form. To begin with, the cumulative tale is almost stage-like in its outlines. Characters are introduced often with the typical phrase

Fig. 16: Artist's Working Sketch for *All The World's A Stage*, by Rebecca Piatt Davidson, illustrated by Anita Lobel

this is or *these are*, which calls attention, as performed drama does, to the fact that the story is about the characters and their interactions with each other. In short, the action is character-driven. Moreover, the characters in the cumulative tale enter and exit from the pages much as actors do from the stage. Indeed, the narrator's function within this format is to present characters and then *do* something with them once they all have been seen or heard. The tension arises from the cumulative nature of the form: once the characters are clustered on the stage together, an inevitable climax seems destined to follow. And it does. At the climactic moment, one character typically alters the story's familiar pattern or starts a new one, and the other characters follow suit, which results in a new and unexpected outcome.

My book is an example. In it, the narrator begins, "This is Young William, his mind all ablaze, who stays up all night writing poems and plays." "This is" and "these are" of course signal the characters' entrances. Following Will is the Muse who inspires him, and she is followed by the Dromio and Antipholus twins from *The Comedy of Errors*, who are followed in turn by Prince Hamlet and so on. Readers who know Shakespeare, however, will notice that these well-known characters are identified not by their names but rather by their characteristics. (While their names are omitted in the text of the book, characters *are* identified and described in greater detail in the back matter at the end of the book.) Kate, for example, is "the maiden saucy and smart;" Hamlet is "the Prince of To Be Or Not;" and Prospero and Ariel are known simply as "the Duke and his airy sprite." These characters take the stage—or the page, as it were—as they take turns appearing in the story. However, this pattern of entrances, introductions, and interactions stops abruptly at the story's climax, when King Leontes (known to my readers simply as "the King whose heart is contrite") bows to his reanimated Queen Hermione, who bows to the character next to her and so on. This new pattern of turning and bowing results in all the characters giving one grand bow to young Will Shakespeare. The story ends when he receives the bow and suddenly understands these players to be the brilliant works of his own mind: "You'll be my players and the world, my stage . . . happy you'll be when you act well your part, and happier, I, making words into art." By shifting the pattern from entering to bowing, Leontes shifts the direction of the story and starts it moving toward its conclusion, which represents a joyful moment of discovery for young Will: "all's well that ends well."

Similar to the climax in the cumulative tale, where characters turn the action by setting a new pattern in motion, the climactic moments of many of Shakespeare's comic plays occur when all the characters are gathered together, old patterns are revealed, and new patterns are begun. In *Twelfth Night*, characters are repeatedly mistaken for each other, resulting in an accumulation of misunderstandings that can be reformulated only when all are onstage together and present to witness what will be revealed and how that revelation sheds new light on the people and events involved. Typically, this all turns on the words of a single character, as in the case of Sebastian, when he gazes after Viola-as-Cesario and wonders: "Do I stand there?" (V.i.227).[1] Once these words are spoken, brother and sister finally have the encounter toward which the story has been moving, and the tangle of mixups begins to unravel. Sebastian and Viola are reunited, Sebastian is understood to be Olivia's real husband, and Orsino learns that Cesario is Viola and thus the woman he will take as his bride. In both the cumulative tale and the play, there is a piling up of characters toward a climax that reassembles them and their relationships in some new and meaningful way.

This cumulative effect is thematic as well as stylistic. At the heart of the cumulative tale is an underlying theme—the power of the imagination, for example. In my book, the characters and their actions underscore this theme either by exercising their own imaginative powers or by affecting the imaginings of other characters. The fact that all these characters meet outside the context of their own play in order to inhabit the imagined world of my book further calls attention to the theme of power through imagining. A similar stylistic-thematic link occurs in *King Lear*, where the theme of self-knowledge is underscored by the self-consciously cumulative format of the play's opening. Lear divides up and parcels out his kingdom, administers the love test, disinherits Cordelia, and banishes Kent—events that happen with dizzying speed in the play's first scene. The story is meant both to begin and to accelerate with Lear's hasty judgments, for it is this immediate piling up of hasty conclusions and rash actions that sets the stage for the painful but necessary realizations that must follow. Indeed, for Lear the arc of change is greater, the wisdom gained is dearer, because the mistakes accumulate so quickly. The real moment of climax comes when he finally is able to understand what was really at stake: peace with Cordelia, with himself, and within his kingdom. The climax, then, could be said to be that moment when his accumulated mistakes have the potential to acquire meaning and therefore to teach him something about himself. The stylistic device of accumulation is thus important because it introduces an extra measure of tension and disorder into the main character's world while also providing the means for an eventual reordering of that world.

Finally, my tale's form allowed me to replicate in a very simple way the metadramatic structure of so many of Shakespeare's plays. Within them, characters often are busy writing and planning other, smaller plays. Sometimes a play ends up being about the writing of plays. The exercise of imagining constantly doubles back on itself, continually calling to our attention the primacy of our own creative instincts and the rewards of creative play. As a tale about a boy writing tales, *All The World's A Stage* reminds us that we, too, have a story to tell about how we came to love language and the many forms into which it can be organized. Just as Will's Muse sings to him, his stories sing to readers whose minds are fresh and fertile. Whether it is the Young Will of my story or the mature Will speaking through his own, his message is the same: embrace and nurture the creative self within!

Note

1. William Shakespeare, *Twelfth Night*, in *The Yale Shakespeare*, ed. Wilbur L. Cross and Tucker Brooke, rpt. (New York: Barnes and Noble, 1993).

5. "All the Colours of the Wind"
Shakespeare and the Primary Student

LOIS BURDETT

Shakespeare is truly part of my life and will stay with me forever. His plays sparkle in my mind, his words are precious jewels in my life and his methods of thought, I collect from afar. And his face I can imagine in my heart.

—KATIE BESWORTH, AGE 7

Katie Besworth (age 8)

Fig. 17: Katie Besworth (age 8) as Macduff

Most students will be exposed to the works of Shakespeare at some point in their educational careers. Traditionally, this initial exposure has been delayed until their high school years, presumably based on the theory that the language and content of the plays are too difficult for younger children to understand. I believe these attitudes underestimate the potential of young students

44

and that, given guidance and encouragement, Shakespeare can be meaningful and fun for our primary students.

Over the past twenty-five years, the study of Shakespeare has become an integral part of my grade two class at Hamlet Public School in Stratford, Ontario. In order to help bring Shakespeare to young students, I have published a series of books entitled *Shakespeare Can Be Fun* (Firefly Books). This series currently offers verse adaptations of eight Shakespeare plays and includes illustrations and written responses by the children themselves.

I have found the study of Shakespeare to be a tremendously powerful medium, which has resulted in dramatic changes for my students. Shakespeare became not an end in itself but a means to an end, and the study went far beyond the plot line of a Shakespearean play. Shakespeare became a friend, not someone to be feared, and language took on a whole new dimension. Seven-year-old William wrote, "The world would be less radiant without Shakespeare's plays, for he warms the world like a burning fire." John, another grade two student wrote, "Shakespeare is like a never-ending song. His words are as powerful as a crocodile's jaws." And Anika, age eight, shared her thoughts in her daily journal: "Shakespeare is like a big piece of chocolate cake. Once you've started, you wish you could go on and on forever in a nonstopping dream."

In this essay I hope to share the excitement of exploring with young children the timeless emotions and ideas of Shakespeare. I particularly wish to address the area of language development and the enhancement of children's communication skills.

Initially, I had no intention of teaching Shakespeare to grade two students. In 1974, I moved to Stratford to accept a teaching position and was surprised to find that all the schools were named after Shakespearean characters. I asked my students, "Why is our school called Hamlet and who is William Shakespeare?" A lively conversation followed. One thought he was a famous boxer. Another believed he was the president of Canada. And my all-time favorite was the boy who responded, "I don't know who William Shakespeare is. I don't know any of the big kids!" It was the children's excitement at making the connection between a historical figure and the name of their school that led me to continue. I wanted the children to be proud of the place in which they lived. Our beautiful city is known throughout the world for its Shakespeare festival, and yet initially, the children knew very little about it.

In keeping with the philosophy that we learn by doing, the whole class became detectives. As they researched Elizabethan times, they began to imagine what it was like to live over four hundred years ago. When the children learned more about Shakespeare's life, they conducted news interviews with their friends, role-playing the parts of William and members of his family. The study quickly spilled over into other areas of the curriculum and rather than a short thirty-minute lesson, it became all-encompassing. In geography, the students used maps to find the location of Shakespeare's birthplace and to follow the route he might have taken to school or to ask Anne Hathaway on a date. During art lessons, life-sized paintings of Shakespeare were created when the children traced themselves. In design and technology, realistic models of the Globe and Shakespeare's birthplace were planned and constructed using lego and building blocks, and props were designed on the computer. Madrigals were sung in music, and in science, herbs were researched and planted. One child became interested in why a thatched roof didn't leak and contacted a local builder. Another student appeared at my door in the summer and seriously announced she'd come to write Shakespeare's last will and testament. Shakespeare became so alive that the children's writing and drawings took on a dramatic quality.

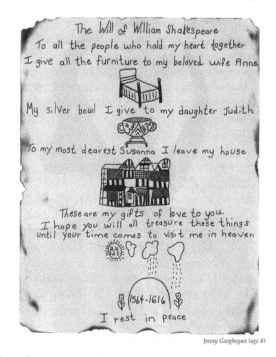

Jenny Geoghegan (age 8)

Fig. 18: Jenny Geoghegan (age 8) writes the last will and testament of Shakespeare

At this point, I began to wonder if the study could be carried one stage further and the students could enjoy an actual performance of a Shakespeare play at the theater. There were plenty of skeptics at the time. It was almost as if Shakespeare was forbidden territory, or at least the preserve of the gifted. Indeed, the first time I took a class of seven-year-olds to a play, I booked seats at the back of the balcony. The students, however, were enthralled, anticipating each new scene with every word and action on stage. People in

Fig. 19: William Shakespeare, by Karolyn Gagnier (age 9)

the audience were amazed that children so young could be so intensely interested and on the edge of their seats for the entire performance. Moreover, the plays often acted as a catalyst between children and parents, and in some cases changed negative opinions the adults had about Shakespeare.

Each year since 1974, a Shakespearean play has become the focus of the school year, and we now book front-row seats. Over this period, the children have studied many plays including: *A Midsummer Night's Dream, Twelfth Night, The Tempest, Macbeth, Romeo and Juliet, Hamlet, King Lear, Much Ado About Nothing, Julius Caesar, As You Like It, The Taming of the Shrew, The Comedy of Errors*, and *The Winter's Tale*.

There has been much discussion regarding the methods by which Shakespeare should be introduced to young children, and whether a play should be approached through the narrative story or the language. I do not see this debate as an either/or proposition, just as I have never subscribed to the theory that reading should be taught solely by phonics or through a whole language approach. A combination of strategies leads to a more fluent reader.

I think of the introduction of children to Shakespeare in much the same way as I do the teaching of a mathematical concept, beginning at the concrete stage, developing through the pictorial stage and finally reaching an abstract understanding. For example, if a child is introduced to the concept of two-digit subtraction with regrouping, the concrete stage might involve manipulating base ten blocks, the pictorial stage might require visualizing the concept with the aid of graph paper and, finally, the abstract stage might include estimating and solving without paper and pencil. I believe both Shakespeare's narrative and language can be introduced simultaneously and the children's understanding will again flow naturally through these various stages.

Let me turn first to the narrative. Unquestionably, the quality of a story is very important. Great stories prompt us to respond as storytellers. When I begin telling the children a simplified story of a Shakespeare play using one of my *Shakespeare Can Be Fun* adaptations, the response to Shakespeare's exciting stories is immediate. They love the intrigue, the comedy, the suspense, and the romance. Only a small portion of the story is shared each day, so that the children can demonstrate their changing perceptions of the characters through role-playing and writing and they become hungry to hear more. At this concrete stage, maps are often used to set the scene and name tags to help the children sort out the characters. At the pictorial level, flannel boards with moveable characters and flow charts are used. At the abstract level, many adaptations by various authors, including Aliki, Bruce Coville, and Marcia Williams are introduced, allowing for more discussion and comparison.

As the children become more absorbed in the role-playing, priceless comments emerge. Seven-year-old Jeremy, as Lysander, remarked to Demetrius, "The fight will be jaw to jaw with madness." I provide the stimulus, the framework, but it is up to the students to organize the information and draw on their own imaginations.

The children learn much more than the plot line of a play. They begin to tap literary talents that they never even suspected they had. As they write diaries and letters pretending to be Shakespearean characters, the dramatic structure allows them to risk expressing their own emotions and thoughts. Their letters become rich in context and contain sensory details and deep insights.

The changes in their writing are remarkable. (In the samples I include throughout this essay, the children's words and spelling have been left in their original, unedited form to give a sense of the development of their communication skills.) Seven-year-old Devon's writing is shown here in September with a story about four crickets and again in April of the same school year, as she shared her evocative description of the witches in *Macbeth*.

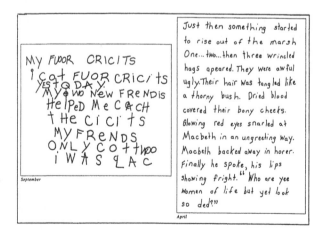

Fig. 20: Devon Searle (age 7) in September and again in April of the same school year

When, then, does the language of Shakespeare become involved? I like to introduce Shakespeare's words as each scene unfolds. The children come to understand the story so well that they are able to predict the meaning from the context and are held spellbound by the beauty of Shakespeare's images. Again, as with the narrative, I see the children moving through the various stages. At the concrete stage, the children role-play various lines, create tableaux from different scenes, move to the beat of his chants, and compose music and dances to accompany the words of his songs. As they move from the concrete to the pictorial, the students view videos and live presentations of professional performances. In some cases, the children even share their displeasure when various lines by Shakespeare are eliminated by directors. At the abstract level, samples of Shakespeare's text are examined and discussed.

During a recent study of *A Midsummer Night's Dream*, my class was introduced to Oberon's speech in Act 2, Scene 1:

> Since once I sat upon a promontory,
> And heard a mermaid on a dolphin's back
> Uttering such dulcet and harmonious breath
> That the rude sea grew civil at her song
> And certain stars shot madly from their spheres.[1]

The children's assignment was to rewrite this speech in their own words, with the proviso that they must include the cliff, the ocean, the music, the waves subsiding, and the shooting star. I was deeply affected by their emotional responses and excited by the quality of their work. Seven-year-old Joy McKeown wrote,

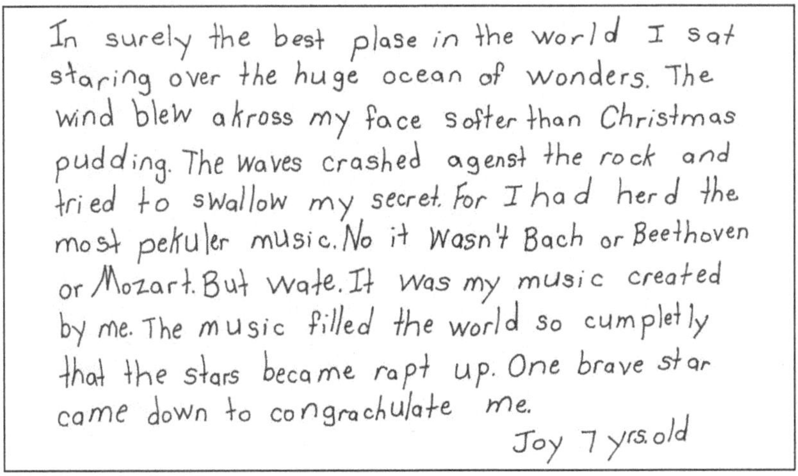

In surely the best plase in the world I sat staring over the huge ocean of wonders. The wind blew akross my face softer than Christmas pudding. The waves crashed agenst the rock and tried to swallow my secret. For I had herd the most pekuler music. No it wasn't Bach or Beethoven or Mozart. But wate. It was my music created by me. The music filled the world so cumpletly that the stars became rapt up. One brave star came down to congrachulate me.

Joy 7 yrs. old

Fig. 21: Joy (age 7)

Courtney Cunningham (age 7) had a different perception of the scene.

One day I sat resting on a cliff as high as a cloud! The wind whisaled a cheerful tune. The waves below rored like canon balls. No one knows what Mother Nacher looks like but at that momint I saw her. She reached out and tuched my face! Then a breeze cot my spine! It was as if life itself was honuring me for a god! I felt like I was a queen! The star of destiny granted all my dreams! Then -SNAP- everything was gone. The waves stoped singing. The wind stoped whistling. Life was captered in the pawm of my hand!

Courtney 7 years old

Fig. 22: Courtney (age 7)

One seven-year-old boy in the room was an elective mute and would not speak while at school. I believe the reason he was able to overcome this problem was due in large part to his desire to take part in the drama activities and to share his writing with his classmates. The following year, he became master of ceremonies at the school concert. This is what Oberon's speech meant to him: "One peaceful evening, I was lying under my secret maple tree on a high cliff listening to the sounds of nature. It was the most beautiful sunset ever. There were reds and oranges, purples and golds. Below me the waves were playing tag, chasing the sun into the distant sky. Then I heard music. It was soft at first, then it grew higher and louder. When I first looked down the waves were pounding against the rocky cliff. Suddenly they were as calm as a sleeping baby. Then out of the gloomy sky, thousands of stars exploded like fireworks. It was beautiful. I wished I could ride those stars. They formed a tunnel. So I crawled through and visited my dreams."

In each of these cases, the initiative to communicate was in the hands of the children. They began to experiment and to make decisions about their own writing. Their words had a dramatic quality and revealed a wealth of knowledge and sensitivity. When we later attended the play at the Festival and heard Oberon's words spoken so eloquently, twenty-five young children gasped in unison and all turned to me with looks of sheer delight. They owned those words! It was one of those teaching moments that I will always treasure.

Children's understanding of Shakespeare can be very deep. One winter morning, seven-year-old Sean arrived at school early. He came to my desk at the back of the room to talk about Shakespeare. "You know," he began, "Leontes in *The Winter's Tale* and Claudio in *Much Ado About Nothing* and King Lear are all alike. They wouldn't believe the truth, even from the people they held most dear. In their minds, they imagined only lies." In our study of *King Lear*, Kelsie (age 7) wrote about this lack of trust in a poem addressed by the Fool to King Lear:

> I never saw such a fool, such a fool,
> Who scorns love, stubborn as a mule.
> Lies are truth, and truth are lies,
> So both heart and justice dies.
> Your scented daisy wilts in the rain,
> You'll never see Cordelia again.
> I wouldn't pick to be a fool you see,
> But that's the life you've chosen to be.

The intensity with which young children convey their feelings can be profoundly moving. During the study of another tragedy, seven-year-old Anika imagined herself as Macbeth.

The deed is done. But oh, it leaves me in terror. I will never see the sweet face of King Duncan again. This is not what I bargined for. My mind will never rest. Darkness fills my head. It surrounds me with dred, and takes away my curage and freedom. These thots will haunt me always and forever efect my brain. Duncan can never be awakined. He is in everlasting sleep. There is no way to free myself now. It is unchangeable!

Macbeth

Fig. 23: Anika Johnson (age 7)

And did the children comprehend the essence of *Macbeth*? Matt (age 7) wrote, "I think Shakespeare wrote the Scottish play to tell the people that bad doesn't pay and what goes around comes around." Morgan (age 7) observed, "There is more to this world than getting to the top. No one will weep at your grave." And Alex (age 7) summarized the play, in his own words: "*Macbeth* is all about pride and blood and spears and swords but mostly it's about power. He started as a good and kind man who protected his country. He tried to become higher and mightier but was never satisfied and became uncivilized."

A recent study of *Romeo and Juliet* with my grade two class evolved into a year-long examination of prejudice. Connor (age 7) wrote, "Why is there prejudice in this world? That's what Shakespeare wanted us to think about in *Romeo and Juliet*. Prejudice is a terrible thing. Violent words sink into your heart forcing you to say something very mean in return! People even use similes and adjectives that are very hurtful. Just because you don't have the same name, the same hat, or the same colour of skin doesn't mean you can't be a team. It is hard to face prejudice. The only way is to speak from your brain and your heart, for they are the masters of your body. Prejudice hurts!" Stu, another grade two student wrote, "Shakespeare spread secrets all over the world. The lesson I think Shakespeare was trying to tell us in *Romeo and Juliet* is that prejudice is horrible. Prejudice is like killing someone's spirit on purpose and its not yours to break. In fact, if you go too far, someone may even be killed. I wish there was serenity all over the world, for it's what's inside that counts. I solemnly swear to never be prejudiced."

As the children became more involved, words with a Shakespearean flair began to appear in the children's own writing. A few years ago, my grade 2/3 class was invited to the Utah Shakespeare Festival in Cedar City to present *Macbeth for Kids*, which I had written in rhyming couplets. Eight-year-old Ellen Stuart described her despair the last day of the performance: "I find all joy has left me. I am as slick and solemn as the snow. I said to myself be brave, be not wounded by the great dagger which doth hang in the air. The great chief of misery did put it there."

And their love of Shakespeare? This letter written by seven-year-old Anika on the last day of school says it all.

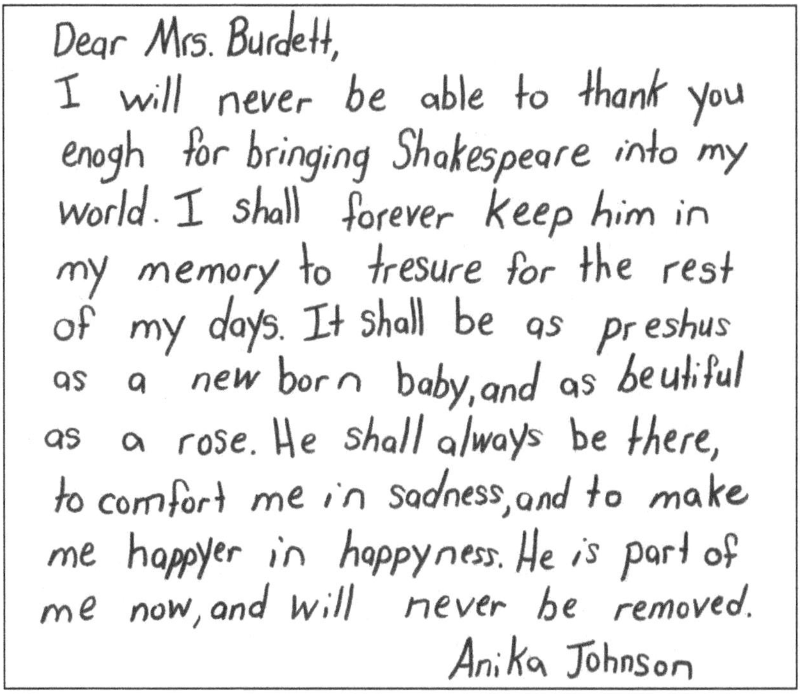

Dear Mrs. Burdett,
I will never be able to thank you enogh for bringing Shakespeare into my world. I shall forever keep him in my memory to tresure for the rest of my days. It shall be as preshus as a new born baby, and as beutiful as a rose. He shall always be there, to comfort me in sadness, and to make me happyer in happyness. He is part of me now, and will never be removed.

Anika Johnson

Fig. 24: Anika Johnson (age 7)

A few years ago, Tom Patterson, the founder of the Stratford Festival, lost his larynx to cancer. The following touching letter from seven-year-old Laura to Tom exemplifies the passion the children feel for Shakespeare:

Dear Tom Patterson,
I have heard! It is too bad you had to have your voice box plucked. I hope this little letter plucks that little bit of grief from your heart and wipes the tears away on your cheeks. Your voice is gone but your thoughts are still here. They will be here forever! You've given us your mind and thoughts will be your voice to guide your heart and talk for you. You have changed the world with your love of plays and the world has changed you. You have also changed us with our likes of Shakespeare. Now it is our turn to be your voice. We will speak for you as long as we live.

This project grew out of the experience of living in one specific community. It was designed to highlight the particular cultural environment of Stratford, Ontario. Now, when I think back over the twenty-five years, it is hard to imagine a time when Shakespeare was not part of my classroom. In our increasingly test-oriented classrooms, drama is often considered a frill. With a return to the basics, perceived frills are out and the three R's in. But just what did the children accomplish? I think of the children on stage and I know their use of oral language has become more fluent and expressive. I remember how engrossed the children were when they attended theater performances. Their powers of concentration and attention have certainly developed. I saw children beginning to take risks and having the confidence to experiment with language in poetry and stories. I heard children talking about their theater and their pride in their town. And most important, I saw children expressing a new confidence in their own abilities. I am not sure what can be more basic than that.

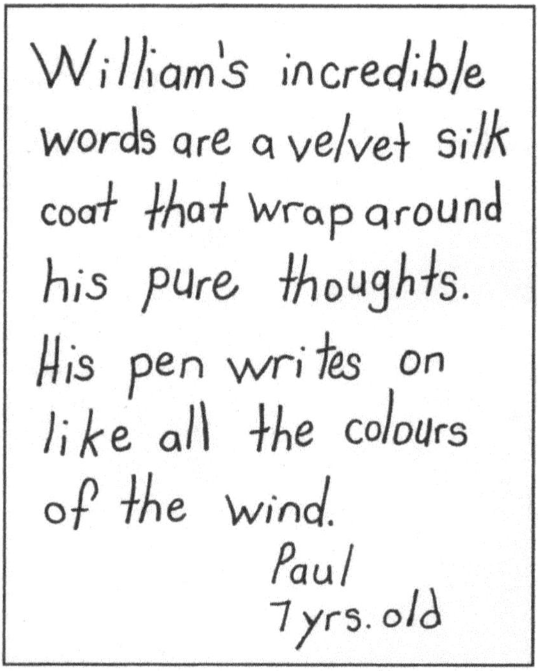

William's incredible
words are a velvet silk
coat that wrap around
his pure thoughts.
His pen writes on
like all the colours
of the wind.
                Paul
                7 yrs. old

Fig. 25: Paul McGarry (age 7)

Fig. 26: Julia Graham (age 8)

Note

1. William Shakespeare, *A Midsummer Night's Dream*, ed. Harold F. Brooks (London: Methuen, 1979), Arden edition, 2.1.149–53.

6.   Nutshells and Infinite Space
Stages of Adaptation

BRUCE COVILLE

This essay comprises some notes on the problems and process involved in adapting the text of Shakespeare's plays to fit the picture book format, with some ancillary thoughts on the matter of interweaving Shakespearean material in young adult novels.

A Bit of Background

Since 1992 I have had the terrifying privilege of adapting five of Shakespeare's plays for publication in storybook format. Though I wish I could take credit for this project, the original idea came from Diane Arico, the editor who first mentioned it to me when I introduced her to an actor who "does" Shakespeare (that is, he performs one man shows in which he appears as the Bard). As we were walking away from the encounter Diane said, "You know, I've been wanting to do a series of Shakespeare picture books for a long time."

With unusual self-restraint, I managed to avoid flinging myself at her feet, clutching her ankles, and crying, "Me, me, me, oh please pick me to do this!" Instead, I simply opined that it sounded like a wonderful idea and that if she ever got around to it I hoped she would consider me for the project—which, to my delight, she eventually did. I say eventually, because it took three years and a shift of jobs before she was finally able to convince the publisher where she worked that the project was a good idea. Her immediate supervisor quashed the idea more than once with a great deal of hand wringing over the imagined criticism we might receive for daring to tamper with greatness.

Eventually, however, Diane prevailed and I was given a chance to adapt *The Tempest* for the picture storybook format. The project proved successful, and I have since adapted four more of the plays, the most recent being *Twelfth Night*. In wrestling with these adaptions I have evolved a five-stage process for approaching the task. The latter part of this essay will describe

Fig. 27: *William Shakespeare's The Tempest*, retold by Bruce Coville, illustrated by Ruth Sanderson

that process. However, before I move into that description I would like to address two other instances in which I have been able to weave Shakespearean story elements into my own work.

The first was in a young adult novel titled *Fortune's Journey*, which tells the story of a young woman leading her recently deceased father's acting troupe west during the California Gold Rush. During my research for this story I discovered that for actors, performing Shakespeare was sometimes big business in the Old West. So I gave my group of worthy players a chance to work within canon, allowing them plenty of opportunity to quote lines at each other and, in one key scene, for the novel's romantic leads to discover an unexpected crackle of connection when they performed opposite each other.

The second interweaving occurs in a middle grade novel (a designation generally meaning a book considered appropriate for 8–12 year olds) called *The Skull of Truth*. In this story a boy who is a chronic liar stumbles into a magic shop where he becomes connected with a skull that compels the truth from whoever bears it. I spent some time flailing about in a search for the proper folkloric provenance for the skull before it struck me that there is one and only one well known skull in all of western literature, and that is Yorick. Immediately the novel came to life for me. Yorick was a jester, of course, and so it made perfect sense for my skull to offer a torrent of wisecracks, bad jokes, and jesterly advice. One of the key scenes in the novel occurs when Yorick offers to show his life story to Charlie (the protagonist). Using a kind of magical sense-o-rama, he spirits Charlie back to Elsinore, where he provides a backstory to the action of *Hamlet*. The scene culminates in the moment when Hamlet holds the skull and proclaims his famous "Alas, poor Yorick" lines, though the young reader experiences it all through Yorick's eyes (or, more precisely, his eye sockets, since he is but bone by this point).

I had two reasons for threading Shakespearean material through these novels. First, it was enjoyable for me as a writer. Second, and more important, I was hoping that if I caught young readers with the thread of story I could also pique their interest in the plays those stories came from. (My faith in this as a method for bringing young readers to Shakespeare is undoubtedly rooted in the fact that the first time I read Shakespeare for myself, rather than as an assignment, was in reaction to reading John Fowles's *The Collector* as a teenager. The novel is deeply larded with references to *The Tempest* and, eager to find out what Fowles was talking about, I went directly to the play as soon as I had finished the book.)

Since I assume that most people reading this will agree that there is value in exciting young people about Shakespeare's work, what I want to discuss here is not the why, but the how—not the reason, but the method.

For me, the tactic—the bait, if you will—is story.

In the introduction to her own book of Shakespeare retellings, the great British children's author E. Nesbit tells how her daughters, after a visit to Shakespeare's home, had tried to read one of the plays. Finding themselves utterly lost, the girls cajoled Nesbit into telling them the story instead: "You will understand when you grow up that the stories are the least part of Shakespeare," she told them, with a level of didacticism that is fortunately absent from her tart and funny novels. "But it's the stories *we* like," replied her daughter, Rosamund.[1]

Indeed, it is stories that children long for, and it is Story that is the entry point for many people to the pleasures of Shakespeare. I think it is sometimes hard for Shakespeare scholars and enthusiasts, having swum for years in the

Fig. 28: *The Skull of Truth*, by Bruce Coville, illustrated by Gary A. Lippincott

sweet ocean of his poetry, to recall the thrill of having one of the plays unfold as story—to remember experiencing it for the first time and being stirred by that ancient question: *What happens next?*

Of course, it's not just children who long for story. I had a chance to interview William Kennedy shortly after he won the Pulitzer Prize for his novel *Ironweed*. When I asked him about the success of the book, he said, "My entire generation is longing for a good story, well told."

If you tell your tale well enough, children, especially, will want to hear it over and over, in a multitude of forms, and will follow it into new venues—

venues into which they might not otherwise have ventured, such as Shakespeare in text or performance.

It may, indeed, be true that the stories are the least part of Shakespeare, but they are also the armature on which all else depends. The hope I hold in doing my retellings is that with an early and pleasurable experience of Shakespeare a child will be able to find his or her way past what I call "the curse of greatness"—the bizarre idea generated by our culture that because Shakespeare's plays are great that they are also too hard for the average mortal to understand and that there is more work than pleasure involved in experiencing them, whether on the page or on the stage.

What I want to describe next is the five-step process I use when I am trying to bring one of those stories to a younger set of readers.

Stage One: Selection

Obviously, the first question to ask if you're going to adapt one of the plays to the storybook format is: which one? Answering this question involves a delicate dance between author, editor, and (alas) the marketing department.

When working for young readers it is helpful to have one or more youthful characters they can identify with, as in *Romeo and Juliet*. Magic is always a big draw for young readers, so plays like *The Tempest* and *A Midsummer Night's Dream* work well. Kids also like the grim and the gory, so *Macbeth* though lacking a youthful protagonist, has a certain appeal.

From the publisher's point of view, a well-known title is also extremely desirable. Thus my suggestion that we do *The Winter's Tale* as a follow-up to *The Tempest* generated considerable consternation among the marketeers, who felt not enough people knew the title, and I was asked to do *Macbeth* instead. *Hamlet*, being among the best known of the titles, has been suggested more than once. My response is that (a) I'm not ready and (b) they're going to have to give me a longer format to work in. In return I occasionally suggest *Cymbeline*, an idea that usually results in a bemused snort, at best.

Political issues also play a role in the selection process. We delayed doing *Romeo and Juliet* because of concerns about glamorizing teen suicide, and I know from conversations with my editor that *The Merchant of Venice*, *Othello*, and *The Taming of the Shrew* are all going to be tough projects to sell in-house.

I think it is interesting to note the degree of correspondence between the plays that I have chosen to adapt and those that other authors have tackled. My adaptations, to date (and in order) are *The Tempest, A Midsummer Night's Dream, Macbeth, Romeo and Juliet,* and *Twelfth Night.* All five of these titles appear in the first volume of Leon Garfield's adaptations, four of

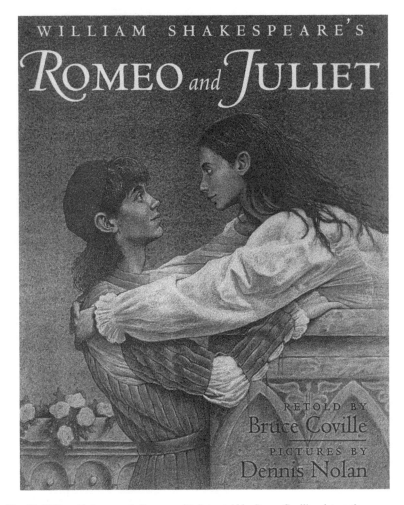

Fig. 29: *William Shakespeare's Romeo and Juliet*, retold by Bruce Coville, pictures by
Dennis Nolan

them appear in E. Nesbit's volume, and four have also been adapted by Lois
Burdett.

Stage Two: Immersion

While the first stage of the process can lead to some tense situations, the next
is pure pleasure, since as soon as the editor and I have agreed on a title I have
an excuse to wallow in the most gorgeous language ever written. I also have
an excuse to indulge my biblophilia, since it's clear (I tell myself) that I need

Fig. 30: *William Shakespeare's A Midsummer Night's Dream*, retold by Bruce Coville, pictures by Dennis Nolan

to have at least three editions of whatever title I'm working on. These in hand, I read the play over and over, trying to find my way into it.

I also begin reading a variety of commentaries. This is partly to further my understanding of the play, of course, but also to help me locate thematic threads that I might pull to the surface when I actually start writing. Alas, because of the intense restrictions on length in this format, this work is usually discarded during the editing process.

For example, when adapting *Macbeth*, I eventually became aware that there was an underlying order to the things the weird sisters say to Macbeth.

In the first draft of my adaptation, their opening conversation with him read as follows:

> *"Greetings, Macbeth, Thane of Glamis," said the first*
> *witch, who always spoke of what had been.*
> *"Greetings, Macbeth, Thane of Cawdor," said the*
> *second witch, who spoke of what is.*
> *"Greetings, Macbeth, who shall be king hereafter,"*
> *said the third witch, who spoke of what was to be.*
> *And with her prophesy of kingship to come, she*
> *planted a hunger in Macbeth's heart that grew until it*
> *devoured all that he loved and valued.*

In order to fit the needs of the book this was eventually trimmed to:

> *"All hail Macbeth, Thane of Glamis," said the first.*
> *"All hail Macbeth, Thane of Cawdor," croaked the*
> *second.*
> *"All hail Macbeth, who shall one day be king,"*
> *hissed the third.*

Whether this is a loss or an improvement I will leave to the individual reader to decide. But even when I am not able to weave these bits of information into the text itself, working them out helps to keep me on track.

In addition to reading the text and commentaries, I try to experience the play in as many forms as possible. For example, I always get an unabridged audiotape version, which I listen to over and over as I am driving around. I find these tapes work best once I already have a solid handle on the play, since the lack of all visual cues can make them hard to understand. Additionally, I try to watch at least two videotaped versions of the play. And, of course, if at all possible I'll see the show in performance.

The one thing I do *not* do at this stage is read other adaptions, at least not until I already have mine in solid shape.

Stage Three: Analysis

As a way of circling the text (and because it suits my anal-retentive personality) I next do a breakdown of the format. That is, I map out the acts and scenes, starting with a simple chart letting me know how many lines are in each scene.

Macbeth, at 2096 lines, is one of the shortest plays, with a lean plot structure. Though it might initially seem that a shorter play would be easier to squeeze into the limitations of my format, this is not necessarily so.

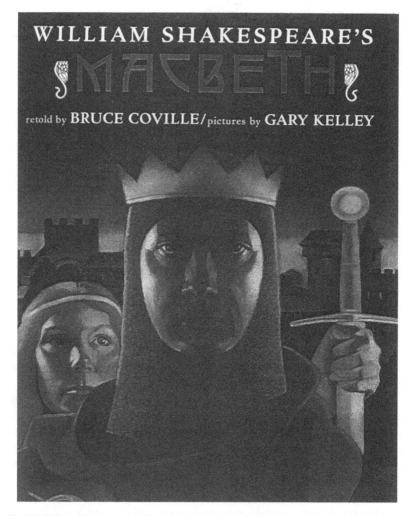

Fig. 31: *William Shakespeare's Macbeth*, retold by Bruce Coville, pictures by Gary Kelley

Macbeth, for example, is so tightly structured that it has no subplots to trim away. Not only that, but questions about plot and motive that can rush past in the excitement of a production—such as what benefit it will be to Macbeth to kill Duncan *after* the old king has declared Malcolm as his heir— can become more glaring when you strip the story down.

Next I write a line or two for each scene to explain the main thrust of the action. This done, I have a one- or two-page document that helps me see the shape of the play. More importantly, writing it out this way helps me find the "bones" of the play, gives me a better feel for its structure.

At this stage I also begin to note lines that I want to use verbatim in the text, some simply because I love them, others because they are well-known enough that they are almost required for the adaptation.

Stage Four: Re-visioning

At some point—usually when I can't avoid it any longer—I sit down and start to write. The hardest thing here is the first line; it seems I have to find that before I can get on with the story. That line may well change later. (In fact, it usually does.) But until I have it, I can't go on.

This stage is where the "magic" (or, at least, the subconscious) comes into play. If I have done my initial work properly, then by this time the story is so well set in my head that the first draft will pour out fairly rapidly. I keep a copy of the play beside me for reference as I work, and pull in dialogue as I can. (A mechanical note: I eventually found it was easier to do this if I make a photocopy of the text, which is much easier to manage when you want it constantly open beside you on the desk.)

The only case in which I have significantly altered the structure of a play was with *The Tempest*, where I untangled the timeline in an attempt to make the flow of events more clear to young readers.

Stage Five: Plunder and Prune

Once my version is in draft form I begin plundering the play for as much original language as I can smoothly massage into the story. This task must be balanced against another less aesthetic but equally important one: keeping the text lean enough to fit the storybook format.

A word about that format: In the picture book world, virtually all books are thirty-two pages in length (two "signatures" of sixteen pages), and a text of one thousand words would be considered lengthy. The "picture storybook" is a designation some publishers use—generally for movie tie-ins, actually—for a book that has a longer text, but where there is still an illustration on every page, and where the illustrations are at least as much a part of the experience as the text. For *The Tempest* I was allowed about 3,500 words to tell the story in a forty-page book. That allocation has crept up in subsequent books, and I can now go to between 4,000 and 4,500 words for a forty-eight-page book.

The first three to five drafts tend to get progressively longer. Then I have to reverse the process; the next several drafts are a time of painful pruning. Basically, I am faced with the warring tasks of putting in as much of the original dialogue as possible while at the same time cutting the text to fit in the format. As anyone who has spent much time writing knows, shorter is harder than longer, and this is the stage where I have to confront that truth on a word-by-word basis, often looking for ways to recast a sentence so that a paragraph will end up a line shorter.

Even with all this pruning, the first manuscript I send the editor will be too long. This is because, over the course of several of these projects, we've decided that it makes more sense for me to leave material in, so that we can discuss (negotiate, argue) our options than it does for me to hand in the tightest possible manuscript, which is my usual preference.

It is during these negotiations with the editor that I may, regretfully, be forced to the conclusion that a character or subplot has to be discarded. Making these decisions can slow me down for some time, as they are very painful.

And Finally ...

Even once the manuscript has been approved and accepted there is a final stage that might be listed: Letting Go.

Just as a playwright must, at some point (at least, these days) release the play to the director, eventually I have to release the text to the artist. Yet revision may continue even after the artist has received the manuscript, because once he or she works out how the text will be divided and what images are to be used, I may need to make additional cuts to accommodate the design of the book.

More pain.

I must say that in this matter of artists I have been extraordinarily lucky, though I doubt anything will top my experience with *The Tempest*.

The artist for this project, Ruth Sanderson, treats a picture book assignment very much as a director or producer might approach a play or film. After working out how she wants to break up the text for illustration purposes, she creates a story board. Then she "casts" the picture book—that is, she assigns roles to friends and family that she will be asking to pose for her. She then hires a costumer to create outfits for the book, and invites her cast to come together for a day of posing as they recreate tableaux from the story.

I was greatly chuffed when Ruth asked if I wanted to appear in *The Tempest*—and even more so when she asked if I wanted to be Prospero. (I had assumed I would be cast as Caliban.) There I am on the cover of the book, staff in hand, commanding the wild waves in their roar.

If Prospero himself can be seen as a stand-in for the greatest word-wizard of all time, then being invited to portray him in my own picture book version of the play offered a kind of symmetry that, were one to believe in omens, would have felt like a blessing on the project.

7. Puck's Gift

SOPHIE MASSON

One afternoon when I was eleven or so, my father came home from work with a sheepish look on his face and a record in a paper bag under his arm. Now, that wasn't an uncommon happening: Papa might wear the same fashion in shirts and trousers for years on end, much to Maman's wry despair, but the shelves at our place groaned with books, bought both new and second-hand, and our record cabinet in the living room was stuffed to bursting with recordings of music from all over the world, and all times. But this particular record was to have a deep resonance in my life, for it marked the first time I ever met the work of the man who was to have one of the deepest influences on my creative life. I can still see it now: dark green, elegant, with a reproduction of an Elizabethan miniature of a gentleman on its cover, it was called *Shakespeare Songs and Consort Music*: songs from the plays, performed by the great English singer, Alfred Deller (1912–1979), who single-handedly revived the lost, exquisite art of the counter-tenor, so popular in Shakespeare's day.

I can still feel the skull-tightening chills that washed over me as I first heard Deller's otherwordly voice. It seemed to me then exactly like the voice of fairytale, the teasing, strange voice, neither quite male nor quite female, that guides and lures the hero through the woods, and into an extraordinary, transforming adventure. Puck's voice, I think of it now.

So it was not through the plays, but the songs, that I first came to know Shakespeare: it was thus that he got under my skin and into my bones and blood. You see, I was not born to Shakespeare's own mother tongue; that brisk, rich, sprawling, beautiful language which was so much more than just a bit player on the stage of his genius. My parents were both born in France, though my mother's direct ancestry is Spanish, Portuguese, and Basque, and my father's French Canadian as well as straight French. To complicate matters, I myself was born in Indonesia, and we lived partly in Australia and partly in France. But it was French that was we children's native tongue, and French that my parents fought their language battles for.

In my family, English was not supposed to cross the threshold. My romantic, moody father wondered aloud how anyone could love in English: it was a tongue fit for business but not much else, he declared. And so, to make quite sure we got a romantic education, he read aloud to us, and encouraged us to read for ourselves, many of the great French classics: poets such as Ronsard and Chrétien de Troyes and Chateaubriand, novelists such as Hugo and Balzac and Dumas and Féval, playwrights such as Molière and Racine and Edmond Rostand. On the other hand, my reserved, analytical mother did not make such a naive comment about English. But in a sense, and despite the fact that as we grew older, she would often point us in the direction of such modern English authors as D. H. Lawrence, Anthony Burgess, and Graham Greene, she felt that the *traditional* or classical literature of England was more of a direct competition with the traditional literature of France, and did not encourage us toward it. She did not think much of modern French literature, apart from a few examples; and she freely admitted the English were "better at modernity," and better at expressing a sense of alienation and nihilism: a rather poisoned chalice, to be sure!

Neither of them censored what we read, however, and as time went on, I read more and more in English, and wrote in it, too, finding a deep pleasure in this language which was not my own but whose richness and flexibility I revelled in. As I was by nature a rather secretive but wildly imaginative child, the intelligent elegance admired by my mother and the swaggering gallantry adored by my father, did not satisfy me entirely. I discovered all those wildly imaginative children's novels penned by secretive English authors: *The Narnia Chronicles*, *The Wind in the Willows*, *The Hobbit*, *The Winnie the Pooh* stories, the novels of Leon Garfield and Alan Garner, and so on. Rapidly, this peculiarly English territory, *l'Angleterre profonde*, if you like, became my favorite hang-out spot. Shakespeare is not so easily approached by a lone child, however, and so for a long while it was only as a songwriter that I knew him, until I reached high school and met the English teacher who was to change things for me.

Mrs. Rose Leaf, English herself, had come to Australia many years before, but still had a strong English accent and a strong working-class sensibility that, despite seventies pieties, never saw Shakespeare as some kind of ruling-class apologist, but always as subversive, funny, tragic, *true*. There was nothing dead about the man whose words sprang from the page in her classes; and her ability to explain the language, the context of the time, the jokes and puns and *double entendres* never weighted down the text but instead clarified and heightened it, so that it came alive and close to us in a most extraordinary way. Her sense of theater too made the plays as plays come to life for us; we fought over the opportunity to read parts in class, we eagerly anticipated the performances we went to as part of the course, and some of us even clamored to have many more plays put on the class agenda. In short, this wonderful teacher made it possible for us to understand that Shakespeare was fun; but not fun in a superficial way: fun in the way that the genuinely exciting, the genuinely moving, the genuinely extraordinary, is.

For me, it was, as we say in French, *un bouleversement.* That earlier experience of Shakespeare as songwriter had planted the seed, but now that seed burst through the ground and into the open air. In Shakespeare, I recognized instantly, as so many have recognized before me, a kindred spirit. This is not as arrogant as it may seem, for in learning to know and love Shakespeare, the passionate yet reserved, imaginative, secretive, but often arrogant teenager that I was learned the true humility that, it seems to me, is a prequisite for any creative artist: a letting go of ego, a lightness of touch. In Shakespeare, though there's such a living, warm, generous human presence, there is not at all the Saturnine self-regard of all too many post-medieval artists. Shakespeare's is a mercurial spirit. And Mercury, or, to give him another name—that famous English name of Celtic origin—Puck, was the messenger of the gods, or the fairies—what you will—and also the Trickster.

Back then, my reading of the plays left me with a great curiosity about their author. I read a lot about his period and about what was known of his life. And in my mind's eye, a picture grew of the person I thought he might have been, making me feel even closer to him. I learned that Will, as I began to think of him, had been steeped as a boy in the rich stories and folklore of his rural Warwickshire culture, and was deeply knowledgeable about all country matters, but also knew the city and court life as an adult. He'd most likely been brought up Catholic, in a time where religious strife was endemic, but was not a dogmatist for any religious viewpoint, though a deep spiritual sense pervades his work. He was a person who had had to scrabble for his living, and had never been able to take anything for granted. He was a courteous, reserved man who partook both of the marginal and the mainstream, an observer who saw courtier and groundling with equal acuity and compassion, a man who could nevertheless conduct his business life with brisk efficiency.

Myself a child whose tangled ancestry and experiences defied simple explanation, I thrilled to the glorious knowledge that you could not categorize him or his characters. They were always people, no matter what race or sex or age or temperament or historical period they inhabited, and were never dead-eyed specimens pinned stiffly down for symbolic lessons. Yet it was not a "guru" kind of experience I had, as a teenager, with Will Shakespeare; not an idolatry either, for I certainly never spent all my time with him, or worshipped at his feet. One or two of the plays, such as *Titus Andronicus*, I positively disliked. But being in his company was a joy, an inspiration always, and in a slow, cumulative, deeply nourishing way, this relationship, which I can only characterize as a friendship, not only inspired me in my creative life but also my relationship with English itself.

The great gifts of generosity, daring, and metamorphosis which Shakespeare brings cannot possibly be overestimated for the young writer in particular, and the young person in general. So in a naive way I tried to emulate Shakespeare: I was very keen, as a teenager, on writing poetry modelled on his sonnets, as well as other forms I loved, such as ancient Celtic bardic stanzas. I did not like to show these poems to anyone, for I was afraid they'd think I was overextending myself—which of course I was. Yet it seemed to me that in Will's work, I could hear a voice whispering to me: relax, he seemed to be saying to me; it's only when you stop worrying about originality that in fact it visits you, for it's like grace, not something you can will into being. What, you're afraid that you'll never measure up to the true English-speakers, that everyone else knows much more than you, that you won't fit in with the crowd: what does it matter? Everyone, whether they're bilingual or not, feels like that, a stranger in their lives, sometimes: it's part of the experience of being human. Just do what you can, what comes naturally, but never imagine that what you write will change the world or even one person's mind . . .

There was another aspect to Shakespeare, his rich sense of the enchanted world, which also connected deeply with me, then, as, indeed, now. As a child, I'd always been a lover of fairy tales, of myths and legends. My father told us many, many traditional stories, often enlivened with bloodcurdling voices and thrilling actions. Sometimes he would tell us these stories in the very places in which they happened, on one of our frequent trips back to France. We would walk in the meadows or in the nearby wood of Goujon, which had the reputation of being enchanted, and he would tell us how the fairy Melisande had appeared from behind a tree to a young peasant girl gathering wood; or how Death had been tricked by the blacksmith Misery into not taking him, and had sat in just *that* apple tree over there; or how see, that well over there, a great treasure was found in it, dating from the time of the Romans, but it was *cursed*; or how, see, in that castle over there, lived a man whom some said was just like Bluebeard. The wood was green and rustling, and full of shifting and mysterious shadows, as well as wild animals such as boar and deer, and many people had been lost in its deceptively gentle depths. Was it any wonder that the stories lived so richly for me, when I could conjure up smells, sights, sounds of real places, situate the stories in known geographies, think that one could just as easily meet a fairy in the woods as another rambler?

When we went for long walks in Australian forests, which preserve very strongly a sense of ancient presence, I saw no conflict between the two enchanted landscapes, but a sense of human linkage. They might not be called fairies in Aboriginal folklore, but the Nyols and Narguns and

Potkooroks that inhabited the folk stories of Aboriginal people were closely related to the unpredictable otherwordly beings of European folklore. And so, when I first read *A Midsummer Night's Dream*, it was both the wood of Goujon, and the Australian bush, that leapt to my mind. And somehow, the reality of these places became even greater, the sense of those ancient forests heightened, and lived experience became, through the medium of a tongue not my native one, and a spirit so sympathetic and subtle, both richer and clearer: Puck doing his usual job of leading astray in order to discover, taunting in order to challenge, yet never deserting you at the crucial moment.

As I grew up and subtly morphed into both an adult, and a published, then professional, writer, Will's presence was very often in my mind. His insights and understandings stayed deep within my work over the years, a nourishing, yet hidden source. For I did not approach Shakespeare directly in my work for a long time after adolescence. In part this was because as I grew into adulthood and realized that Shakespeare was not only seen as a great writer, but as *the* central figure of English-speaking culture, I grew a little shy about my own earlier temerity. An inner, rational voice told me sternly that my earlier insights had been wrong, that I could not possibly understand Will, or truly share in his vision, because I wasn't born to it, by virtue of either nationality or talent. Shakespeare cannot be touched, this voice said. Explore other things, things you can truly understand: and I obeyed, and indeed had many exciting and interesting adventures along the way. But deep inside, almost unknown to my conscious self, my rebellious soul kept the dream alive, just waiting for the moment when it would spring out into view again.

That moment came one morning four years ago, when I was in a Sydney music shop, happily browsing—like my father, books and music are the two things which make me totally ignore the state of my bank balance and shelf space, much to my family's dismay. Suddenly, I caught sight of a familiar name: Alfred Deller. And there it was, newly-released on CD, those *Shakespeare Songs* of my childhood. I stood there for a moment, heart beating fast, a rushing of blood to the head and funny tears starting, before grabbing it quickly, lest anyone else should see it. When I got it home, and put it on, not only did the feeling that had come over me when I first heard Deller's otherwordly voice, singing those robust and beautiful songs, come back to me, but also a new feeling emerged, of excitement, of nervous daring.

I was *ready*, I knew it. The novel I'd dreamed of for years, the one set in the merry, sinister Shakespearean woods of fairy tale and midsummer, was there, waiting for me. And so *Cold Iron*, or *Malkin*, which is its U.S. title, was born: the first of my novels to specifically feature a Shakespearean base, and indeed, with a cameo appearance by Will himself. Based on *A Midsummer Night's Dream* as well as on the lovely English fairy tale *Tattercoats* and folklore about fairies, it was a novel as much sung and declaimed and acted, on the stage of my mind and heart, as written. Writing it was a great liberating experience, an easeful, exciting time of sheer and brilliant fun, going around making up songs and names, colliding worlds together, playing around with mutability and metamorphosis. Written quickly, not at white heat, but at a kind of quicksilver leap, it was a novel whose cadences were such that they made me feel that at last I was truly at home in that tongue which was mine, and yet not mine: that the mercurial spirit of brightness and sadness which danced in it was a gift which at last I was fully able to express gratitude for, and delight in.

And delight is what has also characterized my writing of *The Lost Island*, the Shakespearean-based novel I've most recently been working on. A real magpie motley of a story, based partly on some of the motifs and ideas in *Twelfth Night* and *The Tempest*, it also brings into the mix the Arthurian story of *Perceval* and his quest for the Grail, as well as *Treasure Island*, Venetian intrigue, and Renaissance magic. Set in late-Elizabethan times, like *Malkin*, it is centered around a character whom I love dearly, Hopewell Shakespeare, feckless youngest son of a worthy Worcestershire Puritan farmer, and a distant kinsman of Will's. Hopewell, who has been apprenticed to a wheelwright, spends as much of his time as he can at the Globe with his girlfriend Annie. A bright, lively, naive and heedless young man, rather like Perceval, Hopewell sets off on a great adventure with the saturnine privateer Captain Richard Wolfe: an adventure that will transform his life forever. Like *Malkin*, *The Lost Island* was written at that quicksilver leap of the heart and mind, with a kind of strange, dancing ease, a daring clarity that seemed to guide my very fingers at the computer keyboard.

And like *Malkin*, it first took flight in one serendipitous moment: I had had the basic idea of it for a few weeks or so, but had not been able to think of the right name for my main character. More so, this lack somehow seemed to cripple the idea, to make it creep along rather than flow, for I could not see my hero at all clearly, names meaning a great deal to me. Then, one morning at breakfast, my dear husband David (who was born in Worcestershire) said, "Remember that edition of Shakespeare my sister's students had in Africa? It was called Hopewell Shakespeare, wasn't it? I remember her telling us that one of the kids had said, Hopewell Shakespeare: is that William's brother? Why don't you call your hero Hopewell Shakespeare?"

As soon as the words left his mouth, instantly there he was, Hopewell: standing there in front of me, brightly talking nineteen to the dozen, head full of plans and dreams, live as you or me. Two seconds before, he had not existed; now he was there, impatiently ready to embark on the *Golden Dragon*, and I had to run like mad to keep up with him. Now it seems unstoppable; for in my head are agitating at least two more Shakespearean-themed projects—a novel set in post-Civil War Louisiana, called Malvolio's Revenge; and another, My Brother Will, based on Will's own adolescence as seen by his younger brother Gilbert. Once, I would have been scared stiff to attempt such things; now it seems natural, exciting, and delightful. For that is Puck's gift: the way of the Trickster, who can give you what you want when you least expect it; and grant even airy nothings a local habitation and a name.

Note

For those who are interested: *Shakespeare Songs*, performed by Alfred Deller and Desmond Dupre on lute, is released by Harmonia Mundi, France, HMA 190202.

8. Shakespeare Speaks
Getting the Language Right

GARY BLACKWOOD

I have a confession to make: I've never been to England. In fact the closest I've managed to get is Cape Breton, Nova Scotia. So isn't it rather presumptuous of me to write a novel set in England to begin with, let alone an essay on getting the language right?

Perhaps. But writers are by nature a presumptuous lot. We have to be. Remember the old saw that says you should write about what you know? There's some truth to that, but if writers followed that advice religiously, we wouldn't have *The Wizard of Oz*, or *The Midwife's Apprentice*, or *A Wrinkle in Time*, or Harry Potter. Sometimes we have to write about things beyond the bounds of our own experience.

The fact is, if you want to write a novel about Shakespeare and the Globe Theatre, unless it's a fantasy or an alternate history novel, you're pretty much going to have to set it in England. And Shakespeare is not the exclusive property of the English. He belongs to the world. (Besides, there's always the question of whether or not Will actually wrote all those plays. My theory is that it was Ben Franklin, an American.)

In any case, in order for me to write *The Shakespeare Stealer* and its sequel, it wasn't necessary to know about *England* so much as about England in the early seventeenth century, which is quite a different matter. So, even if I could have afforded to spend a month or two in London—which in 1989, when I wrote the book, I definitely couldn't—I still would have had to depend mostly on books for my research.

Obviously when you're writing a book set in the Elizabethan period, there are a lot more things you need to get right than just the language: What did people wear in 1601? What did they eat? What was it really like backstage at the Globe Theatre? (Nobody really knows for sure, by the way.) Where exactly were things located in London? I had to depend on books for all those sorts of details. And now that *The Shakespeare Stealer* has been

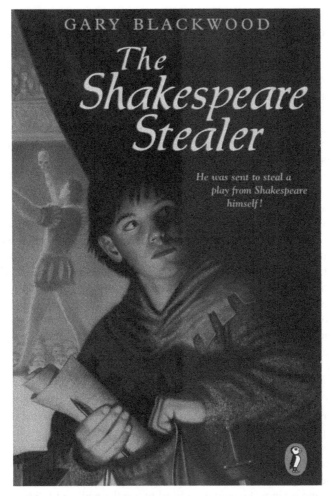

Fig. 32: Cover of Puffin Edition by Greg Call, copyright © 2000 Greg Call, from *The Shakespeare Stealer* by Gary Blackwood

published in Great Britain, I live in fear that one of these days I'll get an indignant e-mail from over there saying something like "You bloody twit; you've put the Tower of London on the wrong side of the river."

With all those other aspects of Elizabethan life to worry about, why go on about such a minor thing as getting the language right? Well, to me it's not a minor thing. I've always been fascinated—obsessed might be a better word—with language, and I think that fact is obvious in all my books. In *The Dying Sun*, which is set seventy-five years in the future, I introduced a number of previously unknown words, plus some new usages for old words.

For example, in the book the Mexican Liberation Army calls gringos *hongos*, which means, literally, "mushrooms." The cars in the story run on "alco." The rural folks often end their sentences with the word "enty?" which is sort of like saying "isn't that so?"—the equivalent of the French *n'est-ce pas*?

For *Beyond the Door*, which is set mostly in a parallel world called Gale'tin, I had to invent whole sentences in the Gale'tinian language. *Moonshine* takes place in the Ozarks during the Great Depression, so the characters say things like "This here we generally just call corn liquor, and I ain't never tasted it. My momma would kill me if'n I did."

By the way, there are some scholars who swear that the dialect Ozarkers used to speak in the era before TV was the nearest surviving relative to Elizabethan English. So maybe I live in the right place after all.

About ten years ago, when I had just started writing *The Shakespeare Stealer*, I got to talking with a fellow author who had published a book that featured a character—a ghost, actually—from the colonial period, and I asked him how he'd gone about making sure the man's speech sounded authentic. "Oh," he said, "I just faked it."

Well, I wanted to do more than just fake it. It had occurred to me that my book, if it ever got published—and for a long time that seemed like a very unlikely prospect—might well be the first exposure a young reader had ever had to Shakespeare and the Elizabethan era. I felt a certain responsibility to give that hypothetical reader as reliable a picture of the time as I could.

So I spent a couple of months digging through books at the Missouri Southern State College library. Luckily for me, someone there was a major Shakespeare buff, so I had a wealth of sources to draw on, including Shakespeare's plays, of course, plus the collected works of several of his contemporaries. Most of those had a glossary that listed all the archaic words and their meanings, and in them I found dozens and dozens of colorful words and phrases and sayings. I would have liked to use them all, but I didn't want too much of a good thing, so I had to leave out such gems as "put your tongue in your purse;" "God's precious potstick;" "Need makes the old woman trot;" "They agreed like two cats in a gutter;" "You have more hair than wit;" "He that would sup with the devil must have a long spoon."

As if it wasn't hard enough to try to approximate Elizabethan speech, I made it even harder on myself by having my main character, Widge, hail from Yorkshire. I could have gotten some sense of what folk from that area sounded like by consulting *Wuthering Heights* or *The Good Companions* or James Herriot's books, but it wouldn't have been Elizabethan. Besides, I didn't want to do dialect, which can be tiresome even for an adult reader; I mainly just wanted Widge to sound rustic in contrast to the Londoners in the book. Some of the peculiarities of Widge's speech come straight from

Shakespeare's rustics—the use of *'a* instead of *he*, for example. Others came from an eighteenth-century Yorkshire dictionary that I stumbled upon—for example, the use of *costard*, which is actually a type of apple, to mean *head*.

To add to the challenge—as if I really needed any more of a challenge—the book is set in the world of the theater, which, then as now, had its own special language. Luckily I had access to dozens of books about the Elizabethan stage in general. As a result I knew that the list of scenes the actors consulted to keep track of their entrances and exits was called the *plot*, and that faking it when you forgot your lines was called *thribbling*, and that what we call the dressing room was called the *tiring-room*, and that the actors were called *players*, and that becoming a player was called *turning Turk*.

To make things even more complicated, I put lots of sword fighting scenes in the book—something that young readers, especially boys, eat up. The moves and the terms used then were very different from those used in modern fencing. Once again I was lucky; I located a volume that was a compilation of three different sixteenth-century instruction books containing literally step by step instructions—complete with illustrations—on how to defend yourself using not just the rapier but also the broadsword and the pikestaff and the dagger.

To top it all off, the whole plot of *The Shakespeare Stealer* revolves around the use of a completely alien sort of language—shorthand. I knew before I started writing the book that a sixteenth-century doctor named Timothy Bright had invented an early system of shorthand. In fact that bit of trivia was what gave me the idea for the book in the first place. I was able to uncover a copy of Dr. Bright's 1588 instruction book titled *Characterie: An Arte of Short, Swift and Secret Writing*, which is supposed to teach the reader how to use his shorthand system.

Unfortunately, his system isn't particularly logical. He doesn't give you a distinctive symbol for each syllable of the language, the way modern shorthand does. All the words that begin with a particular letter or sound do begin with the same sort of little hook or curlicue or whatever—theoretically, anyway—but from there he can go off in any direction. And the number of words he gives you symbols for is sadly inadequate. For example, he lists only thirty common words that begin with the letter R—and some not-so-common words, such as *revile*. Just imagine how many words he omitted that begin with an R.

When I was writing out the passages of shorthand that appear in my books, if I needed a word that Dr. Bright hadn't anticipated, I had to fudge it. In one case, even though I had the right symbol, I blew it. The really astute reader will notice that the symbol for the word *convey* that appears in *The Shakespeare Stealer* is completely different from the one for the same word that appears in *Shakespeare's Scribe*. (If you're the sort who worries about such things, let me say that the symbol in *Shakespeare's Scribe* is the correct one. The one I used in *The Shakespeare Stealer* is actually the symbol for the word *weapon*.)

As tough as it can be to get the language right, the really tricky part is making sure the result is reasonably easy to read and understand. Even if I'd been able to do so, I didn't dare make the characters or the narrator speak the way people in Elizabethan England actually spoke, or it would have been impossible for a young reader. I couldn't even make the characters in *Moonshine* sound the way real Ozarkers sounded in the 1930s, or the reader would have been lost. As important as accuracy is, readability is even more important. I think that about all you can expect to do in a historical novel—especially one for kids—is to give the flavor, the feel of period speech, not try to duplicate it.

Since Elizabethans were fond of wordplay, I included as much of it as possible, as evidenced in this passage from *The Shakespeare Stealer*:

> "I remember well my first faltering steps upon the boards," Mr. Pope said.
> "I'd no idea they had boards so long ago," Mr. Armin said.
> "Oh, we knew how to make boards well enough. It wasn't until your time that we learned how to make an *audience* bored." (*The Shakespeare Stealer*, 1998, p. 131)

Or this, from *Shakespeare's Scribe*:

> "He may vote as he will," said Mr. Armin, "for the will of the company outweighs the will of Will, will he or nil he."
> "And the weal of the company," added Mr. Phillips, "outweighs the weal of Will as well." (*Shakespeare's Scribe*, 2000, p. 68)

Probably the most intimidating task I faced was that of making Shakespeare himself speak. I copped out a bit in the first book, by keeping his appearances to a minimum. But in the sequel it was crucial for the reader to see him and hear him at some length—and not just in everyday conversation, either, but in the throes of creating a new play.

The first thing I had to do was dispense with the notion that he would sound in person the way his writing sounds. I know I don't make nearly as much sense in person as I do in my books, and I assumed that the same was true of Will Shakespeare. But at the same time I couldn't let him sound quite as ordinary as the other characters in the book, so I tried to add a touch of the poet to his speech in passages like this one:

> "Never attempt to write a play, Widge . . . They always betray you. When
> you're only imagining them, they seem so ideal, so full of promise and
> possibility. Then, when you try to get them down on paper, they turn on
> you and refuse to live up to your expectations." (*Shakespeare's Scribe*,
> 2000, p. 174)

Elizabethan speech was more poetic in general than ours, so I made the
prose and the dialogue as graceful as I could without making it seem stuffy.
I also used as many actual words and expressions from the time and as much
sixteenth-century syntax as possible. But I always tried to make it clear from
the context exactly what the meaning was. A number of times I had Widge,
the narrator, come right out and explain a particular bit of slang. For example, as he's climbing into a boat he comments nervously that a few boards
are all that lie "between me and the Land of Rumbelow, that is to say a
watery grave."

No matter how hard you try, of course, you can't please everyone. The
copy editor who worked on *The Shakespeare Stealer* was one of those people who is dangerous when armed with a copy of the Oxford English Dictionary. She checked all the major words and phrases I used in the
book—not just the arcane ones, but *all* of them—to determine whether or
not they were actually in use in 1601. For example, if I'd written "I was hard
pressed to keep up," she noted in the margin something like "There's no evidence that this term was used before 1876" or whenever. Every actor uses
the terms *onstage* and *backstage*, but I couldn't use them because they
weren't introduced until 1790 or whenever; I had to say *on the stage* and
behind the stage. Luckily, by the time I finished *Shakespeare's Scribe* Dutton had another copy editor.

Judging from the letters I get from kids, all the work I put into getting
the language right has paid off. Adam from New York writes, "I liked the
book. I liked the way you had characters talk in sort of a wierd (sic) way. For
example, 'Will they let you go on wi' it?' "

A "reader and fan" named Megan writes, "You made a great choice of
vocabulary and I especially liked the way you made them speak like they
really would have. ('aye')"

However, as I said, you can't please everybody. Ashley from Florida
writes, "I wanted to ask you why the reading was so hard. For example, I still
don't know what Wis means. You said the word a lot and gave no meaning for
the word. This confused me because you said Wis and I did not know what you
were saying. It was hard for me to understand the book because of this even
after my teacher prepared us for how Shakespeare wrote. We studied the way he
wrote by getting worksheets that had words and their definitions. This helped
me a lot but sometimes I was still confused. Wis was not one of the words and
that is why it was still hard for me to understand some of the writing."

Well, as an Elizabethan writer might say, I tried to make it as plain as Dunstable highway, but sometimes you go fishing and catch a frog. I could have used the word *think* instead of *wis*, I suppose, but *wis* is a good word, and, as Shakespeare writes, "Whate'er you think, good words, I think, were best." (*King John*, 4. iii. 28)[1]

Note

1.   *Illustrated Stratford Shakespeare* (London: Octopus Publishing, 1993).

9.　The Players, the Playmaker, and Us

J. B. CHEANEY

London, ca. 1599

Backstage at the Globe Theatre, the actors are in their customary tizzy: chasing down lost props, adjusting capes and swords, running over lines once more, checking the "plot" for entrance cues. Two factors add to the confusion: not only is the Company trying out a new play, but they're staging it in a new theater. Moving in, getting settled, and shaking out the kinks has cut rehearsal time even more than usual; this performance will no doubt be subject to "thribbling" by the actors. The play's author has put much effort into writing a worthy inaugural vehicle, and finds it difficult to be patient with improvisation: "Master Shakespeare, pray do not chide if I must hack Calpurnia's lines—I am suffering with the ague." "Nay, Will, what is this— Et tu, Brute'? Can I not just say, And thou', like an honest Englishman?" "Sir, a word with you. Who is this Cinna the poet I am to play, and for what cause do the people attack him? I am something of a poet myself, and I could add a brief dying speech . . . What's that? They attack him for his bad verses?"

　　The third trumpet sounds, the Company takes a collective breath, and a handful of apprentices and hired men run noisily on stage. *Julius Caesar* escapes from the author's imagination, and into the world's.

Dallas, 1961

In the bug-speckled light of a half-dozen utility lamps, an audience of friends and relatives are gathered to watch a backyard production of *Julius Caesar*. Some of the lines will remind the grownups of high school lit. classes: "a lean and hungry look;" "Beware the Ides of March;" "Friends, Romans, countrymen . . ." But the dialogue takes erratic turns:

The evil that men do lives after them;
The good we can plant with the corpse.

The play was written by my sister and me, with generous helpings of material from *Twisted Tales From Shakespeare*, a book by the humorist Richard Armour. Armour was known for atrocious puns and anachronisms like, "Did you hear anything about a light drizzle of blood in the weather forecast?" The tragic dimensions of Shakespeare's work are left unexplored, but my personal moment of high drama comes in the argument between Brutus and Cassius: "Here is my dagger!" I cry, flipping up a cardboard breastplate. "And here, my heart [altered from ĥaked breast,' for obvious reasons]. If thou be'est a Roman, take it forth; for I know, when thou didst hate Caesar worst, thou lovedst him more that ever thou lovedst Cassius" (Julius Caesar, IV, 3).

Our script is long gone, but forty years later, I *still remember* those lines. A goofy backyard play brought me nose to nose with Shakespeare—hardly a "dignified" introduction, yet it proved to be more effective than many classroom encounters. We have touched noses since: Shakespeare has a way of informing people's lives. Often, like Falstaff, he is "the cause of wit in other men," though it was probably not his ambition to be the world's muse (2 Henry IV, 1, 2, 10). As far as anyone knows, he was only plying his trade.

In his time, writers of drama were called "playmakers"—a descriptive term suggesting a craft. Like a wheelwright, silversmith, or carpenter, the playmaker produced a commodity. Unlike them, his medium was non-material: spoken words. Although some so-called "Oxford wits" dabbled in the form, most of the plays performed on the Elizabethan stage were written by scribblers-for-hire. A few cared deeply about their reputation; others were little better than hacks. They worked on commission or on spec, sometimes collaborated on a project, sometimes came in as script-doctors. Like screenwriters today, they cranked ĕm out to meet an insatiable demand for entertainment.

In general, playmaking was not a prestigious occupation, nor was the playmaker's work "protected." Once accepted, a play became the property of the actors, not the writer. As a member of the company that performed his works, Shakespeare retained some control, but he probably couldn't prevent the Company contributing their own ideas, even during a performance. Hamlet's warning to the traveling players ("And let those that play your clowns speak no more than is set down for them") suggests that at least some of the actors did not approach the text with reverence.

Nor did the audience ever hesitate to express their approval, or their boredom, or their disgust. We will never know how many speeches were altered, how many characters dropped, how many scenes cut or replaced under the direction of the public, who "edited" with the subtlety of a club. But we know that before *The Complete Works of William Shakespeare* joined the Great Books, they first made a place in ordinary English hearts.

Dallas, 1970

Storm clouds gather over the Texas plains, where the students of a small junior college are presenting *A Midsummer Night's Dream* in an open courtyard. With a student body of only about 200, the talent pool is tiny; half the actors have never performed for an audience in their lives. But this play, often described as "magical," has worked a kind of magic on kids who never encountered Shakespeare before, or at least not personally. Over weeks of rehearsal, they have grown into their parts—or rather, the parts have grown on them.

One hour into the performance, magic has transformed the audience as well. They scarcely notice when the light crew cover their equipment with a tarp to keep off the rain. The wind quickens, thunder rolls, umbrellas pop open in the seating area. But nobody leaves—gradually the players realize that nobody *wants* to leave. Imperceptibly, the audience has become part of the play. Helena's "O *weary* night," is a shared joke. Even the clouds get into the act, waiting for a scene change to do their worst.

Audience and cast make a break for the lobby, dripping wet, and quickly set up chairs before the spell can be broken. Every mom and dad and little brother is a member of Duke Theseus's wedding party; we are all audience, we are all players. The fractured performance of "Pyramus and Thisbe" was never more hilarious—our junior-college amateurism is a positive asset. The play has adapted itself to us, and to our circumstances, and become *A Midsummer Night's Dream* like no other.

Shakespeare occupies a unique place in literature: widely regarded as the greatest poet in the English language, yet his life is spare prose. No personal letters survive, no reflections on his work, no self-exposition. The only access we have to his mind is thirty-seven plays (more or less) constituting a landscape so vast that countless scholars have spent lifetimes wandering in it. Given the interactive character of Elizabethan theater, it seems likely that the plays he wrote for the Lord Chamberlain's Men were "works in progress" as long as the Company performed them. And given the unplumbed, open appearance of his mind, they still are.

For Shakespeare, willingly or not, invites collaboration. Since he didn't tell us how his plays were to be performed, we have to determine that for ourselves. I've seen *Julius Caesar* presented as straight history and *Macbeth* as a meditation on gun violence and *The Taming of the Shrew* as feminist tract. These were not all successful, in my opinion but they were all valid. There is no "right" way to do Shakespeare, because his work is never done, never definitive. He teaches us, but we also teach him.

Kansas City, 1990

I've been told to see the new movie version of *Henry V*. Aside from a film clip of Sir Laurence Olivier delivering the St. Crispin's Day speech, I know nothing about the play. But abruptly, one Saturday afternoon in March, I gather up the kids and drive to Westport, where the movie is playing in a small art cinema. I may have been too hasty; some background information would have helped us get into the story. Even so, by the second scene, when Henry half-whispers, "We are glad the Dauphin is so pleasant with us," my daughter and I are enthralled.

It's even better on a second viewing, and doesn't flag much on the third. We read the play, and discover that a lot of material was cut from the text. A comparison with Olivier's 1945 movie reveals a completely different mood and tone. We like Branagh's version better, but why? The production values are more up-to-date, and acting style more visceral—sometimes even vascular (i.e., hammy). But the differences are more than a matter of technique.

I begin wondering what I would do with this play, given the opportunity. . . .

> "*We are* glad *the Dauphin is so pleasant with us.*"
> "*We are glad the Dauphin is so* pleasant *with us.*"
> "*We are glad the Dauphin is so pleasant with* us."

The line can be delivered jovially, sarcastically, menacingly—whose Henry is this? The author's indeed, but also ours. Harold Bloom credits Shakespeare with "inventing the human." That may be an overstatement, but Shakespeare does illuminate the human—from within. He gives us not just characters, but character itself: full-spectrum personality. His greatest creations are wholly themselves, and yet their discovery requires intense participation. It's been said that there are as many Hamlets as actors willing to take him on. What's less obvious is that there is no Hamlet without our contribution; he needs the actor, reader, or scholar to search him out.

Contemporary playwrights take a proprietary attitude toward their characters, who may be memorable and alive, but can't be *ours* in the same way as Lear or Macbeth or Beatrice. Shakespeare only tells us what they say. How they speak, how they affect the others about them, what they really intend—these are largely up to us.

Bolivar, Missouri, 1997

The children are grown and I've turned to writing full time. While my fourth fiction manuscript makes the publishing rounds (unsuccessfully), I've plunged into a new project: *The Playmaker*, a novel about an apprentice in Shakespeare's company. The idea seems inspired. Although structured as a mystery to keep reader interest high, my main purpose is literary. The story will weave itself around the plot of one of the plays, and the overarching theme will explore how art instructs life, and vice versa. (At that time I had yet to hear of *Shakespeare in Love*, Gary Blackwood, or Susan Cooper.)

My protagonist is waiting for me: Richard Malory, an intelligent but rather literal-minded boy from the provinces, who can't understand the purpose of theater at first. Particularly Master Will's plays. A lot of things don't make sense to him: Why do Portia's suitors have to play that guessing game with the three caskets? What makes Lady Constance behave like a madwoman? And why does King Leontes accuse his loving wife of gross adultery, when she has given him no cause for suspicion whatsoever?

That last question has particular resonance for Richard, but ultimately he must supply his own answers. The stage, while it may illuminate his experience, can't reveal what only God knows. The art that he has encountered can show him life, but not tell him how to live it. When it comes to living, everyone (within limits) must be his own playmaker.

And here is where Shakespeare can be particularly valuable to young people today. No subject fascinates them more than themselves. Their world truly is a stage, and they and their peers the players: testing values, trying on attitudes, discovering the roles they can play, and those they can't. They are apprentices at life, just beginning an educational process that should never

Fig. 33: Cover from *The Playmaker* by J. B. Cheaney; cover illustration copyright © 2000 David Kramer

end. They need depth, perspective, balance, and source material. No poet can contribute these better than Will Shakespeare, once we get past a few barriers.

The greatest barrier may be fear. This man has been around for over four hundred years; his language is difficult, his scholarship is massive, his reputation is big and scary. But the playmaker of the Globe would be very surprised to know that he is the terror of modern-day English classes. He should be given his due, and approached in the spirit of a sixteenth-century London audience—who were never shy about expressing their views. Shakespeare was great, but not perfect. Some of his work seems "o'er-hasty," precious, archaic, pretentious—and revised little, as far as we know. A sense of risk and experimentation lingers about him because he seems to have left so much undone. And yet the material we have is so rich and potent that actors and directors can't keep their interpretive hands off it.

Teachers have the same liberty; don't be afraid to question the textbook interpretation of a play. Shakespeare wrote for performance, not English lit. classes; compare movie versions and open the discussion as wide as it will go. How does *Hamlet* look in a corporate boardroom, as compared to a medieval castle, or a *fin de sièle* palace of the last century? What if *Much Ado About Nothing* had to be performed in one hour and fifteen minutes—what should go? How would you update *King Lear*? Does *Romeo and Juliet* work as a story of gang violence set in Verona Beach, California? What's the line between working with Shakespeare and upstaging him? When does a "concept" go too far?

Don't be afraid to experiment with the language. Try paraphrasing speeches, or cutting "expendable" lines. Study a handful of famous quotes from a play out of context (such as "There is a tide in the affairs of men," "Cowards die many times before their deaths," and "The evil that men do" from *Julius Caesar*). Just savor the wording and speculate on meaning and context—then watch the play, or read it aloud in class, and observe how the parts fit with the whole. Rewrite a two-person dialogue, with one character speaking the original text while another responds in contemporary English. Then reverse the roles, and consider what the language adds or detracts. Perform a scene in class in which each character is given only his lines and cues—that way they have to *listen* to each other, and hear the lines with more attentive ears.

Don't be afraid. There are no wrong answers. Shakespeare is one of the few writers who can be appreciated apart from his "worldview," because that worldview is notoriously difficult to pin down. Christians, pagans, nihilists, hedonists, stoics, and cynics all claim him, with justification. But he never fully belonged to any of them. Instead he belongs to all. "He was not of an age, but for all time," wrote Ben Jonson, more profoundly than he knew. Having slipped the surly bonds of ideology, Will Shakespeare is free to roam our minds and mold to our needs.

It's the same kind of freedom he allows us.

II. Interpretation and Critique

10.   Staging Shakespeare's Children

MARK H. LAWHORN

In several recent Shakespeare-related artistic endeavors, a magical force captures the minds and bodies of children. The hero of Susan Cooper's novel *King of Shadows* is an American lad named Nat Field who, while playing a part in a modern London production of *A Midsummer Night's Dream* at a replica of the Globe Theatre, finds himself transported to Shakespeare's London to perform in the same play. In Julie Taymor's film *Titus*, a media-saturated modern boy is carried away by a brutish professional wrestler type down a timewarping stairwell to arrive smack in the middle of *Titus Andronicus*, where the boy becomes Titus's grandson Lucius. Christine Edzard's film *The Children's Midsummer Night's Dream*, in which *A Midsummer Night's Dream* is performed by untrained 8–12 year olds, begins at a puppet theater performance for children. Young audience members and the play's characters magically coalesce in a celebration of the power of Shakespearean drama to appeal to the imaginations of children. When the play's language reaches out irresistibly to the audience as though choosing the young voices as its medium, the relationship between children and playing and words is depicted as an easy, natural one. Peter Holland, director of the Shakespeare Institute, points out that, for young children, Shakespeare's language is no stranger than the other language that surrounds them. During a recent Hawaii Homeschool Association Shakespeare Festival, a parent of a young actor commented on her son's responsiveness to Shakespearean drama, "I guess at this age he hasn't reached the stage where it's uncool or intimidating" (Vogel, B4). Children in fact have a special place in Shakespeare's plays, in which over forty-five child figures appear, an unsurprising number when one considers that about half the population was under twenty years old in early modern England (Brigden, 37).

Children in Shakespeare's plays may perform a number of dramatic functions. First, children may focus attention on adult responsibilities to educate and nurture youth as a means of securing the future of family and the continuity of community values. Such attention may be particularly heightened in situations that depict children as imperiled by their place in a threatening adult society. Second, as sites of moral tension, children in Shakespeare's plays may appear as keen and lively observers of the adult world and as individuals both susceptible to adult manipulations and often capable of resisting base adult influences. In Shakespeare's day, child figures might have worked to offset criticism of the theater as a "destroyer of children" (Crashawe, 170). Third, children may illustrate at times the quickness of youth, entertaining with linguistic cleverness while also evoking a range of cultural tensions such as those between youth and age. The dramatic situations in which children appear may also evoke concerns about processes of maturation, education, moral training, and employment experiences away from home.

Children appeal to desires for domestic, societal, and cosmic order and invoke the bonds of human compassion. Their roles may be diminished, however, by cuts in performance that prevent them from contributing fully to the rich texture and diverse characterization that enhance the plays' structural and thematic concerns involving children, the future political landscape, and the human community. The crucial roles that children may play in contributing to the development of central themes and to the evocation of cultural concerns suggest that cutting them in performance may do serious violence to the structure of a play.

Sometimes a play depends heavily on a child's place in the dramatic scheme of social organization, as *Love's Labour's Lost* does on Moth, the lengthiest child's part in the Shakespeare canon. If Moth is played as an adult, the character's position as clever, young observer of the foibles of the adults around him is obliterated—such is the case in Kenneth Branagh's film adaptation, which also reduces Moth's lines so much that the character is a virtual cipher. Some parts simply require that actors be recognized aurally and visually as children. Moth's lively presence flutters over the many cultural concerns regarding heirship, procreation, pregnancy, cuckoldry, paternity, service, education, and performance that the play's classical allusions, rhetorical figures, and dramatic situations evoke. Moth functions between the worlds of authority and experience, the "silent world of writing" and "the resonant world of speech" (Hawkes, 54). "More authority, dear boy, name more," Armado says when Moth begins to list great men who have been in love. Later, when Moth discourses at some length on singing and dancing as ways to woo women, Armado expresses some surprise that this "well-educated infant" has acquired such knowledge, asking, "How hast thou purchased this experience?" (3.1.24) Moth's response—"By my penny of observation" (3.1.25)—establishes his recognition of the value of learning outside of books and underscores one of the important activities performed by children in Shakespeare's plays—scrupulous observation. Moth's services as a singer for Armado, a herald for the lords' poorly staged attempt to woo the ladies in disguise, and as one of the lower class participants in the Nine Worthies' pageant solidify his position as an acting representative of the performative worlds of poetic drama and song who can bridge the gap between books and experience.

Despite the centrality of Moth to the themes and structural integrity of *Love's Labour's Lost*, the complexity of his language has often been viewed as placing too many demands on young actors. As Miriam Gilbert writes, before 1936, when "Tyrone Guthrie cast a boy, Gordon Miller, in the role so obviously meant for a boy-actor . . . grown-up (though small) actresses and actors had taken the part" (Gilbert, 59). Peter Brook used fifteen-year-old David O'Brien in his 1946 Royal Shakespeare Company (RSC) production, and as Gilbert notes, "recent productions have swung back and forth between petite actresses (such as Amanda Root, Stratford-upon-Avon, 1984) and boys (such as Jo James, Stratford-upon-Avon, 1978)" (59). While the role has been subjected to cuts of various dimensions over the years, none are more surprising than Elijah Moshinsky's extensive cuts in the 1984 BBC version in which an adult John Kane was cast in the role against the advice of series advisor John Wilders (Gilbert, 59–60). There may be ways to preserve the integrity of a child's role, however, even when casting an adult to play the part.

Just before Moth's first entrance in Ian Judge's 1993 RSC production of *Love's Labour's Lost* (1.2), Don Armado walks on stage and pauses a moment to listen to the ending strain of beautifully angelic choral music emanating from somewhere offstage. Two young choristers cross quickly behind him and exit through a gate in a wall. Moth then appears dressed as head chorister and the banter between master and servant begins. The decision to make Moth a choirboy probably had some connection with Armado's command, "Warble, child: make passionate my sense of hearing" (3.1.1), as Luscombe observes (28), and the actor did in fact sing an Elizabethan love poem set to music by the production's composer, Nigel Hess. The problem of projecting a difference in size between Moth and Armado inevitably arose as Luscombe and Daniel Massey (Armado) are about the same height. An effective optical illusion was created in the pair's first scene as they sat on a slanting gravestone with Armado "towering . . . at the top end" as Moth "squatted at the bottom munching a packed lunch" (26). Luscombe's choirboy costume helped foster the illusion of his young age, which he placed slightly higher than the other choristers by making himself head chorister. The Oxbridge setting of Judge's production prompted Luscombe to do some field research observing the choristers at Christ Church Cathedral School in Oxford. Luscombe discovered that the social sophistication and intelligence of the choirboys made "Moth's ease with adult characters seem . . . entirely credible" (25–26).

Judge's production benefited from a willingness to open the play up to possibilities that connected past and present in sensible ways. There is something delightful in the decision to play Moth as a choirboy, with all the rich associations that word has in the history of child performance in England from Shakespeare's time till today. Luscombe's genuine respect for the children he observed at Oxford and his rejection of performance choices that would be "patronizing" are admirable. Luscombe's Moth illustrates how the adult actor's potential disruption to the structural and thematic integrity supported by the child's role may be offset in performance.

Shakespeare's young pages—Lucius in *Julius Caesar*, Robin in *The Merry Wives of Windsor*, the boy in *2 Henry IV* and *Henry V*, Moth in *Love's Labour's Lost*, and Bartholomew in *The Taming of the Shrew*—each reflect their own distinctive qualities. Robin is in service to Falstaff in *The Merry Wives of Windsor*, but the dark-humored prediction in *2 Henry IV* that the boy will end up being hanged because of Falstaff's influence finds no place in the gentler world of *The Merry Wives of Windsor*, where Mistress Page says to Robin, "O, you are a flattering boy! Now I see you'll be a courtier" (3.2.7–8). The intimate connection between master and young servant is sometimes reflected in performance by the almost identical dress of the page and his master (for example, see 1992 RSC *Merry Wives*; 1945 New Theatre *2 Henry IV*; 1946 RSC *Love's Labour's Lost*). Such costuming also suggests the degree to which the adult Falstaff presses his influence on his young servant. Dramatic tensions associated with youth tempted by vice resonate in the figure of Falstaff's page, whose age and size might have stimulated audience affection and concern in ways that the adult Prince Hal would not, perhaps especially among younger playgoers. The page, whose diminutive size is the subject of commentary, has in modern productions been cast from the pre-adolescent (as in Welles's *Falstaff: Chimes at Midnight*) to the late adolescent (as in Bogdanov and Pennington's English Shakespeare Company film of 1989). While the role of Falstaff's page in the histories raises questions about adult responsibilities toward the young, the page may also appeal to young playgoers as a portrait of childhood resistance to, and ultimate wisdom in the face of, adult weaknesses, fears, and follies. The intellectual and moral stature of the character may also have worked to dispel the specter of moral destruction raised by antitheatrical writers who condemned the exposure of youth (including the young performer) to the unsavory world of theater.

A child in *Richard III* evokes concerns of a different sort in an ironic and shocking moment that suggests the perverse range of social decay that Richard's rule epitomizes. The go-between who brings Richard and Tyrell together is a page to whom Richard turns to seek recommendation for an assassin. This troubling moment seems to qualify assertions such as Ann Blake's observation about children in Shakespeare's plays that "they are free from adult vices, and emphatically innocent" ("Children and Suffering," 293).

While the page is often cut in performance or replaced with an adult servant, Jane Howell chose in her BBC/Time-Life production to cast a child in the role, a young looking (ten-year-old?) actor whose voice and facial expressions reflected a sweetness and innocence at odds with the content of his character's speech. The page enters with Buckingham, Catesby, King Richard, and other nobles at the beginning of 4.2. Richard's turning to a child for advice signals his character's downward spiral after having acquired the crown. The decision in Howell's production to have Catesby direct his aside, "The King is angry. See, he gnaws his lip" (4.2.28), to the young page rather than to one of the adult nobles standing nearby may have been a practical choice to remind the young actor that his cue is coming, but it also calls the audience's attention to this young figure who is about to be summoned to center stage. Illustrating his resolve to confer henceforth only with those who are in some way undiscerning—"iron-witted fools / And unrespective boys" (4.2.29–30)—the king calls out, "Boy!" to summon the page for a conference. To Richard's query about a likely assassin, the boy page gives the remarkably unflinching reply, "I know a discontented gentleman / Whose humble means match not his haughty spirit. / Gold were as good as twenty orators, / And will no doubt tempt him to anything" (4.2.37–40). Does the boy's Machiavellian savvy suggest an unformed conscience or reveal one deformed by exposure to the corrupt political environment? To what degree can the page be seen as complicit in the murders of the young princes? How significant is the physical presence of a young body and voice during a scene that centers on plotting the destruction of young bodies and the silencing of young voices? Would the page's youth lessen his culpability by suggesting, as Richard implies, that the boy is "unrespective"? The disturbing image of vulnerable, corruptible youth reflects the potentially far-reaching effects of Richard's influence on the English political landscape. The youth of the actor playing the page could send a kind of dramatic shockwave through an audience in a way that would heighten the sense that the social fabric is hopelessly rending.

Those situations in which children in Shakespeare's plays are positioned as mostly silent spectators and listeners often appear designed to evoke cultural concerns about the children of Shakespeare's time. Antitheatrical concerns about the corrupting influence of playgoing on youth resonate to a degree with present-day concerns about the harmful influences of media violence and overtly sexual behavior on young viewers. In Shakespeare's plays, as in real life, children watch like spies the goings-on of the adults around them, and adults may not fully attend to the presence of children. Both of the recent films *Shakespeare in Love* and *Titus* emphasize the watchful eyes of those youthful spies in the adult world around them. The appearances of a young John Webster in *Shakespeare in Love* evoke several of the cultural concerns mentioned here. The striking visual frenzy at the beginning of Taymor's *Titus* during which the boy beheads one of his toys directly questions the influence of media violence on young people. One of the theatrical jokes of Webster's introduction in *Shakespeare in Love* is the character's admission that he had been in a play before. The laconic lad reveals to Master Shakespeare, "They cut my head off in *Titus Androni-cus*. . . . I liked it when they cut heads off. And the daughter mutilated with knives." In another of the film's reminders that children are ever-present auditors and observers, Webster appears in the audience for the first performance of *Romeo and Juliet* and later comments to the queen that he liked it when Juliet stabbed herself. The joke, of course, is on Shakespeare, who, in the film, does a disturbed double take when Webster announces, "When I write plays, they will be like *Titus*." The audience laughter may be nervous indeed, especially among parents of young children.

In the world of the early modern theater, dramatic considerations of age, size, and sound must have been shaped by practicalities that governed and continue to govern casting decisions. What about a child's role would make it more practical for an adult actor to perform? What actors are available? Is the language difficult? Is the part lengthy? Because answers to these questions shape casting choices and vice versa, a child character often represents a rather wide range of possibilities. Do child labor laws make using an adult actor a virtual necessity in some cases? The legal restrictions that prescribe children's work on stage may tempt directors to cast adult actors in children's roles. The rules covering the use of children in entertainment reflected in Great Britain's Children and Young Persons Acts 1933 and 1963 and the Children (Performances) Regulations 1968 suggest how legal pressures can shape casting choices. Among the many restrictions placed on the use of child actors are those that limit the latest time (10 P.M. for those under thirteen and 10:30 for those thirteen and over) that children may appear on stage and that set forty days as the maximum number a child may perform in any twelve-month period ("Children in Entertainments"). Fourteen other areas are covered by the regulations. Another reason that some adults prefer not to work with children is that the demands of multiple casting lead to increased rehearsal time, a requirement often seen as burdensome on director, crew, and the adults who share scenes with the young actors. Solutions range from casting adults in the roles to making cuts that often render a child's contribution insignificant or puzzling.

Productions of two different plays directed by RSC associate director Greg Doran offer further lessons in casting parts for children in Shakespearean drama. In February of 1999, I attended a session arranged by the Shakespeare Birthplace Trust's Education Centre in which Gregory Doran and Anthony Sher discussed Doran's then current RSC production of *The Winter's Tale*, which I was to see performed later that evening. Asked about his decision to cast a young adult actress in the role of Mamillius, Doran explained that the scenes with Mamillius in them "never get played" when a child has the role.

Doran's decision to cast an adult in a role that presents so few of the potential difficulties mentioned by Christopher Luscombe concerning Moth is dismaying. Mamillius's relatively simple 21 lines pale in comparison with the complexity of Moth's 159 lines. Furthermore, the actor playing Mamillius is free after his exit at 2.1.62 to leave the theater well before the legally prescribed 10 p.m. Moth, on the other hand, must be present throughout the play. Doran's decision, however, to double cast Mamillius and Perdita made it necessary for Emily Bruni, the actress playing Mamillius and Perdita, to be in the theater at the very end of *The Winter's Tale*.

As Mr. Doran and Mr. Sher gamely confessed, it quickly became apparent in rehearsals that staging adjustments would have to be made since Ms. Bruni was taller than Mr. Sher. The decision to have Ms. Bruni play the role of Mamillius while seated in a wheelchair, however, had a deadening effect on the boy's scenes, despite the effectiveness of Ms. Bruni's youthful vocal delivery. Although using the wheelchair to suggest Mamillius's physical vulnerability to the shock that results in his death has a recognizable logic, taking away from Mamillius that freedom of boyish movement that captures his spirit and boyhood kills the character before his time.

Doran's 2001 RSC production of *King John* counters his earlier implication that the limitations of child actors may prevent the full and satisfying realization of a part. Young Joshua MacGuire, who I twice saw play Arthur in Doran's production and who appeared to be about ten years old, brought incredible force and emotional range to the one hundred lines that Arthur is given in 4.1 as he pleads for his life with Hubert. The scene is larger than any written for other Shakespearean children. MacGuire's stage presence, his ability to remain emotionally engaged in each moment of performance and to compel attention to his words—whether standing in the midst of a stage of powerful adults or bound to a chair and successfully arguing for his life with Hubert or balancing precariously on the top railing before falling to his death—established beyond dispute the successful dramatic work a child may perform in such a role. In this play in which a child is used as a political football, Hubert can be seen as a heroic adult figure simply because he recognizes a basic adult duty to protect the child. MacGuire's strong performance, however, also emphasized Arthur's heroism against Hubert's vulnerability. Although Doran chose not to use the approach, it is common for the same young actor to double the roles of Arthur and Henry. As though Arthur has achieved some kind of miraculous rebirth, the image of childhood presented by Prince Henry standing tearfully before his father's body and commenting upon his father's "swan song" works as another forceful reminder of adult duty to the young. Childhood and political power merge in the young figure of Henry III, whose reign of fifty-six years presents a historical lesson to

counter the fears of political instability brought on by a child ruler—a societal anxiety with which Shakespeare deals in other history plays. The rare
possibility that the adult world, by living up to its responsibilities toward the
young, can reap long-lasting political advantages is figured dramatically in
the final scene of *King John* as the boy king is surrounded by kneeling adults.

In the closing images of Taymor's *Titus*, one also has a potentially hope-
ful vision of the future as Young Lucius carries the son of Aaron and Tamora
out of a "theater of violence, of cruelty" (De Luca and Lindroth, 29). The
moment contrasts with the vision of Young Lucius at the end of Howell's
BBC production in which one child's future has been cut off. Howell's conclusion suggests at least two things: the pity reflected on Young Lucius's face
may not endure in the cruel environment of Rome, and even if it does, he will
have to wait until full adulthood to have any real power to act. At the close of
Taymor's film, the young faces on the screen look two ways like the Roman
god Janus. Lucius's eyes are no longer turned toward the camera, but focus
instead on the horizon where a new day is dawning. Over his shoulder, however, we see peering back at us the disturbed-looking gaze of a dark infant,
unable to articulate his questions about the confusing, terrifying, violent,
misogynistic, racist world into which he has been born. Young Lucius has
looked into the eyes of revenge and into these innocent eyes into which we
gaze. By walking out of the circular arena of spectacle that held the play's
theater of cruelty, he is presented as making a choice to break the cycle of
violence that has been so painful to behold. When asked by interviewers
from *Cineaste* why she wanted those who watch her film *Titus* "to view
Shakespeare's play through Lucius's eyes," Julie Taymor explained that
"children are the only . . . way" for the future to realize the "possibility for
fruition, of cleansing, of forgiveness" (29).

Shakespeare's children are purposefully written and may have a penetrat-
ing impact on a play's dramatic realization. Attending to their potential in performance can be a crucial way to capture a play's richness and raise important
questions about the place of children in Shakespeare's world and our own.

Works Cited

Blake, Ann. "Children and Suffering in Shakespeare's Plays." *Yearbook of English
      Studies* 23 (1993): 293–304.
Brigden, Susan. "Youth and the English Reformation." *Past and Present* 95 (May
      1982): 37–67.
"Children in Entertainments: General Notes for Guidance." Solihull, West Midlands:
      Metropolitan Borough Council Education Department.
Cooper, Susan. *King of Shadows*. New York: Aladdin, 2001.
Crashawe, William. *The Sermon preached at the Crosse, Feb. xiiij 1607*, 1608.
Deluca, Maria and Mary Lindroth, "Mayhem, Madness, and Method: An Interview
      with Julie Taymor," *Cineaste* 25.3 (2000): 28–31.

Gilbert, Miriam. *Love's Labour's Lost* (Shakespeare in Performance Series). Manchester and New York: Manchester University Press, 1996.

Hawkes, Terence. *Shakespeare's Talking Animals: Language and Drama in Society.* Totowa, NJ: Rowman and Littlefield, 1974.

Luscombe, Christopher. "Launcelot Gobbo in *The Merchant of Venice* and Moth in *Love's Labour's Lost*," in Robert Smallwood, ed. *Players of Shakespeare 4.* Cambridge: Cambridge University Press, 1998, 18–29.

Shakespeare, William. *The Complete Works.* Stanley Wells and Gary Taylor, eds. Oxford: Oxford University Press, 1988.

———. *Love's Labour's Lost.* H. R. Woudhuysen, ed. (Arden 3). Thomas Nelson, 1998.

Vogel, Scott. "Shakespeare in Lualualei." *Honolulu Star-Bulletin* (August 21, 2001): B1, B4.

11.   Canning the Classic

Race and Ethnicity in the Lambs' *Tales from Shakespeare*

JAMES ANDREAS

What children can read, want to read, and actually do read has long been underestimated, much the way children themselves have been underestimated in the history of Western culture. Until very recently, academic courses in children's literature were rarely offered by English literature departments where, it might be assumed, the focus would be on the texts of the literary canon. When taken by education majors, the function of such courses is often to survey materials available for approved use at the primary school level. Theoretical approaches to the subject are rare and sometimes even discouraged. Such an approach is short-sighted, however, because, at the very least young readers are future consumers of literature, and books are the essential cultural commodities that shape our collective future in a society duty-bound to script and print. Young readers and those who teach and read to them, therefore, play a crucial role in choosing, transmitting, and shaping the literary canon and creating the "classic."

In addition to consuming the steady stream of new materials published every day, children are introduced to existing classics in the hope that they will not only develop their reading habits but acquire a taste for literature of "quality" in the process. Moreover, it is thought that cultural assumptions and norms are appropriately transmitted through books. This chapter will deal with the problem encountered when canonical literature comes to be transmitted to children, as it invariably is. It asks how young readers can be exposed to the uplifting reading and the assumed and perceived moral benefit of texts like Homer's *Odyssey*, *The Canterbury Tales*, *Gulliver's Travels*, and more recently, books ostensibly written for children like *Huckleberry Finn* and *Alice in Wonderland*, without being scandalized by offensive words and subjects and exposed to the transgressive topics and ideologies invariably purveyed by great literary works. To put it more succinctly, this chapter investigates how classics are approved, assimilated, and appropriated for children and how that process has affected the formation and glacial drift of the Western literary canon over the last four centuries. The specimen text for examination will be *Tales from Shakespeare* by Charles and Mary Lamb, because it conditioned almost all future adaptations of the plays for children. The paper will focus on the Lambs' portrayal of Shakespeare's aliens—principally Shylock, Othello, and Caliban—in the narrative versions of their respective plays.

During the five hundred years since the invention of the printing press, various authorizing agencies from Elizabeth's Lord of the Revels to local school boards have devised strategies to contain dangerous literary texts, particularly those targeted at children: revocation of the license to publish, excision, abridgment, bowdlerization, selective translation, indexing, book bannings, book burnings, and, of course, systematic censorship.[1] Over the centuries, the Western public, and especially young readers, have had to be protected from that spectrum of literary production which might suggest a popular or "vulgar," in other words a "folk-oriented," slant. While there has apparently been no discernible bureaucratic conspiracy to sanitize the classics for children, there has been a gentle translation of Shakespeare's tough plays into tales targeted for children, driven in part by market forces but largely by what has been called the "community standards" of decency stringently applied by school boards in the selection of literary textbooks.[2]

Of course, the major weapon against the circulation of books that would challenge children to think and develop independent opinions has been outright censorship. The American Library Association each year updates its list of one hundred books banned in many public and school libraries across the country.[3] Devotees of literature are always shocked that the list includes classics such as *The Chocolate War* by Robert Cormier, *The Adventures of Huckleberry Finn* by Mark Twain, *Of Mice and Men* by John Steinbeck, and *The Catcher in the Rye* by J. D. Salinger, all of which are among the ten most commonly banned books. The *Harry Potter* series by J. K. Rowling and *Brave New World* by Aldous Huxley are listed among the one hundred as are *Slaughterhouse-Five* by Kurt Vonnegut and *Leaves of Grass* by Walt Whitman. However, as effective as censorship has been in challenging the circulation of controversial classics, there are other expurgative means at the disposal of conservative parties which would control the circulation of cultural information.

There is a mode of censorship of great literary texts that has not been recognized and researched at this point in time: converting the potentially dangerous document into a "classic" by co-opting it, as Herbert Marcuse labeled the process, or canonizing it—or, to use the word I prefer, "canning"—sanitizing, and standardizing the illicit content, making it safe for popular distribution, mass consumption, and academic indoctrination for a budding literary public. It is no coincidence that so many of the great classic texts of the ancient and European world are delivered up in translation which can be expurgated or transformed into conventional language to neutralize scandalous content. Nowhere is this process so conspicuous as it is in the reproduction of potentially destabilizing literary works as classics for children. In the process of rendering literary texts like Chaucer's "The Miller's Tale," Shakespeare's *Romeo and Juliet*, and Swift's *Gulliver's Travels* fit for the enjoyment and edification of children, the transformation of the texts themselves often displace the originals in the mind of even the educated public.[4] While nobody would debate the value of making occasionally bawdy, controversial authors like Ovid, Chaucer, Shakespeare, Swift, and Twain generally available to young readers and viewers without scandal, what, we need to ask, is to be sacrificed in the process?

The work of William Shakespeare has long evoked the call to "convert" literary classics into vehicles appropriate for reading and performance by children. In fact, the general process of literary expurgation is known to the world as "bowdlerization," a term that traces back to attempts to expurgate Shakespeare's plays for presentation to children.[5] Following the lead of Charles and Mary Lamb in their *Tales from Shakespeare*, which were designed "to make these Tales (of Shakespeare) easy reading for very young children,"[6] Thomas Bowdler, M.D. and his sister Henrietta Maria Bowdler transformed twenty of the plays by tinkering with the text or blatantly hacking away offending words and subjects after carefully selecting what was thought proper for "a young sister's ear." Both the Lamb and Bowdler projects illuminate the process of transforming classical but problematic texts into icons of moral rectitude which could be safely consumed by children.

In their preface to the *Tales*, the Lambs assert that it is "the subjects"—the presumably dangerous topics—of Shakespeare's plays rather than the language that are most difficult to deal with, particularly for young girls. Girls must not only be protected from offending texts, they must become the standard-bearers of the culture, much like, to get ahead of my argument here, Juliet, Jessica, Desdemona, and Miranda are expected not just to know but to embody and apply teachings in their behaviors when encountering the dangerous "other" in alien families, clans, cultures, and races: "(I)nstead of recommending these Tales to the perusal of young gentlemen who can read them so much better in the originals, their kind assistance is rather requested in explaining to their sisters such parts as are hardest for them to understand: and when they have helped them to get over the difficulties, then perhaps they will read to them (carefully selecting what is proper for a young sister's ear) some passage which has pleased them in one of the stories."(2)

There are several elements in classical literary texts which may constitute sites for offensive material to "young sisters" and children: explicit sexuality, excessive violence, and the so-called vulgar language that is used to describe such activities. However, texts that deal openly with alien cultures and racial issues, particularly biracial sexual relationships, are often targeted for censorship and expurgation, as is indicated in the inclusion of *I Know Why the Caged Bird Sings*, *To Kill a Mockingbird*, and *The Color Purple* on the ALA's list of commonly banned books in the schools.

In the Lambs' reading of *The Merchant of Venice*, the deck is stacked against Shylock from the beginning. As the Jew, he is the "usurer" who lends at "great interest to Christian merchants" (71). His own motives for usury and the traditional endorsement for such activity by his "tribe," so sensitively represented by Shakespeare in his play, are never broached.[7] In fact, the Lambs extrapolate from the text of the play they would abridge, to underscore the "hard-hearted" nature of the Jew and his severity in collecting from his patrons, a vice Shakespeare never mentions in his exposition of the character. "Shylock, being a hard-hearted man, exacted the payment of the money he lent with such severity that he was much disliked by all good men" (71). Antonio is also essentialized, that is, declared a "good man" and "the kindest man that lived, the best conditioned, and the most unwearied spirit in doing courtesies" (71), a characterization that is certainly not sustained in the play. When Portia enters the courtroom disguised as the advocate, Balthazar, she asks in one of the most famous lines in the play, "Which here is the merchant and which the Jew?" (IV.i.169),[8] underscoring the ambiguity in the text regarding the two characters. The Lambs render the line with moral severity: "And now began this important trial. Portia looked around her, and she saw the merciless Jew" (76). And when the judgment turns against Shylock, there is no mention of the cruel and partial "alien law" which has doomed Shylock from the outset. Also, Antonio's insistence that Shylock be forced to covert to Christianity is transferred to the duke, thus sparing the Lambs' hero, Antonio, from the imputation of embarrassing unchristian, unmerciful behavior.

Throughout the tale Shylock's side of the story is left unrehearsed—there is no taunting by Solanio and Salerio, no "rating" of and spitting on Shylock on the Rialto, no cruel baiting of Shylock in the courtroom by Gratiano, and no defense of his Jewishness in the "hath not a Jew eyes" speech. The defection of Jessica is rendered matter-of-factly: "the Jew had an only daughter who had lately married against his consent to a young Christian, named Lorenzo, a friend of Antonio's, which had so offended Shylock, that he had disinherited her" (79). Jessica's betrayal of her father and her sale of her mother Leah's wedding ring—her "turquoise"—is also omitted, although great fanfare is made of the ring trick Portia and Nerissa play on Bassanio and Gratiano at play's end. In fact, astoundingly, the Lambs retain the play's final couplet of Gratiano which surely is an anticlimax to the play's deep moral ambiguity but is as straightforwardly bawdy as anything in Shakespeare: "while he lived, he'd fear no other thing / So sore, as keeping safe Nerissa's ring" (V.i.305–06). Finally, very curiously, the Lambs entirely omit the lottery of the caskets from the play, an action which would certainly have appealed to young readers interested in fairy tales, particularly those with an Eastern ring. In so doing, however, they were spared the embarrassment of Portia's rejection of the black Prince of Morocco solely for his skin color—"let all of his complexion choose me so"—in a game designed to impart the moral that one's choices should not be dictated by superficial concerns and mere appearance.

Although the Lambs reveal little sympathy for Shylock, the "Merchant of Venice," they seem deeply moved by the terrible tragedy of his twin, the "Moor of Venice," as *Othello* is aptly subtitled in the quarto and folio editions of the play. This is all the more surprising given the attitude toward Othello's race in the Romantic period expressed so virulently by Coleridge, surely a hero to the Lambs: "Can we suppose [Shakespeare] so utterly ignorant as to make a barbarous negro plead royal birth? Were negroes then known but as slaves . . . No doubt Desdemona saw Othello's visage in his [Othello's] mind; yet, as we are constituted, and most surely as an English audience was disposed in the beginning of the seventeenth century, it would be something monstrous to conceive this beautiful Venetian girl falling in love with a veritable negro. It would argue a disproportionateness, a want of balance in Desdemona, which Shakespeare does not appear to have in the least contemplated."[9]

The Lambs, on the other hand, uncharacteristically move right to the heart of the racial controversy in the play with none of the blindness about the subject which will mark subsequent considerations until well into the twentieth century. Speaking of Desdemona's consent to elope with Othello, they write: "But among the suitors of her own clime and complexion, she saw none whom she could affect: for this noble lady, who regarded the mind more than the features of men, with a singularity rather to be admired than imitated, had chosen for the object of her affections, a Moor, a black whom her father loved, and often invited to his house" (215). Desdemona is praised for choosing a man of Othello's complexion, granted that he has no other noticeable faults. "Bating that Othello was black, the noble Moor wanted nothing" (215). Moreover, Brabantio is faulted for failing to see beyond the pigment that determines every judgment that follows: "Neither Othello's color nor his fortune were such that it could be hoped Brabantio would accept him for a son-in-law. . . . Desdemona loved the Moor, though he was black . . . and devoted her heart and fortunes of his valiant parts and qualities; so was her heart subdued to an implicit devotion to the man she had selected for a husband, that his very color, which to all but this discerning lady would have proved an insurmountable objection, was by her esteemed above all the white skins and clear complexions of the young Venetian nobility, her suitors." (216) What a wonderful lesson there is for children here, one, indeed, that is far ahead of its time, even today when high school teachers assure me that *Othello* is a play they would not be able to teach to their students, particularly in rural Southern areas. Unlike Portia—and there is a direct comparison being suggested in these Venetian plays—Desdemona truly does see Othello as he is in his own mind's eye rather than judging him, as Portia does Morocco, simply by virtue—or rather the failure—of his "complexion."

There is, too, a straightforward assessment of Iago's motives in undermining the couple's happiness through racial innuendo. The Lambs even relay Iago's fear that Othello, addressed as "the Moor" and "the black Othello" throughout the tale, has done his "office . . . 'twixt (the) sheets" (I.iii.369–70) with his wife, Emilia. The ancient suspects, confess the Lambs, "that the Moor was too fond of Iago's wife Emilia" (219). The jealousy of the suspected sexual prowess of the other is here expressed, however discreetly. The Lambs also clearly identify Iago's stroke of genius that enmeshes the naive and trusting Moor in Iago's web of racial intrigue. He reminds Othello that Desdemona is not to be trusted—with Cassio or any other white Italian—simply *because* she defied her father's wishes and her culture's racial ideology in the very fact that she defiantly married a black man. Iago, the Lambs reiterate, "then came strongly to the point, and reminded Othello how Desdemona had refused many suitable matches of her own clime and complexion, and had married him, a Moor, which showed unnatural in her, and proved to her to have a headstrong will; and when her better judgment returned, how probable it was she should fall upon comparing Othello with the fine forms and clear white complexions of the young Italians her countrymen." (222)

As racist as this remark is, it does justice to the plot of the play, which turns on the fact that Othello's great "flaw" is his ultimate acceptance and embodiment of the xenophobic accusations hurled against him and his race in his own behavior. He himself eloquently acknowledges such a fate when he resorts to revealing the "magic in the web" of the famous handkerchief he demands from Desdemona, a charm he had used to entrap his young wife with spells which are African in origin. He demands the handkerchief which "an Egyptian woman gave to my mother; the woman was a witch and could read people's thoughts. . . . It is a magical handkerchief; a sibyl that had lived in the world two hundred years, in a fit of prophetic fury worked it; the silkworms that furnished the silk were hallowed, and it was dyed in a mummy of maidens' hearts conserved" (223–24). The handkerchief, in short, "enchanted" Desdemona so she might fall in love with and be true to Othello, just as Brabantio had suspected of the Moor early in the play. The child reader is, perhaps mercifully, spared the violent suicide of Othello at the end of the play. However, he also is left uninformed about Othello's final, dramatic condemnation of himself as "turbaned Turk," "circumsized dog," and "base Indian"— in other words, the violent blackamoor and dangerous alien who will be dispatched by the leader of the Venetian forces on Cyprus—Othello himself— in one last act of desperate duty to the state he has served so faithfully.

Shakespeare's other aliens—his strangers who, though useful and attractive to the native cultures of his plays in the short run, are ultimately to be shunned and expelled—are given short shrift by the Lambs. The stories of his two infamous Africans, Aaron the Moor and surprisingly, Cleopatra the African Queen, are not included among the Shakespearean tales narrated by the Lambs. But the collection opens, as does the first folio, with *The Tempest*, certain to be appealing to young readers. It is followed by a rendition of *A Midsummer Night's Dream*. The two plays are really cognates with their emphases upon magic and the manipulation of offending parties. The alien in question in *The Tempest* is, of course, Caliban, an African by his own admission because his mother, Sycorax, is from "Argiers," or Algeria. Ariel is characterized as "ever obedient to the will of Prospero" with "nothing mischievous in his nature," in other words, the polar opposite of Caliban whom he is in charge of and likes to "torment" (4). The Lambs give an orthodox colonial reading to the story of Caliban: "This Caliban, Prospero found in the woods, a strange misshapen thing, far less human in form than an ape: he took him home to his cell, and taught him to speak; and Prospero would have been very kind to him, but the bad nature which Caliban inherited from his mother Sycorax, would not let him learn anything good or useful: therefore he was employed like a slave, to fetch wood, and do the most laborious offices; and Ariel had the charge of compelling him to these services." (4)

The only known source for the play is the account of Sir George Somers's shipwreck in the Bermudas published in 1610, a year before the composition of the play. Caliban is the displaced African, born of an Algerian woman who ruled the island as a black matriarchal culture the residues of which can be detected in some of the islands off the coast of South Carolina to this day.[10] Prospero's arrival on the island is presented as a blessing to Caliban, not the curse of servitude and torture his life becomes as a punishment for the bad "nature . . . (he) inherited from his mother Sycorax," under the cruel mastery of what Aimé Cesaire in his *Tempête* called the "house negro," Ariel.[11] Caliban is not spoken of again in the tale. The comic plot of Stephano, the drunken butler, Trinculo, King Alonso's butler, and Caliban conspiring to overthrow Prospero is entirely omitted as is the reconciliation of sorts between master and slave when Prospero, about to abandon the island to Caliban, confesses that he "acknowledges this thing of darkness, mine."

To conclude with our assessment of the redaction of those plays of Shakespeare for children that feature aliens such as Shylock, Othello, and Caliban in the Christian/European context, the Lambs exhibit for the most part the expected xenophobic tendency to convey the ethnic and racial stereotypes we have all come to recognize. In so doing they strip the plays of their rich ambiguity about the other and mute the compassion for strangers that Shakespeare displays aplenty in the respective plays. The Lambs' Othello, however, represents a glaring exception to this rule, proving that at any given moment in cultural history, there exists a spectrum of reactions to the alien that depends ultimately on individual choice and experience. The culture does not determine racist reaction; it simply predisposes individuals within it to such reactions. No matter how xenophobic the age or culture may appear on the surface, racism exists only in practice—one human being at a time discriminating against another human being.

However, as the appropriations of the Lambs so vividly illustrate, the plays of William Shakespeare have been processed, rendered sanitary, and standardized for popular consumption and safety over the centuries, especially for children. That is the great business of the cultural establishment, not to forbid the transgressive or progressive text but to digest and transform it into a cultural icon which comes to represent the very norms the text sought in its original form to interrogate and even subvert.

Notes

1. On the rhetoric and practice of censorship in Shakespeare's own age, see Annabel Patterson's "Prynne's Ears; or, the Hermeneutics of Censorship" in *Censorship and Interpretation* (Madison, Wisconsin: University of Wisconsin Press, 1984), 52–127. For such practices in contemporary literature textbooks that include the plays of Shakespeare, see James. R. Andreas, "Silencing the Vulgar and Voicing the Other Shakespeare," *Nebraska English Journal* 35 (1991): 74–88.

2. For a teacher's viewpoint on the effects of textbook censorship in the classroom, see Maureen F. Logan, "Star-Crossed Platonic Lovers, or Bowdler Redux," *English Journal* 74 (1985): 53–55. See also James. R. Andreas, "Neutering *Romeo and Juliet*," in *Ideological Approaches to Shakespeare: The Practice of Theory*, ed. Robert Merrix and Nicholas Ranson (Lewiston, New York: Edwin Mellon Press, 1992), 229–42.

3. The entire list is reprinted and updated periodically at the Web site of the American Library Association which can be accessed at www.ala.org.

4. Pertinent here is George Orwell's imaginary conversation with Jonathan Swift about the butcheries of Western censors: Orwell's Swift remarks, "I warn you to beware of all *modern* editors, even of my *Travels*. I have suffered from such damned dishonest editors as I believe no other writer ever had. It has been my especial misfortune to be edited usually by clergymen who thought me a disgrace to their cloth. They were tinkering at my writings long before Dr. Bowdler was ever born or thought of." Orwell, surprisingly enough, defends the censors: "You see, Dr. Swift, you have put them in a difficulty. They know you are our greatest prose writer, and yet you used words and raised subjects they couldn't approve of. In a way I don't approve of you myself," even though, Orwell admits, "I believe *Gulliver's Travels* has meant more to me than any other book ever written." "Jonathan Swift, An Imaginary Interview," in *Orwell: The Lost Writings*, ed. W. J. West (New York: Arbor House, 1985), 112.

5. On the relationship of the Lambs and Bowdlers, see Gary Taylor, *Reinventing Shakespeare: A Cultural History from the Restoration to the Present* (New York and London: Oxford University Press, 1989), 207. This relationship is also in focus in the synoptic article of Laurie E. Osborne, "Poetry in Motion: Animating Shakespeare," in *Shakespeare, The Movie: Popularizing the Plays on Film, TV, and Video*, ed. Lynda E. Boose and Richard Burt (London and New York: Routledge 1997), 103–20.

6. All quotation from the text will be taken from the following edition: *Tales from Shakespeare* (New York: Bantam Books, 1962).

7. For what Shakespeare knew about the Jews and a commentary on his ultimately sympathetic treatment of Shylock, see James Shapiro, *Shakespeare and the Jews* (New York: Columbia University Press, 1996).

8. All quotations from Shakespeare are taken from *The Norton Shakespeare*, ed. Stephen Greenblatt (New York: W. W. Norton, 1997).

9. Quoted in Sylvan Barnett, "Othello on Stage and Screen," in *Othello*, ed. Alvin Kernan (New York: Signet, 1986), 280.

10. Regarding such cultural connections, see James R. Andreas, "Signfyin' On Shakespeare: Gloria Naylor's *Mama Day*," *Shakespeare and Appropriation*, ed. Robert Sawyer and Christine Desmet (London: Routledge, 1999), 103–18.

11. *A Tempest*, trans. Richard Miller (New York: Ubu Repertory Theater Productions, 1985).

12. Alice Reads Shakespeare

Charles Dodgson and the Girl's Shakespeare Project

GEORGIANNA ZIEGLER

In 1882, when he had turned fifty, Charles Dodgson (a.k.a. Lewis Carroll) began floating the idea of preparing an edition of Shakespeare for girls. He wrote in March to the mother of his young friend Marion Richards, telling her, "I have a dream of Bowdlerising Bowdler, i.e., of editing a Shakespeare which shall be absolutely fit for *girls*. For this I need advice, from *mothers*, as to which plays they would like to be included." A few weeks later, on April 5th, he noted in his diary that he had begun "sending round printed request, to lady-friends, for lists of plays of Shakespeare suitable for girls" (*Letters*, 457; *Diaries*, 1971:405), and later that spring he published advertisements in two magazines for women and girls, inviting the readers "to send in their own lists of selections founded on recollections of their own girlhood or on obser-vation of their daughters' reading" (Bakewell, 248).

In October of the following year, he wrote to Alice Cooper, Head-mistress of the Edgbaston High School for Girls in Birmingham, further explaining what he had in mind. He says he had almost given up the project, thinking that Charlotte Yonge, popular author of moralistic novels, had scooped him. But since she was preparing only the history plays to meet the new school board requirements, Dodgson felt free to pursue his own project.[1] He tells Miss Cooper, "My notion is to bring out the plays one by one (at 4*d*. or 6*d*. each), and then everybody can select which they please to make a vol-ume of. I have begun on *Tempest*, but done very little as yet." He continues: "the method I propose to myself is to erase ruthlessly every word in the play that is in any degree profane, or coarse, or in any sense unsuited for a girl of from 10 to 15; and then to make the best I can of what is left" (*Letters*, 513, 514). In February of 1884 the two of them met in Oxford to discuss the proj-ect, and by April of 1885 Miss Cooper was engaged as his collaborator "by marking a couple of plays" (*Letters*, 514, 572). Four years later the project was still on Dodgson's "to-do" list, as indicated in the preface to *Sylvie and*

Bruno, but eventually he felt there were too many other pressing calls on the time of an aging man, and in 1894 he wrote to Mary Brown that he feared the Girl's Shakespeare would never be done (*Letters*, 1031).

I think we can honestly say that the world did not lose a great Shakespearean book by Dodgson's failure to complete the project; nevertheless it is valuable to consider the rationale of this brilliantly creative man in pursuing the idea as long as he did, and to set this rationale within the larger context of Victorian attitudes towards Shakespeare and children, especially young females.

The plays of Shakespeare had been adapted for childhood consumption from at least the 1790s. In addition to retellings of individual plays such as *The Merchant of Venice* and *Hamlet*, a book called *Mother Goose's Melody* presented a whole section of songs from Shakespeare, while in 1807 Charles and Mary Lamb published their enormously successful *Tales from Shakespeare* for younger children, a book still available in modern printings.[2] In the same year appeared the expurgated edition of the plays to which Charles Dodgson referred when he spoke of "Bowdlerizing Bowdler." Although often credited to Thomas Bowdler, the first edition of four volumes, as we now know, was largely the work of his sister Henrietta. Like Mary Lamb whose versions of twenty plays form a large portion of "Lamb's Tales," Henrietta Bowdler must be credited for her major contribution to what became one of the most frequently published editions of Shakespeare in the nineteenth century.

Perhaps capitalizing on the popularity of the Bowdlers' edition of 1807, many other would-be reformers tried their hands at "purifying" Shakespeare. In 1822, the Reverend J. R. Pitman came out with *The School-Shakspeare*, in which he remarked that "the attention of young females, both in schools and in families, has, of late years, been carefully directed to the study of our English Classics," and that in his volume he had excluded "immoral language . . . so that taste may be cultivated, without offence to delicate and religious feelings." In 1876, Henry Cundell produced *The Boudoir Shakespeare*, its very title suggesting an audience in the intimate world of women. According to his own words, his aim was "to strip the text of all that might wound a feminine sense of delicacy."[3] Charles Dodgson knew several of these editions, but he was not satisfied with their efforts. "Neither Bowdler's, Chambers's, Brandram's, nor Cundell's 'Boudoir' Shakespeare, seems to me to meet the want: they are not sufficiently 'expurgated.' " (*S&B*, 282)[4]

Dodgson envisioned "an edition in which everything, not suitable for the perusal of girls . . . from 10 to 17, should be omitted." "Few children under 10," he went on, "would be likely to understand or enjoy the greatest of poets: and those, who have passed out of girlhood, may safely be left to read Shakespeare, in any edition, 'expurgated' or not" (*S&B*, 282). Never mind that Emily Sellwood, later Mrs. Tennyson, fell in love with *Cymbeline* at the age of eight, or that, at about the same age, little Helena Faucit, the future actress, wrote home for a copy of Shakespeare and performed Imogen in scenes from *Cymbeline* at her boarding school. Perhaps these girls were precocious.[5] In the event, the many adults between the Bowdlers at the beginning of the century and Charles Dodgson at the end who felt it necessary to "clean up" Shakespeare for juvenile, and especially, female consumption, operated with the notion that "the child is the measure of all good" (Cohen, 111), and that little girls in particular must be protected from the vulgarities of life as long as possible so that they may grow into pure and loving women. Such a view is epitomized in the recommendation of Sarah Stickney Ellis that appeared in *The Young Ladies' Reader* (1845: 289–90): "It is scarcely possible to imagine a prudent and judicious mother allowing the unrestrained and private reading of Shakespeare amongst her children; but if herself a good reader, thoroughly imbibed with a sense of the beautiful and the pure, it *is* possible to imagine her reading passages from Shakespeare to her family in such a manner, as to improve the taste of those around her, and to raise their estimate of what is great and good."[6]

Various biographical and fictional accounts from the nineteenth century indicate the ways in which this practice played out in real life. Martha Sharpe, a middle-class mother in Cheshire, writes that she has promised her daughter, Molly, "to read a few of Shakespeare's historical Plays with her, in an Evening, when Aunt Kate is gone, & we are quite alone, as a great Treat."[7] The May family of eleven children in Charlotte Yonge's popular novel *The Daisy Chain* (1856) experience Shakespeare in various ways: two of the older children, Ethel and Norman, settle on a window seat to read *Henry V* to themselves, while one of the younger girls declaims speeches from *Julius Caesar* and *Hamlet* aloud to her governess from a book of selections (4–5, 64–65, 85).[8] Mrs. May herself draws on Shakespeare for a moral lesson to them all, speaking to her eldest daughter: "No, no, Margaret, don't go and protest that you love me, more than is natural, . . . that would be in the style of Regan and Goneril. It will be natural by-and-by that you should, some of you, love some one else better . . ." (19).

In the preface to their edition of Shakespeare, Mary Cowden Clarke and her husband Charles summarize the moral agenda which the nineteenth century brought to Shakespeare and declare that "A poor girl, studying no other volume, might become a lady in heart and soul" (i). While it would be grossly generalizing to see the issue divided along gender lines, nevertheless women were some of the strongest proponents for presenting Shakespeare in an unadulterated form. Unlike her predecessor, Henrietta Bowdler, Mary Cowden Clarke did not eviscerate Shakespeare's text in her editing. She may have believed with Emily Shirreff, who wrote a popular book on education, that "The extreme ignorance of early girlhood is a reason for encouraging the first reading of some of our great poets at that age. I would ask the objectors . . . why reading these in private is more objectionable than listening in

public to certain chapters of the Old and even the New Testament . . . ?"
(207) Shirreff goes on to say that if girls do not naturally turn to the objectionable parts of the Bible when they read on their own, why should they be
expected to do the same with Shakespeare? (207) To Mary Cowden Clarke,
Shakespeare *was* the girl's moral preceptor. In an 1887 article for *The Girl's
Own Paper* entitled "Shakespeare as the Girl's Friend," Cowden Clarke
wrote: "To the young girl, emerging from childhood and taking her first step
into the more active and self-dependent career of woman-life, Shakespeare's
vital precepts and models render him essentially a helping friend" (562).[9]

As I have written in a different context, girls of that period "were
encouraged to read Shakespeare as a way of improving the mind, but they
were also provided with essays and books about Shakespeare's heroines as a
way of improving their own characters."[10] In 1832, Anna Jameson used
Shakespeare's heroines as moral examples in her book *Characteristics of
Women, Moral, Poetical, and Historical,* reprinted frequently throughout the
century. Cowden Clarke published her own popular *Girlhood of Shakespeare's Heroines* in 1852, while other writers followed with books discussing the moral qualities of Shakespeare's heroines: in 1859 *The Stratford
Gallery: or, the Shakespeare Sisterhood* by the American writer Henrietta
Lee Palmer; in 1880 *On Some of Shakespeare's Female Characters* by the
actress Helena Faucit Martin; and in 1885 *Shakespeare's Garden of Girls* by
Madeleine Elliott. All of these writers treat the heroines as though they are
real people with lives outside the plays they inhabit. They refer to them as
sisters and see them as offering the kind of guidance one would expect from
real friends and relatives. Elliott says that "we can take their hands in honest
faith and learn from them to appreciate more than ever nobility of character,
singleness of purpose, and purity of ideal" (ii). Elizabeth Wordsworth, head
of Lady Margaret Hall at Oxford, "advocated that a 'well-educated girl ought
to be, at twelve or fifteen years old, in love with Miranda, Cordelia, Desdemona, Portia, and Perdita . . . and many another heroine. She ought to catch
some of their beautiful feeling, their dignity.' "[11] Women were not the only
admirers of Shakespeare's heroines, however. No less a critic than John
Ruskin found his primary examples of womanhood in Shakespeare, who he
said, "has no heroes;—he has only heroines" (92). Ruskin's idealization of
Shakespeare's characters as primary examples of womanhood appears in his
essay "Of Queen's Gardens," part of his popular work, *Sesame and Lilies.*[12]

There is no doubt that the presence of a woman on the throne helped to
focus nineteenth-century British thought on the role and character of women.
Victoria herself "said that her success as a queen depended in large part on
the morality of her court and the harmony of her domestic life" (Springer,
125). The queen patronized productions of Shakespeare's plays at Windsor,
she allowed Helena Martin's book on the heroines to be dedicated to her, and
eventually the queen's image itself became conflated with those of Shake-

speare's heroines. Two political cartoons in *Punch* represent Victoria as Titania from *A Midsummer Night's Dream* (February 23, 1856) and as Hermione from *The Winter's Tale* (September 23, 1865).

This interpenetration of reality with fiction, of real women with characters from plays, returns us to the world of Charles Dodgson, where the real Alice Liddell and any number of Dodgson's other friends and acquaintances were written into the imaginary characters who peopled his Alice books.[13] The man who wanted to "Bowdlerize Bowdler," to clean up Shakespeare, the man who objected to strong language on stage and who quibbled about certain lines or illogical strands of plot that he saw in Shakespeare's plays, nevertheless could *not* stay away from the theater. According to his diary, Dodgson's first public experience of Shakespeare occurred in February of 1855 when he was twenty-three and heard Fanny Kemble give one of her readings of *Henry V*. Dodgson writes, "I can hardly criticize her performance, as I never heard anything of the kind before, nor any Shakespeare on the stage" (*Diaries*, I:62–63), but then in June of that year he saw *Henry VIII* and was so taken with the gorgeous vision of Queen Catherine's dream, that he was hooked. His subsequent diary entries record a number of visits to the professional theater as well as attendance at various amateur home-grown productions, to some of which he contributed prologues.

It is well known that Dodgson loved being around theatrical people—especially the Terry family—and he took numerous little girl friends to see plays or to meet Ellen Terry, even encouraging the older ones who wanted a stage career themselves. When in November of 1879, twelve-year-old Agnes Hull wrote that she would like to see *Hamlet*, Dodgson responds that she is too young, but that in the meantime, "I wish you and Alice would read *Hamlet* and *The Merchant of Venice*, and see which of the two you like best" (*Letters*, 353). Later that month, he writes that he hopes to take her and her sister Alice "to see *The Merchant of Venice* in December or January." He continues, "I think you will enjoy it all the more if you read beforehand exactly what you are going to see. If you only read the regular Shakespeare, you will be expecting lots of things that will never happen" (*Letters*, 354). Realizing the difficulty of Shakespeare, Dodgson, the good teacher, encourages the girls to get the plot ahead of time by reading one of the so-called "acting" editions that presented the plays with the line cuts and transpositions of scenes as they were often staged. A few years later, in July of 1884, he wrote to Beatrice Earle, daughter of an Oxford colleague, saying that he had suggested that Miss Ellen Terry send her a photograph of herself as Beatrice. Terry charmingly obliged. Enclosed with the note was a photograph showing her as Beatrice, and inscribed: "To Beatrice: from 'Beatrice'—Ellen Terry, July 5.84." On the back she wrote: " 'There was a star danced & under that was I born. . . . ' "[14] Reminiscing about him, Terry wrote in her memoirs, "Mr. Dodgson's kindness to children was wonderful. . . . nothing could have been more touching than his ceaseless industry on their behalf" (Terry, 230).[15]

Though his own single attempt at playwriting was not a success, Dodgson's very life was theatrical. This fastidious Oxford mathematician created his alter ego, Lewis Carroll, and performed over and over again—a master of tricks, games and surprises—to generations of little girls.[16] The *Alice* books themselves are full of dramatic moments, strange encounters, and witty, memorable dialogue. Such inherent theatricality has made them eminently performable, whether on stage or, in modern times, in the movies. But if Dodgson was worried about the effect of vulgarity in Shakespeare, he was at least as squeamish about any hint of it in his own work. When, in 1886, he allowed Henry Savile Clarke to mount the *Alice* books as an operetta, he did so on one condition: "that, neither in the libretto nor in any of the stage business, shall . . . anything suggestive of coarseness, be admitted" (Cohen, 434–35). The production evidently had the desired effect, for a reviewer for one of the papers noted, "a more sweet and wholesome combination of drollery and fancy . . . a more refined and charming entertainment—has not been seen upon our stage for many a day" (quoted in Cohen, 436–37).

"Sweet and wholesome" is what Dodgson envisioned for his Girl's Shakespeare as well, but I would like to end this chapter by imagining the kind of Shakespeare Dodgson *could* have created, if he had allowed Lewis Carroll to take over. Then he could have let his mind run through Shakespeare's language and stories, reshaping them into his own fantastic creations, much as his friend the painter Joseph Noël Paton filled a Victorian wood with faeries from *A Midsummer Night's Dream*, or his illustrator Sir John Tenniel admiringly lampooned Shakespearean scenes in his *Punch* cartoons.

It is interesting that Tenniel *also* had a Shakespeare project in mind that remained uncompleted—he wanted to make an illustrated edition of the plays.[17] What a book that might have been if Tenniel and Dodgson had joined their talents with Shakespeare! One can imagine an Alice/Juliet similar to the illustration made by another contemporary artist, Henry Selous, for Cassell's Shakespeare in 1864. Selous's drawing is itself close to one made by Dodgson for *Alice's Adventures Under Ground*, that Jeffrey Stern has convincingly shown was influenced by the work of Dodgson's friend Arthur Hughes, one of the Pre-Raphaelite painters. Dodgson owned Hughes's "Girl with Lilacs," which he hung in his study in 1863, about a year before he finished the *Alice* illustrations (Stern, 171–76). Dodgson's picture shows Alice holding the flask from which she has just drunk the potion that makes her grow too large. In Selous's image, Juliet holds the flask containing the potion that will give her the appearance of death. Both young women are frightened as they contemplate the enormous changes they face at this transitional moment in their lives. Stern writes that both Dodgson and Hughes were fascinated with "the precise moment of change from innocence to commitment, from childhood to adulthood," and they attempt through their art to freeze this moment when

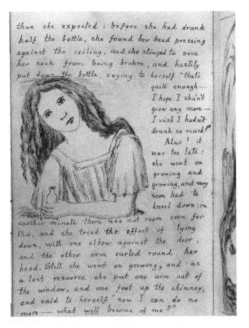

than she expected ; before she had drunk half the bottle, she found her head pressing against the ceiling, and she stooped to save her neck from being broken , and hastily put down the bottle, saying to herself "that's quite enough— I hope I shan't grow any more— I wish I hadn't drunk so much!" Alas ! it was too late : she went on growing and growing, and very soon had to kneel down : in another minute there was not room even for this, and she tried the effect of lying down, with one elbow against the door , and the other arm curled round her head. Still she went on growing, and as a last resource she put one arm out of the window, and one foot up the chimney, and said to herself "now I can do no more — what will become of me ?"

Fig. 34: Alice from Lewis Carroll, "Alice's Adventures Under Ground." British Library Add. MS 46700, f.19v. By permission of the British Library.

Juliet. What if it be a poison, which the friar Subtly hath minister'd to have me dead. *Act IV. Scene III.*

Fig. 35: Juliet by Henry Selous. Illustration for *Cassell's Shakespeare*, ed. Charles and Mary Cowden Clarke (London, c1864). By permission of the Folger Shakespeare Library.

female freshness may succumb to decay (Stern, 176–77). He suggests, without making explicit, a comparison between Hughes's painting of Ophelia (1851–53) holding the rushes she has gathered and looking into the stream, and Dodgson's evocation of Alice gathering rushes in *Through the Looking Glass*, where they fade as soon as gathered and the most beautiful ones are always beyond her reach.[18] But Juliet also changes "from innocence to commitment" when she turns to the Friar for a remedy to her situation. As Helena Faucit, Lady Martin writes in her 1881 essay on "Juliet:" "It is for the actress, in this marvellous and most difficult scene, to show, by her look and manner, how everything that is girlish and immature . . . falls off from Juliet,—how she is transfigured into the heroic woman . . ." and she describes how she felt Juliet's terror when taking the sleeping potion (Martin, 140, 143–44), a terror that registers in the face of the Selous Juliet. Just as Juliet is imprisoned in her father's house by the death-like sleep, so Alice is imprisoned in the rabbit's house by her size and realizes that she has "grown up." Looking at the illustrations by Dodgson and Tenniel for this episode of the Alice story, Donald Rackin has rightly noted how much more psychologically disturbing some of Dodgson's own illustrations are than the ones by Tenniel. In this case, Dodgson's figure of Alice takes up the whole page, "in her fetal position, so horribly crowded in that womb she cannot escape," and with a "dreamy look of terribly sad acceptance" (Rackin, 12). Perhaps Dodgson's edition of Shakespeare would have been more compelling had he illustrated it himself.

To imagine the kind of pseudo-Shakespearean text that Dodgson might have created to accompany his own or Tenniel's illustrations, we can turn to several imaginative pieces he wrote, inspired by Shakespeare. Around the age of thirteen, Dodgson designed and largely wrote eight magazines for the amusement of his family of seven sisters and three younger brothers. In the first of these, called *Useful and Instructive Poetry* (1845), he interpolated his own already-mature wit into a passage from Act 4 of *Henry IV, Pt. 2*, the scene in which Prince Hal keeps vigil beside the bed of his dying father.[19] A brief sample from this dialogue will give an idea of Dodgson's precocious play with words. Prince Hal begins his speech, "Why doth the crown lie here upon his pillow?" But when he gets to the lines: "Yet not so sound, and half so deeply sweet, / As he whose brow with homely biggen bound / Snores out the watch of night," he is suddenly interrupted by the King who says, "Harry I know not / The meaning of the word you just have used." The Prince asks, "What word, my liege?" and the King replies, "The word I mean is 'biggin.' " The Prince enlightens him, all in proper iambic pentameter, that a biggin is a woolen nightcap worn by the peasantry. After one or two other quibbles about words, the King interrupts the Prince when he says, "My due from thee is this imperial crown." " 'Tis *not* your due, sir! I deny it!" the King rejoins, but the Prince responds, "It *is* my liege! How dare you contradict me? /

Moreover how can you, a sleeper, know / That which another doth soliloquise?" Both then fall into an argument about whether the King is asleep, and if he is, how he can hear the Prince's soliloquizing, all based on Dodgson's keen interest in logic, even at the age of thirteen. Beyond the word play and logic, however, lies a deeper restlessness with authority that becomes a dominant theme of the later *Alice* books. Here the son, logically correct, contradicts the father; later when Dodgson writes as Lewis Carroll, he will feminize the conflict between generations, as Alice comes up against the arbitrariness of adult authority figures of both genders: the White Rabbit, the Duchess, the King of Hearts, the Red and White Queens, and others.[20] We can only speculate how he might have rewritten Juliet, Rosalind, Beatrice, Desdemona, Helena, and Hermia—all of whom challenge the assumptions and regulations of the mostly patriarchal figures in their own societies.

Another piece demonstrates the lighter side of Dodgson's imaginative encounters with Shakespeare's texts. In 1871, the rehousing of the bells of Christ Church Cathedral in a structure that was universally considered ugly led Dodgson to create a comical attack against the project, printed as a pamphlet that went through five editions. One section of the spoof is a playlet, in which the Dean of Christ Church alternately plays Hamlet and Lear. He enters saying, "Methinks I see a Bell-tower!" and when the Canons reply, "Where, my good sir?" the Dean says, "In my mind's eye." The Great Bell itself then appears as "Poor Tom" from *King Lear*, "whom the foul fiend hath led through bricks and through mortar, through rope and windlass, through plank and scaffold." The Dean, reverting to Lear, says, "The little Dons and all, Tutor, Reader, Lecturer—see, they bark at me!" to which the Censor responds, "His wits begin to unsettle." The two men then continue their discussion as Hamlet and Polonius: "Do you see yonder box that's almost in shape of a tea-caddy? / By its mass, it is like a tea-caddy indeed. / . . . Or like a tub. / Very like a tub." The episode ends with a take-off on *The Tempest* when the Treasurer as Ariel recites: "Five fathom square the Belfry frowns; / All its sides of timber made; / Painted all in greys and browns; / Nothing of it that will fade." (*Diversions*, 112–15) As in the *Alice* books and elsewhere, Dodgson here bursts the pretentious bubble of authority. Appropriating scenes of madness from the Victorians' "sainted" Shakespeare allows Dodgson to excoriate the wisdom of the Dean, Architect, and Treasurer who have permitted the erection of such an excrescence at the college: "Beauty's dead! Let's ring her knell. / Hark! now I hear them—ding-dong, bell." Beauty and order were fundamental to the sensibilities of a mathematician such as Dodgson. While the nonlogical might reign for a time in the universe of his imaginative writings—and of Shakespeare's—as a way of setting "a mirror up to nature," order is restored in the end. Alice comes back through the looking glass, Lear regains his wits and self-knowledge. The kind of whimsical playing with words and ideas that Dodgson does here—free associating, stretching their boundaries to incorporate the old with the new, Shake-spearean with Victorian—is typical of much of his work, poetry and prose, riddles, and puzzles. If Charles Dodgson had turned his Lewis Carroll mind to Shakespeare, rewriting the plays or the stories from the plays, the evidence is that he would have produced a work, more witty and imaginative than the books by Jameson, Cowden Clarke, and others on Shakespeare's heroines, and much more inviting than the "sweet and wholesome" Girl's Shakespeare he had planned.[21]

Notes

1. *Shakespeare's Plays for Schools.* Abridged and annotated by C. M. Yonge. 5 pts. (London: National Society's Depository, 1883–85).
2. *The History of Shylock the Jew . . . with that of Portia and the Three Caskets. . . .* (London, 1794); *The Lives and Tragical Deaths of Hamlet . . . and the Lovely Ophelia* (London, 1823); *Mother Goose's Melody; or, Sonnets for the cradle . . .* (London, c. 1797).
3. Quoted from Pitman, "Advertisement" and Cundell, "Preface" (3) to their editions of Shakespeare. For a listing of the various editions of Shakespeare used in this essay, see References under Shakespeare. The Princess Victoria was given copies of Lamb's *Tales* and Pitman's Shakespeare (Vallone, 47).
4. On March 15, 1882 Dodgson noted in his Diary: "Received Brandram's *Selections from Shakespeare*: I had fancied it would make my idea of a 'Girl's Own Shakespeare' superfluous—but it does not do so." (*Diaries*, 1971: 404)
5. See Thwaite, 6 and Martin, *Helena*, 3–4.
6. Quoted in Flint, 83. A Quaker who married a Congregationalist missionary, Ellis is best known for her popular series of advice books: *The Women-*, *The Daughters-*, *The Mothers-*, and *The Wives of England*, published between 1838 and 1843.
7. Quoted in Uglow, 42.
8. Yonge may be thinking of B. H. Smart's *Historico-Shakspearian Readings from the Chronicle and Roman plays . . . the Companion Volume to the Practice of Elocution* (London, 1851). Yonge herself as a child read from Bowdler's Shakespeare and received a copy of Jameson's *Characteristics of Women* (see Flint, 192, 199–200).
9. This essay also appeared in *Shakespeariana* 4 (1887): 355–69.
10. See Ziegler, "Queen Victoria, Shakespeare and the Ideal Woman" in *Shakespeare's Unruly Women*, 11.
11. Quoted in Flint, 76.
12. For Ruskin's views on gender, see Weltman.
13. Casting "real" people as literary figures was prominent in the photography of the time. Dodgson photographed his young friend Alexandra Kitchin as Viola in male disguise, which he inscribed with lines from *Twelfth Night* (II.iv. 106–08), "My father had a daughter loved a man, / As it might be, perhaps, were I a woman, / I should your lordship" (Princeton U Library, Lewis Carroll Photographic Archives. Web address: http://libserv3.princeton.edu/rbsc2/

portfolio/lc-all-list.html). See also Julia Margaret Cameron's photographs of family, friends, and servants as allegorical and literary figures.

14. The note and photo are in the manuscript collection of the Folger Shakespeare Library: Y.d.458 (4b, 4a).

15. See also the well-known letter concerning a passage in *Twelfth Night* that Dodgson wrote to Terry's sister Florence in 1874 (*Letters,* 204–05).

16. Edith Arnold, one of his young friends, wrote of Dodgson's rooms in Christ Church: " 'The large sitting-room was lined with well-filled bookshelves, under which ran a row of cupboards. . . . Oh, those cupboards! What wondrous treasures they contained. . . . Mechanical bears, dancing-dolls, toys and puzzles of every description came from them in endless profusion!' " Quoted in Cohen, 234. Edith Arnold was the niece of the poet Matthew Arnold.

17. ". . . despite an offer from his *Punch* publisher . . . to publish the book when he completed it, and with at least two drawings engraved by the Dalziels, the project was eventually abandoned for want of time" (Engen, 119).

18. Stern, 176–77. See *Through the Looking Glass,* chapter 5. Hughes did another Ophelia painting in 1863–64. While Stern sees the implied affinity between Alice and Ophelia, he does not pick up on the Alice/Juliet relationship.

19. *Useful,* 25–27.

20. For an excellent discussion of the relationship between Queen Victoria and the *Alice* books, and of Carroll's undermining and rewriting Ruskin's idealization of girls into queens, see Homans, 85 ff.

21. An earlier version of this paper was read at the meeting of the Lewis Carroll Society of North America, Washington, D.C., May 1999. I would like to thank the members of that Society, and especially David and Denise Carlson of D&D Galleries for sharing information from their catalog of Carrolliana, and Donald and Phyllis Rackin for their comments.

Works Cited

Bakewell, Michael. *Lewis Carroll: A Biography.* London: Heinemann, 1996.

Carroll, Lewis. *The Diaries* . . . Ed. Roger Lancelyn Green. 2 vols. New York: Oxford University Press, 1954; rpt. Westport: Greenwood, 1971. Cited as *Diaries* 1971.

———. *Diversions and Digressions of Lewis Carroll.* Ed. Stuart Dodgson Collingwood. New York: Dover, 1961.

———. *Letters.* Ed. Morton N. Cohen with Roger Lancelyn Green. 2 vols. New York: Oxford University Press, 1979.

———. *Lewis Carroll's Diaries.* Ed. Edward Wakeling. 5 vols. Luton, England: The Lewis Carroll Society, 1993–99.

———. *Sylvie and Bruno.* In *Complete Works.* New York: Modern Library, 1936.

———. *Useful and Instructive Poetry.* Intro. by Derek Hudson. London: Geoffrey Bles, 1954.

Clarke, Mary Cowden. "Shakespeare as the Girl's Friend." *The Girl's Own Paper* 8 (June 1887): 562–64.

Cohen, Morton N. *Lewis Carroll: A Biography.* New York: Random House, Vintage, 1996.

Elliott, Madeleine. *Shakspeare's Garden of Girls*. London: Remington, 1885.

Engen, Rodney. *Sir John Tenniel: Alice's White Knight*. Aldershot, England: Scolar Press, 1991.

Flint, Kate. *The Woman Reader 1837–1914*. Oxford: Clarendon Press, 1995.

Homans, Margaret. *Royal Representations: Queen Victoria and British Culture, 1837–1876*. Chicago: University of Chicago Press, 1998.

Lewis Carroll Observed. Ed. Edward Guiliano for The Lewis Carroll Society of North America. New York: Clarkson N. Potter, 1976.

Martin, Helena Faucit. *On Some of Shakespeare's Female Characters*. 5th ed. Edinburgh: Blackwood, 1893.

Martin, Sir Theodore. *Helena Faucit (Lady Martin)*. Edinburgh: Blackwood, 1900.

Rackin, Donald. "Laughing and Grief: What's So Funny About *Alice in Wonderland*?" In *Lewis Carroll Observed* 1–18.

Ruskin, John. "Of Queen's Gardens," *Sesame and Lilies*. 1865. London: Allen, 1904.

Shakespeare, William. *The School-Shakspeare*. Ed. J. R. Pitman. London: J. F. Dove for C. Rice, 1822.

———. *The Family Shakespeare*. Ed. Thomas Bowdler. 3rd ed. 6 vols. London: Longman, et al., 1823. The Folger Library owns Dodgson's own copy, inscribed (C. L. Dodgson 1875) but not annotated, shelf-mark PR2752 1823j ShCol.

———. *Dramatic Works*. Chambers's Household Edition. Ed. R. Carruthers and W. Chambers. 10 vols. London: Chambers, 1861–63.

———. *The Works of William Shakespeare*. Ed. Charles and Mary Cowden Clarke. London: Bickers, 1875.

———. *The Boudoir Shakespeare: Carefully Prepared for Reading Aloud*. Ed. Henry Cundell. 3 vols. London: Sampson, Low, et al., 1876–77.

———. *Shakespeare: Certain Selected Plays Abridged for the Use of the Young* by Samuel Brandram. London: Smith, Elder, 1881.

———. *The Riverside Shakespeare*. 2nd ed. Ed. G. Blakemore Evans, et al. Boston: Houghton Mifflin, 1997.

Shirreff, Emily. *Intellectual Education*. 2nd ed. London: Smith, Elder, 1862.

Springer, Marlene. "Angels and other Women in Victorian Literature." In Marlene Springer, ed. *What Manner of Woman*. New York: New York University Press, 1977: 124–59.

Stern, Jeffrey. "Lewis Carroll the Pre-Raphaelite 'Fainting in Coils'." In *Lewis Carroll Observed* 161–180.

Terry, Ellen. *The Story of My Life*. New York: Schocken Books, 1982.

Thwaite, Ann. *Emily Tennyson: The Poet's Wife*. London: Faber, 1996.

Uglow, Jenny. *Elizabeth Gaskell: A Habit of Stories*. New York: Farrar, Straus, and Giroux, 1993.

Vallone, Lynne. *Becoming Victoria*. New Haven: Yale University Press, 2001.

Weltman, Sharon Aronofsky. *Ruskin's Mythic Queen: Gender Subversion in Victorian Culture*. Athens: Ohio University Press, 1998.

Yonge, Charlotte M. *The Daisy Chain*. London: Virago Press, 1988 [from 1873 ed.].

Ziegler, Georgianna, with Frances E. Dolan and Jeanne Addison Roberts. *Shakespeare's Unruly Women*. Washington, D.C.: The Folger Shakespeare Library, 1997.

Works Consulted

Clarke, Mary Cowden. *The Girlhood of Shakespeare's Heroines.* 5 vols. London: W. H. Smith, 1850–52.

Jameson, Anna. *Characteristics of Women, Moral, Poetical, and Historical.* 2nd ed. corr. and enl. 2 vols. London: Saunders and Otley, 1833.

Leigh-Noel, M. *Shakespeare's Garden of Girls.* London: Remington, 1885.

Lootens, Tricia. *Lost Saints: Silence, Gender, and Victorian Literary Canonization.* Charlottesville: University Press of Virginia, 1996.

Martin, Helena Faucit. *On Some of Shakespeare's Female Characters.* Edinburgh: Blackwood, 1885.

Palmer, Henrietta Lee. *The Stratford Gallery: or, the Shakespeare Sisterhood.* New York: Appleton, 1859.

Robson, Catherine. *Men in Wonderland: the Lost Girlhood of the Victorian Gentleman.* Princeton: Princeton University Press, 2001.

Thomas, Donald. *Lewis Carroll: A Portrait with Background.* London: John Murray, 1996.

Women Reading Shakespeare 1660–1900: An Anthology of Criticism. Ed. Ann Thompson and Sasha Roberts. Manchester: Manchester University Press, 1997.

13. Strutting and Fretting on the Page

Representing Shakespeare's Theater in Illustrated Books

MEGAN LYNN ISAAC

Students generally arrive in middle and high school classrooms without a great deal of knowledge about how many daughters King Lear has or whom Rosalind loves. Many have never seen a play performed, or at best, have only watched modern musicals or a matinee showing of *A Christmas Carol*. Some may realize Shakespeare was born in the Renaissance, but most will be hard-pressed to explain when the English Renaissance occurred, if any time frame more specific than before World War Two and after the dinosaurs is demanded. Yet, a surprising number "know" that Shakespeare didn't write the plays and that Juliet married Romeo when she was only thirteen, which was a perfectly "normal" age for matrimony "back then." Teaching Shakespeare's plays often means teaching about his world as well. Fortunately, a variety of recent publications, both picture books about Shakespeare's world and adaptations of specific plays make a virtue of this necessity by showing readers the excitement of Renaissance drama and inviting them to explore it further.

Picture books about Shakespeare and the Renaissance world are, without a doubt, an under-utilized resource. The growth of such publications in recent years suggests some positive development in this area, but old myths also persist. A number of well-intentioned, if misguided, reasons are frequently used for dismissing picture books or adaptations of Shakespeare. Many teachers with high standards and admirable goals believe that picture books are inappropriately "easy" for older students—an absence of illustrations somehow being equated with rigor; most such instructors are simply unfamiliar with the current rich diversity of illustrated materials. Others feel that using such books to introduce a play will ruin the surprise. But this view of drama misinterprets where the power of a play lies. Shakespeare's own audiences surely often knew the outcomes of the tales he dramatized; after all, he borrowed them from other plays and from well known historical events. The excitement of a play comes from the revelation in how the story is told much less than in what the outcome will be. Furthermore, due to the fact that Shakespeare's plays are both so historically and culturally distant from modern students, there is a much greater danger that students will lose interest due to confusion than due to too much knowledge about the play! Finally, some teachers believe they are doing students a disservice if they fail to provide them with anything less than "the real thing." Yet, any search for the "real" or a "pure" Shakespeare will soon reveal its futility. Is a text more authentic than a performance? Is a lackluster uncut production better than a breathtaking edited one? Is an authentic performance utilizing an all-male cast preferable to one using women in the female roles? There are not any right answers to these questions. Drama is by its very nature a shifting and transitory art form. No play is ever the same twice. The fact that new artists and new audiences, century after century, bring their own visions and experiences to interpreting the plays is exactly what makes them so special. Picture books and adaptations are not a substitute for Shakespeare's plays, but they are wonderful supplemental and introductory materials—in many aspects little different from the program notes or scholarly introductions more experienced adult fans of Shakespeare carefully peruse before seeing a performance or reading a play.

The more of these picture books a student can study the better. Comparing several will help readers see the way historians and literary critics selectively represent even so focused a topic as Shakespeare and his stage, and the more interpretations of this topic a student reads, the richer and more complex his or her understanding of its possibilities will become. For a student without much experience in theater-going, an unillustrated comparison of the Globe's thrust stage to the performance space available at Blackfriars is almost impossible to envision. The opening scenes of *Hamlet* are easier to follow for a reader who can see the trapdoor on the stage and the stars painted on the canopy above. Picture books, whether distributed among the class and read during the first course meeting as an introduction to the stage or held on reserve in the library for students to peruse at their own leisure, provide the visually orientated information so helpful to students of drama. For students in middle and high schools, these picture books are more exciting, and in many cases more informative, than the brief textual introductions provided in anthologies and classroom editions of the plays. A quick survey of the prefatory materials included in the Bantam, Dover, New Folger Library, Everyman, New Penguin, Oxford School Shakespeare, and Signet Classic editions of Shakespeare's plays demonstrates that only the New Folger Library series provides detailed and specific information about Shakespeare's theatrical world comparable to that provided in many picture books. And, even in this case, the information is much less appealing in its presentation. (Obviously, there are many other popular and inexpensive editions frequently used in schools; these editions merely represent a rough sampling of the field.)

Eight recent titles all offer thought-provoking illustrations and provide well-detailed and specific information that makes them appropriate to multiple audiences—curious adults as well as curious children. In some ways, however, these eight volumes replicate one of the most important divisions within Shakespeare studies—Shakespeare as a theatrical genius or Shakespeare as a literary artist. Both visions of Shakespeare have significant merit. But considering whether one prefers, at least in a specific situation, to focus on Shakespeare's soaring poetry or on the magic of the stage, may help both teachers and students find a focal point to begin their explorations. The first six volumes all have a significant emphasis upon stage history; exploration of a specific play or two is secondary to an exploration of the Renaissance theatrical world.

Shakespeare's Theatre by Andrew Langley with paintings by June Everett (1999) epitomizes the emphasis on Shakespeare as a dramatic master. Designed in part as an architectural record, this picture book juxtaposes a history of the recent construction of Sam Wanamaker's new Globe Theatre with a history of the events that led to the construction of the original Globe in 1599. Everett's delicate and intricately-detailed paintings emphasize the busy complexity of Renaissance London, a modern construction site, and the splendid decoration of the new Globe. This volume provides little information about Shakespeare's biography or the content of his works but elegantly demonstrates the visual splendor of the Renaissance theatrical experience, a dimension of his dramas almost always absent when students meet Shakespeare on the page in the classroom.

Amanda Lewis and Tim Wynne-Jones's amazingly comprehensive *Rosie Backstage* (1994), illustrated by Bill Slavin, also uses the stage as a platform for provoking readers' curiosity about Shakespeare and his works. Rosie's tale is set in Stratford, Canada. Her mother works as a props mistress, and Rosie works at staying out of trouble, without notable success. Lewis and Wynne-Jones intersperse Rosie's adventures backstage, understage, and onstage with a fantastic tour of the multi-faceted work of a professional theater company. The artistry and effort of the behind-the-scenes-staff receives just as much attention as the work of the actors. Her most exciting adventures begin once the ghost of Will Shakespeare himself takes a special interest in helping Rosie learn how to navigate both a modern stage in Stratford and the Globe in London. Rosie's adventures take place during rehearsals for *The Tempest*, *Macbeth*, and *As You Like It*, providing readers with the additional bonus of a casual introduction to these three plays. At almost one hundred pages, nearly evenly divided between text and illustrations, Lewis and Wynne-Jones's book quickly demonstrates that it is more than a simple illustrated tale for children.

Aliki's *William Shakespeare and the Globe* (1999) examines a bit of both the theatrical and literary approaches to studying Shakespeare's work.

The author mimics the five-act structure typical of Renaissance drama to organize her book. Each of the five sections of the story emphasizes a different part of Shakespeare's theatrical development. Most pages are decorated with carefully chosen and colorful quotations from the plays. These aspects of the book's construction serve to prepare readers to meet the plays as literary works. Readers of the plays often consider the five-act structure of the dramas and consider line-by-line the memorable power of Shakespeare's prose, but these elements of play design generally remain an invisible skeleton to theatrical audiences.

Like Langley's book, Aliki spends much of her space detailing the architectural design of Wanamaker's Globe (and by implication the original Globe as well). Little space, however, is devoted to exploring the actor's experiences on the stage; instead Aliki provides a brief, but well-selected, overview of the trials and tribulations of an actor's life. More specifically, she presents the limited historical facts of Shakespeare's life within the context of typical Renaissance practices. Speculations about Shakespeare's motivations and personal relationships are appropriately minimal. She points out that Shakespeare's tragedies and more solemn plays follow the death of his son Hamnet, leading readers toward a cause and effect interpretation of these two events, but she refrains from any direct conjecture. An illustrated glossary of many of Shakespeare's neologisms and paper-doll renditions of his most famous characters encourage readers to explore the plays on their own.

Shakespeare and Macbeth: The Story Behind the Play by Stewart Ross with illustrations by Tony Karpinski (1994) balances the literary and theatrical approaches to studying Shakespeare's works. Using *Macbeth* as an example, Ross narrates the process of writing a play. In his imaginative reconstruction of events, Shakespeare selects his subject (fully aware of King James's Scottish heritage and supernatural interests); proposes his material to fellow members of the King's Men; studies a variety of historical sources; selectively changes and adapts the material to fit his needs; drafts his play with a conscientious awareness of the strengths and weaknesses of the actors available to fill the roles; and once the play is complete, hires a scribe to copy out the parts. Ross helps students of Shakespeare understand not so much where the playwright got his ideas, but what he does with ideas to transform them into literature. Some of the dramatic elements of *Macbeth* are also considered; Ross explains how the symbolism of costumes supports a play's themes, illustrates some of the differences between performing a play at the Globe and at Hampton Court, and demonstrates the collaborative nature of a theatrical performance. But more than anything else, Ross is interested in *Macbeth* as a story—six of the book's final pages tell an abbreviated version of the play. The illustrations in this section are sketchy and dreamlike, in direct contrast to the bold and richly colored pictures that illustrate the scenes of Shakespeare's creative process. These later pictures present a vision of how a reader might imagine the play—with well-armed men on horseback approaching a trio of wind-whipped witches on a stormy moor. These are imaginative visions of *Macbeth*, not ones that would have or could have been found on stage, and they are the last images a reader receives.

In some ways, Diane Stanley and Peter Vennema's *Bard of Avon: The Story of William Shakespeare* (1992) presents the most provocative vision of Shakespeare's life and stage, especially if it is read alongside one or more of the other recent picture book versions of Shakespeare's stage. It is a tidy book. Stanley admits that little is known of Shakespeare's life, but she goes on to construct a biography filled with speculations designed to plug the holes in the fragile historical record. She explains that Shakespeare's parents were probably against his marriage to Anne Hathaway and that the union was not a happy one. She supposes that the great tragedies he wrote in the early seventeenth century were inspired by Shakespeare's horror over Essex's death and the imprisonment of his own early patron, the Earl of Southampton. Neither of these speculations is without merit, but at the same time they are utterly unverifiable. It is just as likely that Shakespeare married Anne Hathaway at his parents' insistence (she was pregnant), than that he did so against their wishes. In presenting such a confident vision of Shakespeare's life, Stanley's narrative risks doing a disservice to readers. Students develop a better appreciation for the complexity of history if it is presented as a puzzle or a skeleton rather than a finished product, a concluded tale.

Bard of Avon does give readers a sense of Shakespeare's theatrical writings; his primary genres are briefly defined and a handful of the plays are quickly summarized. Unlike any of the other picture books discussed, the authorship question and the improbability of the anti-Stratfordian position are raised. The illustrations in this book, however, reflect Stanley and Vennema's interest in a clear or clean view of Shakespeare's world. The paintings are beautifully sharp and precise; every citizen, actor, spectator, and courtier wears a crisp, white collar or lacy ruff. Streets and buildings are uniformly spotless, almost as if every pavement has just been swept and every windowsill freshly painted. In the illustration of theater-goers watching a performance of *Richard II*, the well-dressed groundlings remain a discreet distance from the stage. No one pushes forward to get a better view or picks his neighbor's pocket in this vision of the Globe. In short, the individual physical details of the Renaissance world seem accurately depicted, but the overall aura seems inexplicably clean—a Disneyfied vision of Shakespeare's world, free of warts and wrinkles, rats and refuse.

The most recent and most magnificent picture book on England's famous playwright is, however, *Shakespeare: His Work and His World* (2001) written by Michael Rosen and illustrated by Robert Ingpen. Like Lewis and Wynne-Jones's book, this volume is substantial, ninety-six pages. Rosen's text bridges the distance between Shakespeare's life and the reader's by asking and addressing questions that might seem impertinent but lurk in many reader's minds, like "What's so special about Shakespeare?" He also admits to and explores the holes in our historical records of Shakespeare's life rather than ignoring them or filling them in. Near the conclusion of his chapter on Shakespeare's experiences in Stratford and at school he writes, "But let's face it, we don't really know very much about how Shakespeare spent his childhood and teenage years" (33).

Most of the book is devoted to exploration of Shakespeare's world, but brief discussions of *A Midsummer Night's Dream, Macbeth, King Lear, The Tempest,* and *Romeo and Juliet* are included. Quotations from the plays are also woven through the book to highlight how Shakespeare's language illustrates the Renaissance world. More than any other picture book, Rosen manages to make Shakespeare's language interesting and pertinent to a study of his world. Finally, whether discussing life in Shakespeare's time or how performances of the plays have changed through the centuries, Rosen's text is full of colorful facts and modern insights all expressed in a comfortable and conversational tone.

Robert Ingpen's wonderfully textured illustrations make this volume difficult to put down even for readers initially suspicious about Shakespeare. The pictures glow with light and life whether he is portraying a torch lit vision of the Burbages stealing the timbers of an older theater to use in the construction of the Globe; a misty vision, almost like a Turner painting, of the Stratford marketplace; or the stark but sunny atmosphere of a Renaissance schoolroom. His sketches of Shakespearean characters are also interesting; they almost always force the reader to focus on facial expression or body language. Using his own medium, Ingpen, as much as Rosen, emphasizes the enduring human qualities of Shakespeare's drama.

Instead of focusing on Shakespeare's theatrical world, some picture book authors choose a specific play to adapt. Like Shakespeare himself, these authors and illustrators insist that audiences experience a play visually as well as verbally. And, studying how a play is told in pictures can be in many ways as enlightening as studying the text of the play itself; rather than simplifying what a student learns, such an approach provides the groundwork to transform a young reader into an astute literary and theatrical critic, particularly if two or more versions of a play are compared and contrasted. Although many interesting illustrated adaptations are currently available, briefly exploring just two versions of *Romeo and Juliet* will demonstrate the process.

Margaret Early's *Romeo and Juliet* (1998) uses a highly stylized artistic vision of the play to enhance a reader's interpretation of the story. With only six colors of paint and highlights in luminous gold, the book recalls the illuminated manuscripts of the Middle Ages. Each page is bordered with intricate and delicate patterns, and the illustrations are even more richly detailed.

A careful attention to architectural forms like arches and ceiling beams enhances a very measured sense of depth in these paintings. Early's human figures, on the other hand, are all static, nearly one-dimensional. Romeo and Juliet seem almost doll-like figures posed against backgrounds of great complexity. While this description might seem like a criticism if the paintings were gracing the wall of a museum, as accompaniments to Shakespeare's plays this style seems poignantly appropriate. In this interpretation, Romeo and Juliet are simple lovers caught up in a conflict much larger than themselves and betrayed by coincidences far beyond their powers of prediction.

Early's prose also emphasizes the simplicity of the lovers' tale. The book begins, "Once upon a time, in the fair city of Verona, lived two noble families, the Montagues and the Capulets." Students frightened by horror stories about the complexity or incomprehensibility of Shakespearean verse won't find anything to dismay them in these simple cadences, but they may be prompted to wonder why Early turns to the familiar cadences of fairy tales for her readers. And asking such questions is at the very heart of literary interpretation.

Early adapts other aspects of the play as well. She eliminates many of Shakespeare's characters and the careful layering of conflicts that supports his plot. Here, the attention is almost always on the unquestioned love of Romeo and Juliet. Shakespeare's play frequently highlights the haste of Romeo and Juliet's infatuation and interrogates their course of action. In Early's version, however, the protagonists are emblems of sincere love whose actions are above reproach. To enable this romanticized interpretation of the play, Early makes important choices in her illustrations and text. For example, Romeo is all but relieved of bloodshed. He seems little more than a passive participant in Tybalt's death. In the illustration, a small pool of blood trickles from Mercutio's fallen body, and Romeo stands quietly with his sword drawn while Tybalt rushes forward to impale himself. Romeo's murder of the rival suitor Paris never occurs at all. In Early's text, Romeo is a gentle lover victimized by the violence of Verona, not a participant in its bloody ideologies. Early's *Romeo and Juliet* chooses to celebrate in words and pictures the splendor and purity of romantic love.[1]

Clearly, however, there are other ways to understand this play. In Bruce Coville's *Romeo and Juliet* (1999) with illustrations by Dennis Nolan, a different vision of the tragedy in Verona emerges. Unlike Early, whose Romeo and Juliet appear as small, almost distant, figures amid a rich background, in Nolan's illustrations the youth and vivid individuality of the characters are emphasized. Almost all of the illustrations are narrow vertical panels occupying about one third of a page and illustrating a single human figure, most often, of course, Romeo or Juliet. There is almost no background detail in these pictures at all, so like Shakespeare's plays themselves, which were presented in theaters where scenery was scarce, readers are forced to focus on the characters.

Like Early, Coville and Nolan also show an awareness of the difficulty of adapting the violence of Verona to a format most likely to be read by younger audiences. Whereas Early silently shifts both the visual and verbal elements of the plot to soften the murderous intensity of the story, Coville chooses a fuller interpretation of Shakespeare's tale; limits to the gore and violence are imposed only in Nolan's illustrations. For example, a weapon appears in just one illustration, despite the fact that careful attention is given to detailing the clothing of the characters. Even in the illustrations of Romeo comforting a dying Mercutio or staring aghast at the "deceased" Juliet in the tomb, he is without even so much as a dagger. Yet, in contrast to these bloodless choices, the illustrations are dominated by a reddish aura; the tones of the air, the vague forms of the buildings and paving stones, and even the accents in the characters' clothing are all infused with what might both be described as a rosy hue and a bloody shadow. Intriguingly, however, these choices are in some ways reminiscent of the devices theater companies often employ. Some stage versions of *Romeo and Juliet* revel in combat scenes and oozing wounds, but others rely on the language of the play and subtle lighting effects to convey the violence. Students attuned to considering these interpretive decisions through thoughtful study of several variants of a play will probably have quite a bit to say about their preferences in dramatic interpretation, and are likely to be inspired to try their own hand at Shakespeare— whether it is in the form of textual interpretation, dramatic performance, or illustrative design.

None of these picture books can replace the experience of reading and watching Shakespeare's own words, but the work that they do perform may be equally important. All of these works encourage readers to abandon stuffy, off-putting, and staid impressions of Shakespeare's plays and the world in which they originated in favor of a lively, moving, and personal vision of the Renaissance. They create a context for reading or watching Shakespeare as informed participants and not simply as victims of a traditional curriculum. Whether an instructor aims to present Shakespeare's works primarily as texts to be read or as plays to be watched—literary or theatrical masterpieces— picture books and adaptations recreating Shakespeare's world have much to offer audiences of all ages.

Note

1. Discussion of Early's text is adapted from my book *Heirs to Shakespeare: Reinventing the Bard in Young Adult Literature.*

Bibliography

Aliki. *William Shakespeare and the Globe.* New York: HarperCollins, 1999.

Coville, Bruce. Illus. by Dennis Nolan. *William Shakespeare's Romeo and Juliet.* New York: Dial Books, 1999.

Early, Margaret. *Romeo and Juliet.* New York: Harry N. Abrams, Inc., 1998.

Isaac, Megan. *Heirs to Shakespeare: Reinventing the Bard in Young Adult Literature.* Portsmouth, NH: Heinemann, 2000.

Langley, Andrew. Illus. by June Everett. *Shakespeare's Theatre.* Oxford: Oxford University Press, 1999.

Lewis, Amanda and Tim Wynne-Jones. Illus. by Bill Slavin. *Rosie Backstage.* Toronto: Kids Can Press, 1994.

Rosen, Michael. Illus. by Robert Ingpen. *Shakespeare: His Work & His World.* Cambridge, MA: Candlewick Press, 2001.

Ross, Stewart. Illus. by Tony Karpinski. *Shakespeare and Macbeth: The Story Behind the Play.* Viking: New York, 1994.

Stanley, Diane and Peter Vennema. Illus. by Diane Stanley. *The Bard of Avon: The Story of William Shakespeare.* New York: Morrow Junior Books, 1992.

14. Mediating the Supernatural in Adaptations of Shakespeare for Children

Three Unique Productions through Text and Illustration

DOUGLAS KING

In her preface to *The Best of Shakespeare: Retellings of Ten Classic Plays*, E. Nesbit recounts a conversation with her children upon their first exposure to Shakespeare: "Poring over" a volume of Shakespeare's plays, the children complain, "I can't understand a word of it . . . What does it all mean?" Daughter Rosamund adds, "it's the stories we like," to which Nesbit replies, "You see he did not write for children." Daughter Iris provides her mother with an authorial commission she cannot refuse: "Why don't you write the stories for us so that we can understand them . . . and then, when we are grown up, we shall understand the plays so much better. Do! do!" (Nesbit, 8–9).

Nesbit's anecdote delineates—and sets in opposition—the two primary variables usually considered in the mediation of Shakespeare's drama for children: language and story. The fundamental processes undertaken by adaptors of Shakespeare are normally paraphrasis and narrative interpolation. Shakespeare's language is replaced by paraphrasis, commentary, and explication, and the mediator decides to what extent to include (or reinsert) Shakespeare's original language; commonly the new version contains bits of original dialogue within the context of a dominant paraphrastic structure. The result is that the essential dramatic element transmitted to children is what so often comes to be called the "tale." As Peter Hunt, in his afterword to Nesbit's *The Best of Shakespeare*, notes, this is not an easy task: "Nesbit clearly found, as her predecessors had done, that paring the flesh of Shakespeare's inimitable verse and prose from the plays can leave you with an unmanageable excess of plot, and there are times in her paraphrases . . . where little else is visible." (106) This problem of the tension between language and tale plagues many adaptations designed for children. Most often, the process of adapting Shakespeare's works for children becomes one of privileging narrative over poetics. At its extreme, the result of such privileging is adaptation as plot summary, devoid of narrative eloquence or linguistic suppleness, as in, for example, Marchette Chute's *Stories from Shakespeare.*

However, although Shakespearean adaptations for children almost always sacrifice Shakespeare's language in favor of a distilled essence of tale, such texts also almost always contain a third dimension, an element that print versions of the plays for adults usually lack: the visual. Illustration visually suggests the dramatic action that inheres in the text, and thus serves as a print analogue for the production (stage or film) of a play. Shakespeare adaptor Bruce Coville notes that the roles of adaptor and illustrator are analogous to those of playwright and director; indeed, to expand the analogy a bit, the illustrator also serves the functions of casting director and of costume, lighting, and set designers. The visual element in adaptations of Shakespeare is potentially, and sometimes actually, very effective in enlivening the plays for children. The mediating impact of the visual dimension in such texts is inestimable, especially upon pre-readers who nonetheless "read" the texts (construct a story based upon looking at the pictures), whether with or without a reader to communicate the words to them. Illustration in such texts serves the same role as does the viewing of a stage or screen production: it makes the invisible visible. It transforms the potential energy of what is purely linguistic into the kinetic energy of a visual production. As the marketing slogan for the Oval Projects Shakespeare texts (which I will discuss at length later) states, "the page becomes the stage."

Illustration is perhaps particularly effective in reifying elements appealing to children, with which Shakespeare's plays abound: the humorous, the martial, the magical. One of the key narrative devices from Shakespeare's plays that appeals to young children is the presence of the supernatural.[1] Particularly with plays involving the presence of supernatural forces, the interpreting mediation of the adaptors—authors and illustrators—is influential, as they make decisions that determine whether such forces come across as benevolent, dangerous, fearsome, controllable, and so forth. My intention here is to explore some unique tropes through which three Shakespearean adaptation series use language and illustration as production tools to bring to life the supernatural.

In *Tales from Shakespeare*, Marcia Williams, as author and illustrator, presents seven plays in comic-book form. She uses three familiar modes: panel illustrations; comic-book style dialogue within the illustrated panels (consisting of Shakespeare's language); and sub-panel original narration, which provides the main thread of the story. To these, Williams adds a fourth mediating element, as she creates an imaginary panoply of Globe Theatre denizens who, along with their visually interesting and often amusing activities, provide commentary on the plays. These audience figures are situated in the side and bottom borders of the book's pages, some representing groundlings and some higher-class patrons standing in boxes. In a "Where's

Waldo"-like gimmick, Williams presents somewhere in the audience of each "play" Shakespeare and Queen Elizabeth, who also react to and comment on the proceedings.[2] The imaginary audience constitutes Williams's unique (in my experience) device, one that she uses to often ingenious and amusing effect, as, for example, when the audience responds to the supernatural elements in the plays.

In Williams's rendering of *Macbeth*, observing the scene where the witches prophecy the futures of Macbeth and Banquo, one groundling asks, "Are witches always right?" while another proclaims, "This is too scary, take it away." Observing the scene in which Macbeth returns bloodied from having murdered Duncan, a matron with her eyes closed intones, "I don't think this is quite suitable for children," while directly in front of her a young boy sticks his tongue out in her direction. Williams devotes a full-page illustration to the Act III witches scene, and her Globe patrons react strongly: "Tell me when it's over," "That brew smells poisonous," "This is too bloomin' spooky," and, a mother to her very young child, "Behave, or I'll put you in the cauldron." These mediating tropes—visual and verbal—simultaneously convey and confine the power of the supernaturally-tinged scenes; the audience device creates a distancing effect, serving as an additional layer of mediation for the children receiving the texts. Significantly, the adults in the audience are more disturbed by the potentially "scary" elements than are the children, and the overall effect is comical.

Similarly, in Williams's version of *A Midsummer Night's Dream*, the supernatural world provides her audience members with the strongest reactions. As the conflict between Oberon and Titania develops and Puck and Oberon both employ the flower love-in-idleness to work mischievous magic on sleeping victims, a mother remarks to her child, "Just like you, she's quite sweet asleep," while below a groundling child asks, "Is this good for my education?" to which a woman—presumably her mother replies, "I doubt it, dear." Bottom's metamorphosis into an ass-headed creature brings even greater fascination, as an adult asks, "How do they do that?" while a nearby child asks, "Can we do that to daddy?" Williams depicts groundling children as distracted even from the important business of picking nobles' pockets; as a woman with several children commands, "Get her jewels next" to some of her brood, another child, fascinated with the apparition of the translated Bottom, complains, "Sssh! I'm listening." Williams's depiction of a tremendously detailed cosmos of myriad fairies attending to Bottom causes her audience figures—adults and children—to debate the substantiality of the sprites: A child asks, "Who acts the fairies" (which are, in Williams's rendering, of various minuscule sizes and clearly do not represent actors in the Globe), and her mother replies, "Your imagination acts them, dear." Williams depicts a world in which, though adults too are impressed with the beauty of the fairy world ("Ooh! That's so pretty"), the reality of the supernatural is only to be recognized and appreciated by children. A conversation between two young boys begins: "I'm going to be a fairy when I grow up," to which the other boy replies, "Grownups can't see fairies, stupid."

This theme of the invisibility of supernatural beings permeates Williams's audience dialogue in her rendition of *The Tempest*. Ariel is quickly identified as "invisible to all but Prospero," and the audience is able to see Ariel only when she assumes particular form. On the initial page, Williams depicts Ariel sadistically tormenting Caliban, then taking the form of a star which he struggles to reach. The groundlings—adults and children—debate: "Can you see Ariel? . . . No. . . . I think Ariel's hidden in the star. . . . You don't know nothing. . . . Ariel's just air." Later in the tale, a crying child complains, "I don't like not seeing Ariel." Williams clearly dichotomizes the good spirit Ariel, whom the children regard with affection and frustration at being unable to see her, with Caliban, who is regarded by the audience as monstrous ("I bet he picks his nose") and, like Williams's weird sisters, a bogeyman-figure for children: "If you wriggle, Caliban will get you." Williams's unique contribution to the genre of Shakespeare adaptation is to use image and dialogue to convey Shakespeare's plays—with the supernatural elements prominent—as productions that the reader views over the shoulder of her imaginary Elizabethan audience.

While all adapting authors and illustrators implicitly mediate the supernatural in order to control its reception by young people, and while Williams imagines and depicts the reactions of adult and youthful Globe audience members, Lois Burdett, in her *Shakespeare: for Kids* series, presents texts in which children—her own second-grade students—are actual collaborators. Prior to teaching the plays to her students, Burdett creates verse couplet transformations of the plays—with Shakespeare's language copiously embedded—that are later enhanced and accompanied by children's illustrations and letters that capture her students' reactions to the plays. The results are entertaining and fascinating. For example, whereas in Williams's version of *The Tempest*, Prospero's use of the supernatural is presented as wholly positive, and Ariel and Caliban represent positive and negative supernatural creatures, respectively; in Burdett's *The Tempest for Kids*, Prospero's tempest is presented as truly troubling to Miranda, perhaps even more so than as the scene (I.ii) is commonly interpreted critically and in performance. Burdett's verse tells us:

> Miranda wailed in complete despair,
> "They've all vanished in the storm out there.
> My dearest father, your magic I deplore,
> If you have caused this terrible uproar." (9)

Then, as a student illustration depicts a Prospero looking rather like a zoot-suited mob figure, another student's letter in the persona of Miranda reads,

> Oh, dear father, stop it! Those poor people on that beautiful boat will per-
> ish! It grieves my heart to hear their pitiful cries, ringing in my ears. I never
> thought you were on[3] to torment innocent people so. Well I see I am wrong.
> Their lives are being sucked from their cold, wet bodies. (9)

As Prospero unfolds his tale to Miranda, he is depicted as a saintly victim ("I
am so lucky to have a father like you. Your heart is as pure as glass and your
soul is as gentle as a lamb"), but Burdett's—and her students'—depictions of
the characters retain a notable sense of ambiguity, as for example when a
very fearsome, sorceror-looking Prospero orders Caliban to do his chores.
Caliban's letter as written by a student reveals a keen empathy for the figure
so easily and simply dismissed in traditional renderings of *The Tempest*
adapted for children (e.g., the Lambs dismiss him as simply "an ugly monster
called Caliban," [4] and Nesbit as "a hideous, deformed monster, horrible to
look on, and vicious and brutal in all his habits" [49]):

> You villainous master! I used to care for you and in return this is what I
> get . . . work work work! I was lord of this island until you showed up. I
> know you have great powers but that gives you no right to pick on me. (23)

The children again capture the ambiguous nature of Prospero's use of his
"art" as he concocts, then interrupts, the celestial wedding party with Iris,
Ceres, Juno, and so on. A student's letter as Prospero reads:

> Love was in the air! Tears of joy trickled down my face at this romantic
> scene. Then evil thoughts gripped my mind with a BANG! The sky turned
> black in misery. Caliban's plan boiled in my brain. The game of life and
> death and magic itself will be played once again. (51)

The children seem to view Prospero's human dimension as primary, with
his supernatural powers subsidiary to his flawed, willful character. Similarly,
on the continuum of Macbeth interpretations ranging from the freely-willful
villain to the supernaturally beguiled victim, Burdett's text positions him as
clearly culpable for his actions. As a child's letter written from Macbeth's
point of view puts it, "My conshense has no chanse against my will" (18).

The student creations, visual and verbal, constitute Burdett's unique
addition to the genre of Shakesperean adaptation, and stand as a fascinating
mediating element for readers of the popular texts. The children's responses
to the supernatural are varied, complex, and nuanced, and reflect active
engagement with Shakespeare's texts. Of course, the student responses themselves are (inevitably) shaped by an additional mediating element: the powerful influence of a teacher on her students. It is to Burdett's credit both as
teacher and as adaptor that the resulting products—with the children as collaborators—constitute thoughtful and thought-provoking texts. These texts

stand as productions in themselves, and also serve as play scripts for classes which, like Burdett's, wish to act out the plays.

Both Williams and Burdett create successful variations on and additions to the traditional adaptation formula of abridgement and paraphrasis by incorporating unique mediating elements—Williams with her imaginary Globe productions complete with audience reactions and shenanigans, and Burdett with her students' creative responses included as integral parts of the texts. The full-text Oval Projects editions produced in the 1980s constitute even greater rarities, and give the fullest possible sense of the interpretive possibilities available through illustration-as-production. Because these texts (*Macbeth*, *Othello*, and *King Lear*) are unabridged, one can validly question whether they are particularly conducive to consumption by children. Indeed, Anne Tauté of Oval Projects notes that the texts were not designed for children. However, despite the original production intent, these texts are appealing to and appropriate even for non-reading children precisely because of the prominence of the illustrations. In the absence of the traditionally central mediating elements in children's adaptations of Shakespeare—abridgement and paraphrasis—the illustrator is the only new author, and the comic-book format gives a child a visible production that enhances engagement with the play.

The creative possibilities involved in the illustration of a full text play are vast, and indeed Ian Pollock's Oval *King Lear* is a fully-realized, masterful directorial vision of the play, one that far excels the work in the Oval *Macbeth* illustrated by the artist Von. Oscar Zarate's *Othello* also constitutes a powerful and distinctive production. Though neither *King Lear* nor *Othello* is as imbued with the supernatural as is *Macbeth* (or, say, *A Midsummer Night's Dream* or *The Tempest*), the artists of the respective works both bring to life supernatural elements latent in the plays, making the invisible dramatically visible. Indeed, it would be virtually impossible to create stage analogues for some of Zarate's and Pollock's means of depicting or reifying the supernatural, which are more analogous to non-mimetic film techniques. For example, Pollock's characters are of various, protean, odd, and grotesque shapes, with Lear shaped approximately like Humpty Dumpty while his miniscule Fool most often perches somewhere on Lear's head or body; the Fool's own head size, in many panels, equals or exceeds that of his body.

Pollock actually evokes a supernatural not necessarily intrinsic to Shakespeare's text, in the manner of a film or theater director asserting a strong production vision. In III.vi, the arraignment in the hovel scene (which would almost certainly be cut from any children's abridgement of the play, as indeed it is frequently pared or eliminated in play productions), Pollock gives a brilliant example of the possibilities open to a gifted illustrator exploring imbedded possibilities in the text. Taking Poor Tom's raving line, "Tom will throw his head at them" (that is, at Lear's "little dogs and all"), Pollock depicts Tom's hands holding aloft his head, then in the next frame literally tossing the head at the snarling and snapping dogs. By the next frame, Tom is recapitated, as Pollock has graphically reified the quasi-lunatic metaphor in a fashion achievable in no other medium, save film.

Zarate achieves similarly enlivening effects in his exotic *Othello*, in which his coloration is as bright and bold as Pollock's is muted and pale (with the exception of Pollock's use of red). Again, the artist takes a play not much associated with the supernatural (except, again, metaphorically) and brings to life tropes imbedded in the text. A prime example is I.iii, which visually establishes both Othello and Iago in the context of a supernatural struggle. Brabantio accuses Othello of having used "witchcraft" in his seduction of Desdemona, an accusation Othello ostensibly refutes. Yet in another sense the accusation is true: Othello reveals that it is through his stories of strange creatures and exotic exploits that he has won Desdemona's heart. He has indeed woven tales of "witchcraft." Zarate's illustrations dramatically accentuate the supernatural aspect of Othello's tale. As Othello begins to speak, exotic birds of many colors begin to swirl around his head, and the background of the Venetian senators is gradually (with each succeeding frame) replaced by these birds, then by a full-page view that comprises the speaking Othello with birds above and speech bubbles on either side, while below him is depicted the scene he is describing, complete with "the anthropophagi, and men whose heads do grow beneath their shoulders." As he completes his story in the succeeding frames, the exotic images are gradually replaced by the figures of the senators and the scene of the narrative present.

In his representation of a later portion of I.iii, Zarate again reifies the supernatural as he cleverly objectifies Iago's psychomachia. The artist gives Iago a pet monkey, who returns to the scene immediately after Iago, responding to Roderigo's pledge to "drown himself," identifies humanity with the simian: "Ere I would say I would drown myself for the love of a guinea-hen, I would change my humanity with a baboon" (I.iii.309–11). In the succeeding frames, Zarate's Iago gets drunk while his monkey leers. At scene's end, Roderigo exits and Iago conceives his "monstrous birth." The last frame shows Iago passed out on the table with the monkey sitting on his head, celebrating the fact that he has splattered a tomato all over a painting of three cavorting cherubim (which the artist has introduced earlier in the scene). Thus Zarate visually evokes the three levels of the created world—the animal, the human, and the angelic—in dynamic interplay. Iago's malicious, sub-human tendencies are associated with the animal, with the planned destruction of the human (Othello), and with an animalistic assault on the angelic. The artist has mined the text so as to make visible the verbal, and to produce a powerful vision of the supernatural order.

The Oval *Othello* and *King Lear* demonstrate the power of illustrative vision melded with Shakespeare's unaltered language. Unfortunately, critical reception of the series was mixed (perhaps the most unfortunate factor being that the least satisfactory volume—*Macbeth*—appeared first and thus garnered the most critical attention), and sales were so disappointing that Oval abandoned plans to produce further volumes.[4] The reasons for the critical and popular disappointment with the volumes are complex, and should be the subject of another essay. However, part of the problem no doubt stemmed from the very uniqueness of the project. The volumes, as I noted, were not conceived for children, but yet were most frequently reviewed in such places as children's literature sections of newspapers and journals. The format and prominence of the illustration made such attention inevitable, and, indeed, much of this attention was positive. Project publisher Workman Press specializes in scholastic materials, which again seems to conflict with the producers' intentions with regard to audience. Reviewer David Nokes reflects some of this paradox and tension in his review of Pollock's *King Lear*: "What is most disturbing . . . is the undeniable power of these nightmare images [that] represent a definite interpretation of the play itself. He is more like an artistic director than a mere illustrator of the text and has created a world whose psychedelic effects and haunting caricatures turn *King Lear* into a form of video nasty. . . . The power of this imagery is made the more insidious by the inventive wit of many of the comic details. . . . This cartoon book is clever, violent, iconoclastic, and will, I fear, be very influential with school-age readers (506)."

It is telling that much of Nokes's review would read as high praise for a stage or screen production of the play (or indeed, for a book intended for adults), but instead here turns to the paradoxically negative ("the power of the imagery is made the more insidious by the inventive wit") due to the reviewer's fears and assumptions about the potential effects on young readers. Without doubt, Pollock's and Zarate's depictions of supernatural images and worlds are powerful. Also without doubt, the Oval versions—designed for adult consumption—make these supernatural elements more likely to disturb than do, say, the more gently-mediated versions of Williams and Burdett. However, these facts do not lead me to Nokes's conclusion that such images are thus dangerous for children's viewing. Rather, these texts, as with a PG-rated film, simply call for further mediation on the consumer side— someone to help a young child assimilate the images in the context of the other essential elements of the play: language and story. In this context, the Oval versions, like those of Williams and Burdett, present unique and stimulating visions of the plays as productions.

Notes

1. My implicit focus throughout this essay is on younger children (under 12) rather than on "young adult" consumers.

2. Williams evidently didn't wish to complicate matters by changing monarchs for the plays produced in the Jacobean era.
3. I quote exactly Burdett's texts, which retain her students' sometimes flawed spellings.
4. Indeed, Oval produced a version of *Twelfth Night* that was never printed in the United States because Workman Press refused it.

Works Cited

Burdett, Lois. *Macbeth for Kids.* Buffalo, NY and Willowdale, Ontario: Firefly Books, 1997.

———. *The Tempest for Kids.* Buffalo, NY and Willowdale, Ontario: Firefly Books, 1999.

Chute, Marchette. *Stories from Shakespeare.* New York: Meridian Press, 1987.

Lamb, Charles and Mary. *Tales from Shakespeare.* New York: Bantam Books, 1963.

Nesbit, E. *The Best of Shakespeare.* New York: Oxford University Press, 1997.

Nokes, David. "Vile Jelly." *Times of London Literary Supplement.* May 4, 1984: 506.

Shakespeare. *King Lear.* Ill. Ian Pollock. New York: Workman Publishing, 1984.

———. *Othello.* Ill. Oscar Zarate. New York: Workman Publishing, 1983.

———. *Twelfth Night.* Ill. John H. Howard. London: Ravette Books, 1985.

Tauté, Anne. Telephone conversation. July, 2000.

Williams, Marcia. *Tales from Shakespeare.* Cambridge, MA: Candlewick Press, 1998.

15. "The Play's the Thing"

Genre and Adaptations of Shakespeare for Children

ALISON H. PRINDLE

How are Shakespeare's plays currently being presented to young readers? Is it Shakespeare's sounds, rhythms, and poetic language that are being made accessible, voiced, embodied? Is it the plays as theater—collaborative, shifting under directors' and actors' choices, performed under particular conditions? What do we want to bring from Shakespeare to children? As a college teacher of Shakespeare I brought these questions to a 2000 Shakespeare Association of America seminar called "Playing with the Bard," organized by Naomi J. Miller. For convenience, I focused on one play, *The Tempest*, and on a selection of current illustrated storybook versions of *The Tempest* by Ann Beneduce (1996), Lois Burdett (1999), Bruce Coville (1994), Leon Garfield (1985), Bernard Miles (1986), and Marcia Williams (1998), with reference also to the classic adaptations by Charles and Mary Lamb (1807), E. Nesbit (1900), and Marchette Chute (1956).

All but one of the versions follow in the footsteps of the Lambs, attempting to mediate between children and Shakespeare by presenting the play in narrative form. The essence of Shakespeare, in practice, has become story. While there are a number of fine works for children that emphasize Shakespeare the playwright and actor, the presentation of the plays themselves continues to transform the actor's script into a narrative.[1] In the transformation, one key result is that all the roles which a play offers—director, actor, and even audience—are claimed by the writer. This effort to make Shakespeare accessible, through pictures and storytelling, creates an observer's role for the child, rather than the collaborative, interactive role offered by the original genre, the drama.

The first thing that happens in the move to narrative is that writers try to sort out Shakespeare's plot, with an assumption that a story, especially one for children, should have a linear, chronological order to it. Of the nine versions of *The Tempest* that I've looked at, three resequence events so that the usurpation of Prospero's power in Milan, the abandonment of Prospero and three-year-old Miranda at sea, and their arrival on the island are recounted first to us by the narrator, not by Prospero in a retrospective explanation to the teenaged Miranda. Three of the others introduce us to Prospero, Miranda, Caliban, and Ariel at some length before turning to the storm at sea and the fears and angers of those on board ship. Only Burdett, Williams, and Chute enter the story with Shakespeare, on the desperate decks of Alonzo's ship. Following Shakespeare's condensation of events into a single day, viewers of the play would first accompany those who fear and suffer: the first experiences would be chaotic and distressing. The needs of narrative flatten these moments into the steadying voice of the narrator describing the events which precede the play's action. This approach orients us clearly to the innocent and the guilty, the wise and the monstrous. The storm follows as justifiable and logical, less disturbing or disorienting.

In order to make their narratives more manageable and coherent, several of the authors also suppress, condense, or rearrange later events on Prospero's island. In the play, Prospero himself creates the plot strands: Ferdinand's encounter with Miranda; the conflicts of usurpers and would be usurpers in the group including the "three men of sin"; and the comic triad of Caliban, his new god Stephano, and the jester Trinculo. Each strand has a different tonality; each brings a necessary variety to a play that has little real conflict, since no one in the play can act independently of the magician's control. Burdett, Williams, and Chute are faithful to Shakespeare's sequencing of these three strands of plot. The Lambs suppress virtually all of the events surrounding Caliban and greatly diminish the tensions in the Alonzo-Antonio-Sebastian plot. Beneduce diminishes the power struggles in lines of action involving Caliban and those involving the king of Naples. Nesbit retains the three men of sin, but abandons Caliban entirely after the third paragraph of the story.

For three of the authors, the love story of Ferdinand and Miranda takes precedence over other issues in the narrative. Beneduce's exquisitely illustrated narrative most clearly emphasizes the two young people. From the storm at sea onward, the narrative selections emphasize that all Prospero's actions are done for Miranda's sake. The repentance of Alonzo and Antonio at the end of the story is swiftly achieved and subordinated to the presentation of Ferdinand and Miranda: "The rest of the day passed in a flurry of plans for the voyage back to Naples and the royal wedding, as well as for Prospero's triumphant return to Milan."[2] Prospero's magic seems intended more for Miranda's protection than his own pleasure or power, and he lets it go with no difficulty or regret as Miranda and Ferdinand's joy is expressed: " 'Well, I see I have no further need for magic!' exclaimed Prospero."[3] In Nesbit's rendition, Miranda and Ferdinand also occupy the narrative's central position. The only dialogue in her presentation occurs between Prospero and

Ariel; or between Ferdinand, Miranda, and Prospero. And she, too, emphasizes the return to Naples and the wedding: "So all ended happily. The ship
was safe in harbor, and next day they all set sail for Naples, where Ferdinand
and Miranda were to be married. Ariel gave them calm seas and auspicious
gales, and many were the rejoicings at the wedding."[4] Nesbit draws an additional moral from her narrative, but so little has been provided about Prospero's feelings of revenge or forgiveness, so perfunctory has her
development been of the line of action dealing with the "three men of sin,"
that the moral conclusion seems an afterthought.

The narratives of Miles, Coville, Chute, and Lamb maintain a fuller
presence of the three plots Shakespeare has at work. In each case, however,
their choices reflect the author's interpretive intervention in the play's events.
For Miles, the love story receives much less attention than any of the other
elements; Ariel's relationship to Prospero, the comedy of Caliban's worship
of Stephano, and the violent fantasies of Sebastian and Antonio all receive
more narrative attention than the lovers, who merit only four paragraphs in
Miles's sixteen pages of narrative. It is Caliban, in fact, as a source of comedy,
to which Miles is most drawn. Indeed he adds scenes at the end of the story,
after Prospero has left the island and surrendered his "crystal ball," in which
Ariel attempts to teach Caliban to count and to learn his ABCs, to no avail.
Caliban becomes a kind of relaxed Huck Finn, "drowsily chewing a blade of
grass, with his back to a tree, his legs spread out before him, happily doing
his best not to think about anything at all. He's got his island back at last."[5]

Coville maintains a balanced presentation of the three plot lines. His narrative, however, requires that Miranda's maturation shape the story's structure: from Miranda's three-year-old self in the leaky boat, to her arrival on
the island, to her childhood, education, and isolation on the island, it is her
growth and, by extension, her future that give the story's skeleton. Prospero
is a nurturing, protective father, Caliban a jealous competitor, and Miranda a
wild, free daughter, hoping only "for company her own age" and wishing that
the ship will land on the island (" 'come to our shore,' she whispered long-
ingly").[6] Because Coville has created a kind of prequel to open his narrative,
he has framed Shakespeare's three plot strands in another story, and that
story, of father and daughter, focuses our sympathies and affections on
Miranda.

Moving from a play to a story, then, compels complex decisions to be
made about plot. It also forces the creation of a narrator's voice, and this
voice is a crucial part of the interpretation of the story for readers. Beneduce's voice is reassuring, placing us in a fairy-tale enchantment. Her book
includes Shakespeare's words, through quotation of some of the loveliest language in the play, beginning with the lines, "the isle is full of noises, sounds
and sweet airs, that give delight and hurt not" (which are not identified as
Caliban's), and continuing with two of Ariel's songs, the blessings of Juno,

Ceres, and Iris for the lovers, and Prospero's "our revels now are ended." However, these quotations are set apart from Beneduce's own narrative, and are not connected with the context of the story's actions, serving instead to support the narrator's choice of lyric lightness, with no threat of danger felt; the dialogue, too, consists primarily of positive, enthusiastic, or affectionate statements by the characters.

Miles's narrative voice has a cheerful, avuncular, read-aloud sound. Prospero is introduced with the clear understanding that this narrator will judge the characters: "Now the Duke in this story is called Prospero, and I'm afraid he cannot be bothered to look after his own province, let alone try to take over anyone else's."[7] And, of the early interactions with Caliban, the narrator says, "Prospero tries to teach Caliban manners, but I'm afraid he isn't very successful. Caliban simply will not stop eating with his fingers and slopping his soup all over the table."[8] Such a voice serves well in the task of slipping back and forth between the subplots, when Miles can use such overt strategies as this: "But what about poor Caliban and his two friends? How are they getting on? Well, Prospero decided to teach them a lesson too, like this."[9] Miles's voice dominates the narrative, establishes for us a certain detachment from the events, and underlines the comic nature of the material. Though violence, anger, and evil exist in the story, there is no sense that these are serious presences, emotions that may reveal truths or direct events. Prospero laughs at Caliban's plot and his forgiveness of Alonzo and Antonio is quick and easy, requiring no prompting from Ariel.

Leon Garfield, writing for older readers, does still more with the narrator's voice and control of the story. His narrator both describes and interprets the significance of characters and actions. Like most of the adaptations, his begins with Prospero and Miranda viewing the tempest, rather than with Shakespeare's frightened mariners: "His face was calm; hers was pale and frightened." We see the ship and its sailors, vividly described but at a great distance: "As it heaved and tossed, its masts scribbled frantic messages against the blotchy sky, and its rigging all fell down like a madman's hair. Tiny figures, black as fleas, and with patched white faces, clung where they could; and shrieks and screams, small as the squealing of mice, drifted to the watchers on the shore."[10] Prospero's eyes are triumphant as he explains their enemies were aboard the tempest-tossed ship, and we are never in doubt about the intensity and depth of his anger. Other figures are described in ways that suggest what an actor might bring to the part. Ariel, for example, reports, "with a queer sideways smile," that he has isolated Ferdinand on the island.[11] As Sebastian and Antonio plot to kill Alonzo, they "begin to stroll about, on tiptoe, and to peer and stare among the trees," and as each speaks, he moves through the vegetation, "reassuring himself that a shadow was not a watcher," or "confirming that a bush was not a spy."[12] The narrator's voice also comments on significance directly: Trinculo is "the king of Naples' jester, an ageing fool who lived only in the echo of old jokes. Saved from the shipwreck by a Providence that plainly did not know right from wrong, he wandered across the shore. . . ."[13] Or, of Prospero's "visions" created for Ferdinand and Miranda, he says, "the great enchanter was not without vanity. Seeing the enchantment in which the lovers held one another, he was stirred to show them that his own power was still greatest."[14] And, although the narrator follows Shakespeare in emphasizing that Prospero learns to forgive his enemies, the narrator's final paragraph reasserts Prospero as the superhuman figure in control; after he breaks his staff and casts away his book, Garfield sees Prospero as author in these last lines: "He had no more need of them, nor of the enchanted isle. By his art he had made men see themselves, and, through make-believe, come to truth. Now he, too, like Ariel and Caliban, longed to be free."[15]

Plainly, transforming *The Tempest* from Shakespeare's play to a story for children requires difficult choices. Storybook authors are working within severe length constraints: it is a rare author who is given as much as three thousand words to work with to retell *The Tempest*. And, as Peter Hunt has said about Nesbit's work, to condense any work to such an extent can "leave you with an unmanageable excess of plot,"[16] to which a good writer must respond by paring, eliminating, and balancing what he or she sees as the essence of the work. In the case of these examples of adaptations of *The Tempest*, the responses have created coherent patterns around the play as a love story, as a growing up story, as a jolly, comic story about a foolish, not-very-bright spirit-monster, and as a story about an enchanter wrestling with his own power and vanity. And yet, I think it is also the expectations of the narrative genre which have constrained the resulting works. The linearity of plot and the necessity of adding a narrative voice follow from the move to narrative, not from the length constraints of publishers. Even the version by Coville, which I admire greatly for its elegant precision of language and for its reticent, unforced narrative voice, is a work whose formal difference from the Shakespearean play means that its reader can surrender to the interpretive understanding of the narrator.

In puzzling over these efforts to reach children with Shakespeare's plays, I asked my daughter (now fifteen) and my nephew (now sixteen) to respond to questions about what they liked and engaged with in Shakespeare. My daughter went to her first Shakespeare play at Stratford, Ontario when she was five. My nephew has acted in Shakespeare since he was ten, in a variety of plays, mostly comedies, as a part of his experience as a home-schooler in Colorado. Sarah said that what has always been most powerful for her is the presence of the actor. She remembers particular performers, the way they surprised or compelled attention. The story or plot of the plays seemed to hold little value for her compared with the fundamental magic of the actor speaking and moving as another person, as a character. Russell, the actor, said two things kept bringing him back to Shakespeare: first was the experience of getting to know the character, of being free to figure out what this guy was like, how he spoke, how he would move or look; and second was the collaborative, group effort, as all the kids worked together to create the play. I should add that his drama group worked with cut versions of the plays, but students did the cutting and directing.

As plays, Shakespeare's texts have an openness that requires interaction. No narrator guides the through-line. As plays, Shakespeare's texts offer multiple entry points—all the characters as well as several, varying plot lines. As plays, Shakespeare's texts say you must join in this project before it can come alive: this is collaborative. Our cultural choice of narrative as the form in which Shakespeare should be presented to children has many reasons and justifications. One of these is that we are uncertain of children's capacities to understand his work. We translate his language and his "adult" themes today, much as the Lambs and Nesbit did for previous centuries. I suspect we need to do less translation than we think. But we are also faced with a culture that privileges narrative and that does not easily provide children with the opportunity to see how the theater works.

Yet every parent who has ever gotten a child involved in a good drama program knows how surprising children are: how many ways they find to work on the stage, how long the parts are that they can memorize, and how their imaginations are sparked by back-yard performances. The work by Lois Burdett, an elementary teacher working with second and third graders (whose projects are described in detail elsewhere in this volume), suggests that we are selling both Shakespeare and children short. As Richard Monette says, Burdett's work structures the occasion for elementary students to "reinvent Shakespeare's plays, creating their own unique versions of his stories and his characters."[17] For *The Tempest*, for example, Burdett has written a quick-moving narrative in couplets, avoiding description and commentary to emphasize action and speech. In her *Tempest*, we start, as Shakespeare does, *in* the storm, with disorientation, fear, and powerlessness. In what follows her narrative is not a parent-child story, a love story, a story about power and revenge, a comic turn, or a fairy story. The matter-of-fact tone she uses, which is both energized and concise, never seeks to make the story a type or a theme. Instead we have actions and words and more actions. Description is subordinate to dialogue, interpretation slinks away under the pressure of decision. I love the pacing, the precision, and the conciseness of her rendering of the original text. The stylistic choices include colloquial language and archaic, Shakespearean phrases, in a mixture that will not bother elementary kids, grounding Shakespeare firmly in rhythms and word choices they can enjoy speaking.

Used fully, her books are templates for performance, with the whole class speaking the narrative and individual students miming or speaking as particular characters. Drawings of characters show her students imagining concretely how these people look. Brief letters or comments, written by the students *as* the play's characters, give kids the occasion to speak as someone else and express that person's feelings. (Ferdinand says, "Oh joy! Oh fabulous rapture! Thrills and excitement are heading my way!"; Alonzo writes, "Dear Prospero, I beg your forgiveness. It is more important than the most gleaming sapphire. I was a fool to set you off into that unpredictable ocean. From a shamed, Alonzo."[18]) The kids are clearly both creators and performers of the text, as they write for characters and jointly narrate the play. Burdett is tapping into the essence of the genre.

Marcia Williams's comic book-like renditions of Shakespeare's plays attempt to preserve their dramatic character visually. Three levels of the book operate simultaneously on each page; the outer edge holds spectators and their comments and actions, the central boxes show the actors on stage speaking selected lines, and the actors are framed in narrative boxes that carry the story line. The theater is the Globe itself, in 1599. The drawings are often comic and surprising; the eye must attend carefully to follow the information carried visually. The overall effect is a visual parallel to the experience of the theater, entering the play from several perspectives and seeing three layers of creation at work. While the book does not offer readers a way to become performers, it does make clear that *The Tempest* is a play, and that the audience's participation, through questions and observations, is part of the theatrical reality.

Does this mean that Shakespeare should only be approached through dramatic form? Surely I admire the genuine excellences of all the adaptations I examined. All provide a comfortable entry point for readers, increasing the possibilities that students will approach Shakespeare as a companion, not a distant, peculiar, old-fashioned authority. Yet, if they leave kids with the feeling that theater is like a story, they misrepresent the form. I admire Burdett's work with her students. It genuinely connects children to Shakespeare the playwright and actor. It assumes kids can tangle with difficult material and so constructs for us a different conception of the child. Above all, it establishes the kind of interactive, collaborative relationship with the text that seems to me at the heart of drama as a genre. As a college teacher of Shakespeare, I need to enter into more collaborative relationships with my peers in elementary and secondary classrooms to explore the possibilities they see for their students. I also need to do more to reach my own students who plan to be teachers, to bring these questions about genre to them, so they can discuss the interpretations inherent in these story books for children and the ways narrative forces an author to be director, actor, interpretive audience, and child designer, all at once. Reading more than one adaptation in an elementary classroom may help a teacher not yet ready to become Lois Burdett to communicate Shakespeare's complexity and openness to the students. I suspect that teachers in the public schools are more ready than any of us in colleges and universities to see children as creative, enterprising, and interactive learners, and that they would encourage us to replace the child-to-be-protected with the child-as-player. As British teacher Fred Sedgwick has said in his recent work *Shakespeare and the Young Writer,* "The power of what children learn when they play with Shakespeare's words derives from the fact that play, being active, is bound up with choice: playing with words requires constant decisions. Decisions require thought and thought causes that dangerous thing—learning—about Shakespeare, about words, about life and its glories and problems."[19]

Notes

1. For example, such wonderful works as: Colleen Aagesen and Margie Blumberg, *Shakespeare for Kids: His Life and Times* (Chicago: Chicago Review Press, 1999); Aliki, *William Shakespeare and the Globe* (New York: HarperCollins Publishers, 1999); Amanda Lewis and Tim Wynne-Jones, *Rosie Backstage* (Toronto: Kids Can Press, 1994).
2. Ann Keay Beneduce, *The Tempest* (New York: Philomel Books, 1996), 28.
3. Ibid., 26.
4. E. Nesbit, *The Best of Shakespeare* (Oxford and New York: Oxford University Press, 1997), 57.
5. Bernard Miles, *Well-Loved Tales from Shakespeare* (Twickenham, England: Hamlyn Publishing, 1986), 35.
6. Bruce Coville, *William Shakespeare's The Tempest* (New York: Bantam Doubleday Dell Publishing, 1994), 13, 14.
7. Miles, *Well-Loved Tales*, 16.
8. Ibid., 21.
9. Ibid., 31.
10. Leon Garfield, *Shakespeare Stories* (New York: Schocken Books, 1985), 51.
11. Ibid., 55.
12. Ibid., 61.
13. Ibid., 63.
14. Ibid., 69.
15. Ibid., 74.
16. "Afterword," in E. Nesbit, *The Best of Shakespeare* (Oxford and New York: Oxford University Press, 1997), 106.
17. "Preface," in Lois Burdett, *The Tempest for Kids* (Willowdale, Ontario and Buffalo, NY: Firefly Books, 1999), 3.
18. Ibid., 27, 56.
19. (London and New York: Routledge, 1999).

Works Cited

Beneduce, Ann Keay. *The Tempest.* Illus. Gennady Spirin. New York: Philomel Books, 1996.

Burdett, Lois. *The Tempest for Kids*. Willowdale, Ontario and Buffalo, NY: Firefly Books, 1999.

Chute, Marchette. *Stories from Shakespeare*. Cleveland and New York: World Publishing, 1956.

Coville, Bruce. *William Shakespeare's The Tempest*. Illus. Ruth Sanderson. New York: Bantam Doubleday Dell Publishing, 1994.

Garfield, Leon. *Shakespeare Stories*. Illus. Michael Foreman. New York: Schocken Books, 1985.

Lamb, Charles and Mary. *Tales from Shakespeare* (1807). New York: Parents' Magazine Press, 1964.

Miles, Bernard. *Well-Loved Tales from Shakespeare*. Illus. Victor G. Ambrus. Twickenham, England: Hamlyn Publishing, 1986.

Nesbit, E. *The Best of Shakespeare*: *Retellings of 10 Classic Plays* (1900) Intro. Iona Opie, Afterword, Peter Hunt. Oxford and New York: Oxford University Press, 1997.

Sedgwick, Fred. *Shakespeare and the Young Writer*. London and New York: Routledge, 1999.

Williams, Marcia. *Tales from Shakespeare*: *Seven Plays*. Illus. Marcia Williams. Cambridge, MA: Candlewick Press, 1998.

Works Consulted

Aagesen, Colleen and Margie Blumberg. *Shakespeare for Kids*: *His Life and Times. 21 Activities*. Chicago: Chicago Review Press, 1999.

Aliki. *William Shakespeare and the Globe*. Illus. Aliki. New York: HarperCollins Publishers, 1999.

Bailey, Paul. "An Approach to Shakespeare Through Drama," *The use of English* 36.2 (Spring 1985): 47–56.

Bottoms, Janet. "Of *Tales* and *Tempests*," *Children's Literature in Education* 27.2 (1996): 73–86.

Bottoms, Janet. "Playing with Shakespeare: Or 'Where There's a Will There's a Way,' " *English in Education* 28.3 (Fall 1994): 25–33.

Coleman, Libby. "Shakespeare for the fun of it," *Instructor*, November 1974, 56.

Gibson, Rex and Janet Field-Pickering. *Discovering Shakespeare's Language*. Cambridge: Cambridge University Press, 1998.

Lewis, Amanda and Tim Wynne-Jones. *Rosie Backstage*. Illus. Bill Slavin. Toronto: Kids Can Press Ltd., 1994.

Pollinger, Gina. *A Treasury of Shakespeare's Verse*. Illus. Emma Chichester Clark. New York: Kingfisher, 2000.

Sedgwick, Fred. *Shakespeare and the Young Writer*. London and New York: Routledge, 1999.

Shakespeare, William. *The Tempest*: *A Case Study in Critical Controversy*. Ed. Gerald Graff and James Phelan. Boston and New York: Bedford/St. Martins, 2000.

Teaching Shakespeare through Performance. Ed. Milla Cozart Riggio. New York: MLA, 1999.

Williamson, David. "English Children Are Too Sophisticated for Shakespeare," *The use of English* 38.2 (Spring 1987): 27–32.

16.   Promoting the Original

Perspectives on Balancing Authenticity and Creativity in Adaptations of *The Tempest*

AMY E. MATHUR

Interpreting Shakespeare's plays has inspired, intrigued, and often infuriated scholars, audiences, and directors for centuries. Like a stage production, a picture book adaptation of a Shakespeare play offers the audience an interpretive glimpse into the playwright's original work. Authors attempting to introduce children to Shakespeare's plays may encounter many of the difficulties that directors face when staging a production. Like directors, writers must consciously and carefully decide how to incorporate or preserve the spirit of the original without stifling personal creativity or sacrificing a child's comprehension. Authors of adaptations must utilize a diverse set of techniques to convey fluid meanings and interpretations within a fixed medium. By manipulating troublesome chronology and infusing authentic language into the text, authors create original adaptations that educate and entertain young readers. Through a careful consideration of various adaptations of William Shakespeare's *The Tempest*, including those of Bruce Coville, Ann Keay Beneduce, Leon Garfield, and Lois Burdett, I will explore some literary devices employed in each adaptation which enable the author to preserve Shakespeare's original play while offering children a unique reading experience.

Many of the basic elements within *The Tempest*, such as magic, monsters, and fairies, intrigue and entertain young audiences. Thus *The Tempest* seems like a suitable play to use as an introduction into Shakespeare's writing. However, the original play presents tangible problems for the adapter, including a disjointed sequence of events, confusing subplots, and elevated language that the author must consider while adapting the play for young readers. The creative ways in which authors meet these challenges often displays their commitment to both the original play and to the child's understanding of it.

Although entertaining, Shakespeare's *The Tempest* centers on a thin plot, which contains little character development. The action most crucial to the play's progress and conclusion occurs when Antonio usurps his brother

Prospero's power and casts him out of Milan and into certain death on the sea. Yet Shakespeare opens his play twelve years later on a different ship followed by a remote island scene. For Shakespeare's audience to connect the lives of the passengers on the ship to the inhabitants of the island, the playwright relies heavily on individual characters to provide pertinent background information to the audience. Without numerous speeches about past occurrences, the audience could not follow the play's action or meaning. Shakespeare further complicates his play through his use of numerous subplots. Secondary and tertiary strands, such as the plots made against King Alonso and Prospero's lives, create differences in the play's time frame that an author must address in order to sustain coherence and continuity in an adaptation. Though each of the subplots in *The Tempest* occurs simultaneously, in the narrative or dramatic form they appear successively. The constant shift between individual story lines falsely creates a sense of change in time as well. This sophisticated orchestration of time may confuse the young reader. Unlike Shakespeare, the author of a child's adaptation cannot depend solely on Prospero, Ariel, and Caliban to place the story's action within a sensible historical context. Due to space limitations in picture books and to the young reader's limited exposure to literary flashback or the multi-dimensional plot, the author must decide how to arrange Shakespeare's dramatic sequence in a comprehensible manner. In their adaptations, Bruce Coville, Ann Keay Beneduce, Leon Garfield, and Lois Burdett each address this problem through different methods. How these authors structure their own books sequentially affects more than the basic retelling of *The Tempest*. Rather, as they manipulate the original text the authors each emphasize distinct aspects of the play.

Aware that the complicated order of events may perplex a young reader, Coville "untangled the threads of the story and started at the beginning" (40). Opening his adaptation with Prospero in Milan, he simplifies the play's continuity, so that his reader never looks back to explain the present action. Beginning the narrative with the words, "Once on a time a magician named Prospero served as duke in the city of Milan" (5), Coville highlights the play's protagonist as well. The child reader immediately understands the book as a fantasy story about Prospero the magician. Much like the spotlight in the modern theater, this device draws attention to the main character. From this moment the young reader concludes that the ensuing story will recount Prospero's actions and adventures. By abandoning Shakespeare's construction, Coville also stresses the actual progression of events within *The Tempest*. Employing this strategy, Coville develops the main story in a logical sequence, thereby eliminating a major barrier between the young reader and the original text. Without relying on literary flashback or lengthy informative speeches, Coville focuses the reader's attention on the episodes within Shakespeare's story, not how he told it. Thus Coville encourages the young reader to appreciate Shakespeare's imagination without asking him to decipher his technique.

Like Coville, Ann Keay Beneduce draws her reader's attention to the story Shakespeare tells in *The Tempest*. Beneduce also attempts to clarify the play's development, but does so differently than Coville. Whereas Coville rearranges the story to avoid complications, Beneduce reduces the play by condensing action. In her adaptation Beneduce also opens the story with a look at Prospero. Unlike Coville, though, she introduces Prospero to her reader on his island home. Rather than offering the magician's history, she reports his present condition. Again, this choice alerts the child reader that the following story focuses on Prospero's activity on the enchanted island. However, Beneduce fails to eliminate the need for flashback and repeated explanatory speeches to illuminate the reasons behind the protagonist's future actions. Beneduce's attempt to simplify Shakespeare's play resorts instead to elimination of events. By removing various characters' dialogue or actions, Beneduce seeks to treat only those elements which elucidate Shakespeare's basic story line. This approach leads her to completely disregard aspects of the play's subplots, including the formations of the separate designs on King Alonso and Prospero's lives. Instead of simplifying her narrative, Beneduce actually complicates it. By describing the failure of Caliban's scheme to kill Prospero without initially showing the plan's creation, Beneduce creates a gap in logic that would puzzle the young reader. Such an example demonstrates the author's responsibility to consider clarity and consistency before eliminating any portion of the original piece. Although Beneduce attempts to omit events that might disorient the reader, her approach ultimately produces a rough outline of the play without offering her audience a true sense of Shakespeare's ingenuity.

Leon Garfield displays his creative spin on Shakespeare's play much like Ann Keay Beneduce does. Adapting *The Tempest* not only as a picture book, but also as an identical cartoon version of the book for the *HBO Animated Tales* series, presented Garfield with many constraints. Due to space and time restrictions Garfield extracts certain raw elements of the text to create his adaptations. This practice, which alters the play's original sequence, also eliminates information vital to the child's understanding of the play. Garfield opens his adaptations with Prospero and Ariel watching the enemy's ship at sea, quickly followed by Prospero's call for the storm. Similar to Beneduce, Garfield instantly draws attention to the father and daughter on the island. Through his narrator and illustrations Garfield indicates a connection between the island inhabitants and the ship's passengers. However, the author fails to explain that association, thus constituting the need for informational scenes or speeches. Yet in his extreme compression of the text, Garfield excludes Prospero's flashback scene entirely. Although he offers his audience the reason for Prospero's actions on page 34, for a child reading the book or watching the cartoon the ambiguity Garfield produces from the outset would jeopardize the child's enjoyment and understanding of *The Tempest*.

Garfield continues to create confusion when he introduces two of the sub-plots. When he includes the murderous conspiracies against both King Alonso and Prospero, Garfield mirrors the events that transpire in the play. Unfortunately Garfield's space and time constraints compel him to discard many lines which define the plotting characters' motivations. Confronted with such limited detail, the young reader may decipher the proposed murders, but would not grasp the reasons behind them or their repercussions. By persistently ignoring the catalysts for the story's conflicts, Garfield presents *The Tempest* as a confusing, incoherent play, which reinforces the cultural belief that for young audiences Shakespeare's work remains wholly impenetrable.

Unlike Coville, Beneduce, and Garfield, Burdett adheres more strictly to Shakespeare's original sequence of events in her adaptation. By closely following Shakespeare's text, Burdett intimates that in an adaptation, describing how the original story was told remains as important as retelling it. In her work she displays her commitment to presenting an intelligible adaptation which closely reflects Shakespeare's story and organization. Burdett manages to maintain her devotion to the text without curbing her own artistic interpretation of it.

Burdett approaches the problematic order of events within *The Tempest* differently than her contemporaries. The elements that other authors rearrange or eliminate, Burdett expands upon. As the longest of these four considered adaptations, Burdett treats the play not as a summary or outline of the original, but as an opportunity to introduce children to the overall wonder and richness of Shakespeare's actual writing. To present her reader with such an introduction, Burdett cautiously follows Shakespeare's outline. When encountering problematic moments within the text she refuses to move or reject them. Instead she elaborates upon the points offering the young reader a concrete understanding of the characters or actions, which in turn pulls the reader further into the story.

Once inside the framework of the play, Burdett works not only to inject portions of the subplots, but also to integrate those elements as valuable aspects of Shakespeare's text. Through her elaboration of the murder plots, Burdett details the villainous motives that drive the characters. In doing so, she unites disreputable characters and their story lines through the common theme of lust for power. This construction also enables her to acknowledge Shakespeare's ability to conjoin seemingly unrelated subplots to articulate subtle themes or meanings. Through her willingness to follow the original text and her ability to seamlessly fuse separations in time and subplots through careful explanations, Burdett invites her reader to truly enjoy the intricacies of Shakespeare's writing.

Deciding how to relate the complexity of the action within *The Tempest* presents the author with a problem he or she must face when adapting a specific Shakespeare play. The question of how to incorporate the playwright's original language into an adaptation pertains to any of his plays. Shakespeare's language remains one of the major barriers that deters readers and audiences from approaching his work. A cultural belief exists in which people avoid Shakespeare's plays believing that language used almost four hundred years ago essentially sounds foreign to them. Others consider Shakespeare's language too difficult to decipher or enjoy. Yet for those who perform, watch, or study Shakespeare's plays, his unique and poetic use of language constitutes one of his dramatic accomplishments. For the author who desires to introduce Shakespeare to a young child before cultural perceptions discourage him from discovering the playwright's genius, deciding on the amount of original language to include shapes an entire adaptation. The use of Shakespeare's own language within an adaptation can either dispel or reinforce the popular cultural perceptions of his work the young reader will one day encounter. The ways in which Coville, Beneduce, Garfield, and Burdett utilize Shakespeare's language in their own adaptations allows each of them to address the prevailing cultural belief while emphasizing distinct elements of *The Tempest*.

In their picture books, Coville and Beneduce each include Shakespeare's language sparingly. Writing prose narratives, the authors choose distinct ways to include actual lines from the play. Coville does weave portions of Shakespeare's text into his own work when possible. Generally assigning those original lines to specific characters through dialogue, the author reinforces the connection between Shakespeare and his characters. Coville effectively blurs any distinction between his own language and Shakespeare's so that the child reader enjoys a consistent voice throughout his adaptation.

Contrarily, whenever Beneduce includes actual Shakespearean verse, she deliberately separates that section from the remainder of her text. Rather than eliding distinction between her writing and Shakespeare's, as Coville does, she in effect highlights the difference. Beneduce avoids including Shakespeare's lines within her own narration. Instead she sets off whole passages from the play as illustrations. She instantly segregates the original text from her retelling of it, which in effect separates Shakespeare from the central story told in the book. Beneduce essentially suggests to her reader that Shakespeare's language stands apart from that which he or she can comprehend. Suggesting that an audience must view Shakespeare's words differently inadvertently fortifies the cultural misconception of his language's unintelligibility.

Garfield and Burdett both use Shakespeare's language within their adaptations to produce distinct ends as well. Garfield relies exclusively on Shakespeare's original text to produce the lines within his adaptation. Basically following *The Tempest's* script, Garfield extracts individual lines from the text to provide dialogue within his book. Although Garfield offers his audience authentic Shakespearean language, by randomly selecting individual lines from the text he often loses meaning essential to the child's comprehension. Garfield, in an attempt to sort through much of Shakespeare's complex poetry, often sacrifices relevant information and characterization.

Garfield's work does succeed in emphasizing Shakespeare's original medium. The picture book exists primarily as the screenplay taken from the *HBO Animated Tales* series cartoon. Therefore, Garfield's adaptation reads like a play's script, complete with prompts and stage directions. Reading *The Tempest* in this form places emphasis on the fact that Shakespeare wrote his story to be performed in the theater.

Of these four adaptations Burdett's again follows Shakespeare's play most closely. Writing in rhyming couplets, Burdett repeatedly manages to intertwine the playwright's lines with her own. She constantly incorporates Shakespeare's text into her adaptation without compromising her own creativity or sacrificing her audiences' comprehension. Without breaking her rhyme scheme or poetic meter, Burdett often camouflages any distinction between the authentic and the adapted lines. Being able to include the play's lines so naturally, Burdett invites the reader to admire the poetic beauty of Shakespeare's language while proving that he or she can fully comprehend and appreciate it.

The challenges of simplifying problematic dramatic sequencing and of incorporating original language into the modified text represent a very limited portion of the issues authors must confront when adapting a Shakespearean play for a young audience. However, considering these specific points adequately exemplifies the ways the author's choices affect the child reader's experience in terms of enjoyment and comprehension. In looking at the unique adaptations of Coville, Beneduce, Garfield, and Burdett, one quickly recognizes that the author's manipulation of Shakespeare's text dictates the audience's response to it. Authors can introduce a child to Shakespeare's basic story without demanding that the reader understand the playwright's technique or language. Or through explanation and emphasis, the author may invite the reader to witness the full dramatic complexity and linguistic creativity Shakespeare displayed in his writing. Regardless of individual strategies or choices, authors of such children's adaptations seek to present Shakespeare's plays, not as daunting or inaccessible scripts, but as delightful and intriguing stories which invite the reader to revisit and rediscover the playwright's world.

Bibliography

Beneduce, Ann Keay. *The Tempest*. New York: Philomel Books, 1996.
Burdett, Lois. *The Tempest for Kids*. Ontario: Firefly Books, 1999.
Coville, Bruce. *The Tempest*. New York: Bantam Doubleday Dell, 1996.
Garfield, Leon. *The Tempest*. New York: Alfred A. Knopf, 1993.
Shakespeare, William. *The Tempest*. Ed. Robert Langbaum. New York: Penguin, 1998.

17. First One I and Then the Other

Identity and Intertextuality in Shakespeare's Caliban and Covington's Lizard

CYNTHIA PERANTONI

Dennis Covington's *Lizard* takes its readers along on a journey of self-discovery and self-acceptance, a journey often found in literature, but rarely treated so imaginatively and compellingly. Explicit and implicit parallels with William Shakespeare's *The Tempest* in character, plot, theme, and structure make the two works mutually enlightening. The parallels, which are shifting and ambiguous, provide high school students with opportunities for genuinely heuristic experiences in reading, writing, and discussing.

Covington's hero-narrator Lucius "Lizard" Sims looks different from other people. His unusual face—produced either genetically or accidentally (due to birth trauma)—has led to false assumptions that he cannot think, see, or breathe well. His facial and physical malformities are so severe that he was once mistaken for the victim of a serious car accident (3). He is readily disguised as a dog in order to evade authorities when he runs away (48). He is typecast, so to speak, to play Caliban in a just-barely professional production. He delivers his lines with heartfelt sincerity because he truly empathizes with Shakespeare's "puppy-headed monster" (2.2.148–49). Trying to comprehend and memorize, Lizard often paraphrases his lines, slanting the interpretation. Lizard's life and his brief theatrical career provide a delightful and thought-provoking new spin on Shakespeare's romance, making it more accessible and intriguing to students.

Lizard's journey is as mystical and magical to him as that experienced by the shipwrecked Italians in *The Tempest*. He leaves his home above the café in DeRidder (Is the town so-named because his mother "rids" herself of him?) and travels first to the Leesville State School where he enters a new world which includes albinos whose unusual appearance—ironically—frightens him, especially after he is told they have supernatural vision. Running away with two itinerant actors Sallie and Callahan, he journeys to Newllano (Is this "New Land"—evocative of New World overtones in the apparently Mediterranean island in *The Tempest*?) where he meets the remarkable Rain and her brother Sammy who live in a natural state but not an unspoiled natural state—they have been horribly victimized by a one-eyed preacher. Traveling from Louisiana to Mississippi astounds Lizard as if he'd "traveled a thousand miles . . . from another time" (80–82).

His arrival in the big city, Birmingham, is dulled by his disappointment in the theater, which was recently a kitchen, where they will perform. However, the theme of illusion is extended to setting when Waldo, the director, reminds his disgruntled actors, "This is only the physical space where it takes place. The real play is in the mind, the imagination" (97). Birmingham provides a good art museum where Lizard receives further lessons in aesthetics. Most of all, his initial reaction to Birmingham conjures up the tenuousness of identity in his response to the panorama of people and places that he so abruptly and rapidly encounters (101–102). On his journey he meets a variety of people and grows in understanding not only of himself but also of others; his continuing refrain is that he looks at people "with first one eye and then the other" (6, 31, 96, 138, 164 and elsewhere!).

Structurally, *Lizard* resembles *The Tempest* in the separation of characters into small groups for episodic adventures. From all of this, a new view of Caliban, one seemingly not considered in the vast critical commentary, arises. This is a more highly-personalized, individualized, and sympathetically-portrayed Caliban, given a voice through a young and unsophisticated actor performing Caliban who, in effect, has been Caliban in reality. They remain two distinctly different fictional characters, yet a reading of *Lizard* cannot help but inflect our reading of *The Tempest*. While my students read *Lizard* on their own time, we perform *The Tempest* as readers' theater in class. Until they have finished reading the novel, I try to avoid focusing on Caliban in the discussions which conclude each day's session; however, as they progress through *Lizard*, they become insistent. How lovely, to have them demanding to discuss subtle connections between two works of literature! The intertextuality provides substance for discussions that are often convoluted but always lively. They enjoy inventing ways to "map" their comparisons and contrasts—diagrams, clusters, geometric figures—in an attempt to show all the connections.

Researching literary criticism and theatrical interpretations of Caliban provides a microcosm of the history of social thinking from 1611 to the new millennium, while taking them to a new level of intellectual sophistication. Cross-curricular dialogues arise naturally as students discover remarkable connections with topics considered in their social studies classes. Historically, Caliban has been lizard, fish, monster, ape-man, missing link, devil, noble savage, ignoble savage, poet, Native American, African-American, black militant, aborigine, terrestrial, extra-terrestrial, third-world victim, and allegorical alter ego for virtually every other character in the play and for the members of the audience as well. Caliban has been vilified and idealized. Critics have condemned and commiserated. Some celebrate his importance despite the brief time he is on stage; others deplore the mass of criticism he has spawned considering his "unimportance"! Who—or what—is Caliban? We have little textual evidence to go on: what he says and what others say of him, the latter mostly in the form of insulting epithets hurled at him by unreliable witnesses.

Similar to Caliban, Lizard is subjected to many insults. He is called "Turd Head" by the boys (10) and referred to as "that boy with the squashed head" by the nurse (28) during his brief stay at the Leesville State School for Retarded Boys. He is called or referred to as "deformed retard" (48); "subhuman, humpbacked thing" (59); and "shithead" (77), among other insults. Some observers have invoked the supernatural by pronouncing him "a bad sign" (54). Like Caliban, also, he is told—twice—that he smells just awful. In view of the reactions of others, Lizard seems to have a remarkably accepting attitude about his appearance. He looks in the mirror and sees "just Lucius Sims staring back at me" (3). He eventually perceives his different appearance as part of his individuality. Lizard also has an understated sense of humor about his capabilities: discussing his examination by a nurse trying to measure his height, he comments, "She kept telling me to stand up straight, which I have never been too good at" (11). Novel and play become valuable tools in helping students reconsider their attitudes about "different" people.

Perceptions based on externals often prove illusory in novel and in play. Lizard finds acceptance from Mike and Walrus, from Callahan and Sallie but—most importantly for him—from the lovely Rain, who befriends him without comment about his appearance, perhaps because of her notion about herself and her brother Sammy: "we're what we look like, and we're something else that you can't see" (61). French students have quoted St. Exupéry, *"L'essentiel est invisible pour les yeux"* ("That which is essential is invisible to the eyes.") (47), in discussing this theme.

At the state school, Lucius meets others who are physically and mentally "different." The brothers Walrus and Mike—do they resemble Stephano and Trinculo in ways other than gender and number?—bestow upon him the nickname, "Lizard." Instinctively delighted, he accepts "Lizard" as his true name because of his appearance and his affinity for water (17). (Caliban is identified as fishlike in both odor and appearance although no mention is made of a talent for swimming.) The three form a loose alliance.

Like *The Tempest*, *Lizard* examines the nature of art. Lizard first realizes the uses of art through Walrus, who is neurotically dependent on constant music provided by his portable radio, a prized possession only he is permitted to have. Lizard understands the concession when the batteries run low and Walrus becomes violently frenzied. Mr. Tinker, the brutal attendant at the school who shows no signs of sensitivity other than this pragmatic one, orders Lizard to sing. And he does, amazing himself by remembering Miss Cooley's favorites. Wonderfully, Walrus calms down (15–16). A constant influence in *The Tempest* is ethereal music which Caliban poetically describes:

> . . . the isle is full of noises,
> Sounds, and sweet airs, that give delight and hurt not.
> Sometimes a thousand twangling instruments
> Will hum about mine ears; and sometime voices,
> That if I then had waked after long sleep,
> Will make me sleep again, and then in dreaming
> The clouds methought would open and show riches
> Ready to drop upon me, that when I waked
> I cried to dream again. (3.2.133–141)

The themes of illusion versus reality and of the uses of art are introduced when Lizard becomes acquainted with the theater through Sallie and Callahan, roving actors, and their performance of skits based on *Treasure Island*. His naive response reveals an initial acceptance of illusion as reality. Upset by the performance, he tries to go backstage, fearing Jim Hawkins had been murdered by the pirate. Pushing aside a curtain, he reveals the two actors, rehearsing Prospero's and Miranda's lines (as Ferdinand and Miranda are revealed, playing at chess in *The Tempest*). He is astounded to realize that Jim Hawkins is not only unharmed but female! (23–25) Significantly, the lines they are reading when Lizard bursts in upon them are the exchange upon Miranda's first sight of Ferdinand; she insists he is a "spirit" or "a thing divine" while her father assures her that he is human (1.2.412, 418). These lines coincide with Sallie's first view of Lizard whose appearance is not "divine" but whose moral development is superlative. Perceptions of identity are often illusory.

Although later she denies any emotional attachment (104), Sallie assumes a maternal relationship with Lizard which contrasts with Miss Cooley's rejection of him. She debunks the notion that Lizard is an ominous presence and appreciates the color of his eyes, which she calls "the prettiest green" (54). She teaches him *The Tempest* and helps him learn his lines. She recognizes and compliments his natural acting ability as he identifies with Caliban and performs convincingly (145). Sallie portrays Ariel; she is, indeed, a good and helpful spirit who remains uninvolved emotionally, or tries to! However, Ariel in *The Tempest* is often the tormentor and denigrator of Caliban. In their acceptance of Lizard, Callahan and Sallie also resemble Trinculo and Stephano. Both pairs plan to use their subject; even so for both Lizard and Caliban, the unaccustomed camaraderie and acceptance are meaningful. For the first time in his life, with Sallie and Callahan and their dog Mac, Lizard experiences family feeling.

Callahan's identity is protean. Altered, illusory identity presents itself, not only through his stage performances, but also through his convincing assumption of a series of personae—first as Simonetti, Lizard's "father" to help him escape the state school. Although suspicious from the beginning, Lizard does not recognize Callahan until he peels off false mustache and nose. He is a magician, and the magic that he brings into Lizard's life is that of the theater. Callahan, like Prospero, assumes responsibility but with ulterior motives: Prospero needs a servant and Callahan needs someone to replace an alcoholic actor and recognizes in Lizard's unusual face a perfect Caliban.

Ironically, Callahan himself is an alcoholic—as Lizard soon realizes—who can also be cruel. The parallels shift ambiguously; obviously the similarity in names is no accident! What does Covington intend to imply by giving a Caliban-like name to the character whose role generally seems linked to Prospero's? Callahan drunkenly informs Lizard of painful truths about his identity, for just as the exact nature and parentage of Caliban in *The Tempest* cannot be fixed, Lizard has no valid information and remarkably little curiosity about his parents. Through Callahan, he learns that Miss Cooley is his mother and his father may not be dead. His parents had willfully rejected him. Moreover, some animalistic imagery is associated with Callahan: Lizard has trouble "getting used to Callahan's real face, which [is] narrow and pointed like a fox's" (52).

So much of the critical commentary on *The Tempest* involves comparing and contrasting Caliban with virtually all of the other characters in the play. In the novel, Covington connects, disconnects, and reconnects characters, suggesting varying Shakespearean associations which students delight in discovering. After seeming to abandon Lizard, Callahan does return to help the thirteen-year-old confront the truth of his identity, to reunite him with his friends in Newllano, and with his mother in a newly-honest relationship in which she finally acknowledges him as her son.

Lizard meets Rain, the beautiful creature of nature, and Sammy, her loud and proud brother, under mystical circumstances. Rain weaves marvelous tales of her family's Cherokee origins and unashamedly swims in the nude. There is some connection between Caliban and Rain, perhaps, as native naturals; however, Rain is the victim of rape, not the would-be perpetrator. At first, Lizard did not believe Sammy's claim to being related to Chief Narrow Meadow; however, listening to Rain's story, he accepts it as true. It is a story loaded with disguise and illusion and revenge. Central to the story is the beautiful silver bowl with multiple symbolic applications to theme. According to Rain, the bowl has magical properties: water from it restores primordial purity, emanating from "the imagination of the one who first imagined it" (67). According to Caliban, such beauty once characterized his island, before the arrival of Prospero and Miranda. The bowl, secretly sent with Lizard when he leaves, represents Rain's faith in him and his first commitment to another human. The restoration of the bowl which he had believed, in despair, to have been stolen, suggests the theme of loss and recovery. Believed by Rain, Sammy, and Lizard to be extremely valuable, the bowl is also illusory, not precious silver, but a carnival prize worth only fifty dollars. The symbols are as protean as the characters! However, at its restoration to Aunt Eunice, the rightful owner, the bowl is revealed to be priceless: it represents memories of family life past, associated as it is with family folklore about their roots, a memento of her dead sister, the "Mama" whose wisdom has been so often quoted. They believed it to have magical powers and it had, reputedly, saved the life of an ancestor. Prospero's magic books might well come to mind.

Later, a second seemingly miraculous restoration takes place: Rain has not been murdered by the clergyman who is really a rapist and a murderer. She is rediscovered by Lizard with the same joy with which Alonso and Ferdinand behold one another at the end of *The Tempest*. Ironically, just before he saw the "resurrected" Rain in the courthouse where Reverend Smith will be tried for her mother's murder, he noted that above the water fountain, "the word COLORED had been painted over . . . [leaving] the outline of the letters" (169). His relationship with Rain and Sammy teaches him to identify with a group discriminated against because of race and false assumptions, a group far larger than that consisting of the few differently-formed others that he has encountered. Rain herself represents Lizard's first love interest, but it is love with a sense of responsibility, remarkable in one for whom so very little responsibility had been assumed by others.

Lizard's encounters with Robert Howell, director of the museum, and William Tyson, sculptor and custodian extraordinaire, facilitate his growing understanding. In a wonderful anecdote about Bierstadt's painting of Yosemite, Howell explains that the artist did all that work for "the simple truth of the entire piece—the way the sunlight falls upon that single stunted tree" (115). How significant to Lizard—whether he consciously realizes it or not—must be the fact that the huge mural, with its beautifully normal elements of nature, was created to illuminate a "single stunted tree" which represents "truth"! (114–15).

Later, Lizard discovers to his surprise that the black custodian is an artist himself. Willie J. Tyson shows Lizard his sculpture *Waking on the Other Side*, memorializing the four girls who were killed in the 1963 church bombing (129) so recently in the news again because of the 2001–2002 trial. Through both art and life, Lizard learns again of the damage done through stereotyping those who are "different" and the ease with which such tragic errors might be made. Caliban's aesthetic sense, evident in his ability to appreciate art in the form of music and to rhapsodize poetically about his ethereal island again comes to mind.

After the performance, Mr. Howell's astronomy lesson provides Lizard with another insight. After initial awkwardness because binoculars are not made for "people with eyes like Lizard's," Mr. Howell instructs Lizard to look "a little more to the side . . . distant lights are brighter when viewed peripherally. Sometimes things are clearer when you don't look at them head on . . ." (150). Howell's advice recalls Lizard's continuing refrain: he looks at other people and at himself "with first one eye and then the other." Despite appearances, his vision is not bad at all, just different and perhaps better. His unique experience of the world has inflected his vision and his understanding. He is sensitive beyond his years and certainly beyond the insensitivity with which he has been treated.

When Lizard plays Caliban, he needs no instruction in method-acting techniques. He truly empathizes with the "monster's" resentment of restrictions of his freedom and of his natural urges. He understands the hatred that Caliban would feel toward Prospero because he feels the same hatred toward Callahan both for lying to him and for telling him the truth. Most of all, he understands the pain of having been stuck in a place because of assumptions. Prospero is no hero; having been usurped, he became a usurper. There is justice in Caliban's complaints: "This island's mine by Sycorax my mother, / Which thou tak'st from me" (1.2.331–32) and "You taught me language, and my profit o't / Is I know how to curse" (1.2.362–63). Lizard's paraphrase, if less poetic, is also less ambiguous:

> There was nothing I couldn't do if I'd wanted to, until you came along and ruined it. I thought you were going to be my teacher. You said you'd teach me how to talk, how to count the shells I found on the beach. But you only taught me enough to know that I was nothing but dirt to you. You wanted the island for yourself. You'd been kicked out of your own place, so you came here to steal mine. (120)

At the end of *The Tempest*, Gonzalo marvels, "In one voyage . . . found . . . all of us ourselves / When no man was his own" (5.1.208, 210, 212–13), optimistically not noticing that there has been no change in Sebastian and Antonio. The voyage, as discovery and self-discovery, is significant in both works. Students might well be reminded of the often anthologized e. e. cummings poem, "For whatever we lose (like a you and a me) / it's always ourselves that we find in the sea" (682). In the end, Caliban's expression of a desire to be redeemed—"I'll be wise hereafter, / And seek for grace" (5.1.294–95)—is denigrated and dismissed by Prospero, "Go to, away" (5.1.298). The sincerity and prognosis of his desire for wisdom and grace can only be guessed at. Abandoned, Caliban remains on the island alone. In the novel, Lizard moves on among friends.

Lizard's fate diverges from Caliban's, of course, because Lizard is not Caliban. His unambiguous moral goodness separates him from Caliban. Lizard's redemption is not from a personal moral darkness, but from society's abusive darkness in its failure to appreciate him. Lizard fares far better than Caliban. He has options and some freedom of choice. He has been invited to live with the director Waldo and his wife and to appear in a play. He has been reunited with his mother. We feel that his friendship with Rain will continue. His new-found friends will help him, as he has helped them. Callahan reappears to help with legal details to obtain financial aid. Returning home, Lizard realizes "how wide the sky was above the place where we lived, and how long during the summer it stayed light" (198). We feel assured of a happy future. Lizard knows who he is. Still, he is stunned when a reviewer comments on "his beautifully grotesque mask" (153). He takes seriously the reviewer's failure to separate reality from illusion. A similar instance occured earlier when Waldo directed him, "The limp's great! . . . Keep it!" (121). Metadramatically, Lizard's "handicaps" have become advantages. Reality has been mistaken for illusion! Lizard, however, has learned to accept himself, to value himself, to seek a place for himself in society.

In addition to providing insight into Shakespeare's masterpiece, this novel may help adolescent readers grow in compassion and acceptance of limitations and misfortunes in others and in themselves. We all need to be reminded to look beyond misconceptions based on the physical and the stereotypical to see the individual. Intellectually, students can learn to take risks in reading and responding to literature. They should not fear answering incorrectly, yet they should also be called upon to give textual evidence for their interpretations. So often students come to us wanting the one correct answer to dutifully record on a test to "earn that A." The rich complexities of *The Tempest* and *Lizard* provide an authentic opportunity to discover meaning because truly no one-to-one matching is possible. A multiplicity of connections elicits thought. I remember an assistant principal advising me, at the beginning of my teaching career, "Never ask a question unless you know the answer." Perhaps those questions, the ones for which there may be no answers, are exactly the ones our students need.

Works Cited

Covington, Dennis. *Lizard*. New York: Bantam Doubleday Dell, 1991.

cummings, e. e. *Complete Poems: 1913–1962*. New York: Harcourt Brace Jovanovich, 1968.

de Saint-Exupéry, Antoine. *Le Petit Prince*. Educational Edition. Cambridge, MA: Houghton Mifflin, 1943.

Shakespeare, William. *The Tempest*. Ed. Stephen Orgel. Oxford: Oxford University Press, 1987.

Works Recommended for Further Research

Auden, W. H. "Caliban to the Audience." 1945. From *The Sea and the Mirror.* In *Shakespeare The Tempest: A Casebook.* Ed. D. J. Palmer. London: Macmillan, 1968. 96–105.

Boas, Frederick S. Introduction. Rev. Katharine Lee Bates. *The Tempest,* by William Shakespeare. The Arden Edition. Boston: D. C. Heath and Company, 1916. v–xxv.

Covington, Dennis. *Lizard.* New York: Bantam Doubleday Dell, 1991.

cummings, e. e. *Complete Poems: 1913–1962.* New York: Harcourt Brace Jovanovich, 1968.

de Saint-Exupéry, Antoine. *Le Petit Prince.* Educational Edition. Cambridge, MA: Houghton Mifflin, 1943.

Dover Wilson, John and Arthur Quiller-Couch. Introduction. *The Tempest,* by William Shakespeare. Cambridge: Cambridge University Press, 1921. vii–lx.

Dryden, John. "The Character of Caliban." 1679. In *Shakespeare The Tempest: A Casebook.* Ed. D. J. Palmer. London: Macmillan, 1968. 34.

Frye, Northrup. "Introduction to *The Tempest.*" In *Twentieth Century Interpretations of The Tempest.* Ed. Hallett Smith. Englewood Cliffs, NJ: Prentice-Hall, 1969. 60–67.

Griffiths, Trevor R. " 'This Island's Mine': Caliban and Colonialism." *The Yearbook of English Studies* 13 (1981): 159–80.

Hazlitt, William. "Unity and Variety in Shakespeare's Design." 1817. In *Shakespeare's The Tempest: A Casebook.* Ed. D. J. Palmer. London: Macmillan, 1968. 67–71.

Hirst, David L. *The Tempest: Text and Performance.* London: Macmillan, 1984.

Kermode, Frank. Introduction. *The Tempest,* by William Shakespeare. The Arden Edition. Cambridge, MA: Harvard University Press, 1954. xi–lxxxviii.

Maclean, Kenneth. "Wild Man and Savage Believer: Caliban in Shakespeare and Browning." *Victorian Poetry* 25.1 (Spring 1987): 1–16.

Mowat, Barbara A. "A Modern Perspective." *The Tempest,* by William Shakespeare. The New Folger Library Shakespeare. New York: Washington Square Press, 1994. 185–99.

Mowat, Barbara A. and Paul Werstine, ed. Introduction. *The Tempest,* by William Shakespeare. The New Folger Library Shakespeare. New York: Washington Square Press, 1994. xiii–li.

Neilson, Frances. *Shakespeare and The Tempest.* Rindge, NH: Richard R. Smith Publisher, Inc., 1956.

Orgel, Stephen. Introduction. *The Tempest,* by William Shakespeare. Oxford: Oxford University Press, 1987. 1–87.

Shakespeare, William. *The Tempest.* Ed. Stephen Orgel. Oxford: Oxford University Press, 1987.

Spivak, Charlotte. *The Comedy of Evil on Shakespeare's Stage.* Rutherford, NJ: Farleigh Dickinson University Press, 1978.

Tomarken, Edward: *Samuel Johnson on Shakespeare: The Discipline of Criticism.* Athens, GA: University of Georgia Press, 1991.

Vaughan, Alden T. and Virginia Mason. *Shakespeare's Caliban: A Cultural History.* Cambridge: Cambridge University Press, 1991.

Vaughan, Virginia Mason. " 'Something Rich and Strange': Caliban's Theatrical MetaMorphoses." *Shakespeare Quarterly* 36.4 (Winter 1985): 390–405.

18. Harry Potter and the Shakespearean Allusion

MIRANDA JOHNSON-HADDAD

What is the secret of J. K. Rowling's success? As I write this essay, Rowling has completed four of her projected seven-volume Harry Potter series, and all have been runaway bestsellers. All four are still on the *New York Times* best-seller list; in fact, their phenomenal sales prompted the newspaper to create a separate children's bestseller list. Anticipation for the fourth volume, *Harry Potter and the Goblet of Fire*, was at fever-pitch, with the largest advance order and the largest first printing for any book, ever. On the morning of July 8, 2000, many bookstores opened at midnight and held Harry Potter parties. Those purchasers who had shown the foresight to place an advance order for the book with online retailer Amazon.com waited with bated breath for the Federal Express delivery truck to pull up with the volume—the result of a special arrangement between FedEx and Amazon.com. At my own house-hold we weren't able to hold out for the FedEx delivery; we piled into the family minivan and charged off to the local children's bookstore for a copy. I need hardly add that having two copies did not prove to be excessive, given all the readers (adults as well as children) competing for them; indeed, at one point I wondered whether I had erred in not purchasing a third copy. Later that same day I telephoned my parents, both retired academics in their seven-ties. "We can't talk to you now," said they. "We're reading *Harry Potter*."

So what's going on? Plenty of successful children's books have been written before, though none that have been this successful. (The last chil-dren's book to make it onto the *New York Times* bestseller list was E. B. White's *Charlotte's Web* in 1952.) But never before has a children's author, or any author, inspired the kind of intergenerational and commercial frenzy that J. K. Rowling has set into motion with her Harry Potter series. The explanation for this is, I think, fairly straightforward: Rowling is a master-mistress of literary and psychological allusion. She takes a simple frame-work—the English school story—and overlays it with an extraordinarily rich tapestry of characters and settings, all imagined in marvelous and engrossing detail. And underneath all these characters and settings lies the rock-solid foundation of archetype, myth, and fairy tale. In her *New Yorker* review of the Harry Potter books, Joan Acocella identifies several sources for the books, including the Arthurian legends, "Star Wars," *The Lord of the Rings*, the *Chronicles of Narnia*, Sherlock Holmes, *The Divine Comedy*, and *Paradise Lost* (74). To that list I would add *Tom Brown's Schooldays*; the school stories of Enid Blyton, Elinor M. Brent-Dyer, Noel Streatfeild, and many other English authors; and, as I shall show, the plays of William Shakespeare.

As everybody knows by now, the Harry Potter books have had their share of critics, from hysterical parents and teachers who make the astonishing claim that they are somehow immoral to establishment critics who complain that the Harry Potter books are derivative. Shakespeare himself would have loved that one. Certainly they're derivative—as was Shakespeare, as are fairy tales, as indeed is most literature. In his classic work *The Uses of Enchantment*, Bruno Bettelheim shows us that fairy tales are effective precisely because they evoke deep, unconscious associations within the minds of those reading or hearing the tales, and these associations make the tales resonate on the profoundest levels. It is the same with Rowling's Harry Potter books, which gain power from the complexity and evocativeness of their allusions.

Of particular interest to me is the way that certain tremendously powerful passages in the most recent book, *Harry Potter and the Goblet of Fire*, evoke two early plays of Shakespeare, *Titus Andronicus* and *Richard III*, that share similar themes of kinship and vengeance—themes that are also central to the Harry Potter books. There have been Shakespearean echoes in the books before, most notably in the figure of Hermione, one of Harry's closest friends. Smart, loyal Hermione is the know-it-all girl we all remember from school: the girl who always has her hand in the air, the girl who's already read the course books before the school term starts. (Rowling has let it be known in interviews that she modeled Hermione on herself; why are we not surprised?) Hermione also bears the name of one of Shakespeare's most memorable heroines, the wronged queen of the late Romance *The Winter's Tale*. In the second book in Rowling's series, *Harry Potter and the Chamber of Secrets*, Hermione is one of several students who become paralyzed after glimpsing the basilisk, the terrifying monster that lives in the Chamber of Secrets at Hogwarts school, and that is periodically released to prey upon muggles (that is, non-magical people) and muggle-born wizards like Hermione. "Hermione [lay] on the hospital bed as though carved out of stone" (258). Like her namesake in Shakespeare's play, Hermione temporarily becomes a living statue who is ultimately restored fully to life.[1]

Another, more playful Shakespearean allusion occurs in *Goblet of Fire* when the popular rock group The Weird Sisters has been hired to play at the

Hogwarts Yule Ball: "The Weird Sisters now trooped up onto the stage to wildly enthusiastic applause; they were all extremely hairy and dressed in black robes that had been artfully ripped and torn" (419). The name Weird Sisters is, of course, another appellation for the three witches in *Macbeth*. Light-hearted as this allusion is, it nevertheless puts us on the alert for more such references, and in *Goblet of Fire* we don't have to look far to find them.

In the opening chapter of *Goblet of Fire*, a minor character overhears a terrifying conversation. Old Frank Bryce, of the village of Little Hangleton, upon seeing a light late one night in the supposedly deserted Riddle mansion, stealthily enters the house and follows the sound of voices to an upstairs room. Standing cautiously outside the door, he listens to a conversation that he barely understands but that is clearly sinister and becomes more so by the minute. Readers familiar with the Harry Potter series quickly realize, although Frank Bryce cannot, that the two voices that Bryce overhears belong to Lord Voldemort, the most evil figure in the wizarding world, and his supporter Peter Pettigrew, known as Wormtail. Presently Bryce hears an exchange that appalls him:

> "[Y]ou will have your reward, Wormtail. I will allow you to perform an essential task for me, one that many of my followers would give their right hands to perform. . . ."
>
> "R-really, My Lord? What—?" Wormtail sounded terrified again.
>
> "Ah, Wormtail, you don't want me to spoil the surprise? Your part will come at the very end . . . but I promise you, you will have the honor of being just as useful as Bertha Jorkins." (11)[2]

Thirty one chapters and 625 pages later, Voldemort's prediction to Wormtail is fulfilled with horrifying literalness. Captured by Voldemort, Harry watches helplessly as Wormtail adds three crucial ingredients to a potion that is brewing in an enormous cauldron, a potion that will restore Voldemort to full life and power. The first ingredient, "Bone of the father, unknowingly given," is taken from the grave of Voldemort's father, to whose tombstone Harry is bound. The third ingredient, "Blood of the enemy, forcibly taken," is blood that Wormtail obtains by cutting Harry's arm. But the second ingredient is the most chilling.

> And now Wormtail was whimpering. He pulled a long, thin, shining silver dagger from inside his cloak. His voice broke into petrified sobs.
>
> *"Flesh—of the servant—willingly given—you will—revive—your master."*
>
> He stretched his right hand out in front of him—the hand with the missing finger. He gripped the dagger very tightly in his left hand and swung it upward.

> Harry realized what Wormtail was about to do a second before it hap-
> pened—he closed his eyes as tightly as he could, but he could not block the
> scream that pierced the night, that went through Harry as though he had
> been stabbed with the dagger too. He heard something fall to the ground,
> heard Wormtail's anguished panting, then a sickening splash, as something
> was dropped into the cauldron. (641–42)

Wormtail has indeed contributed something to Voldemort's resurrection that
his other followers would have been compelled to give their right hands to
provide—his own right hand.

For Shakespeareans, Wormtail's sacrifice vividly recalls a similar gesture by one of Shakespeare's most compelling hero-victims, Titus Andronicus. In Act 3, scene 1 of *Titus Andronicus*, Titus receives word from the
emperor Saturninus that there is a way to save the lives of his sons, whom the
Emperor holds prisoner.

> AARON: Titus Andronicus, my lord the Emperor
> Sends thee this word: that if thou love thy sons,
> Let Marcus, Lucius, or thyself, old Titus,
> Or any one of you, chop off your hand
> And send it to the King. He for the same
> Will send thee hither both thy sons alive,
> And that shall be the ransom for their fault.
> (3.1.150–56)[3]

Titus eagerly replies, "With all my heart I'll send the Emperor my hand. /
Good Aaron, wilt thou help to chop it off?" (3.1.160–61). Marcus and Lucius
protest, and Titus pretends to relent; then, while the two of them are off looking for an ax and arguing about which of them will sacrifice his hand, Titus
commands Aaron to chop off his hand, and Aaron willingly complies. As
Titus soon learns however, Aaron has deceived him, and a messenger shortly
arrives bearing the heads of Titus's sons along with Titus's severed hand.

> MESSENGER: Worthy Andronicus, ill art thou repaid
> For that good hand thou sent'st the Emperor.
> Here are the heads of thy two noble sons,
> And here's thy hand in scorn to thee sent back—
> Thy grief their sports, thy resolution mocked,
> That woe is me to think upon thy woes
> More than remembrance of my father's death.
> (3.1.234–40)

Thus far in the Harry Potter series Wormtail has fared better than Titus, for
Voldemort replaces his severed hand with a silver one, though not before

subjecting him to some vicious mockery (645). I suspect, however, that Wormtail will ultimately resemble Titus in other ways as well, for Voldemort always betrays his followers sooner or later.

Soon after Wormtail sacrifices his hand, the scene crescendos to a stunning climax when Voldemort attempts to kill Harry by using the curse that killed Harry's parents and countless others. But Harry fights back, pointing his own wand at Voldemort and using the "Expelliarmus" charm in an attempt to knock Voldemort's wand out of his hand. Neither Harry nor Voldemort is prepared for what happens next, for neither is aware of how profoundly and inextricably their wands are linked, although Harry is aware that the two wands share a common core. As Albus Dumbledore, the headmaster of Hogwarts, will later remind Harry and his godfather, Sirius Black, " 'Harry's wand and Voldemort's wand share cores. Each of them contains a feather from the tail of the same phoenix' " (697), a phoenix wittily named Fawkes that roosts in Dumbledore's office and that saves Harry's life in *Harry Potter and the Chamber of Secrets*. Dumbledore goes on to explain that:

> "[W]hen a wand meets its brother . . . [t]hey will
> not work properly against each other. . . . If, however, the
> owners of the wands force the wands to do battle . . .
> [o]ne of the wands will force the other to regurgitate spells
> it has performed—in reverse. The most recent first . . . and
> then those which preceded it. . . ." (697)

When Harry and Voldemort attempt to engage their wands in battle, each wand emits a burst of light, and then, as Harry and Voldemort struggle to maintain a hold on their vibrating wands, "a narrow beam of [bright, deep gold] light connected the two wands . . ." (663).

> The golden thread connecting Harry and Voldemort
> splintered; though the wands remained connected, a
> thousand more beams arced high over Harry and
> Voldemort, crisscrossing all around them, until they
> were enclosed in a golden, dome-shaped web, a cage
> of light, beyond which [Voldemort's supporters] the
> Death Eaters circled like jackals, their cries strangely
> muffled now. . . . (663–64)

As Harry manages to maintain the connection between his vibrating wand and Voldemort's, Voldemort's wand is forced to recreate, in reverse order, all the spells that it has performed. As a result, Harry sees first a dense, smoky hand ("the ghost of the hand [Voldemort] had made Wormtail") emerge from the tip of the wand, and then the ghostly figures of those whom Voldemort has killed. The first figure to emerge from Voldemort's wand is the last killed: Cedric Diggory, Harry's fellow student at Hogwarts, whom Harry has seen killed only moments before. The wand then produces the ghostlike figures of Voldemort's victims in quick succession: Frank Bryce, Bertha Jorkins, and then Harry's own father and mother, who died thirteen years before while protecting Harry. As the figures emerge, they speak words of encouragement to Harry: " 'Hold on, Harry,' " says the figure of Cedric. " 'Killed me, that one did. . . . You fight him, boy' " urges the ghost of Frank Bryce. " 'Don't let him get you, Harry—don't let go!' " cries the "shadow" of Bertha Jorkins (666). The first three figures begin to circle the enclosure in which Voldemort and Harry confront each other: "[The] shadowy figures began to pace around the inner walls of the golden web, while the Death Eaters flitted around the outside of it . . . and Voldemort's dead victims whispered words of encouragement to Harry, and hissed words Harry couldn't hear to Voldemort" (667).

This scene bears a striking resemblance to a powerful moment in Act 5, scene 3 of Shakespeare's *Richard III*, in which Henry Richmond—soon to be Henry VII—and Richard lie down to sleep in their respective camps on the eve of their decisive battle at Bosworth. As they sleep, the ghosts of Richard's victims enter in turn and circle the stage between the two sleeping figures, cursing Richard and offering words of hope to Richmond. There are eleven ghosts in all, and they too enter in the order in which they were killed, but from first (Prince Edward) to last (Buckingham).

Enter the Ghost of young Prince Edward, son [of] Harry the Sixth, to Richard.
GHOST: (*to Richard*):
      Let me sit heavy on thy soul tomorrow!
      Think, how thou stabbed'st me in my prime of youth
      At Tewkesbury. Despair therefore and die!
      (*To Richmond*) Be cheerful, Richmond, for the wronged souls
      Of butchered princes fight in thy behalf.
      King Henry's issue, Richmond, comforts thee. [*Exit.*]
Enter the Ghost of Henry the Sixth
GHOST: (*to Richard*):
      When I was mortal, my anointed body
      By thee was punched full of deadly holes.
      Think on the Tower and me. Despair and die!
      Harry the Sixth bids thee despair and die!
      (*To Richmond*) Virtuous and holy, be thou conqueror!
      Harry, that prophesied thou should'st be king,
      Doth comfort thee in thy sleep. Live and flourish!
                            [*Exit.*] (5.3.117–30)

One by one, the ghosts of Richard's other victims enter and speak to the sleeping Richard and Richmond. Three of the ghosts tell Richard, "Let me sit heavy on thy soul tomorrow," and all tell him to despair, most cursing him with the phrase "despair and die." All speak words of encouragement and blessing to Richmond, and the names "Henry" and its diminutive "Harry"— names redolent with association in English history and in Shakespeare—resonate throughout the benedictions. The last ghost, Buckingham, speaks a final blessing to Richmond: "God and good angels fight on Richmond's side, / And Richard fall in height of all his pride" (5.3.175–76).

Similarly, the ghosts of Voldemort's victims also give Harry their blessing and what help they can. The last ghosts to appear are the shadows of Harry's father and mother, and at a signal from his father, Harry breaks the connection with Voldemort. The golden cage disappears, "but the shadowy figures of Voldemort's victims did not disappear—they were closing in upon Voldemort, shielding Harry from his gaze . . ." (668). The ghosts delay Voldemort just long enough for Harry to make his escape, back to Hogwarts and, eventually, to safety.[4]

The six chapters that comprise the denouement of *Harry Potter and the Goblet of Fire* have a horrifically nightmarish quality about them, a quality they share with both *Titus Andronicus* and *Richard III*.[5] The haunting atmosphere is due in part to the fact that all three works are concerned with exploring the relationship—the affinity, even—between good and evil. This affinity is always profoundly unsettling to contemplate, but the connection clearly intrigues both Shakespeare and Rowling. Indeed, the idea of a relationship between Harry and Voldemort is proving to be increasingly important in the Harry Potter books. Acocella writes: "[There] is a strange matter—something about the *kinship* of good and evil—that Rowling has been hinting at since the beginning of the series. Harry and Voldemort have a lot in common. . . . There is some connection between these two. (Shades of "Star Wars.") I don't know what Rowling has in mind here. Maybe it's the Miltonic idea of evil as merely good perverted. Or maybe not" (78). Shakespeare's interest in the connection between good and evil underlies all of the history plays. Like Harry and Voldemort, Henry Tudor and Richard III share literal kinship through a convoluted lineage, and Shakespeare presents them, to a certain extent, as the obverse of the other. Richard and Henry hail from the rival lines of York and Lancaster, but Henry Tudor triumphs over the usurper and marries Elizabeth of York, thereby uniting the two families and ending the Wars of the Roses. Whether Harry Potter, like Henry VII, will ultimately defeat his wicked enemy and prove to be the savior of England remains to be seen, but it strikes me as entirely plausible. We already know that names are never accidental in the Harry Potter books: Hermione (who will, I suspect, evoke Shakespeare's Hermione again); Remus Lupin, a werewolf; Sirius Black, whose alter-ego is a black dog; Draco Malfoy, Harry's evil and high-born nemesis; Severus Snape, the dreaded and dreadful potions teacher, who is indeed "severe" but who has also "severed" his former ties with Voldemort; and so on. Harry Potter's own name carries powerful associations with Shakespeare's hero-kings, as we have seen, as well as with English crafts-men-laborers, and indeed with the soil itself—what John of Gaunt calls "This blessed plot, this earth, this realm, this England" in *Richard II* (2.1.50). Harry may well turn out to be both as gracious and as warlike as his Shakespearean namesakes.

The connection between good and evil features prominently in *Titus Andronicus* as well, where it centers specifically on the relationship between parents and children. Titus earns Tamora's hatred by executing her son, and her revenge hinges on the systematic destruction of his children. Titus, in turn, cannot rest until he has avenged his family's wrongs. Even Aaron's wicked-ness is complicated by his paternity; for though he is almost unbelievably evil, he nevertheless proves admirable in his love for his child. Given the fact that the central relationship in Rowling's books is between the orphaned Harry and the parents whom Voldemort killed, her evocation of *Titus Andronicus* and its themes of family destruction and bloody vengeance seems deliberate. Until now, Harry has been too busy defending himself against Voldemort to think of avenging his parents' deaths; but Rowling has been hinting at other deaths to come, and the time of vengeance may well be at hand.

Rumor has it that the fifth volume will be entitled *Harry Potter and the Order of the Phoenix*. I don't want to make too much of this, because Row-ling has changed titles on us before (*Goblet of Fire* was originally entitled *Harry Potter and the Doomspell Tournament*). Nevertheless, the proposed title is tantalizing, given what we know about the link between Harry's and Voldemort's wands. It is also an especially suggestive title for Shakespeare scholars, evoking as it does the Order of the Garter, an elite group of Eliza-bethan nobles dedicated to pursuing the courtly virtues. Acocella observes that "As Harry has grown, he has become more powerful and ambitious and, at the same time, more virtuous" (78). Will Harry, like Hamlet (another Shakespearean hero whose story rests on the themes of vengeance and kin-ship) turn out to be "th'expectancy and rose of the fair state" (*Hamlet*, 3.1.155)? Fans of Harry Potter, and of Shakespeare, can only hope; but we can be confident that whatever Rowling gives us in the next three volumes, they will be rich in every kind of allusion and—thank goodness—thoroughly derivative.

Notes

Throughout this article I am indebted to my son, William Henry Johnson Had-dad, for helping to refresh my memory on various aspects of the Harry Potter books.

1. See *The Winter's Tale*, Act 5, scene 3.
2. Bertha Jorkins is a witch whom Voldemort has tortured for information and killed.
3. All Shakespeare quotations are taken from *The Complete Works of Shakespeare*, 4th ed., ed. David Bevington (New York: Addison Wesley Longman Inc., 1997).
4. In a private communication, Alan C. Dessen pointed out to me that the stage directions that call for each ghost to exit are the work of later editors, and that it is possible that the ghosts remained on stage for the rest of this scene. This staging would increase the similarity to the scene in *Harry Potter and the Goblet of Fire*.
5. One reason why the recent film versions of these plays—Julie Taymor's *Titus* (Fox Searchlight, 1999) and Richard Loncraine's *Richard III* (MGM, 1996)—are effective is because the directors capture the nightmarish atmosphere of each play very succesfully.

Works Cited

Acocella, Joan. "Under the Spell: Harry Potter explained." *The New Yorker*, July 31, 2000: 74–78.

Bevington, David, ed. *The Complete Works of William Shakespeare*. New York: Addison Wesley Longman Inc., 1997, 4th edition.

Rowling, J. K. *Harry Potter and the Chamber of Secrets*. New York: Scholastic, 1999.

———. *Harry Potter and the Goblet of Fire*. New York: Scholastic, 2000.

Works Consulted

Bettelheim, Bruno. *The Uses of Enchantment: The Meaning and Importance of Fairy Tales*. New York: Vintage Books, Random House, 1977.

Propp, Vladimir. *Morphology of the Folktale*. Translated by Laurence Scott. Bloomington: University of Indiana Press, American Folklore Society, 1968.

Rowling, J. K. *Harry Potter and the Sorcerer's Stone*. New York: Scholastic, 1997.

19. Playing with Shakespeare
Making Worlds from Words

JENNIFER LEE CARRELL

Forget poetry, literature, culture, history, and politics: Shakespeare's plays are all about play. Uninhibited, exuberant play.

Since play is all about make-believe, about blowing shining new worlds like bubbles and then—however briefly—walking into them, Shakespeare, you might say, is all about world-making.

In the spring of 1997, I stood at the back of a crowd scattered in bunches across the lawn of Harvard Yard, focusing intently on the monumental stage made by the steps and wide foundation of Memorial Church. The dogwoods were in giggling pink-and-white bloom, and a thin, shivery sun shone through the new leaves of the Yard's huge old trees. Up on the stage, ranged before a row of pillars that Ozymandias would have found imposing, a mysterious flock of fairies had just flown away with all the dangerous slow-motion grace of prehistoric raptors. Now, some rag-tag clowns were earnestly making hash of tragedy as they tried to kill off Pyramus and Thisbe.

Standing at the back of that crowd—five hundred strong—I was weeping, but they were tears of hilarity. The audience was roaring with belly-laughter—but at least they'd seen the spectacle only once. As the director, I'd seen it for weeks. But this *Midsummer Night's Dream* played by Harvard's undergraduate Hyperion Theatre Company was still both eerily beautiful and breath-squeezingly funny.

I am quite sure that I was—and remain—prejudiced in this opinion, but at least I also know that it wasn't mine alone: for several weeks, I found myself approached around the Yard and on Cambridge streets, often by people I didn't know, who said things like "You're the director of that play, aren't you? That's the first time I ever understood Shakespeare," or "I never knew Shakespeare could be that funny—I mean, I knew it was supposed to be, but it just never was."

"It was straight," announced a review passed around the black sophomore class email list. "Did Shakespeare actually write that?!!" the irreverent review went on to ask, answering its own question by declaring "That sh*t is funny as hell!" and "JOLITY. JOLITY. JOLITY."

"easily the best harvard production i have seen," wrote another emailed response, "but i don't think that says enough. it was well cast, hilarious, and beautiful to look at."

Spontaneous, gleeful, flouting all rules of correct writing, punctuation, and even, by some standards, proper manners, these emails left clues as to why this show proved so much fun: but at the time, *Midsummer* was too close for any of us involved to see clearly why it had astonished so many people with delight. From a distance of five years, it's easier to glimpse at least part of the answer: we ignored the rules of adoring Shakespeare. Instead, we took his words up as a game and played with such abandon that we swept our audiences right alongside us.

That Shakespeare is a game of earnest and eagerly generous world-making shared between actors and audience is not an obvious conclusion within either the ivory towers of academia or the bright lights of tradition-bound theater. Weirdly enough, from the late nineteenth to the late twentieth centuries, when Kenneth Branagh's surprise success with *Henry V* in 1989 unleashed a spate of superb Shakespeare films, both institutions came close to adoring Shakespeare right into boring oblivion.

All the time we were rehearsing and performing, I was aware of the marble temple of study known as Widener Library rising directly behind our stage, at the other end of the Yard. At its heart, like the central vault of a Pharoah's pyramid, opens a hushed, tomb-like room that focuses all attention upon a glass-topped table. On display within this altar lie two of the most precious relics of western learning: the first printed edition of the Bible, known as the Gutenberg Bible and the first edition of Shakespeare's collected works, known as the First Folio.

"For worship only. Not for use," the cold surroundings seem to intone in the gravest, priestly voice of Sir Laurence Olivier.

Fancy theatrical productions where everyone's dressed to the nines, sitting stiff and proper in the dark, and determined to enjoy their $50–$80 tickets aren't necessarily much better.

Give me eighteen-year-olds romping in the sun, with their peers lounging on a lawn and hooting with laughter, any day.

Like an old-fashioned fairy-tale princess, the higher we've hoisted Shakespeare on his literary pedestal, the less immediately real his work has seemed. While it's possible to be beautiful and proud from a distance, it's supremely difficult to be either funny or tragic without some urgent sense of flesh-and-blood immediacy.

Lacking details of either biography or staging, all we've got left of Shakespeare are his words. Increasingly, we've granted authenticity and authority to the verbal purity of the printed page, but the more we strive to display these words correctly, the less we play with them. The less we play with them, the more their power dwindles and dries up.

Herein lies the great paradox of Shakespeare worship: At their most powerful, Shakespeare's words are not an end in themselves. They're a means to an end, and that end is storytelling incarnate, the making of a world in which real bodies run their course through a story, imagining and sharing it as they go. On stage or screen, that works out to the difference between play and display.

The two versions of *Romeo and Juliet's* balcony scene filmed by George Cukor in 1936 and Franco Zeffirelli in 1968 make this difference amusingly and startlingly clear.

In the earlier film, Leslie Howard's Romeo prances toward Norma Shearer's Juliet across a neat, glimmering expanse of garden that looks like Hollywood dreaming of the Taj Mahal. Howard tiptoes forward a few steps, then stops, sets, and masterfully delivers two or three lines. The camera briefly cuts to Shearer mooning wordlessly above him in the night, and then it's back to Howard: Move, stop, speak, react, repeat, from beginning to end, presenting the precious verse as if on a silver platter, carefully distinct from both action and reaction.

This is a world made in the finest theatrical tradition to display Shakespeare deftly and devoutly, but beyond its devotion to Shakespearean verse, there isn't a dram of believable passion in it.

Zip forward to Zeffirelli's 1968 film: Leonard Whiting sneaks recklessly across an unruly Tuscan garden, and the viewer sneaks right along with him, watching the bushes lurch as he stumbles, hearing his gasp and fairly sharing his adolescent burst of adrenaline as he glimpses Olivia Hussey sliding into view as young Juliet. As the passions intensify, so does the cause-and-effect intercutting of shots and soundtrack. Words push these characters to move while they speak, and Zeffirelli increasingly focuses attention on the fleeting, apparently spontaneous emotional and physical reactions that the words elicit, rather than on the words themselves. In Zeffirelli's film, the words are one part of a thickly woven world, not the point.

Both imaginatively and emotionally, it is a far more powerful film than Cukor's.

Part of this difference is no doubt due to growing sophistication in point-of-view filming and splicing of soundtrack—but Cukor, who had already made *Little Women* and *Dinner at Eight*, and who would go on to direct *Camille, The Philadelphia Story,* and *My Fair Lady*, was neither novice nor pedestrian when it came to making films. In larger part, the difference between these films stems from a different relative valuation of Shakespeare's words. Cukor displayed them like butterflies pinned to a board; Zeffirelli played them, catching the flash of wings fluttering and floating on a breeze.

First and foremost, Shakespeare's plays are scripts: bare-bones blueprints that can be lifted into all kinds of life. But lifting words from page to stage or screen is a long (and for theater people, addictive) process; most audiences only share in its end-stages.

Many of the greatest twentieth-century playwrights have left detailed stage directions that amount to demands: George Bernard Shaw, Eugene O'Neill, and Samuel Beckett have all scrawled directions that go on for pages, seriously constricting players' freedom to imagine the script as they see fit. Springing from an older, different tradition that did not give much respect to playwrights and had not as yet even dreamed up directors, Shakespeare has proved far more imaginatively generous (whether or not he meant to be or would have been, given the choice). His stage directions are so few and far between as to be virtually nonexistent—and those few that do exist cannot, in any case, be identified with certainty as his.

Many directions, it's true, can be deduced from the dialogue. Lines like "Draw, if you be men" (*Rom.* 1.1.62) and "I was hurt under your arm" (*Rom.* 3.1.103) give a certain shape to *Romeo and Juliet's* fight choreography.[1] At the snickering heart of *Twelfth Night*, when prudish, puritanical Malvolio picks up a stray scrap of paper which he imagines to be a love letter from Olivia and reads "If this fall into thy hand, revolve," theatrical tradition has him spin in unwitting glee (*TN* 2.5.143). Just after acquiring the head of an ass in the magical midst of *A Midsummer Night's Dream*, Bottom's tendency to use words like "nay" and "knavery" fairly begs for some comical, ono-matopoetic neighing and braying (*MND* 3.1.112, 120, 133, 146).

But beyond terse entrances and exits, occasionally expanded to something like "Exit pursued by a bear" (*WT* 3.3.58), explicit stage direction is not a Shakespearean habit. As a result, Shakespeare turns out to be one of the most demanding writers on record, in a different direction from Messrs. Shaw, O'Neill, and Beckett: actors, directors, and sometimes audiences not only all get to join in the theatrical process of world-making—*they have to*.

Beginning rehearsals for a production of Shakespeare is like being handed the dialogue of an epic novel along with the polite demand to return the thing, in five or six weeks' time, if you please, with all the details of narration complete: conjuring up place and period, specific bodies and voices to deliver the words, with actions and absurdities all gracefully worked out and suited, of course, to the most extreme passions human beings can face. It must all make sense, somehow, and it must never, ever be boring.

You have to be borderline crazy to try it.

I was lucky: I learned to play with Shakespeare from some of the finest teachers around, including Marjorie Garber of Harvard, whose quicksilver sense of fun encouraged students to enjoy toying with the many possible meanings of Shakespeare; directors Tina Packer and Dennis Krausnick, the elemental forces behind Shakespeare & Company of Lenox, Massachusetts; and Jane Nichols, actress, acting teacher, Shakespeare & Company faculty member, and extraordinary mistress of clowns.

I learned just as much, in the end, from my students: after earning my Ph.D. in English literature, I was given the luxury of designing a course for Harvard's Freshman Seminar program. In "Shakespeare in Performance," I taught twelve students at a time to analyze Shakespeare's words on the page and various Shakespearean worlds lifted to stage and screen. Then I asked them to do an about-face and work the other way, piecing those words into worlds of their own imagining. We began by close-reading films, learning how films say what they say—looking at details of camera work, editing, sound and music, scene and frame composition, action and movement, choreography, acting, casting, costuming, lighting, and set design. Then we focused on ferreting out the overt and covert implications of what various productions say, discerning the politics, philosophy, and ethics buried within storytelling.

In the three years that I taught this course and a related one in the Expository Writing Program, my students worked (at the rate of four or five per semester) through films including three *Hamlets* variously starring Laurence Olivier, Mel Gibson, and Kenneth Branagh, three *Romeo and Juliets* directed by Cukor, Zeffirelli, and Baz Luhrmann, a pair of *Macbeths* directed by Roman Polanski and Akira Kurosawa (*Throne of Blood*), two *Henry V*'s directed by and starring Olivier and Branagh, a brace of *Othellos* directed by Orson Welles and Oliver Parker as well as a silent third starring Emil Jannings, *Much Ado About Nothing* directed by (and once again starring) Branagh, and three adaptations of *The Tempest*: Paul Mazursky's *Tempest*, Peter Greenaway's *Prospero's Books*, and *Forbidden Planet*. Whenever we could find them close by, we also watched live productions.

Finally, students turned from analysis to creation, using their newly burnished skills to imagine scenes in productions of their own design. The final paper asked students either to start with an idea and build a scene that would convey it, or to start with an image, deduce what its implications might be, and then fill out that picture to create a sharply honed and fully detailed scene with a specific point. For the length of at least one monologue, they performed their productions before the class.

The first year, one hundred students interviewed for the twelve available spots; the twelve who wound up in the class turned out to enjoy tinkering with Shakespeare so much that as the semester drew to a close, they decided to keep up their new pastime, moving from classroom to stage. Thus the Hyperion Theatre Company was born.

To be more exact, freshman Sam Speedie, who began as a straight arrow enamored of neat endings and certainty, and who toted *Sports Illustrated* inside his notebook lest discussions drift toward the dull and the vague, sat up as the lights went down on the American Repertory Theatre's stunning post-colonial *Tempest* and said, "*Let's do it.*" He transformed himself into a visionary founder and tenacious producer of the new student company, badgering students with all kinds of necessary talents into joining, and convincing faculty from young adjuncts like myself to august full professors like Garber to sign on as advisors.

As the opening of Hyperion's first production—*Much Ado About Nothing*—approached, co-directors Monica Henderson and Brett Egan, who were also playing Beatrice and Benedick, came to me for some help. I had no practical notion of how to direct, or even assist in directing. I also had no time to worry about it: I learned in the fiery cauldron of the final weeks of rehearsal.

Shot through with sunlight and laughter, the show was a success that became something of an instant legend among the undergraduates; though I had done no more than help to hold steady the course set by Monica and Brett, I fell deeply in love with the theater's process of play, its endless intense crises and delights.

A year later, I directed Hyperion's spring show of *A Midsummer Night's Dream* from beginning to end.

We were creating a fairy tale, so perhaps it's not surprising that the process kept bringing to mind the musings of another great English world-maker, J. R. R. Tolkien, as he pondered the source of fairy tales' delight. They aren't really about fairies, he decided: They're about building and experiencing make-believe worlds. Again and again, I found myself adapting his language to the subject of Shakespeare, words, and playhouse worlds: "Plays—even Shakespeare's plays—are not in normal English usage stories *about* words and wordplay, but about the worlds in which those words are used and the people who use them. Played well, they contain many things besides the words from which they are made, and the speech and writing that display them: they hold the seas, the sun, the moon, the sky; and the earth, and all things that are in it: tree and bird, water and stone, wine and bread, and ourselves, women and men, when we are enchanted. Plays that are actually concerned primarily with words are relatively rare, and as a rule not very interesting."[2] Admittedly, though, Shakespeare's plays start out nowadays as words, words, words—nothing but words. If these revered and relentless words are to recede from center stage, allowing all the shining and shadowed elements of a full world to billow up around and through them, players and designers have to conjure up actions, costumes, scenery, and sounds that can rise to match and sometimes best Shakespeare's words in importance.

In many of the finest Shakespearean films, the most memorable moments are not only *not* verbal, they're sometimes not even remotely Shakespearean, in the sense of specified or even clearly implied by his words. When they work, though, they are invariably fitting: that is, they convincingly shape or are shaped by genuinely Shakespearean words.

Think of the long tradition of Juliet's hand moving, signaling to the audience her promised return from disguised death to life (a tradition so recognizably iconic that it's parodied in numerous *Frankensteins*); and of Baz Luhrmann's one-upsmanship of this tradition in his *Romeo + Juliet*, as Claire Danes's Juliet stirs in time for Leonardo DiCaprio's Romeo to glimpse it, leaving him to die in ironic agony, realizing his mistake, but unable to alter the progress of poison drunk mere seconds too soon. Think of the slow-motion, close-up and viciously personal blood- and mud-spattered chaos of battle in Branagh's *Henry V*, backed by the eerily focused sounds of single blows grinding through armor and bone, not to mention the grand speechless entrances of the young king cloaked like a prince of darkness as he sweeps in upon his plotting lords, and of the Duke of Exeter, stalking like a burly, armored angel of vengeance into the tight circle of the French court, overripe for a fall.

On the lighter side, think of the young lovers' eyes meeting amid the hormone-driven whirl of dancing in any *Romeo and Juliet*, or Kenneth Branagh's hilariously bumbling bit with the beach chair in his film of *Much Ado About Nothing*, as his habitually suave Benedick is tricked into discovering his passion for razor-tongued Beatrice.

Then there's *Shakespeare in Love* in its entirety, mischievously, cleverly and gorgeously burrowing its way to a romantic comedy that supposedly begets the stage tragedy of *Romeo and Juliet*.

In the alterations, major and minor, that these willfully independent-minded productions have made to Shakespeare, a cry all too often silenced in the classroom becomes audible: *the story's the thing*! Not the words. The story. The brave new worlds the words can make.

To directors and actors, screenwriters and adapters, here's what these films can be heard murmuring under their cinematic breath: Know what story you want to coax these words into telling, and don't lose sight of the shape of that proverbial forest for the infinite flickering of its leaves, much less the trees.

Those words crowding the pages are not there as stone idols or obstacles to be skirted as nimbly or numbly as possible. They are there as raw materials to be tasted, toyed with, tossed about with glee and gravity until they are as comfortable in the mouth as chicken soup or chocolate cake, as necessary and invisible as air, as entertaining, quick, and deftly spun as a juggler's shimmering balls, or as hard-driving as a home-run headed for the moon.

They are malleable, at least in the early stages of world-making. Their first job is to join up with your imagination to spark a new world into being.

Find out why each flowering phrase or abrupt exclamation must be flung out just at a particular moment, in those particular words, in a certain manner and tone of voice. Find out what effect those words have on everyone and everything present: Just as there are no minor characters in a Shakespeare play (only complex characters whose stories do not happen to sit in a given play's limelight), there are likewise no passive listeners on a lively Shakespearean stage. Every phrase is a cue ball that scatters the company of billiard-ball actors anew.

Consider your audience. Does a joke now need a footnote or a mini-lecture to get a laugh? Substitute an intelligible word for that obsolete one, or cut the whole unfunny thing altogether. If the dramatic tension builds better if you shift a speech or even a whole scene from here to there, by all means shift it.

There's plenty of room here (and in many professional productions still a crying need) for scholarly excavations of various words' many layered connotations: given half a chance, fine actors, who tend to be wizards with words, can incorporate such subtleties into mannerisms and expressions of rank, conflict, and romance.

Gradually, as rehearsals go on, a curious but crucial tide should begin to ebb. As the scenes wake to new life and a kaleidoscopic world begins to settle into shape, the spotlit strength of those all-powerful words should begin subside. It's not as if they ever become unimportant. It's just that they begin to engage in their new-made surroundings more fairly, as equals—rarely, if ever, forcing to mind their earlier pride of place as sole founders, preservers, commanders and creators.

This job of marshaling antique words into shimmering, urgent worlds may seem alternately like herding cats or squeezing water from stone, but in the theater, on a film set, or even in a classroom, you won't have to do it all on your own—you shouldn't even try. As a director, you may feel like a ghost-novelist speed-writing from stiff and skeletal dialogue, but unlike that solitary soul, your characters can stop mid-sentence, step out of their roles and talk back to you, suggesting a much better way to proceed. They can do exactly what you ask, quite beautifully, and then just when you think you're satisfied, they impishly improvise—and suddenly your finest plans spin into scenes far more sublime or silly than you—and quite possibly Shakespeare himself—could ever have dreamed up alone.

In rehearsal for Hyperion's *Midsummer Night's Dream*, Will Burke as the fairy king Oberon more than once gave spontaneous performances of such inspired hilarity, cruelty, lyricism, eager mischief, and lust that he sent his sparse house of fellow actors and crew into paroxysms of laughter and chills. His improvisations were neither precisely repeatable nor sometimes reputable enough to dish out on stage, but they rank as some of the finest theater I ever hope to witness. Shaped up and toned down, his sudden, silly dance of invisibility (after which he stood forth in a Superman pose and announced with pride to the startled crowd, "I am invisible!"), and his lascivious fantasy of Titania asleep and vulnerable on her bank of wild thyme became comic linchpins of the show. In the often interminable scene that draws the Athenian lovers together in the third act's enchanted woods, Will's Oberon and Nick Parrillo's Puck twined themselves together in disguise as an oak tree and began a magical, macho contest for control of the confused and fickle mortals. Almost entirely without words, they transformed their characters from mere witnesses to central players in that act's shenanigans.

That's the joy of rehearsal rooms at their best: ideally, they're big, safe, communal playpens, where no idea is greeted as stupid or too silly, and where quite a few are strong enough to make their way on stage.

To audiences and students, ready-made productions whisper a similar message: come play with us. Not on your knees, ready to worship unchanging scripture nailed down to the one true meaning, never to be questioned. Come with your mind and heart open, your belly ready for laughter and your eyes for tears.

You may think you know and love *Hamlet* or *Romeo and Juliet* or *A Midsummer Night's Dream*, each new production will tease, but not *this* one. Not yet . . . though in two or three hours time, we hope that you will.

Meanwhile, we dare you to play.

Notes

1. All Shakespearean quotations are taken from *The Riverside Shakespeare*, ed. G. Blakemore Evans (Boston: Houghton Mifflin, 1974).
2. Adapted and paraphrased from J. R. R. Tolkien, "On Fairy Stories," *The Tolkien Reader* (New York: Ballantine, 1966), 9.

20. Descending Shakespeare

Toward a Theory of Adaptation for Children

HOWARD MARCHITELLO

In the preface to a collection of adaptations of Shakespeare for children, E. Nesbit's narrator describes a scene at an inn on the evening following a visit to Shakespeare's house in Stratford in which children are gathered about a table "poring over a big volume of the Master's plays;" the narrator, with eyes "fixed on the fire" and mind "wandering happily in the immortal dreamland people by Rosalind and Imogen, Lear and Hamlet," is roused by a sigh: " 'I can't understand a word of it,' said Iris." The children, it turns out, cannot read the plays. In response, the narrator declares that she will tell them the story:

> In truth it was not easy to arrange the story simply. Even with the recollection of Lamb's tales to help me I found it hard to tell the "Midsummer Night's Dream" in words that these little ones could understand. But presently I began the tale, and then the words came fast enough. When the story was ended, Iris drew a long breath.
>
> "It is a lovely story," she said; "but it doesn't look at all like that in the book."
>
> "It is only put differently," I answered. "You will understand when you grow up that the stories are the least part of Shakespeare."
>
> "But it's the stories *we* like," said Rosamund.[1]

In response to this defense of "story" and after the children's pleas ("Why don't you write the stories for us so that we can understand them, just as you told us that, and then, when we are grown up, we shall understand the plays so much better" [9]), the narrator—like Nesbit herself—undertakes to write her own adaptations. But, as the narrator has already indicated, the stories she—again, like Nesbit herself—is able to write constitute only "the least part of Shakespeare." I would like to use this anecdote about Shakespeare, children's fascination with stories, and the genesis of a writer's project as a point of departure for my discussion of adaptations of Shakespeare for children. I do so in part based upon my sense that we need to theorize more precisely what is meant by the phrase "Shakespeare for children" and by the largely-mystified term "adaptation." Adapting Shakespeare for children is not only far more complex than is generally believed (by typical adult readers, at least), but it is at the same time an intensive labor that hides its own traces. As a consequence, the politics of adaptation have generally remained undertheorized.

In the most obvious sense, Nesbit's "least of Shakespeare" corresponds to the story of the play at hand and this story, in turn, corresponds to the narrative content of the given play. But what is the nature of this "content" that emerges as that part of Shakespeare that, while "least," is simultaneously the *most* transmittable? Is the "Shakespeare" that is abstracted in adaptation largely a matter of this content? While the "content" of the Shakespeare play—that which in adaptations is repeated or transmitted principally as plot (in the non-technical sense)—is the most immediately obvious and therefore most unproblematically accessible feature of the plays for new or young readers, it is also the most traditional element of Shakespeare. And yet, our understanding of Shakespeare today is more complete, more sophisticated, and more nuanced in large part because we no longer privilege—or even trust—"content" in the ways we have historically. If we consider the challenges to the "traditional Shakespeares" that collectively have served to produce "our Shakespeare," then we would have to look at the effects on criticism of numerous counter-hegemonic discourses, including feminism, new historicism, cultural materialism, post-colonialism, and the new textualism. If "our Shakespeare" has diverged from the one(s) we inherited from previous critical traditions (Romantic, transcendent, new critical, and so on), this is due largely to the demands on our attention made by gender, historicism, race, and textuality. In other words, what we have learned over the last two decades is that "Shakespeare" has become untenable. And this is why our understanding of Shakespeare is being revised; but this necessary revision is confined largely to the work of scholars and critics and teachers. And though this is in itself clearly a valuable, and even indispensable labor, one may well wonder at what point these revisions might enter the popular imagination. Like the Shakespeare of such films as *Shakespeare in Love*, the Shakespeare commonly adapted for young readers enters popular culture, but the image thus projected is merely contemporary and not necessarily *new* in the ways our recent critical work would enable.

What provides for this distinction, then, between the "new" Shakespeare of criticism and theory on the one hand, and the "old" Shakespeare of adaptation on the other, would seem to be an essentially conservative reliance in adaptation upon the transmission of narrative content as embodied in plot.

When one reads Shakespeare for children in which the language (poetics) has been subjected to the most rigorous re-negotiation (which typically means its elimination, sometimes wholesale), what stands as the most thoroughly "Shakespearean" feature of the adaptation is the plot of the play it adapts. Since Shakespearean language and poetics are typically understood as obstacles to comprehension and therefore largely set aside, what emerges in the adaptation is the plot of the given play. It is the plot—approximated through the various practices and techniques of abridgement, summary, and substitution—that enables the adaptations to refer both themselves and their readers to the play.[2] One of the more striking ironies here is the fact that a great number of Shakespeare's plots, if by "plot" we mean something like the story a particular play tells (and a story, moreover, of the kind demanded by Rosamund and the other children represented in Nesbit's collection) are in fact not Shakespeare's but rather the result of creative borrowing—*adaptation*, one could say—by Shakespeare from the works of a variety of other authors. In this sense, then, the stories are indeed the least part of Shakespeare because they are the least Shakespearean.

In his afterword to the recently published edition of Nesbit's adaptations, *The Best of Shakespeare*, Peter Hunt observes that Nesbit, like Mary and Charles Lamb before her, discovered that "paring the flesh of Shakespeare's inimitable verse and prose from the plays can leave you with an unmanageable excess of plot, and there are times in her paraphrases . . . where little else is visible."[3] This statement points to a number of issues I take to be critically important to the various practices of adapting Shakespeare plays for children, among them: the notion of an essential inimitableness of Shakespeare's poetics; the idea of adaptation as a matter of the related work of excision and paraphrase; and the problematical status of plot, which in such adaptations threatens to become "excessive." Taken together, these issues both characterize the aesthetic dangers associated with adaptations of Shakespeare for children and map out the field for discussions of the informing model of the Shakespearean text and its subsequent transmission in adaptations. Is the Shakespearean play fundamentally a matter of poetics? of plot? What is the relation between the two and can one properly stand (or, withstand) the "paring" away of the other?

The answers to these questions may well lie precisely in the nature of the relation posited by the adaptation itself between the original and the re-telling—an issue that has long been overlooked. Though Hunt points to such infelicities as occur in Nesbit's text (he identifies, for example, a certain tendency toward linguistic anachronism), these amount to little and lead Hunt to only a gentle criticism: "Nesbit's versions may occasionally be uneven . . ." (108). After one further, and perhaps tentative, comment—that "it may well be that they achieved their aim of helping children toward the 'real thing' "— Hunt concludes his remarks with a passage from Nesbit's version of *Romeo and Juliet*: "And the tale of all they said, and the sweet music their voices made together, is all set down in a golden book, where you children may read it for yourselves someday."[4]

This gesture toward the "original" (enacted by both Hunt and by Nesbit) that is positioned as simultaneously both the "source" and the "destination" of adaptations for children has a double genealogy that I would like to trace here. On the one hand, this referential maneuver derives from a traditional understanding of the relation posited between signifier and signified; on the other hand, it derives from idealist (as opposed to materialist) conceptions of Shakespeare and the Shakespearean text. In terms of the first branch of this genealogy, the adaptation is intended, above all, to direct young readers to its greater original—the Shakespearean text. This is an entirely conventional maneuver that functions, at least in part, as a justification for writing such adaptations. There are any number of instances of this gesture, from the earliest works adapting Shakespeare for child readers to our own contemporary versions. It is present in Mary and Charles Lamb's 1807 *Tales from Shakespeare*: "The following Tales are meant to be submitted to the young reader as an introduction to the study of Shakespeare."[5] It is present in Marchette Chute's 1987 *Stories from Shakespeare*, the "purpose" of which is first "to give the reader a preliminary idea of each of the thirty-six plays by telling their stories and explaining in a general way the intentions and points of view of the characters," and secondly, to "open a door that to some people is closed and give a glimpse, however slight, of what lies beyond."[6] And it is present, though more ambiguously, in Julius Lester's 1995 book, *Othello, A Novel*: "It is my hope that those who might feel intimidated by Shakespeare will gain sufficient confidence from this exposure to his language to read the original for themselves."[7]

But what is the mechanism of the adaptation that would allow young readers eventual access to Shakespeare's plays? Or, to phrase this same question in another way: what is Shakespearean about the adaptation for children? What is the "story" of *Othello*, for example, that allows for its successful transmission in two radically different textual forms: in Shakespeare's play and in a children's writer's abbreviated version?

Borrowing terminology from the Russian Formalists, we can say that a given adaptation of Shakespeare for children is a narrative that tells a certain "story" (*fabula*) and that the discursive arrangement by which the story is told is its "plot" (*sjužet*).[8] Thus it becomes clear that any one story could be re-told with any number of variations in the arrangement of its particular events; each one re-telling would then constitute a different plot, but all of them would nevertheless narrate the same story. The terms *fabula* and *sjužet* can be helpful in describing the largely-obscured and complicated work that an adaptation represents—particularly when we consider the intentional nature of the claims concerning the relation of adaptation to source-destination. Any given adaptation of a Shakespeare play—and I mean the term "adaptation" in its broadest sense to include what is in fact a range of incarnations: abridgements, paraphrases, re-tellings, summaries, and reconceptualizations or novelizations—intends to retell the story of the play at hand. *Othello*, for example, re-appears as "Othello," the story (as Leon Garfield has it) of "a great general, a man in whom the state of Venice has put all its trust, a black man of immense dignity and splendour who is brought to madness, murder and suicide by the skillful lies of the lieutenant he trusts and calls 'honest Iago.' "[9] Although even a passage as apparently expository as this necessarily represents a certain degree of interpretation (Garfield will hold only Iago responsible for Othello's fall), this opening moment is recognizable as constituting in a most distilled and abridged form the *fabula* of *Othello*, and while there are necessarily great differences between Garfield's abridgment and the *Othello* one reads in the Oxford or Arden edition, for example, there is a corresponding and perhaps more surprising set of differences on the level of *sjužet*—its plot. So, for example, Garfield's version begins in an altogether unfamiliar fashion:

> *The curtain rises on a chapel. Othello the Moor, commander of all the forces of Venice, is to marry Desdemona. But it is a wedding that causes more rage than joy. Not only to Desdemona's father, Brabantio, but to Iago, Othello's ensign.*
> IAGO (*watching Desdemona and Othello*) I do hate him as I hate hell's pains. (*They kiss.*) O, you are well-tuned now! But I'll set down the pegs that make this music, as honest as I am.
> *Iago rushes through the dim and torchlit streets of Venice. He reaches Brabantio's house and bangs on the door.*
> IAGO Signior Brabantio, ho! Awake!
>
> (Garfield, 13)

The theory that underlies this freedom or license with *sjužet* depends upon an understanding of the *fabula* itself as communicable outside *sjužet*—or rather, independently of a particular *sjužet*. Indeed, not only the success of any particular adaptation, but precisely the viability of adaptation altogether depends upon just this theory.

The second branch of the genealogy identified above derives from the informing notion or idea of Shakespeare and the nature of the Shakespearean text itself that reside behind a given adaptation. The story of *Othello* that Garfield's adaptation tells constitutes only one of the narratives that the adaptation conveys—we can identify it as *fabula*$_1$ / *sjužet*$_1$. There is, at the same time, a second narrative—which we can designate *fabula*$_2$ / *sjužet*$_2$—that tells the story of the presiding figures of both Shakespeare and the Shakespearean text that are present in the adaptation, but only to the extent that they are rendered absent or erased. Even as the gesture toward the "true Plays of Shakespeare" (as Mary Lamb wrote) is conventional, so too is the presiding figure of Shakespeare as the informing genius. One could cite many pertinent examples here, including the great and wholly unqualified praise offered by Chute: "William Shakespeare was the most remarkable storyteller that the world has ever known. . . . In all the world of storytelling, his is the greatest name."[10] Similar praise for the very figure of the transcendent Shakespeare constructed by tradition is found in Lester's *Othello* where, in the introduction, he describes Shakespeare's profound ability to access a universal and transcendent human nature: "In the characters of William Shakespeare's plays we find vivid representations of the inner human landscape that is part of all of us. Romeo and Juliet, Hamlet and Ophelia, Macbeth and Lady Macbeth, Othello and Iago, Julius Caesar and Brutus, and other characters transcend the plays to which they belong. Romeo and Juliet, for example, are the purest examples of romantic lovers in the English language, and at some time, most of us have imagined ourselves to be one or the other." (Lester, ix)

These and similar professions of adoration of Shakespeare that frequently attend or preface adaptations of the plays for children and that serve as their justification derive from the romantic definition of Shakespeare as the repository of Western cultural and aesthetic value—a conception that is increasingly difficult to maintain given the current critical re-evaluation of such issues as author/authorship, canon formation, and, for that matter, the politics of cultural and aesthetic valuation itself. In other words, the Shakespeare that informs these texts is precisely the Shakespeare that has been so vigorously de-centered and de-stabilized as a transcendent category over the past twenty years within adult early modern literary studies. The same holds true for the conception of the Shakespearean text that both underwrites and at the same time serves as the objective for a great many adaptations for children. In a manner of speaking, the new textual studies of Shakespeare and textuality have served to dislodge the referent of these "adaptations-as-signifiers."

If this set of assertions holds, if it is the case that we derive from these adaptations two stories—the $fabula_1$ and $sju\check{z}et_1$ story of Othello, say, the "great general," and the $fabula_2$ and $sju\check{z}et_2$ story of the transcendence of "Shakespeare"—then a further consequence is, I would argue, that not only do the adaptations represent these "manifest" and "latent" stories, but they manage to reverse their priority such that the $fabula_2$ and $sju\check{z}et_2$ story of "Shakespeare" becomes primary—the *story* the adaptations tell—while the $fabula_1$ and $sju\check{z}et_1$ story is assigned a secondary position or status—the plot of the adaptation. What we would conventionally think of as the story of *Othello* (that which we read) becomes the plot for the story of "Shakespeare" (that which we would repeat).

In an attempt to locate adaptations of Shakespeare for children that respond in new and powerful ways to this particular challenge—texts, that is,

that establish what I will call a new ethics of adaptation—I find myself turning to the work of Lois Burdett, both in the books in her "Shakespeare Can
Be Fun!" series and in her teaching more generally.[11] Burdett's work suggests that there are two issues that are fundamentally at stake in Shakespeare
for children: the first is the story communicated by the play, and the second is
the story we produce in response to the (story communicated by) the play. In
establishing these two related issues, Burdett introduces an even more important effect: the distancing of the content of the Shakespearean story and the
subsequent privileging of the stories we choose to tell. It is this liberating
gesture, as I see it, that enables the wonderful work Burdett does with her
grade two and grade three students. In their various projects, what becomes
primary is the child's relation to Shakespeare and not Shakespeare as such:
Shakespeare not as pedagogical object but rather as pedagogical site for the
stories we would like to help others to tell. A similar claim could be made for
Marcia Williams's *Mr. William Shakespeare's Plays* in which what could be
considered the monological nature of more conventional adaptations or retellings is replaced by a staged polyvocality—a gesture that similarly serves
to displace the "content" of the plays and offer instead models for multiple
points of entry into and understanding of the plays as sites for the social construction of meanings.[12] From this perspective, any ambivalence about the
larger project of adapting Shakespeare for young readers will find resolution
not in suspension of, but rather in an even greater investment in, the production of Shakespeare for children by both writers and critics/scholars—precisely because every point of entry, like every story we would tell, is also a
point of departure.

Notes

1. E. Nesbit, *The Best of Shakespeare*. Introduction by Iona Opie, Afterword by
   Peter Hunt (New York and Oxford: Oxford University Press, 1997), 8–9. Subsequent references appear parenthetically in the text of this essay.
2. Although I haven't the space to expand my discussion of adaptations to
   include it here, I would like nevertheless to note that among the variety of
   forms that adaptations of Shakespeare's plays for children take—poems, tales,
   picture books, and plays (to name perhaps the most typical)—one in particular
   both represents an especially important form for adaptations today and at the
   same time poses some of the most challenging and difficult questions about
   textual, literary, and cultural reproduction and the politics of adaptation: the
   novelization. While there are a number of important characteristics of the
   Shakespeare novels (as I have come to call these texts) that serve to distinguish
   (alienate) them from Shakespeare's plays as their early modern "originals"—
   for example (and most conspicuously) they have narrators—they are entirely
   unique among adaptations in that they constitute not abbreviated but rather
   self-consciously *expansive* versions of their "source" plays. Rather than a logic

of deletion necessary to the transmission of the Shakespearean "original" in abridged form, the Shakespeare novels deploy a counter-logic of *dilation* in which a "striking out" is replaced by "folding in," in which cancellation is replaced by supplement. And yet, even as these novels stand on their own as distinct and separate aesthetic productions (hence the frequently-applied term "re-imagining") they nevertheless simultaneously re-inscribe their position within a self-delineated referential status: as "novelizations" they function—at least on one level—as signifiers to the Shakespearean signified. This topic constitutes the focus of another discussion of Shakespeare adaptations for children in which I am currently engaged.

3. Hunt in Nesbit, 106. Subsequent references appear in the text of this essay.
4. This passage, in spite of its gesture toward narrative closure, actually occurs in the middle of Nesbit's "Romeo and Juliet"—at the moment *and in place of* the lovers's one night together. While this solution has the immediate value of referring young readers to the Shakespearean original, it also allows Nesbit a tidy way of censoring a scene some might deem inappropriate for young readers (Nesbit, 13).
5. The Lambs' preface to *Tales from Shakespeare* (New York: Signet, 1986) concludes with a more complete—and a more completely ideological—formulation:

> What these Tales shall have been to the *young* readers, that and much more it is the writers' wish that the true Plays of Shakespeare may prove to them in older years—enrichers of the fancy, strengtheners of virtue, a withdrawing from all selfish and mercenary thoughts, a lesson of all sweet and honourable thoughts and actions, to teach courtesy, benignity, generosity, humanity: for of examples, teaching these virtues, his pages are full. (vii)

For a discussion of particular features of the ideologies informing *Tales from Shakespeare*, especially the gender-specific nature of the constructed reader of the *Tales*, see Jean I. Marsden, "Shakespeare for Girls: Mary Lamb and Tales from Shakespeare," *Children's Literature* 17 (1989): 47–63.

6. Marchette Chute, *Stories from Shakespeare* (New York: Meridian, 1987), 10.
7. Julius Lester, *Othello: A Novel* (New York: Scholastic, 1995), Introduction, xiv. Lester continues, identifying a second—though perhaps primary—ambition: "It is also my hope that those who are comfortable with Shakespeare will find a new pleasure in this reimagining" (xvi). Subsequent references appear parenthetically in the text of this essay.
8. For an important and serious reassessment of what I would call the relative cultural prestige of plot, see Peter Brooks in *Reading for the Plot Reading for the Plot: Design and Intention in Narrative* (New York: Knopf, 1984; rpt. Cambridge, MA: Harvard University Press, 1992):

> "Reading for plot," we learned somewhere in the course of our schooling, is a low form of activity. Modern criticism, especially in its Anglo-American branches, has tended to take its valuations from study of the

lyric, and when it has discussed narrative has emphasized questions of "point of view," "tone," "symbol," "spatial form," or "psychology." The texture of narrative has been considered most interesting insofar as it approached the density of poetry. Plot has been disdained as the element of narrative that least sets off and defines high art—indeed, plot is that which especially characterizes popular mass-consumption literature: plot is why we read *Jaws*, but not Henry James. (4)

9. Leon Garfield, *Shakespeare, the Animated Tales*: *Othello* (London: Heinemann, 1994), 13. Subsequent references appear parenthetically in the text of this essay.
10. Chute, 7. Also important for this discussion is Chute's praise of Shakespeare's poetry, which she seems to understand as wholly separable from the "stories" of the plays:

> Shakespeare told his stories for the theatre and so he used verse. And the world is fortunate that he did, for he is England's greatest poet. He combines Chaucer's clearness and Milton's magnificence with Keats' magic and the lovely singing line that has been the glory of so many English poets. He could write about battlefields or country flowers, witches or children, dying heroes or young lovers or chatty old men, and could do it in poetry which is not only perfect in itself but which joins hands with the storytelling, so that the two go together like the words and music of a song. (8)

11. Titles in Burdett's "Shakespeare Can Be Fun!" series (Willowdale, Ontario and Buffalo, NY: Firefly Books) include: *A Child's Portrait of Shakespeare* (1995), *A Midsummer Night's Dream* (1997), *The Tempest* (1999), and *Hamlet* (2000).
12. Marcia Williams, *Mr. William Shakespeare's Plays*. (London: Walker Books, 1998).

Bibliography

Peter Brooks. *Reading for the Plot Reading for the Plot*: *Design and Intention in Narrative* (New York: Knopf, 1984; rpt. Cambridge, MA: Harvard University Press, 1992).

Lois Burdett. *A Child's Portrait of Shakespeare*; "Shakespeare Can Be Fun!" series. Willowdale, Ontario and Buffalo, NY: Firefly Books, 1995.

———. *A Midsummer Night's Dream*; "Shakespeare Can Be Fun!" series. Willowdale, Ontario and Buffalo, NY: Firefly Books, 1997.

———. *Hamlet*; "Shakespeare Can Be Fun!" series. Willowdale, Ontario and Buffalo, NY: Firefly Books, 2000.

———. *The Tempest*; "Shakespeare Can Be Fun!" series. Willowdale, Ontario and Buffalo, NY: Firefly Books, 1999.

Marchette Chute. *Stories from Shakespeare*. New York: Meridian, 1987.

Leon Garfield. *Shakespeare, the Animated Tales: Othello.* London: Heinemann, 1994.

Mary and Charles Lamb. *Tales from Shakespeare.* New York: Signet, 1986.

Julius Lester. *Othello: A Novel.* New York: Scholastic, 1995.

Jean I. Marsden. "Shakespeare for Girls: Mary Lamb and Tales from Shakespeare," *Children's Literature* 17 (1989): 47–63.

E. Nesbit. *The Best of Shakespeare.* Introduction by Iona Opie, Afterword by Peter Hunt. New York and Oxford: Oxford University Press, 1997.

Marcia Williams. *Mr. William Shakespeare's Plays.* London: Walker Books, 1998.

III.   Pedagogy and Performance

21.   The Bard for Babies

Shakespeare, Bettelheim, and the Reggio Emilia Model of Early Childhood Education

SHEILA CAVANAGH

My son Davis came to Shakespeare at an early age. In the womb, he encountered the Folger Shakespeare Library, the Royal Shakespeare Company, the Georgia Shakespeare Festival, and countless video productions and classroom presentations on Shakespearean drama. His first airplane trip, at the age of three months, took him to the Shakespeare Association meeting in Washington, D. C. His passion for the bard, therefore, may not be surprising, but the range of his Shakespearean knowledge and his enthusiasm for Shakespeare's plays is noteworthy nonetheless. Now three, he is conversant with about a dozen plays, several of the related ballets and three Shakespearean operas.[1] He enlists his friends as performers in his productions of the plays, corrects his father when he playfully misquotes famous lines, plans his own operatic versions of *A Midsummer Night's Dream* and *Macbeth*, and begs to see Shakespearean videos as a "special treat." When Georgia Tech cancelled its production of "Romeo and Juliet on Ice," he was inconsolable. In this essay, I will describe my incorporation of Shakespeare into Davis's education at home. Loosely following the educational model of Reggio Emilia, I have provided Davis with a range of Shakespearean materials and encouraged his interest, but the primary motivation has clearly come from him.[2] In this discussion, I will begin by offering a brief overview of the Reggio educational philosophy, then I will detail some of the ways that Shakespeare has become part of Davis's life. I will also speculate on possible reasons for the apparent positive results emanating from this exposure.

"Reggio Emilia" is the term associated with an educational approach used in numerous preschools in Italy and America. Drawn from the practices and philosophical principles developed by Loris Malaguzzi in Italy after the end of the Second World War, the Reggio approach is both "child centered and teacher directed" (*Hundred Languages*, 221). Reggio teachers engage students in complex projects that develop out of subjects that already intrigue these pupils. Thus, if a group of students demonstrates a fascination with pirates, the teacher will help them create a module that capitalizes on this interest, using it as a means to develop additional intellectual and physical skills. According to educator Baji Rankin, Reggio teachers draw the initial idea for a project from the students, then "return it to them in a way that would generate observations, questions, suggestions, hypotheses, and set the initial direction of the project work" (*Hundred Languages*, 193). The pirate topic, for example, might initiate a variety of lessons in history, geography, and art, but would also lead to physical explorations through dramatic play or playground activities. As part of this educational strategy, Reggio Emilio teachers involve their pupils in the planning and the execution of each instructional module.

This philosophy has helped guide the introduction of Shakespeare into our household. Davis and Shakespeare became involved initially through serendipity. Horrified by the prospect of a second ice storm in two weeks, I grabbed videotapes of the *Hamlet* ballet, the *Macbeth* ballet, the "Shakespeare Dance Trilogy," and Gonoud's *Romeo and Juliet* opera off my office shelf so that we would have something to watch if we couldn't go out. Davis had seen the *Nutcracker* a few months before and had always loved music, so bringing more ballet and opera into the house made sense, particularly since we didn't watch or own any traditional children's movies. Davis insisted on watching each of these films and over the next few days, he became completely entranced by the staging, costuming, music, and stories. In keeping with the Reggio model, it seemed appropriate to encourage this interest, so Shakespeare became a regular part of our experience together.

Fortunately, available resources are bountiful. As readers of this volume know, Lois Burdett and Bruce Coville each have a wonderful series of Shakespeare books for children and we have acquired several of these. Initially, however, we started with Michael Bender's *All the World's A Stage: A Pop-up Biography of William Shakespeare* because it includes a scene from *A Midsummer Night's Dream* and provides a number of pictures of the Globe. Staging practices remain a dominant interest of Davis's, so this pop-up book has offered a useful way to describe how the stage is set up, where the audience sits, where musicians might be located, and many of the other questions this inquisitive preschooler generates. The Reggio philosophy supports the cultivation of children's physical and artistic skills in conjunction with their intellectual growth; thus, I have also used this curiosity about staging to work with Davis's fine motor skills and spatial awareness. After spending some time reading and discussing the Globe pictures in Bender's book, for instance, we were able to locate a model Globe that did not require complicated assembly. Although Davis is not at an age where he can complete such a task independently or expeditiously, he enjoys doing such projects in short sessions with supervision. Accordingly, we built our own Globe, which works well for the many puppet versions of *Macbeth, Romeo and Juliet, The Taming of the Shrew*, and *Hamlet* that fill our days. Costumes for live versions of the plays and many of these puppets have been constructed at home also, so that this love of theater continues to fulfill a wide range of educational objectives.

Another of our first purchases was designed for much older children, but this has not diminished its value. Margaret Early's adaptation of *Romeo and Juliet* is beautifully illustrated with colorful medieval images. The bright, detailed pictures depict key scenes from the play, such as Romeo's meeting with Juliet, his duel with Tybalt, the young couple's separation, and Juliet's consumption of the poison. Although the text is too dense even for this avid fan, he is familiar enough with the story to enjoy going through the book together, identifying the sequence of events, and discussing a myriad of questions and problems associated with the play, such as: Why don't the families get along? Why is Tybalt so angry? Why is Juliet engaged to Paris when she's in love with Romeo? Why is Juliet put in the crypt? Why doesn't Romeo know that she is only pretending to be dead? As the months have progressed, his questions have become more complicated and astute, while the play never seems to lose its appeal.

This fascination with *Romeo and Juliet* has also prompted some responses that appear to mirror Bruno Bettelheim's theories regarding the importance of fairy tales in the psychological and emotional development of young children. Although the methods that Bettelheim used in his own practice have come under attack since his death,[3] many of the observations he offers in *Fairy Tales and the Uses of Enchantment* seem parallel to my son's interaction with Shakespeare's plays, particularly in connection with the tragic lovers from Verona. This correlation with Bettelheim's rubrics became increasingly apparent following Davis's first encounter with a live Shakespeare performance. After overhearing Davis performing Shakespeare on the playground, a couple of the teachers at his preschool asked whether he was ready for a traditional production, since they wanted to invite him to the New American Shakespeare Company's performance of *Romeo and Juliet*. Given that he had already been to several concerts and ballets of comparable length, this outing seemed worth a try. Unfortunately, there is a lot of shouting and physical violence in this play and it was too much for a small boy with sensitive ears. Almost as soon as the sword fighting started, he asked to leave, although he unsuccessfully lobbied to return when he was halfway home. We had many discussions about the fighting and its choreography on the ride back and he talked primarily about how frightening it was for him.

By the next day, however, he began to incorporate these scenes into his pretend play and talked about the fights frequently.[4] Soon after, while mounting a production on the playground, he remembered these incidents when he ran into a casting dilemma. After he assigned the roles of Romeo and Juliet, one young friend announced, "I'm a cowboy, bang, bang, bang." Davis paused only for a second, before taking this recalcitrance into stride and determining, "O.K., we'll call you Tybalt. You can be one of the families who don't get along." The play, in abbreviated form of course, then went on without a hitch. Unfortunately, however, within a few days, Davis's own swordplay got out of hand. In his apparent efforts to come to terms with the violence he had witnessed, this normally peaceful boy began to engage his friends in sword battles, often without their prior knowledge or consent. While this activity accords perfectly with Bettelheim's contention that fairy tales (or Shakespeare, I would argue) help children grapple with the recognition of "the propensity of all men [sic] for acting aggressively, asocially, selfishly, out of anger and anxiety" (7), it seemed inappropriate for group play and we finally restricted sword fighting to evenings with daddy. Nevertheless, Shakespeare, like Bettleheim's fairy tales, "confronts the child squarely with the basic human predicaments" (8). Unlike many children's stories, where good always triumphs and evil characters generally reform, Shakespeare's plays offer a much more complex view of the world, wherein, as Bettleheim notes, "good and evil are omnipresent in life and the propensities for both are present in every man" (9). Notably, the Reggio model offers a similar interpretation of the malice in fairy tales, with some educators arguing that characters such as the wolf in "Little Red Riding Hood" enable children to "understand and learn how to cope with their own and others' feelings" (226). Both Bettelheim and Reggio teachers, therefore, suggest that the frightening aspects of fairy tales provide valuable fodder for emotional growth.

Davis's interaction with Shakespeare suggests that this theory holds true with these plays also. Although he has only seen the ballet, operatic, and picture book versions of *Romeo and Juliet*, his simultaneous attraction and revulsion toward the fighting and the deaths indicates how he has assimilated these aspects of the drama into his emotional development. Over the past several months, we have engaged in increasingly complicated discussions about death and dying, pretense, the difference between acting mean and being mean, and the distinction between performing a role on stage and what an actor is like in real life.[5] He often asks whether the "bad" characters "turn friendly" at the end,[6] just as he repeatedly reminds me that the angry or violent characters are really just actors pretending to behave this way. Similarly, when he was casting a production of *Twelfth Night*, he forgot Toby's name, referring instead to "the man who drinks too much alcohol." He then asked a series of questions about what it means to drink too much and why someone would do it. Although I am not a professional psychologist, it seems obvious that Davis uses these plays in part to make sense of difficult and frightening aspects of his world. Since he knows that they are not "real," he creates a buffer zone to facilitate discussions that would be too scary in another context. Although not all the plays perform this function for him, *Romeo and Juliet* has remained a primary exemplar of Bettleheim's contention that some stories are important for children because they help them address "the need to be able to feel fear" (280).

Since violence on the stage is often overwhelming and inappropriate for this age group and that portrayed on screen is unacceptable for a small child, Davis has primarily encountered the tragedies through ballet or opera.[7] *Macbeth* remains one of his favorites, possibly because its story correlates with lessons he learns at home and school, such as the importance of sharing and of being patient. Thus, his synopsis of the play states that "Macbeth wants to be king, but he doesn't want to wait his turn." Over the months, however, he has especially enjoyed watching the comedies and would doubtless be devouring even more if his parents did not restrict his viewing. The Shakespeare Collection from the Stratford Festival, Trevor Nunn's *Twelfth Night*, Adrian Noble's *A Midsummer Night's Dream*, the animated *Tempest*, and even the 1956 Russian *Twelfth Night* have all been watched with pleasure and apparent comprehension, but the undisputed hits for this three-year-old aficionado have been Sam Taylor's 1929 version of *The Taming of the Shrew*, starring Mary Pickford and Douglas Fairbanks and Max Reinhardt's 1935 rendition of *A Midsummer Night's Dream*, featuring Olivia de Havilland, Mickey Rooney, and James Cagney. Each of these films is presented in black and white and neither is very long: the former runs about sixty minutes, the latter lasts just under two hours. Both have become sources of endless delight, and an invitation to a viewing of either film has evolved into a sure sign of favor.

These particular films have much to recommend for young viewers. The first, released only a year after the first talking movies, simplifies the original plot, but is generally presented with humor and limited violence. Presuming that one does not require small children to be exposed to complete, unadulterated texts, this rendition is a good choice. Enough of the original language was retained that Davis is hearing Shakespeare's words, but since the plot has been pared down, he does not have to keep track of an endless cast of characters. His viewings are always punctuated with lots of questions, which I answer readily, suppressing my ingrained impulse to point out ambiguity and nuance.[8] Like this film's probable target audience, Davis is intrigued by the story, but is most interested in the performances of the main characters. He wants to know what they are doing and why. He laughs at the physical humor and is pleasantly perplexed by the vision of Petruchio explaining his taming techniques to a large dog. He recommends this play to all his friends and while I hope he will be less complacent about the gender issues when he's older, right now, his enjoyment seems unproblematic.

The Reinhardt film is more complicated, but equally popular. Like many adult viewers of the play, Davis pays relatively little attention to the confused lovers, but enjoys watching Titania, Oberon, and Bottom. Victor Jory's rather intimidating Oberon prompts a host of questions about this character's relative goodness or evil, while Titania's glittering, diaphanous costumes and Bottom's transformation provoke lengthy discussions about magic, theater, Puck's motivation, and the mechanics of Bottom's meta-morphoses. All of these characters appear regularly in Davis's puppet shows and dramatic play and he informs me that he would like to stage an operatic version wherein Bottom is played by the statue of a complete donkey.

Whether or not Davis will enjoy Shakespeare as an adult remains to be seen, of course, but Shakespearean drama clearly plays a significant role in his imaginative life as a child, and he has enjoyed many related perfor-mances, including the Atlanta Ballet production of *Romeo and Juliet* and the Georgia Shakespeare Festival's two-hour "Camp Shakespeare."[9] Although my son's literary and dramatic interests extend far beyond this one author, he readily distinguishes between Shakespeare and other writ-ers; thus, when I told him that the schedule for Atlanta's Center for Pup-petry Arts was in my office, he looked at me quizzically and asked: "why is it there? 'The Sorcerer's Apprentice' wasn't written by Shakespeare." As Davis learns to categorize the world, Shakespeare clearly occupies a dis-tinctive place.

The Reggio model of early childhood education emphasizes following the interests displayed by individual children, and Bruno Bettelheim accords his highest literary recommendation for fairy tales, not Shakespeare. It would, therefore, be foolhardy to maintain that proponents of either philoso-phy would necessarily support this use of Shakespeare in the developmental process of small children. My own experience, suggests, however, that Shakespeare can help parents and educators attain key educational aims, even when children are quite young. Shakespeare offers compelling stories in addition to characters who face important challenges and who frequently find themselves in diverting and perplexing circumstances. Action packed and linguistically challenging, these texts offer opportunities for a range of phys-ical, emotional, and intellectual activities that can provide great satisfaction even for very young children. Although Davis's friends have not had the same kind of exposure to Shakespeare that he has enjoyed, they still partici-pate in the plays and are beginning to create their own renditions now that they have been introduced to the main characters and plot elements. Knowl-edge of Shakespearean drama may or may not be valuable for all young chil-dren,[10] but my admittedly limited experience suggests that it offers more benefits than we ordinarily recognize.

Notes

1. I am revising this essay while Davis is four and a half. His passion for Shakespeare continues unabated, but he now revels in the swordplay and death scenes that used to worry him.

2. According to the Reggio model, the fact that Davis became interested in Shakespeare per se is not as important as the significance of developing projects from whatever topic he becomes attracted to. For Reggio, dinosaurs, teddy bears, or Shakespeare would be equally useful starting points for an educational experience. Recognizing that my sample set is statistically nonexistent, I would still argue that one of the reasons this subject has remained of such fascination is because it is so rich. For a child who is attuned to language, music, costuming, and other aspects of staging, Shakespeare provides an invaluable educational resource. Obviously, Davis knows that I teach Shakespeare, but this connection only accounts for part of his abiding passion for these plays. My experiences suggest that age should not be a deterrent to introducing these materials, although Davis has encountered only modest success in his efforts to include his friends in his love for Shakespeare. He is a good marketeer, however, and recognizes his audience. Thus, when *As You Like It* was performed at Emory, he kept trying to entice his friends into joining him, announcing that "they wrestle, you know."

3. Two recent biographical accounts of Bettelheim detail this controversy. Richard Pollak excoriates Bettelheim, while Nina Sutton offers a more sympathetic portrayal, but both discuss the criticism that has surfaced since Bettelheim committed suicide.

4. He had a similar response to the Mouse King in *The Nutcracker*. Initially hesitant to enter the theater because he was afraid to see this character, he subsequently announced that the Mouse King was his favorite part of the ballet and he enacted this role for weeks at preschool.

5. These questions recall one of Bettleheim's observations about fairy tales, "the child who is familiar with fairy tales understands that these speak to him in the language of symbols and not everyday life" (62).

6. He asked, for example, whether "Poor Tom" becomes "happy Tom" at the end of *King Lear*.

7. He was mesmerized, however, by the Georgia Renaissance Faire's thirty-minute version of *Macbeth*. Although there were several comic lines and funny pieces of stage business added, most of the lines were directly out of Shakespeare.

8. Notably, Bettelheim argues that children cannot readily understand "the complexities that characterize real people" and that "ambiguities must wait until a relatively firm personality has been established" (9).

9. Fortunately, Davis accepts that he cannot attend plays after bedtime, so he did not object to missing the Center for Puppetry Arts presentation of "Wrestling Macbeth," which was billed as being suitable for adult audiences only.

10. The video distribution company, Facets, sells a film from the "Baby Einstein" series called "Baby Shakespeare," which its Web site describes as "a one-of-a-

kind visual and auditory field trip into the rhythm of classic poems and the beauty of nature, specifically created for very young children." I have not viewed this video, which is offered at www.facets.org.

Works Cited

Bender, Michael. *All the World's A Stage: A Pop-up Biography of William Shakespeare*. San Francisco: Chronicle Books, 1999.

Bettelheim, Bruno. *The Uses of Enchantment: The Meaning and Importance of Fairy Tales*. New York: Alfred A. Knopf, 1986.

Early, Margaret. *Romeo and Juliet*. New York: Harry N. Abrams, 1998.

Fried, Yan. *Twelfth Night* (Russia, 1956). Chicago: Facets Video, n. d.

Gounod, C-F. *Romeo et Juliette*. West Long Branch, NJ: Kultur Films, 1994, VHS.

Hamlet Ballet. West Long Branch, NJ: Kultur Films, n. d., VHS.

The Hundred Languages of Children: The Reggio Emilia Approach to Early Childhood Education. Edited by Carolyn Edwards, Lella Gandini, and George Forman. Norwood, NJ: Ablex Publishing Corp., 1993.

Macbeth Ballet. West Long Branch, NJ: Kultur Films, 1984, VHS.

Noble, Adrian. *A Midsummer Night's Dream*. Burbank, CA: Buena Vista Home Entertainment, n. d., VHS.

Nunn, Trevor. *Twelfth Night*. Fine Line Features, 1996, VHS.

Pollak, Richard. *The Creation of Dr. B: A Biography of Bruno Bettelheim*. New York: Simon Shuster, 1997.

Reinhardt, Max. *A Midsummer Night's Dream* (1935). Farmington Hills, MI: CBS/Fox Video, 1985, VHS.

The Shakespeare Collection. Quebec, Canada: Canadian Broadcasting Company, 1996, VHS.

Shakespeare Dance Trilogy. New York: V.I.E.W. Video, 1993, VHS.

Sutton, Nina. *Bettelheim: A Life and a Legacy*. Translated by David Sharp. New York: BasicBooks, 1996.

The Tempest, Shakespeare: The Animated Tales. New York: Random House, 1992, VHS.

22. Visions of Shakespeare in a Montessori Classroom

REGINE EBNER

Children are not what they seem. They are not just adorable offspring, both fun and annoying. They are not just cerebral mush waiting to develop (slowly) into surgeons, writers, and accountants. Children are far more capable than we can even know. They are, in fact, master learners from the very beginning, efficiently and thoroughly chronicaling their environment, its meaning, logic, and purpose. If we wait until, say, age six to begin teaching them to read, write, and compute we have missed a thousand opportunities to expand their learning and their ability to learn. If we wait until, say, eleven or fourteen to teach them world culture, history, and literature, we have fundamentally misunderstood their abilities and even their humanity. Like water finding its own level, children will learn whatever we place before them, whenever we place it there.

I have seen six year olds deeply absorbed by the magic of ancient Egypt. I have seen eight year olds fascinated by the Periodic Table and the chemistry of the Primordial Soup. I have heard nine year olds recount in elaborate detail the stories of the gods and goddesses of ancient Greece. And I have seen seven year olds draw delicate, lovely pictures of Puck and Titania from *A Midsummer Night's Dream.*[1]

The works of William Shakespeare are not what they seem, either. Many adults cringe at the thought of reading the great plays and envision each page as a dense thicket to be hacked through. In fact, Shakespeare's plays are classic stories and fairy tales like Peter Pan or the Knights of the Round Table told in elegant poems for all people to know and love. This is certainly what the children in our classroom came to believe.

When I made the announcement to my class of seven to ten year olds that we were about to begin our unit on William Shakespeare, a loud cheer went up. The noise was no different, really, than if I had announced a pizza party or trip to the skating rink: wild, rollicking, gleeful, sustained. Why such fervor? Earlier, with red velvet timelines, muffin hats, telescopes and globes, we had studied the Renaissance and the children had come to view this period as a series of great and glorious events (the printing press, world exploration, the study of the heavens). And right there on the time line, next to Queen Elizabeth, was a hand drawn picture of William Shakespeare and a card which read "greatest playwright of all time." So, when I made my announcement several months later, the children welcomed him. In a way, they had been waiting for him.

Maria Montessori studied the way children learn by observing them directly (what an idea!). She writes of the "absorbent mind," by which she meant much more than the adage "children are like sponges."[2] The minds of children genuinely work differently from those of adults. They operate unburdened and unhindered. They take in information as a whole, in one motion, of a piece. Hence: the absorbent mind. In a Montessori classroom, all subjects are taught with hands-on materials. To best illustrate how a child learns, let's take an example from math: there is a Montessori math material called the Long Division Tubes. It is a complicated, multifaceted piece of educational equipment designed to teach long division in concrete form. The Long Division Tubes are a series of racks with test tubes carrying beads, which are counted out by numeral and place value. It takes adults weeks of practice to master it. The children always learn it in one lesson. Why? The child's mind does not labor over parts and pieces, does not balk at many linear steps, does not grow weary at what lies ahead. Instead, the child works in present time and takes in meaning as a whole, unafraid.

And this is what happened when we presented Shakespeare's plays and language: the children caught the new rhythms of the language deftly and the rich meanings quickly. He was no different to them than, say, a geometry board.

I often suggest to friends that if they wish to learn about something—anything—they should pick up a children's book about that subject (the Middle Ages, simple machines, Native Americans, fossils) and read it cover to cover. They will probably learn all the most important and interesting facts they will ever need to know, and they will learn them in an enjoyable fashion. Children can and will enjoy learning about virtually any subject as long as it is presented in a clear, interesting, inviting method. (This does NOT mean that young students must be extravagantly entertained or cajoled with bright colors and loud noises.)

When we create a unit for the classroom, we must first understand the subject well ourselves so that we can find its essence—its most important features—and translate them into concrete materials. With the Shakespeare unit, I wanted the children to know and understand 1) the basic stories and plots of the plays *A Midsummer Night's Dream* and *Macbeth*,[3] 2) the life and times of William Shakespeare himself, and 3) last but perhaps most important, some of the *original language* in each play.

We began our unit with a read-aloud of Bruce Coville's *Macbeth*.[4] The plan was to study *Macbeth* and *A Midsummer Night's Dream*[5] as one example each of a tragedy and a comedy. Research had also revealed that these two plays had the most resources available at the time for children. Later, when we began *A Midsummer Night's Dream*, we would follow the same series of steps as for *Macbeth*. The read-through of Bruce Coville's story version was a great jumping-off point for the class. This beautifully crafted retelling easily established for them the characters and story line, the place, time, and mood. The previous year, we had studied the Middle Ages in great depth, which the class adored (knights, castles, illuminated letters, unicorns!), so they grasped immediately the dark, medieval setting of *Macbeth* and its place in history.

The initial reading took place over two days so that we could stop and discuss the people, events, and themes as they happened. Quickly, the children grasped the tragic implications of Macbeth's murderous behavior ("Never hurt someone just to get what you want," said one, "Macbeth ruined himself," said another). At this time, I also introduced a material designed to teach Story Analysis—main character, villain, plot, theme, and so on—using abstract felt shapes and labels, and the children began to think about these concepts as they read.

We moved from there to a set of handmade story cards. Remember, in a Montessori classroom, everything (every idea, concept, subject) is presented in concrete form via hands-on materials. Many of these can be purchased for the youngest children ages three through six but as you move up in level fewer and fewer materials are available and teachers must design and make their own. In the case of an elementary unit on Shakespeare's plays, nothing at all existed and everything had to be originally conceived and created. Using the great illustrations by Gary Kelley from the Coville adaptation,[6] I made a set of matching cards which tell the story of the play. These consisted of the *pictures*, a matching *name* for each, and a *quote* for each one from the original play. Thus the children were seamlessly introduced to the original Shakespearean language which they then read and practiced every day. In a Montessori classroom, independent study is fostered over group learning. Instead of everyone doing the same thing at the same time, everyone pursues individualized assignments and works independently. In this way, the educational materials can be passed around and used by everyone.

The three-part story cards were only the beginning, of course, of a parade of handmade, hand-illustrated materials that taught many aspects of our Shakespeare experience: *comedy/tragedy/history cards*, drawn as masks, and accompanied (as are all matching cards) by information cards describing the three main types of play with examples of each; *biography cards* with line drawings of Will, Anne, the cottage, and the Globe; *a basket of objects* from the Renaissance for the children to lay out and explore; the *Renaissance Time Line*, a long strip of sewn-together red felt panels bearing dates and tied with gold ribbon, accompanied by illustrations, labels and information cards from world exploration to Queen Elizabeth and Copernicus; large calligraphied *maps of England* to draw; and *quotes from the plays* on blank pages for the children to translate and illustrate.

They wrote lucid translations of the Shakespearean language into modern: "Is this really a knife I see in front of me, or is it only a mirage?" They painted delicately illuminated alphabet books: C is for Character, G is for Guilt, I is for Illusion. One wrote U is for Unhappy; "many of the people in Shakespeare's plays were unhappy." They cut and sewed colorful story scenes with felt: Midsummer fairies with sparkly wings, Macbeth witches all dressed in red, lots of Bottoms with donkey heads.

We then decided that to be truly authentic and to illuminate these as plays not just literature, we must stage them. We had to cast about for a director, since drama is not on my list of fortés. Help arrived in the form of Mark Peterson, a parent in the school, student of Shakespeare, and onetime stand-up comedian. He hit it off immediately with the children, and we all got on famously. The few times he had to be absent during the eight-week rehearsal period, there were loud groans. To the surprise of some, we chose to stage *Macbeth*. Though we questioned the violence in *Macbeth*, we decided the story was especially strong and meaningful to this age group. They understood surprisingly well the concepts of pride and ambition and even the notion of being pressured into something by someone stronger (peer pressure!), was particularly relevant.

In the Montessori classroom all subjects and tasks are taught in sequential gradations, from simple to complex. For example, to teach pouring to toddlers, one begins with large white beans, moves on to medium brown beans, then to rice, then to water, all to build in success for the child. And so are all subjects taught. We began our stage experience with simple theater games, such as passing an invisible ball, doing mirror-imaging with a partner, and so forth, all leading up to the actual auditioning for parts. This was a tricky situation for us because, in Montessori, we eliminate competition as much as possible (one person's success means another's failure). But Mark had a very positive and encouraging manner and the children were surprisingly brave, stepping up to recite their lines with enthusiasm. Sometimes, this very enthusiasm produced odd results as various Macbeths contemplated their murderous deeds with smiles and enjoyment rather than grief and horror.

To give memorable parts to as many people as possible, we decided to select certain scenes sequentially and leave out some of the subplots. We would also have several Macbeths and several Lady Macbeths. We made another decision that would later prove a troublemaker: The class had learned about cross-gender casting in Shakespeare's time, and that men played women's parts. We took it a step further and cast several girls as Macbeth, partly to give them the opportunity and partly to get some of our best readers for those parts.

This worked out fine until one day, one of our star girl-Macbeths got up to rehearse and froze in her tracks. We took her aside and discovered that someone had made fun of her playing a boy. Sadly, even though the entire class came to her defense and support, she refused ever to return to the part. She refused to participate at all, in fact and chose instead to hand out programs on the day of the performance. Gender identity can be a critical issue during the preteen years.

And thus, we had formed a gallant and dedicated theater troupe which broke into rehearsals of *Macbeth* at least twice a week. The result was a moving and delightful spectacle of young children in dark tunics and flowing dresses gracefully performing some of the greatest writing for the theater. Lady MacDuff, as played by an ambitious ten-year-old, sounded wistful and alone; the sleepwalking Lady Macbeth called out tragically. And our final Macbeth brought the crowd to its feet with his dramatic and forceful, "Of all men else, I have avoided thee, But get thee back, my soul is too much charged with blood of thine already!"[7] And everyone applauded deliriously at the end.

To close out our unit, which had lasted twelve weeks instead of the usual six for most special units, the children created original final projects. These consisted of three parts: a *hands-on material* of something related to William Shakespeare, his life or plays, an *oral presentation* of that project to the class and a written three-to-five-page *research paper*. They came forward, one by one, with gold-tipped Globe Theatre models, forest dioramas with tiny Pucks and felt-clothed witches with fiery cauldrons. One of my favorites: a wooden bed with doll Queen Elizabeth asleep upon it to illustrate the royal audience dreaming the play; another: a magic show, complete with black curtain, scarves and a donkey head to demonstrate the role of magic and illusion in both *Macbeth* and *A Midsummer Night's Dream*. And one confident girl decided to pen her own Renaissance play about the unrequited love of one Catherine. . . . There were many projects like these of great wit and charm and all the projects revealed the love and understanding the children had for the material. The children themselves had become enthralled captors of Shakespeare's great visions and, in so being, turned into creators themselves, inspired by those visions.

In the classroom, we seek to guide children along certain paths. We introduce them to ideas, stories, histories, sciences, artists, literature. And always the children surprise us. They surprise us with their minds, their accomplishments and creativity, but mostly they surprise us with their willingness. They have immeasurable courage and willingness to learn and love all things and, in this case, they honored our greatest playwright with their intelligence, their devotion, and their passion.

Today, if I offered them a choice between a pizza party and a new Shakespeare play, a loud cheer would rise up again. And it would not be for the pizza party.

Notes

1. Shakespeare, William. *A Midsummer Night's Dream.* Shakespeare Made Easy, Barron's Educational Series, London: Hutchinson Pub. Co., 1984.
2. Montessori, Maria. *The Absorbent Mind.* Holt, Rinehart and Winston, 1967.
3. Shakespeare, William. *Macbeth.* Shakespeare Made Easy. Barron's Educational Series, London: Hutchinson Pub. Co., 1985.
4. Coville, Bruce. *William Shakespeare's Macbeth.* New York: Dial Books, 1997.
5. Coville, Bruce. *William Shakespeare's A Midsummer Night's Dream.* New York: Dial Books, 1996.
6. Kelley, Gary, illustrator. *William Shakespeare's Macbeth.* New York: Dial Books, 1997.
7. Shakespeare, William. *Macbeth.* Act V, Scene 7, Line 33.

Bibliography

Aliki. *William Shakespeare & The Globe.* New York: HarperCollins, 1999.

Burdett, Lois. *Macbeth for Kids.* Buffalo, NY: Black Moss Press, 1996.

Claybourne, Anna and Rebecca Treays. *The World of Shakespeare.* London: Usborne Publishing, 1996.

Ganeri, Anita. *The Young Person's Guide to Shakespeare.* New York: Harcourt Brace & Co., 1999.

Garfield, Leon. *Shakespeare Stories.* Singapore: Imago Publishing Ltd., 1985.

Koscielniak, Bruce. *Here, Here, Mr. Shakespeare.* Boston: Houghton Mifflin Company, 1998.

Nolan, Dennis, illustrator. *William Shakespeare's A Midsummer Night's Dream.* New York: Dial Books, 1996.

Ross, Stewart. *Shakespeare and Macbeth The Story Behind the Play* . New York: Penguin Books, 1994.

23. Shakespeare Steps Out

The Primacy of Language in Inner-City Classrooms

JANET FIELD-PICKERING

That night he took away the first volume of the "Faerie Queene," and he went through it, as I formerly told his noble biographer, "as a young horse would through a spring meadow—ramping!" . . . He *hoisted* himself up, and looked burly and dominant, as he said, "what an image that is—'sea-shouldering whales!' " (Clarke, 126)

In 1996, the Folger Shakespeare Library began the outreach project *Shakespeare Steps Out* in several District of Columbia public elementary schools. With the exception of yearly Shakespeare scenes festivals for both elementary and secondary students, the educational programs at the Folger had previously concentrated on secondary school teachers and students, reflecting the general emphasis in English curriculum on teaching Shakespeare at the high school level. We began to see, however, that a strong trend was emerging for teaching Shakespeare to younger students.[1] Shakespeare is trickling down to the elementary curriculum, and the Folger began its work in direct response to this opportunity and to the requests of D.C. public school teachers for enrichment in reading, language arts, and humanities education at the elementary level.

Shakespeare Steps Out targets schools that are, like most D.C. public schools, predominantly African-American, but we also strive to reach schools that are located in underserved and economically disadvantaged areas of the city. The program takes a multidisciplinary approach to the teaching of Shakespeare in grades three through six, with an emphasis on history and social studies, music, dancing, language, visual arts, and performance. Classroom activities include dressing students in period costumes, teaching students Elizabethan dances, and discussing daily life in Shakespeare's time to provide students with a lively approach to history and social studies. We provide each classroom with a book corner—a mini-library of

Shakespeare resources featuring posters, books on Shakespeare, the Globe
Theatre, Elizabethan life and times, and Shakespeare adaptations.

We expected the book corners to have a built-in appeal for the teachers
as much-needed resources for their classrooms; surprisingly, we found that
the children were drawn in increasing numbers to the books for independent
reading. We also discovered that activities that focused more directly on
Shakespeare's language—such as marching around the room in iambic pentameter, drawing pictures in response to hearing a descriptive passage like
"Queen Mab" read over and over again, directly engaging students in language play or acting out short scenes from *Macbeth* or *Romeo and Juliet*—
were the activities that the children clamored for.

It seemed important to ask why. Are these inner-city children responding
to Shakespeare's position as a cultural icon? In a school district that includes
elementary schools with a decided emphasis on multi-cultural or Afro-
centric curricula, why the great interest in one of the original "dead white
males?"

In the winter of 1997–98, I talked to children in grades four, five, and six
at Shaed, Davis, and Whittier elementary schools, as part of my informal
research on the appeal of these books, particularly the Shakespeare adaptations. I focused on Marchette Chute's *Stories from Shakespeare*; Beverley
Birch's *Shakespeare's Stories: Tragedies*; *The Children's Macbeth*, illustrated by Meredith Johnson; Von's comic book *Macbeth: The Folio Edition*;
Oscar Zarate's comic book *Othello: The Illustrated Edition*; and *Under the
Greenwood Tree: Shakespeare for Young People*, with an introduction by
A. L. Rowse and illustrations by Robin and Pat DeWitt. The Chute and Birch
adaptations are fairly traditional retellings of Shakespeare's stories—more
modern versions of Lamb's *Tales from Shakespeare*. *The Children's Macbeth*
is a large-format paperback that provides a cut script of the play and resembles a child's coloring book. The Von and Zarate comic books seem geared
towards a teenaged or adult audience and include the entire texts of the plays
in their captions, and *Under the Greenwood Tree* is a collection of lavishly
illustrated poems and passages.[2]

As a rule, the students held very definite opinions about the books, and
they were very enthusiastic about taking time out from their regular class-
work to talk to me about them. The students at Shaed Elementary School
were the youngest. As fourth graders, their comments were decidedly less
sophisticated than those of older students, and their attention spans were
short. But as we spoke, their comments suggested a real familiarity with the
books, as they insisted on finding and reading aloud representative passages
to support their opinions. One girl indicated her strong preference for Chute's
Stories from Shakespeare by saying, "Shakespeare's words add an accent to
the page—they jump off the page at you." All the students at Shaed were particularly impressed with the *Macbeth* comic book (their teacher deemed the

Othello inappropriate) and *Under the Greenwood Tree. Macbeth* elicited several responses. One boy responded that the picture "looked kind of real when Macbeth got his head chopped off," and another child suggested, "The drawings show the movements that come from the words." Some students preferred *Under the Greenwood Tree* because the poems with illustrations "tell the action—tell the story quickly in just a few words."

At Whittier Elementary, the teacher selected the students I spoke to, and they were all girls. *Under the Greenwood Tree* was their favorite because of its combination of "beautiful pictures and beautiful words," although they were concerned that it might be, as they put it, a "girly" book. They didn't like the comic books as much; comparing the response of these students to students at the other two schools suggests there may be a gender bias in the reaction of these girls. In general they thought that Von's comic book *Macbeth* was "too violent" with "too many characters." Another student thought that Zarate's *Othello* comic book contained too many "X-rated" words and thought the pictures were violent. The students at Whittier were unanimous in their opinion that the comic books were too mature for anyone younger than fifth or sixth grade and that the *Othello* was inappropriate for even sixth grade.

The girls' response to the Chute and Birch adaptations suggests that the Chute version was the more popular of the two. One student "loved" *Stories from Shakespeare*; she praised it as "a great book with very good stories, particularly *Love's Labour's Lost*." Another student reviewed Birch's *Shakespeare's Stories* by objecting to the "very sad and horrible pictures with people stabbing people and swordfights" that filled the book, even though she realized that the book was centered on Shakespeare's tragedies. In discussing *The Children's Macbeth*, the group was impressed with the cutting of the play, but one girl claimed she "didn't get the pictures." The brief discussion that followed revealed that the group felt that the family depicted in the illustrations was obviously white and this annoyed them. In retrospect, this exchange seemed to be one of those moments in which a teacher discovers that what seems to be a localized difficulty that students experience with a book leads to a larger insight about materials we include in the curriculum. Shakespeare's words alone can avoid alienating students in allowing them to read them and supply their own pictures; illustrations of Shakespeare's stories inhibit that vivid imaginative leap.

The tendency of adaptations to mediate student response to Shakespeare's language was raised by yet another insightful set of comments by the children at Whittier, which addressed the problem of reading adaptations instead of the plays, or at least cut versions of the plays. One girl staunchly defended, yet qualified, her response to her favorite book, *Stories from Shakespeare*, by stating, "You can read it and it tells you information, but you understand more about the play by acting it out." Another student added,

"*Doing* what the words say makes you feel your part" and acting it out "makes it more fun to study."

At Davis Elementary, the most popular books were the comic book versions. Several students commented about the vivid illustrations (in particular the decapitation of Macbeth). One fifth-grader liked the comic books because "the pictures show love and hate. You can tell if a character is good or bad." Most of the children responded to the style of the illustrations by agreeing that they showed "action" in the case of *Macbeth* and "passion" in the case of *Othello* (although many of the children thought that the illustrations in the Zarate *Othello* were inappropriate for their age group, with naked characters and "dirty pictures"). They regarded the Chute and Birch books as belonging to the particular category of "story book." In general they liked the fact that these books included more details about setting and the characters' feelings and emotions, but they also liked the snippets of Shakespeare that Chute provided. They seemed to feel that the presence of Shakespeare's words was important to the books. They were confused by unfamiliar words, but responded to the sounds of the language. This was apparent when one boy pulled out his favorite lines of Macbeth in Chute's adaptation: "Will all / great Neptune's ocean wash this blood / Clean from my hand? No; this my hand will rather / The multitudinous seas incarnadine, / Making the green one red" (173). His fellow students continued to repeat, "the multitudinous seas incarnadine" over and over as they rolled the sounds around on their tongues and trotted back to their desks to prepare for their next lesson. There was no irritable reaching after meaning or definition. The sounds, words, and context were enough.

The students at Davis were not only definite in their opinions about the books themselves; they had a strong preference about how to approach the books: they wanted to read the books aloud or hear someone else read to them. The students who read aloud stumbled over unfamiliar words (and were readily corrected by their peers), but they persisted. The desire to read or hear the books aloud has a lot to do with classroom practices in elementary schools, but it seemed to be particular to the Shakespeare adaptations, rather than to books about Shakespeare and his life and times that were also included in the book corners. The students at Davis made a clear distinction between books and plays, and seemed to respond best to adaptations that included sections of Shakespeare's text. As one young boy stated in talking about both the comic book version and Chute's retelling of *Macbeth*, "You get more of the magic and spells from Shakespeare's words." *Under the Greenwood Tree* appealed to a number of the students at Davis because of its mix of colorful illustrations and passages from Shakespeare. The usual comment was that each page told a short story through both the poetry and the pictures. They also responded to *The Children's Macbeth*: they liked the implications of its title and wanted to color the illustrations and act out the whole play.

Interviews, though informal, provided a basis for identifying which books these students liked best. The students at all three schools seemed to share certain preferences. They responded to books with illustrations that they described as either "gory" or "girly," as long as they were colorful and imaginative. When they were exposed to books that they considered too mature for their age group, they self-censored the materials. They liked owning the books and keeping them in their classrooms. They responded to the "action" and stories and characters in Shakespeare's play.

But the children's most consistent response involved an almost physical reaction to the sounds and rhythms and images of Shakespeare's poetry, and they preferred books that included actual passages from the plays. A clear desire for Shakespeare's words crept again and again into conversations with these children, along with a strongly-stated preference for either reading the plays aloud or performing them. I began to question the value of introducing Shakespeare to students primarily through stories and adaptations.

In her introduction to *Stories from Shakespeare*, Marchette Chute tackles directly what most people (and presumably children) fear in approaching the works of William Shakespeare: "The average person does not like to be told what to do, and he might begin to study a play like *Romeo and Juliet* with the conviction already formed in his mind that he is not going to enjoy himself. He starts to read the first act . . . and finds a great many Italian names that he cannot keep apart and speeches full of long words. So he puts the book down, convinced that Shakespeare is much too difficult to be read for pleasure and that the whole subject is overrated" (10). Chute clearly states her intent in publishing the collection of stories: "Its purpose is to give the reader a preliminary idea of each of the thirty-six plays by telling the stories and explaining in a general way the intentions and point of view of the characters. It will not give much conception of Shakespeare's vastness, his wisdom, or his profound knowledge of people. . . . But it may open a door that to some people is closed and give a glimpse, however slight, of what lies beyond" (10).

I'm not sure that children approach Shakespeare with the same trepidation that Chute assigns to "the average person," but I'm all for opening doors to Shakespeare study for elementary students. My experience with the children of *Shakespeare Steps Out* has clarified the importance of Shakespeare's language in any study of Shakespearean material with the critical revelation that students respond to the language on a level that often seems distinct from the level of its precise meaning. It is crucial to let elementary students have direct access to Shakespeare's language by allowing them to respond to words and short passages in a context in which their engagement with the language is more physical than just the act of reading it aloud, or having it read to them.

The quotation that is the epigraph of my paper—Charles Cowden Clarke's image of a young horse ramping in a meadow to describe the young John Keats responding to a line in Edmund Spenser's poem *The Faerie*

Queene—somehow encapsulates my experience in working with inner-city children. In the title of the following lesson plan created for the students of *Shakespeare Steps Out*, I have changed "ramping" to "romping," for the rhyme as well as to emphasize the sheer physicality of this particular sequence of language activities and to convey the giddy, collective excitement that this exercise induces in students. In the activities with language, sound, and rhythm that this lesson plan presents, the meanings of the words are not irrelevant, but they are somewhat beside the point. This lesson was created to allow students to experience Shakespeare's language whatever their command of all the intricacies of its meaning.

Romping and Stomping with Shakespeare:
A Lesson Plan for Elementary Students

Introduction and Objectives

In introducing Shakespeare to elementary school students, the best place to start is with the rhythm of the language in Shakespeare's songs. Children respond to the sound and beat of Shakespeare as much as they respond to his wonderful stories and characters. Shakespeare's songs are also short, self-contained (in terms of what's going on in the rest of the play), and often include vivid images and word pictures.

The meter of Shakespeare's poetry is predominantly iambic. That is, a unit of iambic meter, called an iambic foot, consists of a soft stress followed by a sharp one: da-DUM. (A good example of an everyday word that acts as an iambic foot is toDAY.)

Shakespeare wrote most of his poetry in iambic pentameter, five units of iambic beat to a line:

> *"But SOFT, what LIGHT through YONder WINdow BREAKS."*
> *daDUM daDUM daDUM daDUM daDUM*

But a lot of the songs from his plays are written in iambic tetrameter, four units of iambic beat to a line:

> *You SPOTted SNAKES with DOUble TONGUE*
> *daDUM daDUM daDUM daDUM*

This meter is common in songs and in children's poetry. Dr. Seuss is a great example:

> *i DO not LIKE green EGGS and HAM*
> *i DO not LIKE them, SAM i AM*

The first part of this lesson will engage children in a number of activities that explore rhythm and meter. In the second part of the lesson, students will create a series of "living pictures" to illustrate the song.

This lesson is divided into parts, but the whole lesson will probably take one to three block periods.

Part One: Rhythm and Meter

1. Ask the children to place their hands over their hearts and feel the daDum, daDum, daDum of their own heartbeats. Tell the students that Shakespeare used the rhythm of the heartbeat in his poems and plays. Have them practice beating out this rhythm on their desks, and tell them that this rhythm is called iambic.

2. Next have the students stand up and gather in a big circle. Tell them to face right and start marching around the room to an iambic beat. Starting with a softly placed left foot followed by a sharply stomped right, have the students circle the room twice, marching to the beat.

3. Now add words. Get out your Dr. Seuss and read aloud sections of *Green Eggs and Ham* as the students continue marching around the room. Call out a line, and have the students repeat it. Continue this back and forth until you feel you have fully established the rhythm.

4. Continue marching to the same beat while substituting the words to Shakespeare's "A Winter's Song" from *Love's Labour's Lost*. Again call out each line and ask the children to repeat it:

> *When I-ci-CLES hang BY the WALL,*
> *And DICK the SHEPherd BLOWS his NAIL,*
> *And TOM bears LOGS inTO the HALL,*
> *And MILK comes FROzen HOME in PAIL,*
> *When BLOOD is NIPP'D, and WAYS be FOUL,*
> *Then NIGHTly SINGS the STARing OWL,*
> *Tu-WHIT; Tu-WHO, a MERry NOTE,*
> *While GREASy JOAN doth KEEL the POT.*
> *When ALL aLOUD the WIND doth BLOW,*
> *And COUGHing DROWNS the PARson's SAW,*
> *And BIRDS sit BROODing IN the SNOW*
> *And MARian's NOSE looks RED and RAW,*
> *When ROASTed CRABS hiss IN the BOWL,*
> *Then NIGHTly SINGS the STARing OWL,*
> *Tu-WHIT; Tu-WHO, a MERry NOTE,*
> *While GREASy JOAN doth KEEL the POT.*

At the end of this activity, your students should have a good sense of Shakespeare's meter and should be well on the way to memorizing one of his songs.

Part Two: Meaning, Movement, and Living Pictures

1. Create and give each student a handout of "A Witches' Spell" from *Macbeth*. Point out that Shakespeare often plays with the meter of fairy songs or witches' chants. Ask the students to beat out the rhythm of this poem on their desks. They may have a little trouble at first, but they may come up with something like this:

    The WEIRD SISters, HAND in HAND,
    POSters OF the SEA and LAND,
    THUS do GO, aBOUT, aBOUT,
    THRICE to THINE, and THRICE to MINE,
    And THRICE aGAIN, to MAKE up NINE.
    PEACE! the CHARM'S WOUND UP

    Then have the students get up and gather into small circles of three, pretend to be witches, and move to this new meter. Encourage them to join hands, or to dance, or to change directions—whatever the passage moves them to try. Then discuss reasons why Shakespeare might have used a different meter for supernatural characters. Is the rhythm more chant-like? More spooky?

2. Create a handout for "A Winter's Song." Discuss unfamiliar words and anything that the students may have missed in hearing and repeating the poem as they marched around. Try to see if the students can guess the meanings of unfamiliar words through context or sound. A few words or phrases that might cause problems are "blows his nail," "keel the pot," "saw," and "crabs," but don't be a stickler for the exact meaning. Give your students the chance to use their imaginations. (You can always refer to a decent dictionary or the glossary attached to the New Folger Edition for definitions or suggestions of what the words might have meant in Shakespeare's time.)

3. Divide your class into six small groups. Assign one line from the first stanza of the song to each group; the whole class will act out the refrain. Do the same for the second stanza.

4. Give the small groups three to five minutes to think about how to act out or pantomime their lines in front of the class. Tell the students that they are going to make a living, moving picture out of the poem as you read the poem aloud.

5. While the small groups plan and practice what to do, circulate around the room and encourage students to use their bodies, imaginations, space, sounds, and movement to stage their lines.

6. When all the groups are ready, discuss with the whole class what they want to do to act out the refrain. Practice once or twice.

7. Perform the "living picture" at the front of the room.

Evaluation/How Did It Go?

Ask yourself the following questions. Did your students have fun stomping out Shakespeare's meter? Did they get a sense of how different rhythms can reinforce or affect the sound and meaning of different poems? Did they work together to use their imaginations and create a living picture to illustrate a poem? After working on all the activities on "A Winter's Song," do they almost have it memorized?

The activities presented in this lesson allow students direct access to both Shakespeare's language with all its sound and sense and to the prodigious powers of their own imaginations.

I want to conclude by raising some questions about the political implications of teaching Shakespeare or adaptations of Shakespeare in inner-city elementary schools.

In *Savage Inequalities*: *Children in America's Schools*, Jonathan Kozol uncovers a significant fact about what public education really means in American cities, including Washington, D.C.: "What startled me most . . . was the remarkable degree of racial segregation that persisted almost everywhere. Like most Americans, I knew that segregation was still common in the public schools, but I did not know how much it had intensified. . . . Most of the urban schools I visited were 95 to 99 percent nonwhite" (3). Do some urban elementary schools avoid teaching Shakespeare's language out of a fear of it being "too advanced" or "too hard" both for students and their teachers in inner-city schools? Are adaptations of Shakespeare viewed as more accessible? Although not limited to personnel in inner-city schools, is teacher insecurity with Shakespeare's language a significant part of the problem? When I tried the lesson plan at one school, the principal sheepishly admitted that she had never grasped the concept of iambic pentameter throughout her entire college and graduate school experience, but she didn't seem to be bothered by learning it along with her students, stomping around with the best of them.

Is Shakespeare viewed as alien or culturally oppressive in schools where the majority of the students are nonwhite? The articles documenting the push to teach Shakespeare at the lower grades generally recount experiments at suburban schools. Before the Folger started *Shakespeare Steps Out* and intensified its elementary outreach efforts, most of the D.C. schools that performed scenes in the yearly Children's Festival were from magnet, charter, or private schools, which attract a higher percent of white and middle-class students. How do we address teaching Shakespeare in a two-tier educational system with certain schools set aside for nonwhite and economically disadvantaged children, and with magnet or charter schools set aside to discourage white and middle-class flight from our nation's cities?

The sixth grade girls at Whittier objected to the illustrations in *The Children's Macbeth* as exclusively picturing white children, but they seemed to have no difficulty in enjoying the text of *Macbeth* that the book provided. In the six years that *Shakespeare Steps Out* has been offered in D.C. public schools, I have been astounded by what the elementary students and their teachers have taught me. There is no fear of Shakespeare as alien, or culturally oppressive, or too difficult for any students or teachers to grasp. There is only keen joy to be found in an intense and meaningful encounter with his language.

Notes

1. The trend can be documented by articles on a K-8 Shakespeare curriculum at an elementary school in New Jersey reported in both the *Christian Science Monitor* (May 29, 1997) and in *Phi Delta Kappan* (February 1997) and in an article on teaching *The Tempest* to third graders in *Shakespeare in the Classroom* (Spring 1997).
2. Since 1997, and partly as a result of these interviews, we have replaced some of these titles with books such as Marcia Williams's *Tales from Shakespeare*, and all of the brilliant Shakespeare adaptations by Bruce Coville.

Bibliography

Birch, Beverly. *Shakespeare's Stories: Tragedies*. New York: Peter Bedrick, 1988.

Clarke, Charles Cowden, and Mary Clarke. *Recollections of Writers*. London: S. Low, Marston, Searle, and Rivington, 1878.

Chute, Machete. *Stories from Shakespeare*. New York: Meridian, 1987.

Geisel, Theodor Seuss. *Green Eggs and Ham*. New York: Beginner Books, 1960.

Hyle, Rebecca. "Teaching *The Tempest* to Third Graders." *Shakespeare in the Classroom* 5.1 (1997): 64–66.

Kozol, Jonathan. *Savage Inequalities: Children in America's Schools*. New York: Crown, 1991.

Macbeth: The Folio Edition. Illus. Von. New York: Workman, 1982.

Othello: Illustrated Edition. Illus. Oscar Zarate. New York: Workman, 1983.

Shakespeare, William. *The Children's Macbeth*. Illus. Meredith Johnson. Santa Barbara: Bellerophon, 1996.

Shakespeare, William. *Under the Greenwood Tree: Shakespeare for Young People*. Intro. A. L. Rowse. Owings Mills, MD: Stemmer House, 1988.

Thompson, Neal. "A School Makes Much Ado About Shakespeare." *Christian Science Monitor* May 29, 1997: 1, 12.

Wood, Robin H. "Shakespeare in an Elementary School Setting." *Phi Delta Kappan* February 1997: 457–59.

24. "Your Play Needs No Excuse"

Shakespeare and Language Development in Children

KRISTEN L. OLSON

Operating from the premise that "education begins at birth," The English Nanny and Governess School in Chagrin Falls, Ohio, trains its students to view their work as education, rather than as child care, and instructs them in such subjects as psychological development, behavior, creative play, art, and literature. The Language Arts curriculum I designed while teaching and serving as Program Coordinator in Language, Communication, and Early Childhood Literature there from 1998 to 2000, focused on the connections between literature and language acquisition and development. The students, who had weekly day-long in-home practicum sessions with families, introduced their children to Shakespeare's poetry not only by reading aloud, but also by extending the reading experience in creative play sessions. The nannies designed games and other creative play exercises to be used in conjunction with readings of Shakespeare's poetry as they had traditionally done for the non-Shakespearean texts used in the course. For example, activities associated with reading a story such as "Peter Rabbit" might include planting a garden like Mr. MacGregor's, writing answer stories from the perspective of one of Peter's sisters, or making sock puppets and acting out the story, depending on the age of the children involved and the pedagogical objective of each exercise.[1] The theoretical components of the course examined poetic techniques used by children's authors such as Dr. Seuss, A. A. Milne, and Robert Louis Stevenson—rhetorical strategies similar to those used in "L"iterature typically considered much more "sophisticated." My objective in including Shakespeare in the Language Arts curriculum was to explore the important developmental influences available through exposure to Shakespearean poetic structure.[2]

The Language Arts curriculum was designed to help the Nanny School students consider the basic tenets of language function from a linguistic perspective, based on a Chomskian understanding of language as a system of pattern recognition and manipulation and on Steven Pinker's extension of this principle, which frames human language ability as uniquely "instinctive[3]." The course asserted that literature functions by picking up on this instinctive capacity for language creation by building on the fundamental aspects of pattern recognition and the manipulation of pattern as part of literary structure. The lectures examined the differences between animal communication systems, which are generally characterized by fixed symbolic relationships, and human language, which demonstrates a flexible application of assimilated rules determined by the user's experience with the language (or languages) to which he or she is exposed.[4] Classroom discussion further considered other "instinctive" aspects of human language, such as a cognitive tendency to create narrative, which often functions as a mnemonic strategy; why we have an easier time, for example, remembering how to tie a bowline by remembering the steps as a narrative, "The rabbit runs out of the hole, around the tree, and back down into the hole," than as an arbitrary series, "Line A passes vertically upward through loop A, behind line B, then vertically downward through loop A."[5] We then explored children's stories and poems identifying the ways in which these fundamental principles are used as governing structural guidelines in well-known children's texts. Early-reader books from the *Beginner Books* series, such as Dr. Seuss's *Hop on Pop* and *Green Eggs and Ham*, use pattern recognition as the source of their "fun." In *Green Eggs and Ham* the humor comes from the repetitive intensification of all the conditions under which green eggs and ham are known to be repugnant, and the ultimate overturning of this insistence capitalizes on the hyperbolic quality of this emphaticness. Repetition and pattern are the foundation of such stories' language-play, and also are the driving force of their narrative. Seuss's books for more advanced readers, such as *And to Think that I Saw It on Mulberry Street* and *Thidwick the Big-Hearted Moose*, use repetition also, but they further employ a narrative structure that builds as a pattern is repeated and extended: the boy's fantasy of what he might see on Mulberry Street as he walks home from school grows item-by-item, propelling the story, which grows as the image does, just as Thidwick's predicament predictably intensifies as additional guests take up lodging on his horns, similarly building to the narrative's climax.

The course then looked more closely at poetic structure, focusing on the manipulation of sound patterning and the interplay of pattern when rhyme and meter are considered together, paying particular attention to instances in which the structural patterns within a poem embody its thematic ideas. In A. A. Milne's poem, "Happiness," for example, the reader can "hear" the child depicted in the poem splashing through the puddles as the poem progresses:

> John had
> Great Big
> Waterproof
> Boots on;
> John had a
> Great Big
> Waterproof
> Hat;
> John had a
> Great Big
> Waterproof
> Mackintosh—
> And that
> (Said John)
> Is
> That.

> (*When We Were Very Young*, 6)

Even if a child listening to the poem is unaware of where Milne's line breaks fall, the poem still audibly divides itself into its "marching" rhythm, making the listener feel he or she is stomping through the puddles as he or she listens. Similarly, the poem, "Halfway Down" directs its listener to the space it describes imaginatively:

> Halfway down the stairs
> Is a stair
> Where I sit.
> There isn't any
> Other stair
> Quite like
> It.
> I'm not at the bottom,
> I'm not at the top;
> So this is the stair
> Where
> I always
> Stop.
>
> Halfway up the stairs
> Isn't up,
> And isn't down.
> It isn't in the nursery,

> It isn't in the town.
> And all sorts of funny thoughts
> Run round my head:
> "It isn't really
> Anywhere!
> It's somewhere else
> Instead!"
>
> (*When We Were Very Young*, 81)

This evenly-balanced poem guides the listener to the figured "step" in its middle, "stopping" briefly at that imaginative locus. Children as they read or listen are not counting lines or scanning metrical feet, but they can quite easily intuitively perceive where these patterns direct attention and how they activate the poem's overall structure to illustrate the experience it describes. In such poems, "lived" experience is connected to "imagined" or "read" experience in the *mimetic* patterning of the language. A similarly *mimetic* example by Robert Louis Stevenson captures the experience of swinging in the movement of its lines:

> How do you like to go up in a swing,
> Up in the air so blue?
> Oh, I do think it the pleasantest thing
> Ever a child can do!
>
> Up in the air and over the wall,
> Till I can see so wide,
> Rivers and trees and cattle and all
> Over the countryside—
>
> Till I look down on the garden green,
> Down on the roof so brown—
> Up in the air I go flying again,
> Up in the air and down!
>
> ("The Swing," *A Child's Garden of Verses*, 39)

The lines *sound* evenly balanced, like the arcs in the parabolic motion of the swing, and the movement of the words captures the sense of acceleration as the swing heads toward its lowest point by articulating a greater proportion of metrical syllables. The poem also conveys a sense of "suspension" while the rhythm causes the reader to pause, waiting to continue with the articulated syllables in the appropriate time, yielding the same sensation that one would feel "hanging" in the air before swinging back in the opposite direction. These "children's" authors thus invoke structural pattern to embody meaning within their texts, a technique that plays on the same principles that "adults' " poets recognize and activate in the shaping of linguistic and cognitive expression through the resonance of pattern in more "complex" forms. Children are able to recognize and respond to these principles easily since patterning is fundamental to language.

Shakespeare is one of the most adept manipulators of linguistic pattern and resonance, so it is natural to expect children to be responsive to the resonance of pattern available in Shakespearean poetry. Though they certainly would not be able to recognize the multiplicity of nuance inherent in a sonnet—indeed, Helen Vendler attests to discovering new possibilities and meanings as she thinks through familiar poems, citing this experience as her primary objective for writing *The Art of Shakespeare's Sonnets*[6]—children are clearly sensitive to the play of pattern and symmetry available in Shakespearean language, and their own linguistic development can be enhanced by exposure to these experiences of pattern-rich language. In choosing samples of Shakespeare's poetry to present to young children I therefore paid close attention to issues of pattern and to the relationship of pattern and narrative. Word-play, by which I mean "sound-play" as much as "connotation" and "polysemy," remained a focal issue, as did metrical pattern. In addition, I selected poems that were easily adapted to creative play and/or environmental enrichment activities that could extend the reading experience—sonnet 18, for example, provided a good opportunity to visit a garden or a history museum to compare different kinds of plant life, to explore the differences between "buds" and "leaves," deepening the associative experience and awareness of connotation in subsequent readings of the poem. In addition to sonnet 18, I used sonnets 8, 30, 46, 87, 98, and 116. I also selected the following passages from Shakespeare's dramatic poetry:[7] *Rom.* 1.5.92–105, *TN* 5.1.388–407, *Mac.* 1.1.1–12 and 4.1.1–45, *MV* 2.7.65–73, 2.9.63–72, and 3.2.131–38, *MND* 1.1.180–203, 2.2.9–24, and 5.1.349–76, *Cym.* 4.2.258–75, and shorter blank verse passages such as *Tmp.* 3.2.131–41, and *Tim.* 4.3.439–43.

Activities created by Nanny School students were centered primarily on extending the reading experience by helping to forge the connection between lived experience and read experience. Several of the exercises suggested by Rex Gibson and Janet Field-Pickering's *Discovering Shakespeare's Language*[8] were effective in involving the children with rhyme and meter. For example, in a game called "Round the Cauldron Go," the children were asked to march in a circle to the rhythm of the witches' speeches in *Macbeth* as the text was read aloud to them. The children were instructed that when the reader paused they could, in time with their marching, chant, "Double, double toil and trouble: fire, burn; and, cauldron bubble." They would begin marching with the reading of the line, "Round about the cauldron go," and the reading would continue as follows:

READER: Round about the cauldron go;
In the poisoned entrails throw.—
Toad, that under cold stone
Days and nights has thirty-one
Swealter'd venom, sleeping got,
Boil thou first in the charmed pot.
CHILDREN: Double, double toil and trouble:
Fire, burn; and cauldron, bubble.
READER: Fillet of a fenny snake,
In the cauldron boil and bake;
Eye of newt, and toe of frog,
Wool of bat, and tongue of dog . . .
CHILDREN: Double, double toil and trouble:
Fire, burn; and cauldron, bubble.
READER: Adder's fork, and blind-worm's sting,
Lizard's leg, and howlet's wing,

.   .   .   .

For a charm of powerful trouble,
[In the cauldron] boil and bubble.
CHILDREN: Double, double toil and trouble:
Fire, burn; and cauldron, bubble.
READER: Scale of dragon, tooth of wolf;
Witches' mummy; maw, and gulf,
Of the ravin'd salt-sea shark;
Root of hemlock, digged in the dark . . .
CHILDREN: Double, double toil and trouble:
Fire, burn; and cauldron, bubble.
READER: Add thereto a tiger's chauldron,
For the ingredients of our cauldron

.   .   .   .

Cool it with a baboon's blood:
Then the charm is firm and good.
CHILDREN: Double, double toil and trouble:
Fire, burn; and cauldron, bubble.

(*Macbeth,* 4.1.4–38)

In this exercise, the children experience a physical recognition of the metrical pattern of these lines. In addition, the circular pattern in which they march replicates the imagined stirring of the cauldron's contents, thus the children are enacting not only the metrical pattern but also *mimetically* dramatizing the action of stirring being described.

Another exercise, involving Sonnet 98, forged a link between dramatic enactment and imaginative experience. The consecutive images from the sonnet were isolated and the children were asked, in each instance, to find as many ways as they could of "enacting the image":

> From you I have been absent in the spring,
> When proud pied April, dressed in all his trim,
> Hath put a spirit of youth in everything,
> That heavy Saturn laughed, and leaped with him.
> Yet nor the lays of birds, nor the sweet smell
> Of different flowers in odour and in hue,
> Could make me any summer's story tell,
> Or from their proud lap pluck them where they grew;
> Nor did I wonder at the lily's white,
> Nor praise the deep vermilion in the rose;
> They were but sweet, but figures of delight,
> Drawn after you, you pattern of all those.
> Yet seemed it winter still, and, you away,
> As with your shadow I with these did play.
>
> (Sonnet 98)

The children were given time to think of as many representations as they could, working through, out loud, the various possibilities and their appropriateness, demonstrating a strong intuitive feel for when something "fit." They were prompted by their nannies with questions such as, "Show me, how would April act to show he is 'proud'?" and "What would he be wearing 'in all his trim'? How would his clothes fit and look? How would you look and feel wearing such clothes of your own? Show me how you would look at yourself in the mirror." This dramatic enactment of each image proceeded progressively, as the children would attempt in turn to make their laughs heavier and heavier and then quick and light, ultimately being asked, "Pretend you are the very heavy character with the very heavy laugh again; would it be hard, as that person, to make a light laugh when you feel so heavy? What if you had to 'leap' at the same time? Show me how you would leap." In essence, the children were led through acting out, piece-by-piece, a close reading. Invariably, children would recognize connections between different image enactments: that "plucking" a flower is a quick, decisive action that fits the tone of someone with pride wearing their best clothes, or that the actions for "praising" were similar to the actions for showing one's own pride.[9] In other contexts, lines demonstrating a specific rhetorical figure were presented, with the children acting out "what the sentence does," turning around or upside down, to represent a chiasmus, for instance, in an extended level of *mimetic* physicalization of a poetic line. While the process of enacting close readings followed a series of prompts and questions not unlike what might be used in classroom discussions with college-age students, the additional cognitive task of physical enactment as a basis for imagination reinforced the link between the imaginative and the *mimetic* function of poetry, and the recognition of interconnected ideas and actions fostered an awareness of the structural resonance inherent in the interplay of ideas within a poem.

The nannies' reactions to working with these texts corroborated central theoretical issues raised in several of the essays in this volume. I have been particularly interested in two ideas: the first being the division of story from poetics, and the second being the influence of visual materials as a component of the adapted text. Howard Marchitello's careful distinctions in "Descending Shakespeare: Toward a Theory of Adaptation for Children" between *fabula* and *sjužet* remind us to remain keenly aware of the subtlety of this difference, especially when contemplating the varied mechanisms of reception affected when genre modes are transposed. As many contributors who produce adaptations have observed, in the name of "access" adaptations re-cast the narrative structure of the original, usually into linear prose. Both Marchitello and Alison Prindle in " 'The Play's the Thing': Should Genre Take Precedence in Representing Shakespeare?" cite Edith Nesbit's rationale that this format makes difficult material "easy reading"; that it answers children's call to "write the stories for us so that we can understand them . . . and then when we are grown up, we shall understand the plays so much better," (Nesbit, 9) an objective that seems simultaneously promising *and* deleterious. The continued re-publication of Charles and Mary Lamb's *Tales from Shakespeare* and the contemporary success of Bruce Coville's and Lois Burdett's adaptations clearly bear out the effectiveness of accessibility, but the perception of Shakespeare's language as "inaccessible" has put up many seemingly unnecessary barriers that persist well into adulthood.[10] The ultimate objective of many adaptations is to use Shakespeare's language as much as possible, but, as Coville acknowledges, there is often little room for it in a "lean" format. Marchitello cites Peter Brooks's identification of plot-driven narrative with a "pervasive historicism" characteristic of nineteenth-century historical ideology, an important assertion with regard to poetic structure in that it suggests how such "re-tellings" indeed become subject to an inherent linearity that sacrifices some of the pedagogical "value" in Shakespeare's own work. To follow up on Marchitello's example, the plot of *Othello* can be preserved, but not its poetry—by which I do not mean its authentic language, but rather the balance of structure inherent in the original composition, a concern deeply intrinsic to other plays, as Amy Mathur's discussion of *The Tempest* in "Promoting the Original: Perspectives on Balancing Authenticity and Originality in Adaptations of *The Tempest*" demonstrates. We come to understand plays such as *The Tempest* and *Othello* compositionally, even spatially, to borrow a term from Vendler's aforementioned discussion of the Sonnets[11], in patterns that resist linearity. One could not paraphrase a string quartet; its "meaning" is inherent in the multi-dimensional relationships in its formal structure. Shakespeare's compositions are similarly structured, much of their meaning being produced in the resonance of dramatic features set in counterpoint with one another. Shakespeare's *language* is not only a matter of syntax and diction but of structure and the interplay of pattern. Thus, while adaptors express a strong desire to preserve Shakespeare's "language" or "poetry," this terminology is most often invoked in reference to the level of "word" rather than to the level of "poetics." What I find most interesting, however, are the adaptive strategies that have been used to compensate for the perceived loss of Shakespeare's language, since these compensatory strategies demonstrate the attempt to recover a sense of poetic multi-dimensionality within the constraints of a linear narrative.

This is especially apparent in Coville's account in "Nutshells and Infinite Space: Stages of Adaptation" not only of his own process, but also that of his illustrator, Ruth Sanderson. Coville's line counts provide him with a sense of poetic proportion. Further, his description of the balance between image and word in the "picture storybook" format activates the interdependent relationship maintained between these modes of representation, much like the dynamic characteristic of Renaissance emblem literature, in which picture and text illuminate one another in a balanced exchange, as in a dialogue. Coville likens Sanderson's process to that of a director moving, through performance, to what is an essentially emblem-like illustration that enacts the dynamics of the story. Indeed many contributors address the issue of how to "translate" dramatic action—something experienced while *viewing* a play—into an adapted genre; a quality that Prindle characterizes as "absolutely essential." Coville and Sanderson's use of visuality addresses this desire in a textual medium. The interaction between text and picture restores the three-dimensional quality of the poetic structure in Shakespeare's drama, counterbalancing the limiting linearity of the "lean" prose narrative, a connection that the children are poised to make when they themselves transgress these cognitive boundaries. This principle of enactment can be extended, both theoretically and pedagogically, to the way the experiences of other contributors to this volume are discussed in relation to the awareness of Shakespeare's language as well as his "stories." Lois Burdett's experiences with second- and third-grade students over the course of the school year described in her essay, "All the Colours of the Wind," detail a progressive interaction with each play, and an accordant aptitude for, and appreciation of, an increasing complexity of interrelation between plots as well as words. Similarly, Janet Field-Pickering's description of activities in "Shakespeare Steps Out: The Primacy of Language in Inner-City Classrooms" manifest enactment, not simply of scenes or situations, but of language. By physically enacting the rhythm of iambic tetrameter or pentameter by marching to it, dancing to it—as she tellingly says, "whatever it MOVES them to try," the children are producing a *physically mimetic* experience of the poetry.

A deeper understanding of Shakespeare's poetry in each of the instances described begins with an *enactment* of it. The nannies similarly observed children not only delighting in these activities, but also recognizing and replicating patterns when they recurred in other contexts. Games such as those described facilitate the development of language acquisition by expanding on the human tendency to recognize, and revel in, systems of patterning. Moreover, dramatic play helps children further understand the activity of representation, a concept fundamental not only to language but to all aspects of human artistic expression and understanding.[12]

Literary patterning intrinsically taps into children's natural propensity for structure, something that is manifested more complexly in their developing linguistic sophistication—what we begin to identify as "poetry." The evolution experienced by Burdett's students is clearly observable in their own writings, which show an amazing development in cognitive sophistication. In particular, the difference between the student "Devon's" writing is interesting in terms of what he has "learned" about linearity. His first story, "My Fuoor Cricits," is entirely linear, with no sense of temporal flexibility or multi-dimensionality in terms of description. In contrast, his April description of the witches in *Macbeth*, while it tells a linear story—the witches rise out of the marsh and confront Macbeth—shows an awareness of the time sequence being described as well as the dramatic manipulation of time ("Just then," "Finally"). In addition, his narrative shows further signs of poetic complexity in its use of nested phrases and figurative language. This is a child who understands poetry and who manipulates relation and shape. Indeed, most of the examples Burdett provides evince this ability to recognize and produce an extended level of signification inherent in what we would identify as "poetic" structure. In each of these instances, the students have developed an awareness of the multi-dimensionality of Shakespearean literature made available through the construction of *mimetic* responses that resist the *diegetic* linearity of an adapted prose narrative. This is what seems to me to be most essential about Shakespeare's poetry for all of the consciousnesses, of whatever age, that encounter it. As Burdett acknowledges, "Shakespearean language [begins] to creep naturally into [children's] own role-playing and written stories." An excellent example of this influence can be observed in seven-year-old Laura Bates's letter to Tom Patterson, which employs the rhetorical figure of the *chiasmus*: "You have changed the world and the world has changed you." While this student has not been specifically instructed to use or even identify this rhetorical figure, she certainly understands the dynamic of reciprocality inherent in *chiastic* structure and easily activates it in her own expression of thought, similar to the way in which children infer more fundamental linguistic rules, such as the formation of plurals. Children have an innate ability to appreciate Shakespeare because they have an innate ability to recognize pattern and structure and the other fundamental building blocks of language, open as they are to language acquisition. Accordingly, it remains important to question the overwhelming emphasis placed on introducing children to the plays as opposed to the poetry, what Doug King in "'This is Too Scary, Take It Away': Mediating the Supernatural in Adaptations of Shakespeare for Children" identifies as "the privileging of narrative over poetics" as the easiest means by which to access Shakespeare's complexity. Only two collections devoted to Shakespeare's poetry, Gina Pollinger's *Something Rich and Strange: A Treasury of Shakespeare's Verse* and *Under the Greenwood Tree*, edited by Barbara Holdridge, are currently in print, as compared to the wide array of publications centering on adaptations of Shakespeare's drama. Even Pollinger's collection seems obliged in its title to soften its presentation from "poetry" to "verse" in an effort to alleviate what Tiffany Conroy characterizes in "Presenting Shakespeare's Life and Times for Young People: An Outline Using *A Midsummer Night's Dream* and Susan Cooper's *King of* Shadows" as "Shakes-phobia," and a perception of poetry as "too complex" for children.

The Nanny School students' observations paralleled closely the demonstrated propensity for linguistic complexity evinced in Burdett's experiences with her own students,[13] overwhelmingly supporting the assertion that young students are able to interact with Shakespeare's language *and* the intricacy of multiple plots. The Nanny School exercises and, in particular, Burdett's approach to the layers of textual structure in Shakespeare's drama draw on a process similar to that used by mature readers confronting, and embracing, the polysemy in Shakespeare's poetry. We take poems and break them down, piece-by-piece, and then, perhaps most importantly, reassemble them and appreciate the whole, multi-dimensional structure at once, in all the directions in which it moves. Children can do this too, because they can "do" language—they have the innate ability to perceive pattern and to understand linguistic structure. The spellbound rapture Burdett describes in her students as they marvel at a performance of *A Midsummer Night's Dream* is what we try to help all of our students gain access to (in grades thirteen through sixteen as well), not because we teach it to them, but because we help them to find it for themselves. Thus, the aim of this project has not necessarily been to suggest something akin to the "Mozart effect" in Shakespeare for children, but has rather been to investigate the ways in which relatively "sophisticated" literature embodies fundamental language principles that can be accessed and activated in children whose language skills are in the early stages of development, reinforcing similar "lessons" gained from exposure to texts more typically classified as "children's literature." Indeed, I have found many of these strategies to be pedagogically effective for college students with both limited and extensive literature background. The experiences within the Nanny School curriculum explored ways in which Shakespeare, whose poetics remain so rich in pattern, can allow us to tap and develop the innate affinity children have for language and their desire, like ours, to explore its possibilities, allowing the artistic imagination to "go on and on forever in a nonstopping dream" (Anika, age 8, Burdett).

Notes

1. Students are trained to observe the important cognitive and developmental distinction between asking children to dramatize each event as the story is read aloud and asking the children to become responsible for reconstructing the narrative on their own.
2. While it provided many promising insights for future exploration, the development of this study was constrained by two limitations. Each Nanny School term comprises only twelve weeks, making an extended study of development in the children difficult. Also, as the Literature instructor I did not have direct contact with the families myself, so I could not observe the children's responses directly. Students kept journals detailing the reactions of their children to the literature and activities that were part of each week's practicum experience. Rather than serving as a log, however, I asked the students to focus their journal writings on their own assessment of each activity's success: Did the children respond well to the reading? Did they ask to hear it again? Did they enjoy the activity? Did they create their own extension or elaboration of the activity? And most importantly, why does the nanny think this happened? What does she think is the crucial element of the poem or project that activated something in the child's mind? Moreover, the primary aim of the journal was to serve as a pedagogical experience for the nanny, rather than as a case-study of her charges, functioning as a means through which the nanny herself could recognize and articulate language development-related issues as part of her own learning process.
3. Steven Pinker, *The Language Instinct: How the Mind Creates Language* (New York: William Morrow, 1994). See also Pinker, *Language Learnability and Language Development* (Cambridge, MA: Harvard University Press, 1984) and "A Learnability Paradox," in *Learnability and Cognition: The Acquisition of Argument Structure* (Cambridge, MA: M.I.T. Press, 1991).
4. A typical example of children's inference of linguistic "rules" is observable in the formation of plurals. A three-year-old child will be able to appropriately complete a sentence that calls for the formation of a plural. When shown a pair of ducks, and told, "Here is a duck. Here is another duck. There are now two ____," the child will say, "ducks." To prove that the child is applying a rule and has not independently learned the words "duck" and "ducks," the experimenter substitutes a fabricated word, "wug," in reference to a picture of a cartoon bird. The same sentence completion exercise follows: "Here is a wug. Here is another wug. There are now two ____," . . . "wugs." The fact that the child had never been taught the word "wug" or "wugs" proves that he is applying a rule, invoking a recognized pattern in his use of language. See Peter Gordon, "Level Ordering in Lexical Development" *Cognition* (1986): 21, 73–93.

5. Aboriginal "songlines" are an extended example of this cognitive property.
6. Helen Vendler, *The Art of Shakespeare's Sonnets* (Cambridge, MA: Harvard University Press, 1997).
7. References are to Arden editions.
8. Rex Gibson and Janet Field-Pickering, *Discovering Shakespeare's Language* (Cambridge: Cambridge University Press, 1998).
9. Similar exercises are detailed throughout Fred Sedgwick's recent volume *Shakespeare and the Young Writer* (London: Routledge, 1999). The Nanny School project transpired before the appearance of this volume and would have benefited by incorporating some of the exercises Sedgwick describes. In particular, the chapters "Single Lines and Single Speeches" and "Bright Smoke" provide excellent exercises with similar pedagogical objectives to those related here.
10. It proved much more difficult in many cases for the nannies themselves to access Shakespearean text with any level of comfort than it did for the children to do so.
11. Vendler, *Passim.* In particular, see her introduction to the volume.
12. Note also Sedgwick's description of the value inherent in the physicality of "play," and its various theoretical incarnations, in his overview of that concept in his introduction.
13. Sedgwick, too, frequently chronicles his surprise at underestimating his young students' abilities to comprehend and manipulate complex and subtle abstract, figurative concepts.

Works Cited

Brooks, Peter. *Reading for the Plot: Design and Intention in Narrative.* New York: Knopf, 1984. Reprint, Cambridge, MA: Harvard University Press, 1992.

Carroll, David W. *Psychology of Language.* Belmont, CA: Wadsworth, 1986.

Gibson, Rex and Janet Field-Pickering. *Discovering Shakespeare's Language.* Cambridge: Cambridge University Press, 1998.

Gordon, Peter. "Level Ordering in Lexical Development." *Cognition* 21 (1986): 73–93.

Language: An Invitation to Cognitive Science. Vol. 1. Eds. Daniel N. Osherson and Howard Lasnik. Cambridge, MA: M.I.T. Press, 1990.

Milne, A. A. *When We Were Very Young.* New York: Penguin Putnam, 1992.

Nesbit, Edith. *Best of Shakespeare. The Children's Shakespeare*, 1900. Reprint with a foreword by Iona Opie and an afterword by Peter Hunt. Oxford: Oxford University Press, 1997.

Pinker, Steven. *The Language Instinct: How the Mind Creates Language.* New York: Harper Collins, 1995.

———. *Language Learnability and Language Development.* Cambridge, MA: Harvard University Press, 1984.

———. "A Learnability Paradox." In *Learnability and Cognition: The Acquisition of Argument Structure.* Cambridge, MA: M.I.T. Press, 1991.

Pollinger, Gina. *Something Rich and Strange: A Treasury of Shakespeare's Verse.* New York: Larousse Kingfisher Chambers, 1995.

Shakespeare, William. *Cymbeline*. Ed. J. M. Nosworthy. The Arden Shakespeare. 1955. Reprint, London: Routledge, 1989.

———. *Macbeth*. Ed. Kenneth Muir. The Arden Shakespeare. 1951. Reprint, London: Methuen, 1987.

———. *The Merchant of Venice*. Ed. John Russell Brown. The Arden Shakespeare. 1955. Reprint, London: Routledge, 1991.

———. *A Midsummer Night's Dream*. Ed. Harold F. Brooks. The Arden Shakespeare. 1979. Reprint, London: Routledge, 1990.

———. *Romeo and Juliet*. Ed. Brian Gibbons. The Arden Shakespeare. London: Methuen, 1980.

———. *Shakespeare's Sonnets*. Ed. Katherine Duncan-Jones. The Arden Shakespeare. London: Thomas Nelson & Sons, 1997.

———. *The Tempest*. Ed. Frank Kermode. The Arden Shakespeare. 1954. Reprint, London: Routledge, 1988.

———. *Timon of Athens*. Ed. H. J. Oliver. The Arden Shakespeare. 1959. Reprint, Surrey: Thomas Nelson & Sons, 1997.

———. *Twelfth Night*. Ed. J. M. Lothian and W. T. Craik. The Arden Shakespeare. 1975. Reprint, London: Routledge, 1988.

Stevenson, Robert Louis. *A Child's Garden of Verses*. New York: Penguin Putnam, 1978.

Under the Greenwood Tree: *Shakespeare for Young People*. Ed. Barbara Holdridge. Owings Mills, MD: Stemmer House, 1994.

Vendler, Helen. *The Art of Shakespeare's Sonnets*. Cambridge, MA: Harvard University Press, 1997.

Zipes, Jack. *Fairy Tale as Myth*, *Myth as Fairy Tale*. Lexington: University Press of Kentucky, 1994.

25. Players, Playgrounds, and Grounds for Play

Play v. Theater v. Realism in a Touring Children's Version of *King Lear*

JOHN BARNES

Players and Play

Play is what children do instead of work. An adult who says she needs time to play means she has been working too much. In current slang a player is a man who pursues relationships without being serious about them, i.e., not working at them. Yet in theatre and sports, a "player" is a participant, the person actually doing the work.

In the 1992–93 school year, the Three Rivers Shakespeare Festival (3RSF) sent out its Young Company—graduate students from the Pitt theatre department—to present *King Lear* to elementary school children. Most of the grad students involved were paid to do it as part of their assistantships. Hence the players were working. The work they did was to play in front of the children, who, instead of playing, were expected to sit still and watch.

Playing always involves pretending. In games played by adults, the pretense is of seriousness—anyone playing basketball must pretend that it matters to him which hoop a ball goes through under what circumstances, anyone playing chess must pretend that she cares whether the king is in check. Anyone who cannot pretend that the game matters is no fun to play with.

In children's pretend play, though, the children do not merely pretend that the game itself is serious. Children "playing army" pretend that they are soldiers and that their neighborhood is a battlefield. "Playing Barbies" means pretending that Barbie's life is real. This is the sense of "play" as "act" or "represent," and is closely connected to "playing" in the theatre.

Both children's playing and the adult actor's playing require conventions. Some are sweeping: how far in time and space the sacramental process is allowed to alter the meaning of what we see and hear, e.g., that people moving around in the lighted area are part of the performance, and people sitting in the darkened area are not; or that if you are playing cops and robbers

231

on Saturday, you cannot wait until Monday to "shoot the bad guy" and get him from behind during school recess. Some conventions dictate what pretend situations can and cannot occur within play: no French critic ever enforced the canons of neoclassicism as strenuously as outraged children protesting that "She's not on that show!" or that "Spider-Man can't be in the same time as Robin Hood!" The actor is the character until the curtain call, and then the actor is the actor; the monster may have to answer a question from his mother before he can resume being the monster. There is a right way to express or simulate every situation—the "victim control" rule for stage combat, or the unwritten rule that a toy plane must be flown with the hand so that it always moves nose first, and while it is flying one must make engine noises.

On the playground or on the stage, conventions are violated at peril, as we tell any novice student in directing class; if actors touch audience members in suggestive ways, they may be touched back; if actors verbally abuse the audience, their performance may be disrupted by infuriated spectators. By delimiting the boundaries within which play is serious, conventions permit players and audience alike to take things seriously enough to have fun.

In the great game that is our theatre as a whole, most artists are not paid, and the few who are mostly teach rather than practice. In this sense, the contemporary theatre is mostly playing at playing—which is why the participants must take it seriously. In the theatre subculture the most extreme praise/blame is expressed by "professional/unprofessional." To be "professional" is to treat one's theatre work seriously and to know the requisite traditions and customs; to be "unprofessional" is to behave as if the production, tradition, or one's fellow artists do not matter. Professionalism is a matter of taking the game seriously enough to collaborate in it, with all the other artists, living and dead, understanding that the game matters more than one's own desires.

Other children will not play with a child who has too much imagination about the conventions of the game. If rules and givens of the game constantly change at the whim of one or more players, those who play more seriously can no longer win, those who do not invest themselves into the game wholeheartedly are assured of winning, and the final outcome, being purely the wish-fulfillment of the overly-imaginative and under-invested child, will be much too predictable.

The graduate students of the 3RSF Young Company had to be professional because they were only playing at a professional situation. They were directing, designing, and performing for money, but the money wasn't sufficient for anyone to stay in such a job on a long-term basis. The jobs were intended as resumébuilders. Hence I was thoroughly serious about being contracted to design and construct the set for *King Lear* on a budget of $750, just as the director, the stage manager, the other designers, and the actors were thoroughly serious about their work.

Grounds for Play

The drive to play appears to be innate and powerful. Despite the pressure against play exerted by generations of television, supervised activity, school, child labor, and reading, children still play (though not nearly as much as would be good for them).

Play not only allows the young to try on many of the attributes and situations of adulthood in an environment without lasting consequences, but also to enact (and hence powerfully reinforce) expected cultural standards of behavior. No child elects to play a coward, and most of the traditional sins are remarkable for their absence in children's pretend games; the villains are generally motiveless, or at worst greedy or aggressive. Children's play is openly conservative, reinforcing rather than challenging the accepted; the adult theatre is populated with people who like to pretend that they are innovating, but theatre that innovates to any great extent is generally incomprehensible and dull to most of the audience, and most "innovative" or "experimental" productions of the present day are merely repeating experiments that were first tried in the 1890-1920 period and were repeated frequently throughout the whole twentieth century.

Conservatism of play dominated 3RSF's production of *King Lear*. As in most Shakespeare festivals, most 3RSF productions are "concept" productions—that is, the director and designers choose a period and place different from the nominal, and apply it as an organizing metaphor. Such productions have dominated Shakespearean production since World War Two, and are now the absolutely conventional way of presenting Shakespeare.

This dominance is natural. Concept productions offer several advantages to the producing organization—much greater visual variety in a season, the option of choosing recent periods and places (and hence being able to costume and decorate out of second-hand stores rather than build everything from scratch) to reduce budget, and clear "sound-biteable" statements from the artistic team that can be easily explained to local media. For the modern audience, concept productions make Shakespeare far more accessible, by providing readable visual cues to textual situations (few people today know the significance of an unbraced doublet, or would be able to recognize one in a picture, but put Hamlet in a tuxedo with the shirt undone, and the visual metaphor carries the necessary information). The right choice of period and place can also clarify relationships between character groups—e.g., setting *Troilus and Cressida* during the American Civil War, with Trojans as Rebs. A well-chosen metaphor focuses audience attention on the issues the director wants to emphasize (e.g., in many productions of the Bolingbroke plays on chessboards, *Richard III* in fascist states, or *Romeo and Juliet* on a racial, religious, or class divide). Moreover, over time, festival audiences are trained to become better "readers" of concepts, reinforcing the tendency.

It was perfectly natural, then, for the 3RSF to decide that the Young Company touring productions should be directed and designed around concepts, supposedly to provide easier access for children, teachers, and parents, and to train future audiences to identify the concept and use it to make sense of the production.

3RSF thus chose to set *King Lear* in the Chicago of the 1920s, in the hope that the sense of lawless struggle between violent, treacherous forces would be clearer in that context than in either Renaissance or pre-Roman Britain. Now, given that the audience was children, for whom 1925, 1595, and 255 B.C. are all equally "olden times," it is dubious that the concept provided any better access. Indeed, the pre-show preparation packet sent to elementary schools included about as much material about the 1920s as it did about *King Lear*.

The choice of concept also created a contradiction that had some impact on design and presentation: it only further emphasized the play as one of Shakespeare's most sanguinary, savage, and cruel. But the grounds of public schools are an area that the "adult," "working" world strongly wants to see supervised; many subjects are thought unsuitable for either children's play or children's plays. Hence at the same time that the cast was being equipped with wide-lapeled pinstriped suits and fedoras, and (prop) Tommy guns for their violin cases, the textual basis for comparing the Britain of Lear with the Chicago of Capone was being excised as far as possible.

Play resists censorship the way the Internet does: not by direct opposition, but by flowing around the censor like a flood around a levee. Children try to keep as much material as possible within the game, and artists try to do the same with performance, by the simple expedient of hiding the offensive parts. Children who are not supposed to have toy guns avoid observation when playing at gunfighting, games that involve swearing or nudity are kept at a distance from adults, and when passing adults are pretend monsters, only very young children will actually point at the adult and shout. Similarly, actors in *King Lear* learned early on to avoid visual reinforcement of the more extreme violence and cruelty in the dialogue; since few in the audience could understand what was being said, if the actors did not physicalize it, it generally passed without offense.

Playgrounds and Playing Areas: Realism v. Theatre

Children's play may be vital to psychocommunicational development, nurturing the subjunctive habit of thought needed for many of the mental and emotional skills of adulthood—abstraction, teamwork, planning, empathy, and comparison of consequences, among many others. This includes the child's development of metacommunication, learning that "You be an alien and I'll be an Earth astronaut" is appropriate in playing space explorers, and meaningless in playing house or doctor. This is the sort of mental map needed for learning the difference between gossip and indiscretion, or between appropriate behavior in the staff lounge versus in the conference room. That is, subjunctive—"as if"—play permits children to practice behaving in accord with a sense of place.

Spaces create rules for play. In sports and in realism, spaces must be restrictive and dense with meaning. There is no feasible way of playing basketball on a baseball diamond, nor hopscotch on a shuffleboard court. Realistic theatrical spaces are created exclusively for a given situation or script, often very narrowly so; although *A Doll's House, Who's Afraid of Virginia Woolf?*, *The Homecoming*, and *The Man Who Came to Dinner* all take place in a parlor, it cannot be the same parlor. Some children's playground designers deliberately create sculptures that have a single intent; children can be heard telling each other that this tower is a rocket ship so we only play space explorers on it, or that jungle gym is shaped like a castle so we can't play that it's the police station.

Such spaces have densely interconnected meanings—any point in the space will be significant at most moments. No one confuses the significance of stealing third with the significance of stealing home; if anyone other than Archie Bunker sits in Archie Bunker's chair, something is immediately meant.

In scenography, realism is both the hardest problem to solve and the easiest one to grasp: the space must appear to the audience as an everyday space in which people live, move, and interact, yet a performance space requires many other things—raised places at the back; a number of places to sit greater than the maximum number of actors on stage at a time; clear physical relationships between actors, doorways and other shapes that frame and emphasize actors; discrete planes of lateral motion to make depth identifiable, multiple pathways between points to prevent repetitive rhythms, and so on. Both of these requirements—that it look just like a living room and that at the same time it be a performance space—are constraints on the designer, whose set will in turn impose constraints on the director. The Cain's-mark of ineffectual designers and directors of realism is when we see violations of these constraints: the actor who climbs onto a couch or table to declaim (because there is no suitable high place available), the wall marked by a "chainsawed" partial wall (because the designer was not clever enough to place it outside sightlines), the recurring lineup of four people in a single plane (because they must go to the same spot and there's only one way there). In realistic scenography, the intersection of "realistic" and "performance" constraints becomes part of the rules; to violate them is to cheat. Designing for realism, in short, is a sport.

Designing for theatre is play, much like children's pretend play—it calls for a space in which meaning is sparsely interconnected, created by the players moment to moment. In theatre this is variously called the empty space, the open stage, the plataea, or simply the bare stage. For children, this is "the playground." In such spaces there are relatively few constraints; one may be on a starship at one moment and in an ice-age cave the next. Bare stages and playgrounds are spaces in which people play with each other, freely assigning meaning to continue play; realistic stages and sports fields are spaces with which people play, drawing meaning from the interrelation of space with play.

What Kind of Space for Lear?

Physical, textual, and budgetary constraints demanded that our *King Lear* be theatrical rather than realistic. The set had to fold down to go into the back of a van, in which a substantial amount of space was already reserved for costumes. Costume changes had to be rapid for four people to play so many characters, and thus had to be in full view of the audience (since either blackouts or entrances and exits would take far too much time). Finally, the spaces into which the show would be mounted varied greatly, with all four major configurations (end-stage, alley, thrust, and arena) possible, with some raised, some depressed, and some floor-level playing areas. Setup time of more than two hours could not be counted on, so the sets needed not just lightness and ease of assembly, but also the ability to reconfigure quickly to solve unanticipated problems such as pillars in important sightlines, very wide and shallow end stages, or thrust spaces with no rear entrance.

The text itself further compelled a bare stage; there are essentially four kinds of spaces in the play—court, military camp/fortress, docks/port, and barren heath—and scenes are set in more than one of each. Many scenes in the original are brief—about half are less than ten minutes— and many cuts for the 3RSF version had further reduced the average scene length, in part because rapid changes are often useful in maintaining the attention of younger children.

Finally, $750 did not go very far; at that time, for example, a simple raised $4' \times 8'$ platform cost about $85 when built from scratch, a plain $4' \times 8'$ scenic flat cost about $60, and specialty flats (doors, windows, etc.) could run as much as $135. Even a very small conventional endstage set would have required between four and six platforms and about ten flats, perhaps three of which might be specialties. This would mean a minimum cost of around $1100, and would of course be too heavy and bulky to haul, too visually inflexible to support the narrative, and too difficult to modify quickly for local physical constraints.

The production needed a set consisting of a few durable, lightweight, cheaply-constructed pieces; able to stand free of each other and at least somewhat three-dimensional (so that when they were arranged for different spaces, they could remain functional regardless of the angle the audience saw them from); usable for all the four basic locations (so that they need not be carried in and out of the playing area during the rapid scene changes); in reasonable accord with the 1920s/Chicago/amoral-violent-power-struggle concept.

After some discussion and a great deal of conceptualizing (mainly quick pencil sketching), I settled on six "roscoes," as we dubbed them: plywood versions of the standard lifesize head-and-shoulders pistol target, which could either be slipped onto metal poles that stood on lightweight circular bases, or hung from the bar of a costume rack, facing outward (the costume racks doubled as backdrops for most spaces). Two notches in the shoulders allowed a mini-flat (5′ tall by 3′ wide) to be hung on the roscoe, completely covering it (which then, visually, became a painting on a stand).

The roscoes were light enough for even the smallest actor to lift and carry by the back hook or support pole. "Wearing" a painting in its shoulder notches, a roscoe could serve as a signboard for the setting, and only four paintings were needed, one for each of the basic locations. Sitting on its stand and wearing a costume, a roscoe could play a character, as a kind of puppet. Hung facing outward from a costume rack at the back of the stage, several roscoes in costumes could become a crowd or an army. In principle, the roscoes were a set of toys or fixtures like a playground jungle gym or slide— able to be many different things with just a shift in description, a change of hat or coat, or a quick move by any of the actors.

Play Trumps Design; Any Space for the King?

During the first three weeks of rehearsal, the roscoes were being assembled and their physical bugs worked out. Scenic pieces rarely if ever work perfectly the first time, and among other issues, a whole day each went into perfecting the slip-mounting to the pole, the hook for the horizontal bar, and the fitting of the shoulder slots to the L-brackets of the paintings, so that pieces could be handled quickly and surely. Meanwhile, rehearsals proceeded.

This was a very playful and creative cast, and they had a playful and creative director who also had enough self-confidence to allow the actors to explore and improvise and adjust her concepts as they worked together. The director and actors worked and revised scenes on their feet in the kind of continuous give-and-take that characterizes the best rehearsals.

As a basis for deciding what to do about the roscoes, they had only a brief oral presentation I had given them. Time did not permit the customary building of a set model, and in any case a half-inch scale model—which would have consisted of six 2.5″ tall roscoes and four playing-card-sized paintings, all sitting on a 10″ square of cardboard—would probably not have communicated effectively into their fundamentally kinesthetic rehearsal process. Drawings, too, would have been meaningless—six roscoes, put them where you like. Consequently, what they had to do was "play like" they had roscoes—that is, use chairs or small stands as "pretend" roscoes.

My oral presentation had stressed that the roscoes supported a wide range of flexible improvisation in staging. Without any controlling, repeated messages about the physical limitations of the roscoes, over time, in the rehearsal process, the expected "pretend" roscoes became much more than the delivered roscoes could ever be. For example, the actors issued challenges from the battlements of the fortress, not realizing that there was nothing to stand on behind the painting. Some extremely rapid scene changes were planned in which paintings would be running on and off stage, barely pausing at the roscoe that held them. Actors expected to be able to stand unobserved behind a painting that was only three feet wide and suspended a foot off the floor. The expected roscoes had become magic scenery of the imagination, like the playground slide which can become a spaceship to Mars one minute, and a medieval castle the next.

The real roscoes, of course, could never live up to such expectations. They were like toys in television commercials that are made more appealing with up-close photography and quick cuts to suggest motion—without subtitles to the effect that the toy does not move by itself, does not act of its own volition, and is only a few inches high.

There is a reason why those subtitles are legally required. The real roscoes could not be the set of the company's dreams; they were three-dimensional sketches of scenery, not "real" scenic pieces; their transformability required that they be played with—they couldn't do it on their own. When they were at last delivered, the cast was severely disappointed, and the director chose to cut and reduce the role of the roscoes in several ways, including eliminating the paintings.

Gradually, as the show toured to more schools during the spring, the cast did make more use of the roscoes as puppets and to represent crowds, because they continued to improvise and found that they were useful for that kind of play. But the vision they had created in rehearsal, in the spirit of play, was never realized in the "real" play—which played, in turn, in front of people who should have been playing, but were watching adults play for them, while the adults played at working at play.

Did What the Players Played Play on the Playground?

The great majority of children probably found the play incomprehensible (as did more of their teachers than would be likely to admit it). Severely edited to be performed by just four actors in a little over an hour, and visually re-set to "Chicago in the Roaring Twenties," *King Lear's* connection to Shakespeare, apart from the dialogue itself, was attenuated. In any case the themes and ideas were thankfully far from the experience of most children—futility, old age, sheer bloody-minded brutality, the perversity of fate. Yet obvious though it was that we were communicating a message of little relevance to a mostly uninterested audience using confusing (and often self-contradictory) conventions, the company remained serious about the play and tried to maintain a high standard of "professionalism"—perhaps the most successful playing associated with the production.

26. Presenting Shakespeare's Life and Times for Young People

An Outline Using *Midsummer Night's Dream* and Susan Cooper's *King of Shadows*

TIFFANY A. CONROY

I: New Materials, New Attitudes

As a teacher of introductory college literature courses and Shakespeare courses for adult learners, I have heard a great deal about students' reactions to Shakespeare. I begin any course or unit on Shakespeare by soliciting information about which plays the students have already read, under what circumstances, what their reactions were to those plays and if they have recently read or viewed any Shakespeare for their pleasure, that is, outside formal school settings. Beyond the usual one or two students who really care about literature, the typical reactions reveal several things: first, that the middle school and high school presentation of Shakespeare is largely limited to the page. Few students ever get the chance to read scenes aloud, let alone actually participate in the production of a Shakespeare play. Second, students usually read only tragedies and histories (*Julius Caesar, Macbeth, Hamlet*), which seem to have bored them to death, and they cannot recall any themes which they related to, nor do they feel that those works were in any way entertaining to read. Third, they all claim—adults too—that Shakespeare's language prevents them from reading the plays for pleasure just as it precluded their enjoyment of them in grade school. Fourth, it emerges that they know very little if anything about Elizabethan culture, theater, or Shakespeare's life. All of these symptoms amount to a condition I, almost jestingly, diagnose as "Shakes-phobia."

So why is it that Shakespeare is making a popular comeback at the turn of the century? Shakes-phobia is melting away and I have a few ideas about why. Most visibly, the movies are repackaging Shakespeare, his era, and his works—Kenneth Branagh and the like have spent the last two decades adapting Shakespeare in true cinematic style—even a new musical *Love's Labour's Lost*! With popular actors, lavish effects and costumes, and plenty of hype, the stodgy old BBC videos have been blasted away by our most popular and accessible form of entertainment. In the age of TV, video, and the Internet, the conventions of film are comprehended, nay, *internalized* by the majority of people. Almost every student I had in class two years ago had seen *Shakespeare in Love* and at least one major film version of a Shakespeare play that was produced in the last ten years. Interestingly, as we read scenes and then watched them on video, I found that the students needed very little prompting to notice and analyze such things as scenery, props, costumes, music, and characterization. This is their comfort zone; once they get excited about the connections between film and text it is only a small jump to get them on their feet performing and, perhaps someday, into the theater as well.

As a scholar and cultural observer I find there are other developments that have led to advances in the treatment of Shakes-phobia. Due to the "lit. crit." vogue in New Historicism and its related fields, (feminism, Queer studies, and so on), the text is no longer an abstracted creation from the brain of a superman. Thus, we view the text as a product of its culture and believe that in order to understand it we must immerse ourselves in the world of its genesis—its laws, its customs, its traditions, its sights, sounds, and smells. Furthermore, despite some suspicious "Bardolatry" tendencies in *Shakespeare in Love*, the artist/writer is no longer the Romantic genius-hero—we put writers on trial for their sexism, racism, classism, you-name-it-ism—rather, the author is not above the foibles of humanity, not even Shakespeare. To wit, the Shakespeare of *Shakespeare in Love*, as my students readily recall, was a man who shared the needs (ahem), of all young men, and he was cute enough, despite his "nerdy" occupation, to get the woman he wanted. Heck, even the queen is "cool" in this movie! While iconoclasm might be driving the Bard out of some fanatically revisionist college curricula, it also brings about a certain domestication of Shakespeare, casting his life and times in a light that is more human than divine.

Almost a century after John Dewey, educators have managed to alter pedagogical methods in nearly all academic subject areas. Interaction, activity, and exploration are not just for shop class and home economics (neither of which actually seem to exist anymore). Instead, the student-centered approach applies to literature and mathematics as well. We have finally realized that to get students of any age, but especially young ones, to engage with a strange, far-off world and its products we must engage their natural curiosity and readily activated imaginations. Of the new books for young readers I have gathered to construct this syllabus, nearly every one puts the reader directly into the world of Shakespeare with all its variety—food, dress, music, politics, theater—and each presents his life as the experience of a real man who was not solely a writer, but also a father, a businessman, and an actor. I found that this approach not only appeals to the very young, but also to the college students and adults I have in my classes—after all, they are there because they have been intrigued by the films they have seen and their curiosity has been aroused by the Bard's mystique and ever-enduring cultural appeal. I might not have my adult and twenty-something students make fake swords and stage a duel, but I do get them up on their feet, speaking, imagining, *participating* in Shakespeare's world and words. What's more, they are beginning to like it, and as I look at all of the wonderful books and films being produced I foresee a generation of "Shakes-*philes*" coming up through the ranks and into my classroom . . . and yours.

II: Using Susan Cooper's *King of Shadows* as a Course Cornerstone

Originally, I had intended to survey a small selection of new books for young readers on the life and times of Shakespeare. But one of those books, Susan Cooper's *King of Shadows*, so deeply moved and impressed me that I decided to place her book at the forefront. Furthermore, I wanted to do something that might have some practical application in the classroom. This is why I decided to take the materials at hand and assemble a rough outline that I hope some of my readers will be able to adapt into a syllabus to suit their own purposes.

This outline aims to present a unit that would accompany or precede the study and/or performance of a Shakespeare play. The primary texts are *A Midsummer Night's Dream* (MND), Susan Cooper's *King of Shadows*, and supplemental selections from other plays mentioned in her book: *Henry V* (H5), *The Tempest*, and Sonnet 116. I think MND is an apt choice not only because it is central to Cooper's novel and shares its themes of imagination and playing with reality, but also because many students feel more comfortable reading a Shakespearean comedy. I have used the play in the classroom and find that students truly enjoy it. It seems to have something for everyone: young lovers, magic, moronic would-be actors, and the like.

Secondary texts are drawn from the excellent books for "children" which I have gathered: *Shakespeare and the Globe* (Aliki); *The World of Shakespeare* (Claybourne and Treays); *Bard of Avon: The Story of William Shakespeare* (Stanley and Venemma); *Shakespeare for Kids: His Life and Times, 21 Activities* (Aagesen and Blumberg); and *Shakespeare's Theater* (Morley and James). For the teachers' research purposes, or for use in more advanced/mature classes, I include Burgess's *Mouthful of Air*; *The Riverside Shakespeare* (particularly for its criticism and background materials); *The Bedford Companion to Shakespeare*; and Somerset's *Elizabeth I*. All students will enjoy the New Globe Web site and the films I have included. Film, as I indicated, is a vital tool in the contemporary classroom, and the Internet is an invaluable resource with many more useful Web sites devoted to Shakespeare than I could possibly list here. The Internet Shakespeare site is a good starting point—http://web.uvic.ca/shakespeare—with many useful links for students and teachers.

Hopefully, this outline based upon Cooper's short novel can be altered to suit many levels of learners, from middle school to introductory college and adult learners. A teacher should choose to emphasize certain things based upon the particular class demographics and dynamics. Thus, I have included more information than it would be possible to cover given the limitations of classroom contact time. It might seem odd to center college or adult lessons around a young adult novel, but I have given the book to several older students (and to my mother), and they really enjoyed it—it has served to feed their fantasy without insulting their intelligence in the slightest bit. Its length and the ease of its prose are useful for the community college or adult learner setting because reading the novel will not detract from the demands of work or other classes and will allow plenty of time to carefully study MND, the scenes, and the Sonnets.

III: The Outline

Preparatory Lesson: Since the book *King of Shadows* does not deal with Shakespeare's pre-London life, do a lesson on Shakespeare's biography. *Shakespeare for Kids*, in addition to its activities, is particularly strong and concise on this topic; the books *Bard of Avon* and *Shakespeare's Theater* also have a few pages devoted to biography. Depending upon which edition of MND you use, you can refer to the brief biography provided in the introduction. Maps of Stratford, pictures of Shakespeare's homes and school, and the family tree all serve to place Shakespeare in his historical context with visual reinforcement. *Shakespeare in Love* could be assigned or viewed in class to get students geared up for what is to come, although it isn't really a biography, nor does it give a complete or entirely accurate picture of the age.

> Activities: Give students a list of the characters in the film *Shakespeare in Love* and have them gather biographical information on them and compare them with the film's representation. At the end of the course you could revisit this film and see if the students think the depictions of Shakespeare, Queen Elizabeth, and so on are more or less accurate/believable than Cooper's characters.

Chapter 1: Cooper's book opens with the contemporary Company of Boys in rehearsal prior to their trip to London. We meet Nat and his fellow actors as Arby, their irritable, dictatorial teacher/director runs them through some common theater games. Since one of the goals in this course is to get students on their feet, acting out what they are reading in MND, do some of these games in class.

> **Game 1**: A trust game is illustrated in the opening—one student stands in the center of a group of three or four other students (you need to match

sizes/weights here), and the central person closes his eyes and maintains a stiff body position while free falling into the arms of the other students who gently catch and push the student on to the other catchers. It is interesting to hear students' reactions after doing this exercise and to ask why it might be important for a group of actors, teammates, or co-workers to trust each other.

Game 2: The circle game has a variation I would suggest using—everyone stands or sits in a circle. You may use a ball for the students to toss around to determine order, or students can call out the name of another student (which is good if the students don't know each other already). Put a line or two from MND on the board that everyone will call out. The goal is to say the line slowly, loudly, and clearly.

Language: The dictionary *Coined by Shakespeare* published by Merriam-Webster is highly entertaining and students are often surprised to find how many common words made their debut in Shakespeare's writings. *The World of Shakespeare* has two pages on Shakespeare's language.

MND Preview: In addition to discussing the characters encountered in this chapter, particularly Arby and Nat, this would be a good time to begin MND. Nat introduces the play here himself, so a list of characters and a review of the general plot would be helpful. *Shakespeare's Theater* has a two-page illustrated synopsis of MND, (34-35).

Note: This syllabus is not directly concerned with MND; you should proceed with assignments of readings in MND at whatever pace seems appropriate to your class, or you might hold off until the end of Cooper's book and do MND afterwards. The best method is to begin slowly—with selections, poems, scenes—and then accelerate. As the amount of supplementary material decreases, you can increase the use of Shakespeare's texts and spend more class time on film critique, discussion, rehearsal, and performance.

Chapter 2: Nat and the Company of Boys go to London and rehearse at the New Globe.

The theater: How Elizabethan theater worked. "Act 3" in *Shakespeare for Kids* has plenty of good information and pictures; *Bard of Avon* has several pages to help here as well. *Shakespeare's Theater* is the most comprehensive on this topic, covering theater and the business of theater, from classical to medieval times. Aliki's book is particularly good on the rebuilding of the Globe, as is the Globe Web site: http://www.shakespeares-globe.org.

Language: The Early Modern accent is brought up in this chapter. This is worth pointing out to your students, and Anthony Burgess's book *A Mouthful of Air* has a chapter on Elizabethan pronunciation. Students might have already noticed that much of the verse in MND does not really rhyme, so if you can imitate the accent in a few lines you can illustrate how they might have rhymed in Shakespeare's day.

Characters in novel: Arby's mysterious nature is hinted at, (14, 19-20, 26). You might subtly point out his peculiarities, unless you would rather go back to them after the "mystery" is solved. Nat begins having his "episodes"—the class could speculate about what is happening to him.

MND: There is a great deal of quotation from MND here to read over. The acrobatics of Puck are pointed out in the blocking. This would be a good time to discuss Puck specifically if you are reading the play. Perhaps assign some kind of informal or formal essay on his character based upon gathering quotes from the text. On the more creative end, students could come up with sketches of him. Any characters would lend themselves to this sort of exercise; moreover, getting students to represent characters visually helps them understand how directors and actors use their imaginations in transposing Shakespeare's texts to the stage or screen.

Nat: Nat's problem dealing with the loss of his father is reiterated at the end of this chapter. This theme runs through the entire book, and his emotional attachment to Shakespeare is related to his need for a father figure.

Chapters 3 and 4: In **chapter 3** Nat has a dream; in **chapter 4** Nat wakes up in Elizabethan London, a loan to Shakespeare's Lord Chamberlain's Men.

> **Elizabethan life**: Issues to cover include plague, sanitation, clothing, food and ale, language, and public executions. *Shakespeare for Kids* is great for this, and has activities to illustrate almost all aspects of everyday life. *The World of Shakespeare* also has some very useful, highly pictorial pages on the beliefs and culture of the era. For advanced classes, *The Bedford Companion to Shakespeare* has essays on Elizabethan life.
>
> **Richard Burbage**: Almost every children's book I have listed in the bibliography makes mention of Richard Burbage. He should be discussed in terms of the theater business, the original "Globe," a.k.a. "The Theater," and the practice of apprenticeship.

Chapters 5 and 6: In **chapter 5** we find Nat in a London hospital diagnosed with bubonic plague; **chapter 6** takes place in the Globe when it was new, 1599.

> **Plague**: There is a fun activity in *Shakespeare for Kids* to make a pomander ball, these as well as flowers and herbs were thought to sweeten the air and thus prevent the plague. (You could also explain the "Ring Around the Rosy" song, if anyone still knows it, which is about the plague.) Certainly, it is emblematic of the gulf between our eras to discuss scientific—or not-so-scientific—ideas about how diseases spread.
>
> **The theater**: The Globe Theatre inside and out. *Shakespeare's Theater* and Aliki provide clear diagrams of the house and backstage areas as well as mention of the prices and the behavior of the typical crowd—it is always interesting to discuss the differences between audience behavior then and now, with any level of students. Experiment with audience behavior—have a few students practice reading short speeches with the class sitting quietly. Then have them recite the speeches with students wandering around, talk-

ing and heckling. Discuss both experiences from the point of view of the audience and actors.

Fools and clowns: We meet Will Kempe as he quits the company. A lesson on fools, clowns, and minstrels could be inserted here—list Shakespeare's other buffoonish characters and point out how Bottom represents one of that type. *Bard of Avon*, Aliki, and *The World of Shakespeare* have brief sections on the fool characters.

Nat: Nat is truly affected by meeting Shakespeare, a feeling not every student could relate to, so you should have students equate Nat's hero with one of their own and think about how they would feel in the presence of someone so admired and famous.

Books and manuscripts: Nat notices Shakespeare holding a bound manuscript. This would make for an interesting discussion on the history of printing, and a chance to use another one of the activities in *Shakespeare for Kids*: making a book. It could be used later to copy out lines from MND or Sonnet 116 when that is introduced later in Cooper's novel.

Training: Boys' training and rehearsing includes acrobatics, mime, fencing, and vocal work. Also, boys played female parts. *Shakespeare's Theater* has an illustrated guide to a typical day in the theater, and *The World of Shakespeare* has a section on modern day rehearsals in "Performing Shakespeare." There is an activity in *Shakespeare for Kids* on making a sword and staging a sword fight. If that is inappropriate for your class you could show the sword fight from the end of *Hamlet*. There are very few modern equivalents to the boys' training, but the Chinese film *Farewell My Concubine* has scenes depicting boy acrobats training for the traditional opera around the turn of the twentieth century. In China, boys were used to play female characters in the opera just as they were in Shakespeare's England.

Nat and Elizabethan childhood: Nat is beginning to have "political" problems in the company with Roper, the bully-type. One could equate the Boys' Company stereotype Roper spouts to the idea that kids from private school are "sissies" or something similar. For older students you might point out how this is really a matter of class differences. It is also important to note that these children have no childhood. In Elizabethan times notions of childhood, especially adolescence, were different from today's.

Chapter 7: Nat sees more of Elizabethan London, specifically the entertainment of the "Liberties."

London: The discussion of the Liberty areas outside the walls of London can be superficial or in-depth according to one's students. Nat's experiences of the city are rather explicit, from the initial crossing of London Bridge and observing its "sanitation" to the infected child-whore, beggars, and the bearbaiting episode of this chapter.

Theater and politics: Some commentary on the relationship between the Puritans and the theater would be useful. This is also a good time to discuss Queen Elizabeth's patronage of the theater. According to Somerset she even had her own company called "The Queen's Men." Compare the "culturally conservative" elements in our era that try to subdue the unsavory in the media with the Puritans' censorship. Discuss the theater and its political and moral implications against the function of film, the Internet, printed media, and so on, today.

Animals: Bearbaiting, or more specifically, Nat's reaction to it, serves to point out differences in ideas about animal rights and humane treatment. While on the topic of the Queen's fondness for theater, you might also mention that she was quite fond of bearbaiting as well as hunting and cockfighting. The Somerset biography has a handy index to help you find all sorts of tidbits on QEI. See also *Bard of Avon*, *Shakespeare's Theater*, and Aliki on the Liberties and the Queen.

Plays: Other popular plays of the day are mentioned—for example, *The Devil's Revenge*—a brief list and summary of other Elizabethan plays will reveal how sensational they were—full of violence and sex, not unlike our own popular films and TV shows. You might point out the depiction of John Webster in *Shakespeare in Love* as a sex-and-violence-minded youth. Webster went on to write *The Duchess of Malfi*, a play notable for gore and incest.

Nat: Nat has more troubles in this chapter with Roper, and we see how personal rivalry can ruin a group effort. At the bearbaiting we glimpse Nat's personal memory of blood and begin to suspect he's been through even more than we know about already.

The theater: The "plot" posted backstage—something I always used to make for myself to refer to during a performance. Have the students pick a character from the play and make up a "plot," imagining what his/her blocking, props, and costumes might be.

Chapter 8: This chapter finally gets to the truth about Nat's past.

> **Shakespeare**: Shakespeare acts like a real man here: fatherly, concerned, with a tragic past of his own (see *Shakespeare for Kids* on Shakespeare's son Hamnet). As Lois Burdett's work demonstrates, young people are quite fascinated with the darker side of Shakespeare's life—perhaps it makes the Bard seem more human.
>
> **London**: At the end of the chapter, in order to go over the Oberon/Puck scenes more closely, Nat is invited to stay at Shakespeare's house, which is near the theater. Keep a modern and an Elizabethan map of London up in the classroom, or photocopy them for students' reference.

Chapters 9 and 10: More of Nat in hospital in **chapter 9**—the nurse sings a sixteenth-century lullaby. Then, **chapter 10**, at the Bard's house—Shakespeare works and is visited by a strange man . . .

> **Music**: There are many tapes of early music, so play some secular vocal music to give a sense of what it sounded like. An a cappella quartet called the *Anonymous 4* and the *Tallis Scholars* are good choices.

Politics: The Essex controversy is more specifically introduced here. The actual historical facts differ, but the main ideas and events are preserved. Remember not to give it away too soon, because a lot of the suspense at the performance of MND depends on not knowing the outcome. The *Shakespeare for Kids* book and Somerset's biography provide details on these events as they actually unfolded. Shakespeare's "thribbling" at the end of this chapter in *Henry V* refers to Essex's activity in Ireland attempting to suppress rebellion and to muster forces against Spain.

Characters: "Kit" (Christopher) Marlowe is mentioned—he was murdered. As with many of the figures mentioned in Cooper's book, Marlowe was a real person, and he is also depicted in *Shakespeare in Love*. List the names and assign the students to investigate their identities. Each student, or groups of students, could do one or two names and then present findings to the class.

The theater: The "book keeper," otherwise known as the "prompter," is the person who will shout out a line to an actor who gets tripped up on his lines. Have someone be "on book" while other students are rehearsing or performing.

"Thribbling" or improvisation. As Nat mentions, Shakespeare's actors had to perform up to five different plays per week. Sometimes, instead of getting a line from the book keeper, an actor would just improvise. Clown/fool characters did this very often as part of their acts: they would engage in banter with the groundlings, or dance and sing as the spirit moved them. Nat mentions Shakespeare didn't like this and that it was part of why he dismissed Will Kempe, the famous clown. It can be fun to have students look at a short dialogue passage from the text for ten minutes and then get up and do it "off book." This accomplishes two things: they learn what improvisation feels like and they also get a chance to put the meaning of Shakespeare's words into their own words.

Henry V: Two scenes are appropriate for this chapter: Act 3, scene 4, with Katherine and Alice; and Act 4, scene 4, which is the one Nat steps into in place of Roper. Both of these are very funny once you get a handle on the pronunciation; no knowledge of French is required. Give the story of H5 first and introduce the cast of characters. The use of French is interesting in terms of the history of the English language: since the Norman invasion of 1066 French has heavily influenced English, indeed it was the language of the court for many years.

Chapter 11: After the performance.

Superstition?: Once word spreads of Nat's heroism people suspect he is using magic. Later we find some people are afraid of Nat and make a sign in his presence to ward off the "evil eye" (111). Much of what passed for medicine in this period was categorized as a type of magic. People believed in witches—both "white" and "black"—astrology, alchemy, ghosts, and fairies. Moreover, their lives were governed by religion much more than ours is today, although their "superstitions" were often in conflict with the

Church. *The Bedford Companion* discusses religion and *The World of Shakespeare* has a spread entitled "Elizabethan Beliefs." These topics can generate a good deal of conversation and debate—are we in fact any "smarter" than the Elizabethans?

Sonnets: Shakespeare gives Nat a copy of Sonnet 116. Have the students copy it out and discuss its meaning. How does it relate to Nat's problems? In *Shakespeare for Kids* there is an activity on writing one's own sonnet.

Chapters 12 and 13: In **chapter 12** Nat is delirious and disoriented in the hospital; **chapter 13** is the day of the performance of MND at the Globe.

Note: The class has now covered most of the historical and cultural facets of Elizabethan life, so you can now focus on MND, both reading and performing it, and any film versions you want to share can be used to supplement the next two chapters. The more recent one works because it has many famous contemporary film and television actors in it, which increases its "coolness" factor. The older version from the 1930s is charming and features a very young Mickey Rooney as Puck.

> **The theater**: Elizabethan "special effects." Rolling a ball on the floor of the "heavens" to make thunder, the use of cannons (which eventually burned down the globe—see Aliki, *Shakespeare's Theater*), and the others mentioned on page 115 in Cooper.
>
> **Crime and Punishment**: The thief, "cut-purse," episode before the play begins illustrates Elizabethan "crime and punishment" and the rough behavior of the groundlings. Most punishments were public, including executions, which were often rather gruesome.
>
> **Nat**: From this point until the end of the novel discuss Nat's attachment to Shakespeare and his coming to terms with his father's suicide.

Chapter 14: The play.

> **MND**: Armin as Bottom with the ass-head—discuss the sort of effects and costumes used and the role of imagination. Nat mentions computer graphics—Are we more or less imaginative because of technology?
>
> I strongly suggest acting out the "Pyramus and Thisbe play." Note that they end the play with a dance, which was common for many Elizabethan performances.
>
> Perform and interpret the final scene and Puck's farewell. This appears in the film *Dead Poet's Society*, which, again, will earn you "coolness points" if you show it.
>
> **Elizabeth I**: Hippolyta makes her appearance dressed as the Queen and the crowd goes wild—Aliki has a good drawing, quite flattering, of QE1 and Somerset's book has reproductions of contemporary portraits of Elizabeth, including one of her in a white dress. Now you may finish discussion of the Essex rebellion attempt and its aftermath.

Chapter 15: Meeting the Queen; **chapter 16**: After the play.

> **Elizabeth I**: We know that Shakespeare's plays were favorites of the Queen and that she had many private performances (see *Shakespeare's Theater, Shakespeare for Kids,* and Somerset), but it is very unlikely that she would have ever gone to a public theater. *Shakespeare in Love* depicts the same unlikely event.
>
> **Nat**: Discuss Nat's urge, on pages 14445, to change the past. If you went back in time would it be right to try to change things? Nat must leave the Chamberlain's Men and Shakespeare promises him a place in the company when he comes of age.
>
> **Shakespeare**: On page 145 a mention of Shakespeare's lawsuits. This is one of the ways we know details about him—most of our information comes from public records and documents—you might read his will in class—with the "second best bed" line and such.

Chapters 17 and 18: Chapter 17 another dream; **chapter 18** finds Nat awakened in the London hospital of 1999. He rejoins the company in time to perform Puck in MND again.

> **Nat**: Not surprisingly, Nat has "culture shock." He snaps, loses his temper. Discuss what is happening to him and see if any students have experienced culture shock. Moreover, he finds paint on his body from his Puck makeup circa 1599—was it just a dream?
>
> **Shakespeare today**: When Nat is in rehearsal he is angered by the costumes and staging, which are different from what he has experienced with Shakespeare's company. Many films and stage versions alter the traditional ways of presenting Shakespeare. The recent *Romeo+Juliet* and Ian MacEllen's *Richard III* are both set in modern times. What would Shakespeare think? How would your students update MND?

Chapter 19: Nat tells his story, Sonnet 116, and the real Nathaniel Field. **Chapter 20**: Conclusion, Nat's confrontation with Arby—Arby is Richard Burbage!

> **The Tempest**: Arby gives Nat the Sonnets and *The Tempest.* As Shakespeare promised he wrote another fairy character for Nat, Ariel of *The Tempest.* Introduce *The Tempest* and compare Puck to Ariel—select some speeches and compare the plots and sprites' relationships to Oberon/Prospero.
>
> **Nat**: He is somewhat pleased to know he saved Shakespeare's life, but still longs for a deeper connection. There is a picture of the real Nathan Field in the first volume of the Riverside Shakespeare, plate 11.
>
> The existence of *The Tempest* seems to comfort Nat—he believes that Shakespeare really cared for him and left something behind for him, something his father seems not to have done. His aunt gives him his own father's poetry and promises to talk about him. Has Nat come to terms with his past?

The *New* Globe: Sam Wanamaker is mentioned in this final chapter. Aliki and, of course, the Globe Web site, contain further details on the New Globe Theatre.

IV: Concluding Thoughts

Depending upon the level you teach and the facilities available, this unit could be ended with a video screening of a play—*Midsummer Night's Dream* would be a natural choice—or the class's own performance of all or part of a play or a collage of scenes. Even in a class situation that you may initially feel is not performance-friendly, getting the students to act is immensely useful. Some of my students who seemed to hate the notion of performing, even in a casual manner, ended up reporting that the experience helped them in public speaking and was, (gasp!), fun. So be the "bad guy" and force your students to do this work. I always get up myself and do scenes, which provides a model and shows that class is a place where everyone can make of fool of herself.

Since this outline was first inspired, I have used the book *King of Shadows* and performance activities to complement my teaching *A Midsummer Night's Dream* and *Othello*. The experiences I've had differ widely, from the self-motivated classes of adult learners to the younger, more Shakes-phobic community college students, but overall I have found that this approach can cure Shakes-phobia in a matter of weeks.

Works Cited

Books

Aagesen and Blumberg. *Shakespeare for Kids: His Life and Times, 21 Activities.* Chicago: Chicago Review Press, 1999.

Aliki. *William Shakespeare and the Globe.* New York: Harper Collins, 1999.

Burgess, Anthony. *A Mouthful of Air.* New York: William Morrow, 1992.

Claybourne and Treays. *The World of Shakespeare.* London: Usborne Publishing, 1996.

Cooper, Susan. *King of Shadows.* New York: McElderry Books, 1999.

McDonald, Russ, ed. *The Bedford Companion to Shakespeare: An Introduction with Documents.* Boston and New York: Bedford Books of St. Martin's Press, 1996.

McQuain and Malless, eds. *Coined by Shakespeare.* Springfield: Merriam Webster, 1998.

Morley and James. *Shakespeare's Theater.* New York: Peter Bedrick Books, 1994.

The Riverside Shakespeare, 2nd ed. Boston and New York: Houghton Mifflin, 1997.

Shakespeare, William. *A Midsummer Night's Dream*, Henry the Fifth, and *The Tempest*.

Somerset, Anne. *Elizabeth I.* New York: St. Martin's Griffin, 1991.

Stanley and Vennema. *Bard of Avon: The Story of William Shakespeare.* New York: Morrow Junior Books, 1992.

Web Sites

http://www.shakespeares-globe.org
http://web.uvic.ca/shakespeare

Movies

A Midsummer Night's Dream. Dir. Michael Hoffman. Perf. Kevin Kline, Michelle Pfeiffer, Rupert Everett, Stanley Tucci, Calista Flockhart. Fox Searchlisht Pictures, 1999.

Dead Poet's Society. Dir. Peter Weir. Perf. Robin Williams, Sean Leonard. Touchstone Pictures, 1989.

Elizabeth. Dir. Shekhar Kapur. Perf. Cate Blanchett, Geoffrey Rush, Christopher Eccleston, Joseph Fiennes, Richard Attenborough. Polygram, 1998.

Farewell My Concubine. Dir. Chen Kaige. Perf. Zhang Fengyi, Gong Li. Miramax, 1993.

Hamlet. Dir. Kenneth Branagh. Perf. Julie Christie, Charlton Heston, Derek Jacobi, Rufus Sewell, Kate Winslet. Colombia, 1996.

Henry V. Dir. Kenneth Branagh. Perf. Kenneth Branagh, Derek Jacobi, Brian Blessed, Ian Holm, Paul Scofield. Renaissance Films, 1989.

Henry V. Dir. Lawrence Olivier. Perf. Lawrence Olivier, Felix Aylmer, Vernon Greeves. Two Cities Films, 1944.

R+J. Dir. Baz Luhrmann. Perf. Leonardo DiCaprio, Claire Danes, John Leguizamo. Fox, 1997.

Richard III. Dir. Richard Loncraine. Perf. Ian McKellen, Annette Benning, Robert Downey, Jr. UA, 1995.

Shakespeare in Love. Dir. John Madden. Perf. Joseph Fiennes, Gwyneth Paltrow, Geoffrey Rush, Judi Dench, Simon Callow. Miramax, 1998.

West Side Story. Dir. Robert Wise. Perf. Natalie Wood, Rita Moreno. MGM, 1961.

27.   Understanding Texts and Contexts

Teaching Shakespeare to Future High School Teachers

PAMELA J. BENSON

I think most specialists in Elizabethan and Jacobean literature who teach at state colleges must at times have a sense of futility about teaching English majors, as I do, because so very few of our students take our courses out of particular interest in the subject, and even fewer will go on to graduate school. Few have ever read *Utopia*, *Doctor Faustus*, or even the poetry of Donne before, and few will ever reread them. In this context, how different teaching a Shakespeare course is! Not only have students read a play or two and maybe even seen a movie or a production of one of them before taking the class, but many of them have a very immediate and practical interest in the material: they are future high school teachers and will frequently be called on to teach Shakespeare's plays throughout their careers. Rhode Island College, where I teach, is a former normal school and still educates most of the teachers in the state. Half of all English majors are also secondary education majors, and they are required to take a Shakespeare course; thus, even though my Shakespeare courses are not based in the College of Education, I routinely teach students who want to be able to rely on my course to prepare them to teach the plays. If I do it right, they will hand on their knowledge and draw on what they have learned year after year, so I feel that the quality of the job I do really matters. I am not just pouring water into sand. What I teach will have a very long-lasting effect.

Because of my sense of the importance of what I do in my Shakespeare courses, I have given a lot of thought to who my students are and what they bring to my classes, what they need and how I can best give it to them. The undergraduates are primarily working class and lower middle class; they attended public or parochial schools and were not the most ambitious in their high schools, though often they are very smart; thus, most did not take advanced placement or honors courses. My department requires that they take an introduction to literary analysis course before taking Shakespeare, so they may have become more sophisticated about literature in general; however, I have to help them apply this knowledge to reading Shakespeare's plays.

Neither the students nor I approach the courses as teachers' education. They do not expect to be taught how to present Shakespeare to their students; rather, they expect to learn about Shakespeare. I respond to this expectation that the focus of the courses is on Shakespeare and not on pedagogy by assigning a substantial number of plays, by providing students with knowledge about the material and cultural context in which Shakespeare worked and wrote, but most of all by trying to develop in them the capacity to think about Shakespeare's works and to have a sense of what kinds of questions open them up in exciting ways. My goal for them is that, when they are on their own preparing their lessons, they will have the confidence and ability to discover what it is that they want to teach about whatever work their district or department has chosen rather than simply attempting to recall the details of a single interpretation that they were taught. Everything I do in class is calculated to make them desire to make this discovery, to make them confident that they can make it, and to prepare them to discover significant and exciting aspects of the texts. To this end I do not simply teach them my readings of the plays; rather, I offer myself as a model reader, and I present my voice as one among many—theirs and those of other scholars and directors, whose interpretations I cite. This openness goes against the initial desires of many students who want to be given one reading on which they can rely forever (and certainly for the exam), the reading that they will hand on intact to their students.

I have designed oral and written exercises that stimulate excitement about the plays, demonstrate to students that a range of interpretations is possible, and demand examples and clear reasoning in support of any interpretation offered. I hope that these exercises, together with class discussion, provide students with the analytical tools and confidence to discover and develop an approach to any play that they have to teach when they no longer have the support of a teacher and fellow students to rely on.

When teaching Shakespeare's plays, I first need to make the students aware of the complexity of the language and give them the tools to analyze it and to develop interpretations of the plays based on their understanding of what is going on. One way I encourage students to do this is by requiring that each one do a close analysis of a brief passage from one play and present this analysis to the class in an informal ten-minute-long oral report and to me in a formal paper. They are not allowed to use any critical materials for this assignment; whatever they say about the passage has to be what they were able to figure out with the sole assistance of the Oxford English Dictionary (OED), which is easily available in print and electronic forms. I give them careful written instructions for this presentation and provide a "passage worksheet" that the presenter fills out as research for the paper (see appendix). This form focuses the students' attention on characterization, plot, figurative language, and vocabulary. I have each one fill in a worksheet at least once for practice before using it to prepare the oral presentation, and I write comments on this practice sheet, so that each person has the opportunity to see the kind of thing he or she needs to work on before addressing the class and being graded. As a result of this preparation, even the weakest student almost always has plenty to say, and many are led to speculate and even invite debate or ask for help solving a problem.

This exercise benefits the presenters because they discover how rich the text is, how rewarding time spent reading carefully can be, and how involved they can get in thinking about literary questions. Most students say that careful reading led them to change their minds about what they thought the passage meant on the most literal level and also that such careful reading helped them understand characters and themes much better. The three most valuable aspects of the assignment are the awareness of the power of words that comes from using the OED, the practice it gives students in working with figurative language, and the exposure it gives to the possibility of multiple readings of a single passage.

Many students are really excited by what they find in the OED; most simply, this is because they do not know the meanings of many words in the plays, but even more I think this is because it so often opens up puns and other kinds of multiple readings that they never dreamed existed and they are very stimulated by their discoveries. Using the OED also requires them to make judgments and defend them—obviously, not all possible sixteenth- or seventeenth-century meanings of a word are ever present, and they must decide where they want to draw the line and be ready to explain their reasoning when called on to do so in the discussion that follows the presentation.

Most students find the analysis of figurative language to be difficult. Students who are bewildered by it usually have no idea why it is used or how to understand it. They quickly guess what it is trying to say and translate it into a single adjective (Hamlet is worried) and ignore other connotations introduced by the analogy. As this reluctance to come to terms with figurative language is a persistent problem in the class, I teach the analysis of figurative language every day both by pointing out some figures in the course of discussion and analyzing them myself and by taking one example and breaking it down into its component parts and getting people to express their associations with the terms and then as a group to select the ones that seem relevant. By the end of the semester, most people feel much more confident of their ability to understand and analyze figurative language.

As a result of each oral presentation, both the presenter and the rest of the class are exposed to multiple readings of a single passage. Through working so closely with a passage and with the OED, most students discover that they have become aware of ambiguities in the passage; they learn to notice when they have doubts instead of suppressing them and plowing their way through with a master interpretation that they brought ready-made to the play. In addition, listening to so many presentations over the course of a semester exposes students to the ways other people read and arrive at conclusions; over and over they say, "I hadn't thought of that but now that I hear the evidence . . ."

I also encourage students to consider each other's readings by requiring that the presenter end his or her presentation by asking the other students some questions about the passage and the interpretation offered. I urge the presenter to take risks in these questions—to invite dissent from their views or to find something they didn't understand fully and ask the class to try to solve the problem, but often presenters find this question period very difficult, not because they are shy, but because they ask leading questions whose answers they have already imagined, and the discussion quickly fizzles. After class, when I discuss the presentation with the presenter (and assign the grade, without which they seem unwilling to put in the effort to prepare carefully), I take special care to talk with him or her about the kind of questions asked and about how to formulate more open questions. I encourage students to respond to other people's clever ideas in their written papers, which are due a week after the oral presentations.

The second goal I set for myself is to situate the plays historically and culturally. I want students to become aware of Shakespeare's period as other—"Shakespeare not our contemporary" might be my theme. I always teach about manuscript and print culture and about the physical properties of the Elizabethan theater, and I also include several other cultural contexts. I have taught about the role of women, political theory, Italian culture, early modern psychology, the city of London, and witchcraft, though not necessarily all in the same semester.

The topic of the quartos and folios, Shakespeare's "foul" papers, and memorial reconstructions comes up as students open their books and first see the text on the page because, whatever edition I use, there are puzzling indications about Qs and Fs and emendations. I used to just tell students that all this was something they did not need to worry about, but I realized that I was wrong. Students are interested in the production of the texts, the representation of Shakespeare in the folio, the physical qualities of early modern books—all these make Shakespeare more real to them by locating him in a time and place. So I now bring in facsimile editions of the folio and quartos, a couple of early modern editions, and a manuscript leaf so they can see the paper and ink and handle objects that were around in the sixteenth century. I also bring in copies of the Agas map of London and a map of modern London because seeing the Thames and the boats, barges, and ships, the narrow streets, the many churches, the details of life—such as the laundry drying on the grass—brings them up against the difference of the material conditions of people's lives and, also, stimulates them to imagine the early modern settings of the plays. A former student who is now a teacher told me that seeing the "visuals" was one of the most memorable and useful parts of the course. They made the period seem "not totally removed from real life."

I include the topic of the material theater because I think it is important to think of the plays as literary texts interpreted by actors and completed by an audience and because high school teachers have told me that performance plays a large part in their teaching of the plays. (I myself have used performance only once, and it was not a great success because at a non-residential college where many students have full or nearly full-time jobs, it is difficult for them to get together to rehearse—or so they told me loudly. I always feel as though the lack of performance is a weakness in my courses.) I want students to become aware of how much information about movements and expressions and costumes is given in the lines characters speak and to think about the connotations of seeing people move their bodies and faces as described. For example, the observation that a person is kneeling to another often provokes disgust and leads to a useful discussion of hierarchy and the probable response of an early modern audience to the same action. To get students thinking about the kind of space, actors, props, and costumes Shakespeare was working with, I assign the essay "The Shakespearean Stage" by Andrew Gurr. I also suggest that students look at the Globe Web site, show them postcards of productions at the Globe, and tell them about my experience as a "groundling" in the summer of 2000. Then, I ask students to select a scene and write a description of how they would block it and costume it using features of the Elizabethan theater; they must indicate the lines in the text that led them to put characters in a specific place, make particular gestures, and wear specific pieces of clothing. I make this assignment in the second week of the semester; it is usually very popular and effective. Visualizing the action of a single scene seems to wake students up to the action of all subsequent plays in a way that just being told about the theater does not.

In addition to using Gurr's essay and visual images of the Globe, I try to teach intellectual, literary, and social context by means of primary materials, but because I realize that very few teachers will have the time to go to the library and find primary texts to use, I coordinate primary readings with specific plays that are frequently taught or choose texts that have general application. For example, most students do not know what to make of the nurse and of Juliet's relationship with her mother in *Romeo and Juliet*, so I explain about wet-nurses and give them a selection from *The Countess of Lincoln's Nursery*; this also clarifies several of Lady Macbeth's comments. With *Macbeth* I teach "News from Scotland," a report of a witchcraft investigation; this shows them how real witches seemed to the audience, helps them appreciate how very peculiar the witches in the play are, and shows James I's personal involvement with the topic. (I gather this reading also helps with *The Scarlet Letter.*)

Among the primary materials I use are other versions of the plot story. These are of three types: sources, movies, and children's books derived from the plays. All three help the students form a sense of the plays as live drama and of the difference between the story and the particular way Shakespeare represents it. Discussion of sources of all kinds (Plutarch, Holinshed, and so on) forms a major strand that runs throughout the semester, but I am especially interested in Shakespeare's response to and representation of Italy, so when I have students read a tale, it is Italian. When teaching the tragedies, I assign the story in Cinthio's *Gli Hecatommithi* that was the source of *Othello*; when teaching the comedies, I assign the story from Boccaccio's *Decameron* that was the source of *All's Well that Ends Well*. I ask each student to make a list of six differences between each play and its source and discuss what difference each change makes in the play. In making this list, students become aware of Shakespeare making choices in plotting, in character development, in figurative language, and in themes, to name but a few. For example, when they notice that Giraldi's Desdemona attributes her troubles to Othello's race and condemns intermarriage, they are shocked and return to *Othello* with a sense that the play is doing something more subtle with race and with a desire to understand what that is. Since race, of course, is a subject that they will have to confront if they teach *Othello, The Merchant of Venice*, or *The Tempest*—among other plays—this exercise has the added benefit of giving them some sense of the issue in the culture in which the play was written. Looking at the source gives students the sense that they are seeing Shakespeare at work; they become aware of the pre-existence of a story that is different from what he made of it, and those who have been instructed in narrative theory recognize a phenomenon that they have studied. Many also begin to think about how the "showing" of plays differs from the "telling" of stories because they see what Shakespeare does with material presented by the narrator.

The film I use to come at these narrative topics as well as cultural difference when teaching the tragedies is Kurosawa's *Throne of Blood*. I chose this rather than a filmed production of a play because its strangeness (many of my students have never seen a foreign film, let alone a Japanese one), its alterations of the story (Lady Macbeth's miscarriage, for example), its visual development of elements that occur as metaphors in the play (ominous birds, for example), and its kinship with the original despite the change in location and language help students recognize the power of Shakespeare's original and ask complex questions about loyalty, free will, ambition, and creative influence and tradition. Kurosawa's characters do not feel quite right if thought of by their Shakespearean names rather than their Japanese ones, and so the film provokes students to go back to the text to test their sense of what Shakespeare's characters were like and to discover what clues Kurosawa was following.

My teaching of the third kind of version of the plays, adaptations and retellings of the plays for children, is directed specifically to my students' future as teachers. Since Shakespeare is our focus and not children's literature per se, I ask them to evaluate the texts and pictures with the special task of forming an opinion of the books' success as pre-texts. For example, when teaching *A Midsummer Night's Dream*, I ask the class to look at John

Updike's *Bottom's Dream*, a picture book with line drawings that includes songs set to music by Felix Mendelssohn and is illustrated by Warren Cappell. I use this book because I think that it gives a sense of riches beyond itself that will prompt a child to want to see or read the play on which it is based and because it captures something of the original so that when the child encounters the play itself he or she will feel it to be familiar, though, of course, far more complex and still more delightful and engaging. Since I think Shakespeare's precise and highly connotative vocabulary and figures of speech are essential to the experience of a Shakespearean text, I ask students to consider whether Updike's language resembles that in the original play, and I suggest that the illustrations (like Kurosawa's images) do some of the work done by language in the original play; they pick up some of the figurative language, convey emotion or mood, clarify action, and provoke wonder.

As the above description shows, my course requires a lot of hard work on the part of the students and myself, and they (and I) often complain at how much time and attention it takes to get a good grade (or do a good job), but over the years I have repeatedly seen such improvement and engagement in the text in students of all levels of ability and read enough positive comments about the assignments in the anonymous student evaluations of the course that my department requires to feel that our joint effort is worthwhile, even inspiring.

Note

Before writing this essay, I consulted with two former students who became high school teachers, Carla Oliveira and Susan Murphy Mack. They helped me to understand how the courses that I had taught them had prepared them for teaching, and I not only kept their comments in mind as I wrote, but I revised my current courses to make use of their advice.

Appendix

Shakespeare Passage Worksheet

1. Location of passage—play, act, scene, lines.
2. Speaker(s) and occasion (what has happened or is happening?)
3. Outline of the organization of the passage. What parts does it break into, and what is the main idea or point made in each section? Outline using line numbers.
4. Why is the character making this speech? Is he/she persuading someone, lamenting something, trying out an idea, etc.? Justify your interpretation.
5. Is this passage verse or prose? If verse, copy one line and scan it to the best of your ability.

6. Analyze one figure of speech (metaphor, simile, personification, etc.) and explain what it contributes to the passage.
7. Analyze one or two allusions to people, places, or myths and explain what they contribute to the passage. (If there are any.)
8. Look up one word in the Oxford English Dictionary, list the meanings that apply, and discuss its use in the passage.
9. Note any indications of gestures, movements, or facial expressions in the passage.
10. Why does this passage matter right now when it happens and in the play as far as you have read (character development or revelation, role in plot, themes, important words, suspense, etc.)?
11. Say anything else you want.

Works Cited

" 'Agas' Map, The." In *The A to Z of Elizabethan London*, compiled by Adrian Prockter and Robert Taylor. Lympne Castle, Kent: Harry Margary in association with Guildhall Library, London, 1979.

Boccaccio, Giovanni. "Giletta of Narbona." In *Italian Tales from the Age of Shakespeare*, edited by Pamela Joseph Benson. London: J. M. Dent, Everyman, 1996.

Cinthio, Giovambattista Giraldi. "The Source of Othello." In *Othello*, ed. Alvin Kernan. Signet Classic. New York: Penguin, 1998.

Clinton, Elizabeth. "The Countesse of Lincolnes Nurserie." In *The Paradise of Women: Writings by Englishwomen of the Renaissance*, edited by Betty Travitsky. Contributions in Women's Studies, Number 22. Westport, CT and London: Greenwood Press, 1981.

Gurr, Andrew. "The Shakespearean Stage." In *The Norton Shakespeare*, edited by Stephen Greenblatt et al. New York: W. W Norton and Co., 1997.

Kurosawa, Akira. *Throne of Blood*. 1957.

Updike, John. *Bottom's Dream adapted from William Shakespeare's A Midsummer Night's Dream* (with music by Felix Mendelssohn and illustrations by Warren Cappell). New York: Knopf, 1969.

Works Consulted

Benson, Pamela Joseph, ed. *Italian Tales from the Age of Shakespeare*. London: J. M. Dent, Everyman, 1996.

Bevington, David. *Action Is Eloquence*. Cambridge, MA and London: Harvard University Press, 1984.

Gurr, Andrew. *Playgoing in Shakespeare's London*. Cambridge: Cambridge University Press, 1987.

Kermode, Frank. *Shakespeare's Language*. New York: Farrar, Straus & Giroux, 2000.

28.   Redistributing the Riches

Shakespearean Adaptation in *Moss Gown* and *Mama Day*

CAROLINE McMANUS

> Bill was an adapter, certainly, so he was—and very well
> he adapted too—considering.
> —CHARLES DICKENS, *Nicholas Nickleby*

To many American students today, whatever their ethnic background, Shakespeare seems utterly foreign. Linguistically, historically, nationally "other," Shakespeare is not perceived to be a part of mainstream contemporary American culture but rather an icon of a highbrow elite. Yet how many students realize that Shakespearean drama constituted a dominant form of popular entertainment in nineteenth-century American frontier towns, that Walt Whitman frequently "declaim[ed] some stormy passage from Julius Caesar or Richard" to passersby while riding in buses down Broadway, that a young Ulysses S. Grant played Desdemona in a performance of *Othello* staged in Texas by the Fourth Infantry Regiment in 1845 just prior to the Mexican War?[1] Lawrence Levine has argued that Americans once felt free to take liberties with Shakespeare, who was "seen as common property to be treated as the user saw fit," but now assume that Shakespeare is "the possession of the educated portions of society who disseminate . . . his plays for the enlightenment of the average folk who [a]re to swallow him not for their entertainment but for their education, as a respite from—not as a normal part of—their usual cultural diet."[2]

I'd like to extend Levine's materialist metaphor—Shakespeare as "property," "possession"—and propose that Shakespeare has become to our students a King Lear figure, ready to dispense the riches of his kingdom only in response to sufficiently lavish praise. In our own appreciation of Shakespeare's plays, do we inadvertently teach our students to mouth rote words of adulation, as Goneril and Regan do? Or do we encourage them to emulate the more honest Cordelia, who professes to love her father "according to [her] bond" but, fully aware of his shortcomings, respectfully refuses to join the public flatterfest?[3] Despite Cordelia's initial reticence, her love ultimately proves the strongest and is, in its deliberateness, perhaps the type of response we should encourage in our students.

To help students approach Shakespeare more deliberately, teachers might create a unit that reads one of his plays intertextually with its own sources and with later adaptations, particularly recent American ones. One such unit might feature *King Lear*, which is ideally suited to an adaptation focus, especially now that both the 1608 and 1623 editions are readily available and illustrate the instability of "the" Shakespearean text even in its own day. *King Lear* could be read with any of the following: the twelfth-century source material from Geoffrey of Monmouth's *History*, early modern versions such as Holinshed's or Spenser's, the wonderfully outrageous (to us) eighteenth-century adaptation by Nahum Tate (in which Lear lives and Cordelia is not hanged but survives to marry Edgar), and Jane Smiley's 1991 novel *A Thousand Acres*. One might begin the unit with adaptations of *King Lear* for children, such as Mary and Charles Lamb's 1807 rendition and the 1987 *Moss Gown* by William Hooks, who sets his retelling in tidewater North Carolina. A particularly effective companion to *Moss Gown* would be Gloria Naylor's 1988 novel *Mama Day*, which also possesses a southern setting and a matchmaking conjure woman. *Mama Day* actually revises several Shakespearean texts, reminding us that his plays were, like her novel, adaptations, reshapings of other plots and characters into dynamic new works that provided popular entertainment and addressed contemporary sociopolitical concerns.

"Adaptation" assignments, suitably tailored to students' ages and abilities, might include a compilation and analysis of Shakespearean allusions in advertising and popular culture, including such examples as Theo's rap version of *Hamlet* on "The Cosby Show," Henry V's St. Crispin's Day speech in Danny De Vito's *Renaissance Man*, and even a Bud Light commercial's paraphrase of "To be or not to be." A more formal paper could compare Henrietta Bowdler's 1807 version of *Romeo and Juliet* in *The Family Shakespeare* with recent "bowdlerized" versions designed for use in middle schools.[4] Students could even be asked to create new adaptations of Shakespearean texts (poems, short stories, screenplays, illustrations), drawing, if they wished, on their own cultural backgrounds or incorporating their first languages. No matter what the assignment, students should be asked not only to describe the similarities and differences between the Shakespearean text and the adaptation, but also to comment on the sociopolitical significance of both the original and the adaptation, the "cultural work" the texts perform.

Even students not reading at grade level can exercise this type of critical inquiry if they begin with a children's book such as *Moss Gown*, commenting on the text's representation of family, gender, and race relationships. Hooks conflates the Lear and Gloucester plots by rendering Candace's father "almost blind" (of natural causes rather than sadistic violence) to signify his lack of emotional awareness.[5] Given the book's intended audience, it provides a "kinder, gentler" Lear: the father is less arbitrary and cruel; he spends many days "pondering what to do with his lands" before he makes a decision (5), and in the distribution scene he grants his older daughters his lands but admits that his youngest daughter will always have his love (12). Retha and Grenadine, too, are much less cruel; they are merely greedy, whereas Regan and Goneril are lascivious and violent as well. Rather than being staged in all its painful brutality, Retha's and Grenadine's expulsion of their father is recounted briefly and indirectly: the father, upon arriving at Candace's marriage celebration as a pathetic wanderer, tells the servants "a tale of two cruel daughters who had squandered his wealth . . . and turned him out to sleep in the fields and beg for his food" (42).

Candace, not her father, is the one turned out by the sisters into the storm. Unafraid as the cruel wind "drew her closer and closer to the murky, gray-green swamp," Candace "rode the wind lightly, letting it toss her to and fro like a floppy rag doll" until it "set her softly" on a bed of moss (15–16). The hurricane's wind, associated in *Mama Day* with the legendary conjure woman Sapphira, is simultaneously harsh and kind, figuring the potency and unpredictability of the beautiful witch woman who gives Candace a moss gown and promises to return when needed. She is thus analogous to Kent, the faithful servant, as well as Cinderella's fairy godmother. (Hooks's use of "Cinderella" elements is a logical choice, given the clothing motif that runs throughout *King Lear* and the competition of the sisters for wealth and power, a desire mystified in "Cinderella" as love of the handsome prince.) Still passive, "pulled by a force she could not control" (20), Candace travels to another mansion, where she becomes a servant. Summoning the gris-gris woman to dress her, Candace gratefully dons the now-shimmering moss gown for three successive nights of dancing, during which her young master falls in love with her. As in Nahum Tate's version, Candace marries well and welcomes her father to her new home, thus providing the "kind nursery" Lear desires but never receives from Cordelia in the Shakespearean text. Candace communicates her love for her outcast father when he tastes the bland food she has had prepared and she repeats the words that initially displeased him: "I love you more than meat loves salt" (11). This folk-tale element predates Shakespeare's play, usefully reminding students that *Moss Gown* is not merely an adaptation of *King Lear* but that both texts are adapting earlier sources.

Despite its inclusion of the mysterious, quasi-maternal gris-gris woman, *Moss Gown* does not radically revise Shakespeare's play in light of contemporary concerns about race, class, and gender. Perhaps even more conservative in its depiction of feminine desire than *King Lear*, *Moss Gown* uses

Grenadine's and Retha's single status to underscore Candace's "reward"—a wealthy man. By foregrounding the "Cinderella" courtship narrative, *Moss Gown* replaces Shakespeare's exploration of filial love with a traditional romance in which a woman secures a husband with her physical beauty rather than her integrity.[6] France's words, "Fairest Cordelia, that art most rich being poor / . . . / Thee and thy virtues here I seize upon" (1.1.250–52), reveal the superficiality of the young master's declaration of love: "Rags and tatters could never hide your beauty!" (38). In fact, the young master has *not* previously looked past the rags to notice Candace's beauty, even when given a hint by an old woman seated near the door during the ball: "No one left. . . . Except a poor serving girl dressed all in rags" (32). Moreover, Candace takes no initiative to assist her father as Cordelia does. Although the 1608 *King Lear* carefully explains France's absence and names a male general (4.3.7–8), the 1623 text does not, moving directly from Albany's exit at the end of 4.2 to Cordelia's martial entrance in 4.3 "with drum and colors." As we learn in 4.4.25–28, Cordelia was the motivating force behind the French invasion, and the gentleman in 4.6 refers to "her" army (line 216). Following the reunion of father and daughter in *Moss Gown*, it is, significantly, Candace's husband who invites the old man to live with them. Cordelia's filial love takes precedence over her matrimonial bond, whereas Candace "successfully" transfers her duty from patriarchal father to husband, which is figured in architectural terms; the young master's house (he has no given name) is "as fine and grand as the white-pillared mansion of her father" (20). Once Candace has been safely ensconced in upper class domesticity, the autonomous gris-gris woman disappears from the text.

Ironically, the black conjure woman who facilitates both Candace's marriage and her reunion with her father helps a white woman to maintain, even expand, her property, among which, presumably, slaves figure prominently. "Snow-white" plantation houses (5) don't keep themselves. As Valerie Sayers observes, "black children cannot fail to notice that the story's black characters will return to swamp and kitchen" (29). Students analyzing Donald Carrick's illustrations, described on the book jacket as "elegant watercolor paintings" that "capture all of the drama and magic of a romance filled with happy endings," might notice the spatial politics of the initial pages: the immense white patriarch dominates the left-hand page and a concerned female slave is positioned in the lower corner of the right-hand page below the text, almost off the page altogether. This is arguably one way of translating Lear's dominance in 1.1 into visual terms, but what is also insidiously communicated is the subordinate status of women and black servants. (This composition echoes that of the cover illustration, in which the turbaned gris-gris woman watches the dominant, central Candace from a lower right-hand position in the woods, and anticipates that of the reconciliation scene, in which yet another turbaned black woman watches approvingly from the right, although here Candace and the two black servants are all placed above the now-humbled father.) Although the magic-working gris-gris woman twice takes visual precedence over Candace, her activities are those of a servant, as she helps Candace dress in the gown she has labored intensively to make: "Gris-gris woman work all night, / weave a gown so fine, / stitch in stars and pale moonlight, / Gris-gris, gris-gris, grine" (16). By drawing attention to the physical process and cost of making magic (similar to the slave woman's sacrifice of sleep in order to make her family's clothes after working for her master during waking hours), this description does demystify the fairy godmother myth to some extent but, given the numerous visual parallels with female slaves throughout the text, works also to naturalize the gris-gris woman's efforts on behalf of a white girl. Significantly, the witch woman is last seen standing ramrod straight behind Candace's stooping father at the wedding, as if literally supporting the patriarchy. Our students, very much a part of a visual rather than an aural culture, need to be taught to think critically about the images they see, even the seemingly innocuous ones illustrating children's books.

Like *Moss Gown*, Naylor's *Mama Day* also reworks Shakespearean material, but in doing so clearly challenges racist, masculinist ideologies. Naylor is far from reverent. As Cocoa remarks, after George has asked her out again after a miserable first date, "Surely, he jests. I swear, that's the first thing that popped into my head when you asked me out again. I don't know where that phrase came from—had to be something from my high school Shakespeare. . . . Just proves that Shakespeare didn't have a bit of soul—I don't care if he did write about Othello, Cleopatra, and some slave on a Caribbean island. If he had been in touch with our culture, he would have written somewhere, 'Nigger, are you out of your mind?' "[7] Yet Naylor's novel rewrites, in addition to numerous African-American-authored texts, precisely the plays to which Cocoa alludes: *Othello*, *Antony and Cleopatra*, and *The Tempest*, as well as *Hamlet* and *King Lear*. George, like Othello, is a black man who has achieved success in the dominant white culture; the degree of his assimilation is marked by his first love interest, the pale-skinned, red-haired Shawn. The lack of faith that ultimately kills George, however, is not suspicion of Cocoa's fidelity but rather an inability to believe in Mama Day's magical alternative to his empirical world view. George's recollection that he and Cocoa were "Star-crossed. Yeah, that's what we were. Always missing each other" (129) clearly alludes to *Romeo and Juliet*, yet George and Cocoa are much more mature lovers, their love more closely resembling that of Antony and Cleopatra in its constant renegotiation of power and control. *Antony and Cleopatra* is evoked primarily in the novel's structure and setting, the matriarchal, magical, Egypt-like realm of Willow Springs being juxtaposed with the masculine, rational, Rome-like world of Manhattan. *Mama Day* also echoes *Antony and Cleopatra*'s and *Romeo and Juliet*'s positioning of the male lead's death prior to that of the female protagonist, thereby giving her additional prominence. Unlike Juliet and Cleopatra, however, Cocoa does not take her own life. Tempted to do so (recall that her given name is Ophelia and that she has earlier struggled against madness during the illness caused by Ruby's poison), she is ruled by Mama Day and refrains: "I wasn't ready to believe that a further existence would be worth anything without you. There was just too much pain in it. Yes, I thought often about suicide and once made the mistake of voicing it. I had never seen Mama Day so furious. . . . There ain't no pain—no pain—that you could be having worse than what that boy went through for your life. And you would throw it back in his face, heifer?" (302). Cocoa eventually remarries and bears children, naming one of them George. Naylor thus subtly rebukes the tenets of tragic Shakespearean love suicide, positing instead a life-affirming heroics of endurance and hope.

Naylor's vision does not deny tragedy, however, and other Ophelia figures in her text do commit suicide by drowning. Most explicitly, Cocoa's great-grandmother, also named Ophelia, goes mad following the drowning of her daughter Peace in a well and leaps from a bluff into the Sound below screaming her baby's name (117). George's mother, supposedly a fifteen-year-old prostitute, places him on a stack of newspapers before drowning in the Long Island Sound.[8] Unlike Hamlet, however, he is not consumed with disgust at her promiscuity. Stung when Cocoa calls him a son of a bitch, he recounts his mother's fate, maintaining that she retained a degree of Ophelia-like innocence: "Later, her body washed up down there. I don't have all the pieces. But there are enough of them to lead me to believe that she was not a bitch" (131). Neatly reversing Shakespeare's text, in which the loss of Hamlet's love and her father's death break Ophelia's heart, and Gertrude's heart is "cleft in twain" by her son, Naylor's women break the hearts, both figuratively and literally, of their men: George dies when he overtaxes his heart, weakened by rheumatic fever, in his attempt to save Cocoa's life, and Sapphira breaks, perhaps stabs, Bascombe Wade's heart (118, 151).

The novel alludes frequently to *King Lear*, using it as a benchmark for intellectual sophistication. George recalls of Cocoa, "You were Harold Robbins in general and James Michener when you wanted to get deep. I hadn't read any fiction more recent than Ernest Hemingway and Ralph Ellison, remembering with a sinking heart the worn copy of *King Lear* I could have been spending my evening with" (60). Like Lear, George both desires and fears to be incorporated into women's households. His macho obsession with football parallels Lear's homosocial horseplay with his knights, both serving as a means to avoid meaningful connections with women. Yet once introduced to Mama Day and her sister Abigail, Cocoa's grandmother, George relishes being mothered. George is, however, like Lear, tragically unable to save the life of his beloved. His test (reminiscent of Ferdinand's seemingly meaningless task of carrying logs in *The Tempest*) is to carry John-Paul's staff and

Bascombe Wade's ledger to Mama Day's hen house and bring back whatever he finds.[9] Rather than returning with open, bloody hands and an awareness that women (symbolized by the ferocious setting hen) can also fight for their loved ones (George has tried to save Cocoa alone rather than joining forces with Mama Day), he lashes out violently, thinking he must emulate Lear, who "kill'd the slave that was a-hanging" Cordelia (5.3.275). George, however, suffers a heart attack and achieves peace only when he dies at Cocoa's side.

The most pronounced allusion Naylor develops in the novel is to *The Tempest* as she transforms the Shakespearean island into one of the Sea Islands off the Georgia/South Carolina coast. Its resident mage is not the patriarchal Prospero but the matriarchal Mama Day, whose given name, Miranda, suggests that her magic will be motivated by the kind pity evinced by her namesake during the "shipwreck" in 1.2. Many African and Caribbean reworkings of *The Tempest* empower Caliban, thus using the master's language to curse the oppressor. Naylor, in contrast, revoices the experience of Prospero's other pupil, Miranda, in rescripting the play. Shakespeare's Miranda possesses only a distant memory of women who attended upon her, whereas Naylor's Miranda, in her role as midwife, forms the center of a matriarchal community.[10] In addition, Mama Day is linked to her goddess-like ancestress, Sapphira, who has been able to secure possession of the island for her sons as Sycorax was unable to do for Caliban.

This privileging of the feminine, a restoration of Shakespeare's "missing mothers," is only one of the significant ways Naylor's novel makes Shakespeare's texts her own. Most germane to the focus of this essay, Naylor also draws attention to the ways Shakespeare can be taught and read. Cocoa's education at Willow Springs High School apparently encouraged her to identify with Shakespeare's Moors, Africans, and Egyptians, but the language difference—"Surely, he jests"—suggests that for her, Shakespeare is simply too alien, too temporally distant for meaningful appropriation. George's identification with Shakespeare's tragic heroes prevents him from embracing an alternative feminine, communal ethos and thus exposes the danger of an unquestioned assimilation to a dominant white culture that valorizes the individual. As Mama Day observes, "Tradition is fine, but you gotta know when to stop being a fool" (143). I, for one, *am* a traditionalist in many ways, but I also owe it to my students to help them make their own decisions about the Shakespearean tradition—whether or not to read his plays, which ones, and how. My hope is that they will learn to appropriate Shakespeare for themselves as Naylor does—with respect, humor, and wisdom, but also with a healthy skepticism.

The December 22nd ritual described in *Mama Day* calls for the members of Willow Springs to walk the main road, carrying candles, giving gifts, and exchanging the greeting "Lead on with light." Alterations in the enactment of this rite, however, are apparent: the "younger ones done brought a few . . . changes that don't sit too well with some [using sparklers instead of candles, for example]. . . . There's a disagreement every winter about whether these young people spell the death of Candle Walk" (110–11). However, Naylor's narrator is philosophical about these changes: "You can't keep 'em from going beyond the bridge [to the mainland], and like them candles out on the main road, time does march on." The wise Mama Day, despite her awareness that Candle Walk alters slightly with each generation, remains calm: "It'll take generations, she says, for Willow Springs to stop doing it at all. And more generations again to stop talking about the time 'when there used to be some kinda 18 & 23 going-on near December twenty-second.' By then, she figures, it won't be the world as we know it no way—and so no need for the memory" (111). This commentary can be read as an argument for the openness to adaptation that I am advocating. Just as Mama Day accepts the transformation of cultural traditions as inevitable and believes the pronouncement of Candle Walk's demise premature, so reports of Shakespeare's canonical "death" are greatly exaggerated by those participants in the culture wars who decry what they perceive as the pernicious encroachment of ethnic and "popular" literature into the curriculum. This literary diversity may, in fact, enhance students' understanding of and appreciation for Shakespearean drama, as they realize that his plays constitute a rich legacy to claim, and perhaps to redistribute, in ways meaningful to themselves.

Notes

1. Lawrence Levine, "William Shakespeare and the American People: A Study in Cultural Transformation," *American Historical Review* 89.1 (1984): 40, 50.
2. Ibid., 54, 47.
3. *King Lear*, 1.1.93. All references to Shakespeare's plays are taken from *The Riverside Shakespeare*, ed. G. Blakemore Evans, 2nd ed. (Boston and New York: Houghton Mifflin Company, 1997) and will be cited in the text.
4. For additional suggestions, see Martha Tuck Rozett, *Talking Back to Shakespeare* (Newark: University of Delaware Press, 1994).
5. William H. Hooks, *Moss Gown* (New York: Clarion Books, 1987), 41. Subsequent references will be cited in the text.
6. As Valerie Sayers notes in her review of *Moss Gown*, "the young reader needs more of Cordelia here, less of Cinderella." *The New York Times Book Review* 92 (August 9, 1987): 29.
7. Gloria Naylor, *Mama Day* (New York: Ticknor and Fields, 1988), 64. Subsequent references will be cited in the text.
8. Naylor's 1992 *Bailey's Cafe* rewrites this episode; George is actually the product of a virgin birth, his mother an Ethiopian Jew named Mariam who dies in waters of ritual purification.
9. Like Mama Day, Candace also orchestrates a riddling love-test; the dinner prepared without salt prompts her father's admission of his need for her. Both

women reverse Lear's strategy, however, in that their tests are private, intended to instruct rather than humiliate.

10. Both Peter Erickson, *Rewriting Shakespeare, Rewriting Ourselves* (Berkeley and Los Angeles: University of California Press, 1991), 142, and Valerie Traub, "Rainbows of Darkness: Deconstructing Shakespeare in the Work of Gloria Naylor and Zora Neale Hurston," *Cross-Cultural Performances: Differences in Women's Re-Visions of Shakespeare*, ed. Marianne Novy (Urbana and Chicago: University of Illinois Press, 1993), 157, make this point in arguments to which my own is clearly indebted.

Bibliography

Erickson, Peter. *Rewriting Shakespeare, Rewriting Ourselves.* Berkeley and Los Angeles: University of California Press, 1991.

Hooks, William H. *Moss Gown.* New York: Clarion Books, 1987.

Levine, Lawrence. "William Shakespeare and the American People: A Study in Cultural Transformation." *American Historical Review* 89.1 (1984): 34–66.

Naylor, Gloria. *Mama Day.* New York: Ticknor and Fields, 1988.

Rozett, Martha Tuck. *Talking Back to Shakespeare.* Newark: University of Delaware Press, 1994.

Sayers, Valerie. Review of *Moss Gown, The New York Times Book Review* 92 (August 9, 1987): 29.

Shakespeare, William. *The Riverside Shakespeare.* Ed. G. Blakemore Evans. 2nd ed. Boston and New York: Houghton Mifflin Company, 1997.

Traub, Valerie. "Rainbows of Darkness: Deconstructing Shakespeare in the Work of Gloria Naylor and Zora Neale Hurston." In *Cross-Cultural Performances: Differences in Women's Re-Visions of Shakespeare.* Ed. Marianne Novy. Urbana and Chicago: University of Illinois Press, 1993). 150–63.

29. Learning by Playing

Performance Games and the Teaching of Shakespeare

GREG MAILLET

Though most people today admire Shakespeare and believe he should be taught both to adult students and children of all ages, many also question, often based upon unhappy high school experiences, whether an art so clearly intended for public performance can possibly be presented effectively within a classroom setting. In part, it was the serious difficulty of helping university English students experience the joys of Shakespeare in performance that prompted me to found an amateur acting troop, ACTIO, that is dedicated to exploring how performance enhances, affects, and effects the meaning of literary texts. Though only some of its exercises can be brought into a classroom, ACTIO has altered my pedagogy enough that if someone now asks how I teach Shakespeare, my first response is to say that our class plays with "the Bard" through performance games that seek the spirit of each play we study. To borrow from that great actor and theorist of the theater, Hamlet, we seek to use performance to "hold the mirror" of our human "nature," body and soul, so as to reflect the splendor of Shakespeare's art, without attempting to "pluck out the heart of [his] mystery" (*Ham.* 3.2.20, 348).

This answer may seem to lack academic rigor, but play, though often deemed useless and derided as "child's play," has long been a serious philosophical subject. From Plato to Aristotle, Kant to Schiller, Nietzsche to Derrida, diverse worldviews have considered play both a sign of creative freedom and a means to develop the human personality.[1] Although Appolonian and Dionysian thinkers have often argued for, on one hand, the superior value of structured, goal oriented games or, on the other, spontaneous, undisciplined, supposedly trivial play, many traditions have learned to combine and value both.[2] Erasmus, the most famous exponent of the religious humanism that chiefly formed Elizabethan England, not only translated the New Testament back into Greek, but also developed an educational program that, though highly disciplined, also advised a "gentle method of instruction" in

269

which "the process of education will resemble play more than work."[3]
Though some may not understand, Erasmus notes, that the "playful methods
I have outlined serve a serious purpose," he insists that "play and childhood
go naturally together," and therefore teachers should strive "to give the
course of study the appearance of a game."[4]

Gentle Will Shakespeare, the star pupil of the humanist program, mocks
its rigidity in an early comedy, *Love's Labour's Lost*, but eventually draws
heavily on its curriculum to create drama that fuses the intellectual and moral
qualities of classical and biblical drama with the popular qualities of his
native English tradition. Although Elizabethan players were often regarded
as the social equivalents of bear-baiters or circus clowns, the posthumous
publication of Shakespeare's First Folio marks one of the first times in European history that plays are deemed worthy of being preserved as books and,
eventually, studied for their educational merits. Why? Though the plots of
Renaissance drama are often called "arguments," reflecting their connection
to logic and rhetoric, in Shakespeare it is a play that Duke Theseus calls for,
in *A Midsummer Night's Dream*, when he wants something "to ease the
anguish of the torturing hour" (5.1.37). The same play had earlier portrayed
the magical, irrational allure of drama when Puck, embodiment of childlike
mischief, happens upon the rustic, English "mechanicals," translated from
medieval England to the forest of Athens, and proclaims: "What, a play
towards? I'll be an auditor, an actor, too, perhaps, if I see cause" (3.1.74–75).
In later Shakespeare, though, there is often a more serious rationale for
drama; in *Hamlet*, "the play's the thing" not merely to create emotional
chaos, but also to "catch the conscience of the King" (2.2.593–94). Hamlet,
unlike Puck, has clearly learned the Aristotelian concept of *mimesis*, and
knows that the "purpose of playing . . . was and is to hold, as 'twere, the mirror up to nature," an act with ethical, historical, and political purposes: "to
show virtue her own feature, scorn her own image, and the very age and body
of the time his form and pressure" (*Ham.* 3.2.19–23).

Due in part to these diverse dramatic purposes, the world has played with
Shakespeare ever since. However, due also to his present status as "high culture," and to the practical problems created by four hundred years of linguistic
change, in teaching Shakespeare today the opposition between "game" and
"play" remains, in many ways an unanswered challenge: is there—can there
be—a structured, competitive game which helps its players develop not only a
greater factual knowledge of Shakespearean drama, but also to participate in,
perchance to perform, the spirit of play at its heart? An imaginative U.S. company, Aristoplay, has produced an exciting new game, aptly called "The Play's
the Thing," which successfully meets so many aspects of this challenge that it
is worthy of serious study; even its failures, in my view, suggest many avenues
for further exploring how performance based games might become valuable
aids in the teaching of Shakespearean drama.

At the core of Aristoplay's game is the comedic Shakespearean invitation, to each player, to "entertain the offered fallacy" (*Err.* 2.2.189) and imagine themselves an unemployed Elizabethan whose goal is to act in as many Shakespearean scenes as possible. Or each player can choose, more specifically, to be a famous Shakespearean actor, such as Edward Alleyn, or even a post-Restoration actress like Elizabeth Berry; information on these players is included in the game's "programme," which explains the rules and offers further reading on Shakespeare's age and theater. The play begins on a square representing the Globe Theatre and, once inside the bare stage, players gradually acquire the cards needed to perform and even, perhaps, land upon "rave review," a square on which "comic antics" might "draw big laughs," Queen Elizabeth herself might applaud, or, most exciting of all, Shakespeare himself might "play opposite" you.

Each player's imagination is thus both engaged and relaxed, and the only initial suggestion is more of the same; the Globe's stage design could be pictured, and aspects of it, such as "hell-mouth," could be included in the play. Also, the picture of the stage audience does not include the Globe's social or physical divisions, thus missing a chance for actors to choose whether to play to the groundlings or earn the nobility's favor. More seriously, the stress on the individual actor could be modified to allow for occasional team play, perhaps organized according to rival theater companies of Shakespeare's day, such as the Admiral's company versus the Lord Chamberlain's. To further encourage group activities, Aristoplay might borrow some of the exercises offered by the Folger Shakespeare Library's online "Performance Institute;" their "Ghost Story," for example, retains the lead actors of Hamlet 1.5., but casts everyone else as a chorus in order to intensify the Ghost's call for Hamlet to take revenge.

Still, Aristoplay should be applauded for creating an identity or fantasy game not based, as countless future video games are likely to be, on players pretending to be actual Shakespearean characters; at first this idea might sound appealing, and virtual reality technology will make it appear even better than the real thing. One need not be a Luddite, however, to safely predict that such games will likely be based on rewriting Shakespeare's plays, not learning them in their actual textual forms; such exercises will be interesting, amusing, thought provoking, like staging one of Shakespeare's sources or a Charles Marowitz play, but not likely to reproduce the sublime aesthetic experience of Shakespeare's plays. Further, video technology is likely to reduce the role of language, of human words, in any performance game, and that will take us away from rather than into the world of Shakespeare's plays. Even if video games do retain some language component, they are likely to rely on artificial rather than human technology, and are therefore less likely to exercise the human wit that can be applied outside of the game's context.

Aristoplay's approach to teaching the content of Shakespeare's play can also be applauded. Each play is presented as a color-coded pack of cards, and is divided into thirteen scenes: each scene includes plot, character, and quotation cards, all of which include questions. Players must have three such "scene" cards, including the plot card, to "play" when they land on the board's "perform" space; then, a player must answer one question correctly from each card in order to "win" the scene and lay the cards face up, to be counted as points. In a very Aristotelian way, players thus learn the preeminence of plot in Shakespearean drama, and its integral connection to character and thought. The way the cards are played, though, effectively addresses one of the greatest barriers faced by any Shakespeare game, the players' widely disparate knowledge of the plays. "The Play's the Thing" allows anyone to play because a "novice" simply reads the cards and lays them down, competing for points in a manner akin to the card game "fish." An "apprentice," though, passes the cards to the left and answers a "level one" question that includes choices, while a "scholar" passes the cards and answers "level two" questions recalled purely from memory. During the course of a game, players may also win more cards by answering "cue" cards based on similar levels. Aristoplay's inclusive approach and commitment to learning is also enhanced by one other key factor: players are permitted, if they wish, to study their cards during the course of the game, thus allowing diligent players to make up their knowledge deficiency during the course of a game, while more knowledgeable players can retain a challenge by refusing to look. Yet this option does not make the game as easy as it first sounds. Players normally have more than seven cards in their hand, and currently Aristoplay offers a total of nine different plays, so players can choose to employ multiple decks, or plays, within the same game. A minor deficiency of this card system, however, is its numbering: why number scenes from 1–13, rather than according to the Act/Scene divisions of the plays themselves? Efficiency, in this case, works against knowledge.

More problematically, the cards, in most cases, do not ask questions about or encourage learning of the most unfamiliar aspect of Shakespeare's plays—his language. Although both educational and capitalist advocates of Shakespeare commonly claim, despite the cries of countless schoolchildren, that most of Shakespeare's words are still current, their claim conveniently forgets the numerous "false-friend" words like "weeds" or "maid," or the many common Shakespearean words no longer in use, such as "fain." If either type of word is functioning as a sentence's subject or verb, an entire sentence of otherwise understandable words becomes incomprehensible to most modern readers. Although there are activities, as noted elsewhere in this volume, that do demonstrate the value of "sound-play" exercises in which children can explore connotative meaning without being certain of denotative meanings, it must also be recognized that some Shakespearean passages do require explanatory translation. Often, denotative resources such as the OED, or the lexicons of Schmidt or Onions, will not limit the range of interpretation, but intelligently expand it.[5] Like corresponding visual and historical aids, the suggestion of denotative meanings can enhance students' concrete sense of Shakespeare's world and help them to inhabit imaginatively the interior of his plays.

"Fain, fain," then, should Aristoplay create a fourth category card, "language," to precede the quotation card and focus upon the linguistic difficulties likely to arise from any serious study of Shakespeare's plays. This category need not be dry, or pedantic, and could not only correct mistaken interpretations of particular words, but also suggest the multiple meanings often present in single Shakespearean words. While some language cards might be designed to exclude or correct mistaken meaning, others could, as a prelude to the game's acting component, employ a technique familiar to the Elizabethan grammar school, *imitatio* and have students translate, or rewrite Shakespeare's poetry in order both to comment on its meaning and imitate its rhythm and linguistic techniques.[6] For more advanced levels, language cards might even teach Elizabethan rhetorical devices, but attitude and attention to detail is more crucial here than technique. As John Barton, the longtime Royal Shakespeare Company director, aptly reminds us, "Elizabethans loved" words, "they relished them and they played with them." Thus, especially for us prospective Shakespearean actors, "until we love individual words we cannot love language, and if we don't we won't be able to use it properly."[7]

Despite the absence of a "language" category, "The Play's the Thing" is likely to increase most players' knowledge of Shakespeare's plays. Yet it is also a game of chance as well as of intellect, since luck of the draw determines how quickly one compiles three cards from the same scene, and roll of the dice determines how often one lands on "perform," or on other squares where one might win more cards. Or, one may land on a "stage mishap," in which, for example, "the lead actors forget their lines" or the "plague forces all playhouses to close;" then, players may have to discard a card, or pass one to the right. Similarly, the board also includes four "duel" spaces, which when landed on allow one player to challenge another to bet up to three cards, and then duel by rolling the dice—high roll taking all. Ironically, but aptly, to win a duel may ultimately hurt one's cause, since cards still in one's hand at the end of the game are deducted from the final score. These are simple but historically and theatrically authentic touches that add a dash of fun and unpredictability to the game, and prevent it from being one that the most intellectual students always win. In order to make Shakespeare more accessible within the average school, these are not trivial gimmicks, but invaluable features that help the game to be played and enjoyed by all.

What should be the most popular feature of "The Play's the Thing," however, is actually the most problematic. Billed as a "dramatic introduction to

Shakespeare," the game's rules call for players to act lines from Shakespeare only if, when they land on the "Perform" space, they choose the fourth and most difficult category, "Actor's Choice." Here the player may "perform" the plot card by reading the plot line in a dramatic fashion, like a narrator or chorus, and may convey the "character" card through mime, both interesting variants. But for the "quotation" or "script" cards—the latter is a fourth type of card which is "performed" only if the first three categories are answered correctly, and which consists of actual lines from the plays numbered by the traditional act/scene format—the game's rules require the player to "recite it from memory." This demand is unrealistic for most players, except those with significant preparation time. An obvious variation of the game, and the program does suggest creating one's own variations, is to allow players from the "novice," "apprentice," or "scholar" levels of the game also to try the "actor's choice" options on the "plot" or character" cards, and then to give a dramatic reading of the "quotation" and "script" cards, after, perhaps, answering the quotation question correctly, and offering an interpretation of the character they are reading. Recitation by memory could be retained as an option for players that do have time to rehearse or memorize. In either case, the script cards could be a much more effective dramatic introduction to Shakespeare if more than one actor could participate in the scene; again, the creation of rival theater companies could encourage this, although the script cards would need to be doubled, at least, to allow for more dialogue and interaction between players.

Rival companies would not, however, help to address the other major problem with the "actor's choice" category, especially the "script" cards: its point scoring system. Whereas the other categories are basically objective, this category suddenly becomes entirely subjective; cards are won, and placed face down, to quote the program, if "the majority agrees (by applause) that you performed well." This is a noble attempt to introduce an element of goodwill into the game ("Be kind to your fellow actors, and they will be kind to you!," exhorts the program) and to stimulate the standard Shakespearean epilogue's call to "Give me your hands, if we be friends" (*MND* 5.1.428). But, as a regular practice, it is unworkable, divisive, and at odds with the other elements in the game that fairly reward both knowledge and effort. It is particularly problematic because, whereas players receive ten points for every other card played face down, "script" cards are worth twenty points and, in the current rules, open only to players in the "actor's choice" category. Especially in the often rowdy, sometimes cruel classroom environment, basing the evaluation of amateur acting ability upon popular acceptance or rejection could easily produce a fear of acting Shakespeare, the opposite of Aristoplay's goal. To again cite Erasmus, both the "motives of victory and competition" and "the fear of disgrace and desire for praise" are "deeply rooted in children," and educators must "exploit these motives to advance their education,"[8] not try to deny their existence.

No easy solution exists, but other scoring options could be offered. The simplest would apply only to actors reciting from memory, who could automatically be granted their points if they correctly spoke at least, say, 85% of the script card's words. For the more common dramatic readings, though, the problem is tougher. For novices, one option is to award a set amount, perhaps ten points, to anyone brave enough to act a script card, and applause would be a normal reward. For the higher levels, a different option would be to guarantee five points for anyone attempting to perform a script card, and then ten points for any performance that no other player feels could be topped; in that case, applause would follow naturally. However, if another actor wants to try and "steal the show," he or she could perform the same script card, and then the other players could vote for the superior performance, using paper or show of hand. The winner of the "duelling players" would win the script card, worth ten points, a sum that is probably small enough to procure honest votes from around the "stage," or table. Also, if the initial actor loses, he or she would still add five points to their total, since after all that player had answered the initial three cards correctly; on the other hand, if the challenger lost, he or she would give up two cards, either to the player whom he or she had the audacity to challenge or, if unwanted, to the discard pile. A competitive, exciting, audience response element would thus be retained, but not one likely to radically alter the outcome of the game or, more tragically, to scare away potential actors from the joy of playing Shakespeare.

The possibility, alternatively, of helping the average student not only to learn about but actually to enjoy performing Shakespeare makes it essential that performance games such as Aristoplay's be both encouraged and constructively criticized. "Learning," to paraphrase one of Shakespeare's greatest players, Falstaff, is "a mere hoard of gold kept by a devil," unless play (a healthier spirit than "sack"), "commences it and sets it in act and use" (*2H6* 4.2.110–13). Though I have focused here upon attempting to do so through the structured play of a game, rules are only necessary or effective insofar as they engage students and enable them to experience the actual content of Shakespeare's plays, particularly its language and gestures, how they "suit the action to the word, the word to the action" (*Ham.* 3.2.16–17). Aristoplay's game, though flawed, does allow for and even encourage creative variations that could enhance its authenticity even further, and teachers can also find numerous other performance exercises in resources like the Folger Library's Performance Institute, or in a number of other essays in this volume that suggest how to allow children of all ages to play with Shakespeare. So far from being an elitist method that requires trips to professional theaters (whether in Stratford upon Avon or Canada's own Stratford, Ontario), or even expensive video equipment, a performance pedagogy's crucial trait is the spirit of play. The most important performance space to illumine is each of our students' own "mind's eye," the oft "distracted globe" atop each of their own shoulders (*Ham.* 1.2.184; 1.5.97), which must be lively, attentive, and alert to the subtlety, nuance, and diction of Shakespeare's language. As John Barton puts it, aptly summarizing his own directorial method: "Playing Shakespeare is at bottom to do with playing with words . . . Yes, playing in every sense of playing: playing a game, being zestful, using our wits, spending energy and enjoying oneself. If the actor enjoys the word games, the audience will enjoy them too."[9] Similarly, if teachers find enjoyable, creative ways to play with the Bard, then their students will too. To return, finally, to Hamlet, with a nod to Aristoplay, "the play's the thing" wherein we can help our students catch, or perhaps be caught by, the intellectual depth, ethical passion, and aesthetic beauty of Shakespearean drama.

Notes

1. See Spariosu.
2. Slethaug.
3. Erasmus, 324.
4. Erasmus, 340–41; also, see Gordon.
5. See, for example, Janet Field-Pickering's discussion, in this volume, of the song of Winter, from *Love's Labour's Lost*. In general, Shakespeare's songs, such as Ariel's in *The Tempest* or the songs in *As You Like It*, are a good place to show the importance of both denotative and connotative meaning.
6. Such exercises cannot substitute for Shakespeare's language, but they can introduce it to students and help them enjoy it. ACTIO, in fact, was commissioned last year by the Saskatchewan Department of Education to write an unusual *imitatio*, a "rap" version of the sleepwalking scene in *Macbeth*; though we still doubt its aesthetic merits. I have been persuaded to include it in an appendix here.
7. Barton, 47–48
8. Erasmus, 340.
9. Barton, 117.

Works Cited

Barton, John. *Playing Shakespeare*. London: Methuen, 1984.

Erasmus, Desiderius. *A Declamation on the Subject of Early Liberal Education for Children*. Trans. Beert C. Verstraete. *Collected Works of Erasmus: Literary and Educational Writings 4*. Ed. J. K. Sowards. Vol. 26. Toronto: University of Toronto Press, 1985. 291–346.

Gordon, Walter M. *Humanist Play and Belief: The Serio-Comic Art of Desiderius Erasmus*. Toronto: University of Toronto Press, 1990.

Onions, C. T. *A Shakespeare Glossary*. Rev. Robert D. Eagleson. Oxford: Clarendon Press, 1986.

Schmidt, Alexander. *Shakespeare Lexicon and Quotation Dictionary*. 1902. 3rd ed. Rev. Gregor Sarrazin. 2 vols. New York: Dover, 1971.

Shakespeare, William. *A Midsummer Night's Dream*. Ed. Peter Holland. Oxford: Oxford University Press, 1994.

———. *Hamlet*. Ed. G. R. Hibbard. Oxford: Oxford University Press, 1987.

———. *Henry IV. Part 2*. Ed. Rene Weis. Oxford: Oxford University Press, 1997.

———. *Love's Labour's Lost*. Ed. G. R. Hibbard. Oxford: Oxford University Press, 1990.

———. *The Comedy of Errors*. Ed. Stanley Wells and Gary Taylor. *William Shakespeare: The Complete Works*. Oxford: Clarendon Press, 1988. 258–77.

Slethaug, Gordon E. "Game Theory." *Encyclopedia of Contemporary Literary Theory*. Gen. Ed. Irena R. Makaryk. Toronto: University of Toronto Press, 1993. 64–69.

———. "Play / freeplay, theories of." *Encyclopedia of Contemporary Literary Theory*. Gen. Ed. Irena R. Makaryk. Toronto: University of Toronto Press, 1993. 145–49.

Spariosu, Mihai I. *Dionysus Reborn: Play and the Aesthetic Dimension in Modern Philosophical and Scientific Discourse*. Ithaca: Cornell University Press, 1989.

———. *Play, Poetry, and Power in Hellenic Thought from Homer to Aristotle*. Durham: Duke University Press, 1991.

The 1995–96 Folger Library Shakespeare Institute; *Shakespeare Through Performance Project*. Ed. Tom Gandy. January–February 2000 (http://www.tamut.edu/english/folgerhp/folgerhp.html).

The Play's the Thing: A Dramatic Introduction to Shakespeare. Game Creator: Annie Dean. Game Developer: Lorraine Hopping Egan. Ann Arbor, MI: Aristoplay Ltd., 1993, 1999.

Appendix

ACTIO Rap Version of *Macbeth* 5.1.

DOCTOR: The lights are on
GENTLEWOMAN: But there's no one home
DOCTOR: Her eyes ope wide
GENTLEWOMAN: But is anyone inside?
DOCTOR: Her eyes light up
GENTLEWOMAN: But her senses are shut
DOCTOR: She keeps rubbin her hands
GENTLEWOMAN: Can't she see they're not cut?

LADY MACBETH:
    Yes here's a spot
    That I've still not got
    One, two, three, four
    Out damned spot, out the door

    Hell is murky
    Blood is everywhere

Why did Duncan
Wear such red underwear?

ALL TOGETHER:

Yes there's a spot
That she still hasn't got
One, two, three, four
Out damned spot, out the door

LADY MACBETH:

The Thane of Fife
Won't let me be clean
He had a wife

Can't you hear her screaaaaaaaaaaaammmmmmmmm!

To bed, to bed
There's knocking at the gate
What's done is done
I've sealed my fate.

ALL TOGETHER:

Yes there's a spot
That she still hasn't got
One, two, three, four
Out damned spot, out the door

DOCTOR: My mind she has mated
GENTLEWOMAN: She's amazed my sight
DOCTOR: God, God, forgive us
GENTLEWOMAN: For the horror of this night!

ALL TOGETHER:

Yes there's a spot
That she still hasn't got
One, two, three, four
Out damned spot, out the door

30. Reimagining Shakespeare through Film

GREGORY COLŃ SEMENZA

A colleague recently explained to me that she hesitates to use film in her college-level Shakespeare course because of a limited film vocabulary and a more "general uncertainty" about how to proceed. Such feelings are not uncommon, nor is the root of the problem difficult to identify. Whereas the potential usefulness of film has become an increasingly central—even clichéd—topic in discussions of Shakespeare in the classroom, most published studies have focused on the use of film for the explication of specific plays. Such studies offer excellent models to be emulated but do precious little in the way of inspiring creative and confident pedagogical experimentation with film.[1] Like my friend, most of us who teach prefer not to teach other people's stuff.

In this essay, I suggest how instructors of high school and college students might use film to teach the complexities of Shakespearean drama, as opposed to the "meanings" of his individual plays. I call this the genre-based approach to the use of film. Specifically, I highlight the use of film for teaching such difficult concepts as textual indeterminacy, metatheatricality, and intertextuality. This approach has several particular strengths to recommend it: first, it requires of instructors only the most rudimentary film vocabulary. While any thorough presentation on Kurosawa's adaptation of *Macbeth* would demand knowledge of the myriad technical details that constitute filmic meaning, the genre-based approach allows English instructors to operate within their own discursive field of expertise.[2] Second, the genre-based approach empowers students by helping them to understand *how* Shakespeare creates art. Instead of bestowing upon them the knowledge of what happens in *Othello*, we help them to cultivate analytical skills which they can employ time and time again in their later readings of Shakespeare and other dramatists. A fundamental concern of many instructors is that using film in the classroom will foster complacency in our students—that the relatively

279

passive act of watching a movie will become a substitute for the more active process of reading. One particular risk is that students will learn a good deal more about Branagh's Shakespeare than about Shakespeare's plays. The third benefit of the genre-based approach is that it ensures that Shakespeare, and not Branagh, will remain the focus of the course. In short, it is an approach that encourages students to reimagine Shakespeare as a playwright, as opposed to reimagining Hamlet or even *Hamlet*.

Using film is a complex matter, of course, and I do not wish to suggest that my colleague's ambivalence is unreasonable. Nor do I wish to suggest that the genre-based approach to film will allay such feelings. The most basic problem is determining when film's usefulness as a way into the literary text is overshadowed by the power of the film text itself. Ironically, ambivalence and uncertainty may be the greatest weapons for dealing with such a problem. After all, such feelings keep us alert to what is working and what is not.

That said, I hope that what follows will serve as a practical guide for teachers who are considering the use of more film in their Shakespeare classes. The concepts upon which I focus are somewhat arbitrary; a number of other dramatic concepts—soliloquy, costuming, or *deus ex machina*—could just as easily have been highlighted. The point of the essay is not to offer a template for imitation but, instead, to define a conceptual approach for the use of film that will be adaptable to a wide variety of teaching styles.

Textual Indeterminacy

In order to counter the aversion to Shakespeare that many young students express, teachers may find it helpful to highlight the indeterminacy of the play text. *Textual indeterminacy* suggests the impossibility of finding the "real" meaning behind any particular textual utterance. While one's ability to figure out an author's—or a single word's—precise meaning is inherently limited regardless of the text under consideration, the problem is exacerbated when one turns to Shakespeare's plays. As is well known, individual Shakespeare plays exist in multiple and sometimes incomplete forms, and textual variants are common from one version of a play to another. Furthermore, there is considerable evidence of joint authorship in many cases, whether we mean by this the collaborative work of Shakespeare and Fletcher in *The Two Noble Kinsmen* or the obvious hand of an actor in the *Q1* text of *Hamlet*. Most usefully, an emphasis on textual indeterminacy calls attention to the flawed goal of even *trying* to locate the "real" meaning of a text. Instead of advancing a New Critical notion of the text as a puzzle to be solved, textual indeterminacy suggests how a reader makes meaning out of ambiguity. That is, focusing students on textual indeterminacy replaces the relatively passive act of finding out what a text means with the more active goal of making a text mean something. Eradicating the notion of a solitary or fixed textual "meaning" behind, say, *Romeo and Juliet* frees students to interpret the play's multiple meanings from their own individual perspectives.

In highlighting indeterminacy, we also focus attention on a central characteristic of Shakespeare's art. If one of the playwright's most enduring contributions to the development of drama as a literary form is his subtle defiance of generic expectation, then his deliberate use of indeterminacy may be described as one of the primary means by which he challenges his audiences. For example, students are usually taught that the traditional classification of *Measure for Measure* as a comedy depends upon the assumption that Isabella consents to the Duke's request, "Give me your hand, and say you will be mine" (5.1.492).[3] Her silence famously complicates this assumption. The central problem of the play stems not from a deterministic authorial stance but, rather, from the indeterminacy of the play text.

Film is a particularly useful medium for demonstrating textual indeterminacy and for encouraging students to think about why certain interpretations are more persuasive than others. A wise strategy is to introduce the concept early on in class, even before students have read an entire play. In the first week of my "Introduction to Shakespeare" class, I ask students to consider clips from three separate versions/adaptations of *Romeo and Juliet*— the play with which they are typically most familiar. I juxtapose the equivalent of the Capulet Ball scenes from Franco Zeffirelli's 1968 film, Jerome Robbin's *West Side Story* (1961), and Baz Luhrmann's excellent revisionist film of 1996. Students are asked to read the scene (1.5) before class. After the viewing, I initiate conversation by asking a deliberately vulnerable question such as, "Which of these films offers the most *accurate* interpretation of the scene?"

At first, students will defend Zeffirelli's film because of its period costumes, relatively minor textual emendations, and seemingly conservative cinematography. With a push in the right direction, however (and many times I am not needed to provide it), the conversation will invariably turn as students begin to reflect on the naiveté of the question. "What do you mean by the word 'accurate,'" they will ask. "Isn't Luhrmann's comedic playfulness more 'accurate' than Zeffirelli's sobriety? So what if *West Side Story* is a modernization? Didn't Shakespeare also modernize old stories? Why should the actors wear period costumes? Did Elizabethan actors do so?" Students quickly begin to see how each film adds something new to their understanding of the play, which demonstrates, in turn, the indeterminacy of Shakespeare's work. After the exercise, students are comfortable enough to apply the concept of indeterminacy to other plays they will confront during the semester. They are also considerably more confident that their own interpretations will not be dismissed as "wrong."

Film can be used effectively throughout the semester to provoke debate and conversation about specific textual controversies. I usually show my

students the ending of Sam Taylor's *The Taming of the Shrew* (1929), starring Douglas Fairbanks and Mary Pickford. After Katherine has delivered
her final lines, she looks directly at the camera and offers a memorable wink
to her audience. Class conversation, which follows the viewing, is based on
a simple question: "Is there textual evidence to support such an interpretation of the *denouement*?" Students are asked to consider what is and what is
not determinable in the text and, in addition, to assess the persuasiveness of
one particular interpretation of Shakespeare's controversial scene.

Herbert R. Coursen claims that when students are exposed to multiple
productions of the same script, "Their writing takes a leap towards maturity,
an inevitable consequence of their suddenly enhanced powers of observation."[4] The point is certainly worth emphasizing. Once students learn that
there are multiple valid ways to interpret a text, their goals as writers shift.
Instead of working to *reveal* the meaning that is *in* the text, students begin to
construct meaning from without. By juxtaposing multiple productions of a
single scene in a play or by considering one radical production in relation to
the scene, we encourage our students to become active makers—as opposed
to relatively passive finders—of meaning.

Metatheatricality

Metatheatricality is a term used by critics to define a play's recognition of its
own generic characteristics and limitations. When Prologue asks in *Henry V*,
"Can this cockpit hold / The vasty fields of France," the character calls attention not only to the physical conditions of the Globe Theatre but also to the
boundaries between the theatrical and the real (11–12). Devices such as the
soliloquy and the *aside* can be described as metatheatrical because they
acknowledge the presence of a real audience and, at the same time, the limitations of realism on stage. Metadramatic conventions such as the *induction*
and the *play-within-the-play*, on the other hand, complicate boundaries
between the real and the imagined by highlighting the constructedness of the
act of viewing a play and the difficulty of determining its borders.

The success of a film or television adaptation of Shakespeare depends
largely on the director's ability to accommodate the self-conscious theatricality of the play. Highly metatheatrical plays like *Richard III* offer special
problems, since their meanings often hinge on their conflation of realism and
theatrical artifice. Richard's determination to "*play* the devil," for instance, is
far more enticing to a live audience, which is aware that "Richard" is merely
the temporary construction of a player. Such a realization, in turn, promotes
reflection on one of the play's central ideas that, "Nor more can you distinguish of a man / Than of his outward show" (3.1.9–10). In transferring
Shakespeare's plays from stage to screen, a director risks flattening such productive signifiers into mere words, words, words.

Richard Loncraine's film of *Richard III* (1995) highlights the cinematic medium in order to accommodate the metatheatricality of the play. As James Loehlin and others have shown, Loncraine develops, through allusion, an ongoing dialogue between his and other famous Hollywood films.[5] This dialogue helps to establish what Kenneth Rothwell has described as "meta-cinema," a flexible, playful space within an otherwise realistic medium.[6] Allusions to films such as *White Heat* and *The Godfather* remind viewers that the film's realism is an illusion and thereby uphold Shakespeare's own conflation of artifice and realism. When students are taught to recognize such strategies of accommodation, they begin to perceive the basic differences between film and theater, as well as the complexities of Shakespeare's language and art.

A productive class exercise might begin with a dissection of the opening scene of Loncraine's *Richard III*. Henry VI and Prince Edward are attacked in the Lancastrian field headquarters by an invading army. The invasion is signaled by the barking of a dog at a large brick wall that eventually collapses under the pressure of a tank. The barking informs the audience that Richard is among the invaders ("dogs bark at me as I halt by them" [1.1.23]). Commandos in gas masks flood the room firing machine guns. One dark figure, breathing heavily through a mask shoots Henry at point blank, removes the mask, and stares directly into the camera. Now contrast the first scene of George Lucas's *Star Wars* (1977), which begins with rebel soldiers aboard a fortified galactic cruiser. An imperial invasion is signaled by a loud screech before a sealed door, which gives way under the blasts of Storm Troopers. Moments later, enter Darth Vader breathing heavily through an oversized helmet. To signal that the allusion is deliberate, Loncraine prefaces his opening scene with a Morse-code tickertape that announces the civil war—a tribute to the famous scrolling captions with which *Star Wars* begins.

Juxtaposing these two scenes helps students to grasp the meta-cinematic accommodation of metatheatricality. In addition, the teacher should point out the benefits of such accommodation for the film. After Loncraine has established the playfulness of the film space and, consequently, shattered the audience's expectation of realism, nothing is off limits. Richard can now look and speak directly into the camera lens as if offering an "aside" to the audience or speaking in soliloquy. Each student's enhanced awareness of the different expectations of movie and theater audiences will translate into a more nuanced ability to confront drama on its own terms.

The opening of Olivier's masterful *Henry V* (1944) lends itself to a simpler but equally effective demonstration of meta-cinema. Both Olivier and Branagh have gone to great lengths to accommodate the highly self-conscious Prologue/Chorus figure of the play. As we have seen, this character repeatedly calls attention to the limitations of the playhouse: "Can this cockpit / Hold the vasty fields of France?" In the context of the film, the character seems to be saying that the fields of France and the massive battles of *Henry V* would be more suitable for the realistic medium of film. No wise director would risk cutting the Prologue/Chorus figure as a solution, mainly because of the vital exposition he provides throughout the play. In Olivier's case, the artifice of drama is precisely what he wishes to highlight, since his film acts out a fantasy of the glorious impending victory of the allied (i.e., British) forces over Germany.

The opening scenes of the film take place in a replica of the Globe Theatre—that lamentable "wooden O"—but ever gradually, the scene fades into the more realistic fields of France. In such a way, Olivier captures the very metamorphosis of drama into film. His point is not only to celebrate the limitless possibilities of film, however; it is also to celebrate the power of drama and the human imagination ("'tis your thoughts that now must deck our kings" [28]). More importantly for us, the film is a celebration of Shakespeare's craft. Olivier's film asks our students to imagine an artist struggling to overcome the limitations of his medium and calls attention to the strategies he employs to accomplish this feat.

Teachers may wish to balance their use of Olivier's *Henry V* with some clips from Kenneth Branagh's film of 1989. Whereas Olivier goes to great lengths to emphasize the differences between film realism and theatrical artifice, Branagh interrogates the idea that film requires from its audience less of a suspension of disbelief. The Chorus, played by Derek Jacobi, delivers the opening lines of the play as he winds through the wires of a crowded Hollywood movie set. By reminding us of the constructedness of film, Branagh, like Loncraine, creates a meta-cinematic vocabulary capable of communicating Shakespeare's metadramatic language. Moreover, by obscuring the apparent differences between filmmaking and playwriting, Branagh questions Olivier's binary conception of the two arts. When viewed together in class, the openings of both films raise important questions about both the limitations and the unlimited potential of drama.

Intertextuality

Of the three concepts discussed in this essay, *intertextuality*—a term used to describe the innumerable ways in which one text is linked to or influenced by other texts—is by far the most difficult for students to grasp in abstraction, primarily because they are so often unfamiliar with the texts that Shakespeare appropriates. Still, I believe the effort it requires to teach the concept is worthwhile, especially since so much of the pleasure of reading Shakespeare stems from an awareness of his relentless manipulation of earlier texts and conventions. On a simpler level, it is sometimes difficult to understand even the basic meaning of particular passages without a sense of how they engage other texts. The mechanicals' hilarious rendition of "Pyramus and Thisbe" in *A*

Midsummer Night's Dream, for instance, often falls flat for students who are unfamiliar with Ovid or the myth in general. Furthermore, teaching students about the intertextuality of Shakespearean drama helps them to deconstruct further the intimidating myth of Shakespeare as a genius, writing in solitude.

In the class period after our viewing of *Star Wars* and *Richard III*, I ask my students to reflect on the implications of Loncraine's allusion to the more famous film. About half of the hands in the class usually go up. What students perceive immediately about Richard is that he has much in common with Darth Vader. Both are deformed. Both have made conscious decisions to embrace evil. Both kill mercilessly. And both are far more interesting than their hyper-virtuous enemies. At the same time, Richmond's cartoonish goodness is as apparent as Luke Skywalker's. Such parallels call attention to these early characters as dramatic types, and they provide a starting point from which students can begin to chart the development of character over the course of Shakespeare's career. Most importantly, they expose the simplicity of absolute categories such as good and evil, encouraging students to consider context as the *sine qua non* of all judgment.

Students are quick to grasp and eager to discuss the numerous implications of any allusion to popular films like *Star Wars*. The teacher should be equally quick to inform them that they have just demonstrated a basic understanding of intertextuality. The teacher should also take numerous opportunities during the course of a semester to point out how Shakespeare's plays acquire added meaning and depth as a result of their engagement with other texts. Here the possibilities are limitless. An obvious choice is to provide students with excerpts from Sylvester Jourdain's *A Discovery of the Bermudas* and Montaigne's "Of the Cannibals" while they are reading *The Tempest*. In what ways does Ariel's reference to the "still-vex'd Bermoothes" (1.2.229) alter our view of Prospero's island and, more specifically, of Prospero's slave? How does the fact that Caliban's name is a near anagram for "cannibal" complicate the character further? By focusing on the manner in which Shakespeare's island monster emerges out of English fantasies or fears about the mysterious inhabitants of a New World, we may re-read Caliban as a *victim* of humanity rather than as a threat to it. Though *The Tempest* explicitly advances a notion of Western society as cultured and superior, it also subtly reveals the hypocrisy of that notion. One result of this revelation is that even Prospero, the play's hero, becomes less distinguishable in nature from his "thing of darkness." When students are encouraged to see how Shakespeare engages other texts, their understanding of the complexity and ambivalence of his plays is considerably enhanced.

I have tried to establish some practical guidelines for a creative use of film in the Shakespeare classroom. I recommend using film to help students reimagine Shakespeare as a human being and a working artist. If they are encouraged to learn more about Shakespeare the writer than *Julius Caesar* the play, they will leave our classrooms armed with analytical skills that they can exercise over and over again in their future encounters with other Shakespearean and non-Shakespearean plays. The method I have referred to as the genre-based approach to film allows English teachers to teach what they know best: literature.

On the other hand, I can easily imagine that the concepts I have chosen to highlight here—textual indeterminacy, metatheatricality, and intertextuality—might cause a reader who is uncertain about film to denounce it once and for all. How can we possibly expect a sixteen or seventeen year old to comprehend the function of metatheatricality in *Richard III*? A fair question. And yet, I would prefer to reverse the equation by asking how we can convey the complexity and charm of *Richard III* to readers who have little understanding of the unique ways in which drama operates? The astonishing variety and current availability of Shakespeare films invites us to tackle complex performance issues through a relatively new language that excites and stimulates our students. Be creative. Be ambitious. As the other essays in this volume make clear, even the youngest of our students can handle the challenge.[7]

Notes

1. There are few exceptions to this rule, but some of the best include the opening section—"Theories, Techniques, and Resources"—of H. R. Coursen's *Teaching Shakespeare with Film and Television* (Westport, Connecticut: Greenwood, 1997), 1–103; Michael J. Collins's excellent essay on the uses of film to teach comedy as a genre ("Love, Sighs, and Videotape: An Approach to Teaching Shakespeare's Comedies," in *Teaching Shakespeare Today: Practical Approaches and Productive Strategies*, ed. James E. Davis and Ronald E. Salomone [Urbana, Illinois: National Council of Teachers, 1993], 109–116); and James Hirsch's "Picturing Shakespeare: Using Film in the Classroom to Turn Text into Theater" (in Davis and Salomone, ed., 1993, 140–150).

2. For a useful overview of film terms every Shakespeare teacher should know, see David Kranz, "Cinematic Elements in Shakespearean Film: A Glossary," in *Teaching Shakespeare Through Performance*, ed. Milla Cozart Riggio (New York: Modern Language Association of America, 1999), 341–60. For instructors of literature, the best general overview of film terms and concepts remains Joseph M. Boggs, *The Art of Watching Films* (Palo Alto, Calif: Mayfield, 1985).

3. Quotations from Shakespeare are from *The Riverside Shakespeare*, 2nd ed., ed. G. Blakemore Evans (Boston: Houghton Mifflin, 1997).

4. Coursen, "Uses of Media in Teaching Shakespeare," in *Teaching Shakespeare into the Twenty-First Century*, ed. Ronald E. Salomone and James E. Davis (Athens, OH: Ohio University Press, 1997), 193.

5. Loehlin, " 'Top of the World, Ma': Richard III and Cinematic Convention," in *Shakespeare the Movie: Popularizing the Plays on Film, TV, and Video*, ed. Lynda E. Boose and Richard Burt (London: Routledge, 1997), 67–79.

6. Rothwell, "Representing *King Lear* on Screen: from Metatheatre to 'Metacinema,' " in *Shakespeare and the Moving Image: the Plays on Film and Television*, ed. Anthony Davies and Stanley Wells (Cambridge: Cambridge University Press, 1994), 211–33.

7. I have listed in the Works Consulted section what I believe to be the ten most useful works for *teaching* Shakespeare on film and television.

Works Cited

Boggs, Joseph M. *The Art of Watching Films*. Palo Alto, Calif: Mayfield, 1985.

Collins, Michael J. "Love, Sighs, and Videotape: An Approach to Teaching Shakespeare's Comedies." In *Teaching Shakespeare Today: Practical Approaches and Productive Strategies*, edited by James E. Davis and Ronald E. Salomone, 109–16. Urbana, IL: National Council of Teachers, 1993.

Coursen, H.R. *Teaching Shakespeare with Film and Television*. Westport, CT: Greenwood, 1997.

———. "Uses of Media in Teaching Shakespeare." In *Teaching Shakespeare into the Twenty-First Century*, edited by Ronald E. Salomone and James E. Davis, 193–200. Athens, OH: Ohio University Press, 1997.

Hirsch, James. "Picturing Shakespeare: Using Film in the Classroom to Turn Text into Theater." In *Teaching Shakespeare Today: Practical Approaches and Productive Strategies*, edited by James E. Davis and Ronald E. Salomone, 140–50. Urbana, IL: National Council of Teachers, 1993.

Kranz, David. "Cinematic Elements in Shakespearean Film: A Glossary." In *Teaching Shakespeare through Performance*, edited by Milla Cozart Riggio, 341–60. New York: Modern Language Association of America, 1999.

Loehlin, James F. " 'Top of the World, Ma': Richard III and Cinematic Convention." In *Shakespeare the Movie: Popularizing the Plays on Film, TV, and Video*, edited by Lynda E. Boose and Richard Burt, 67–79. London: Routledge, 1997.

Rothwell, Kenneth S. "Representing *King Lear* on Screen: From Metatheatre to Metacinema." In *Shakespeare and the Moving Image: The Plays on Film and Television*, edited by Anthony Davies and Stanley Wells, 211–33. Cambridge: Cambridge University Press, 1994.

Shakespeare, William. *The Riverside Shakespeare*, edited by G. Blakemore Evans, 2nd ed. Boston: Houghton Mifflin, 1997.

Works Consulted

Ball, Robert Hamilton. *Shakespeare on Silent Film: A Strange Eventful History*. New York: Theater Art Books, 1968.

Boggs, Joseph M. *The Art of Watching Films*. Palo Alto, Calif: Mayfield, 1985.

Bulman, J. C. and H. R. Coursen, eds. *Shakespeare on Television: An Anthology of Essays and Reviews*. Hanover, NH: University Press of New England, 1988.

Coursen, H. R. *Teaching Shakespeare with Film and Television*. Westport, Conn: Greenwood, 1997.

Davies, Anthony and Stanley Wells, eds. *Shakespeare and the Moving Image: The Play on Film and Television*. Cambridge: Cambridge University Press, 1994.

Jorgens, Jack. *Shakespeare on Film*. Bloomington: Indiana University Press, 1977.

Kranz, David. "Cinematic Elements in Shakespearean Film: A Glossary." In *Teaching Shakespeare through Performance*, edited by Milla Cozart Riggio, 341–60. New York: Modern Language Association of America, 1999.

Leach, Susan. "Shakespeare and Video." In *Shakespeare in the Classroom*. Buckingham: Open University Press, 1992.

McMurtry, Jo. *Shakespeare Films in the Classroom: A Descriptive Guide*. Hamden, CT: Archon, 1994.

Willis, Susan. *The BBC Shakespeare Plays: Making the Televised Canon*. Chapel Hill, NC: University of North Carolina Press, 1991.

31. Performing Pedagogy

EDWARD L. ROCKLIN

I am not the first to say that teaching is a performing art. Over the years of my close work with teachers more than a few of them said, "Teachers are actors. We perform." They did not mean that they were in show business but rather they were the vehicle by which the script (the curriculum) becomes a source of interest, a personal and intellectual goal to an audience inevitably heterogeneous on many variable-affecting attitudes toward learning.
—SEYMOUR B. SARASON[1]

Prologue

Over the twenty years that I have taught Shakespeare's plays at two universities, I have not only worked with several thousand students but have also concentrated much of my practice and writing on working with hundreds of teachers, ranging from novices to veterans. I have worked with K-12 teachers in New Jersey, Illinois, Pennsylvania, and, for the last fourteen years, in southern California. And throughout this time I have been struck by how uncomfortable many teachers, even very experienced teachers, become when they have to teach drama, and particularly Shakespeare's plays, to their students. As I have observed how such teachers teach the plays of Shakespeare and as I have listened to undergraduate and graduate students describe how they have been taught to read Shakespeare in earlier classes, it has become clear that a majority of teachers in K-12 systems are most comfortable using the strategies they have mastered for teaching students to read prose fiction.

But to read Shakespeare's plays as novels (or, for that matter, as poems) means ignoring their theatrical life—ignoring, that is, the way in which performance serves to shape not merely different but divergent, conflicting, even contradictory realizations of the same playtext. Yet once they learn to read drama as drama—a form that speaks in what the American director Harold

Clurman calls *another language* (Clurman, 18) many of these teachers and teachers-to-be discover how exciting it is to read employing drama's own strategies.[2] And they become eager to master this language because they recognize that learning to speak this language offers them an opportunity to excite their own students in reading these plays.

Since these teachers have made it clear that it was their own training that made them uncomfortable with teaching drama, one logical response was to design courses that offered opportunities for them to learn to teach plays as drama, incorporating both literary and theatrical practices. Starting in 1994, I have designed several courses specifically to teach methods of teaching drama in general and Shakespeare's plays in particular. The first course is English 590, Pedagogies of Dramatic Literature, offered as part of Cal Poly Pomona's M.A. program. In addition, in my role as regional director of a site of the California Reading and Literature Project, I have conducted three summer institutes with a major drama component; and conducted two drama workshops for teachers to immerse themselves in, test out, and adopt the model, adapting it for grades 4–12.

In this essay, I focus on the challenge of conducting courses which invite teachers and teachers-to-be to adopt a performance approach to teaching Shakespeare's plays—noting also that they will need to adapt such an approach to the students they are teaching in the K-12 and community college systems in which they work or plan to work. The essay is divided into two parts. In the first part, I articulate the challenge of designing and conducting such courses. In the second part, I describe two of the opening activities I use to immerse the participants in the approach—the point being not only to immerse them in the deep end of the pool before they have time for strong resistances to emerge, but also to move through experiences which introduce them to the multiple dimensions and exciting payoffs of such an approach.

Framing Challenges

There are a number of challenges we confront when we create a performance-based pedagogy for dramatic literature that we can employ in our classes in middle and high schools, in community colleges, colleges, and universities. But one way to formulate these challenges is to suggest that a pedagogy of dramatic literature encompasses three linked yet separable areas of study: first, drama as written text; second, performance as the translation of that text from page to stage realization; and third, pedagogy, or teaching considered as a form of action in which the teacher creates designs through which students learn both about performing and through performing.

Obviously, the tripartite focus of our subject means there is a tripartite set of interlocking objectives. The first objective is for the participants to develop their ability to read a play's text in terms of its logic both as a literary work and as the blueprint or score from which the players create a theatrical event. The second objective is for the participants to learn to ask some of the questions by which actors and directors, having studied the design of the playtext, treat that text as a script which invites their co-creative efforts to transform the words on the page into the performance on the stage. (I am always very explicit that this approach does not teach acting, nor does it demand training as an actor for either teachers or students.) The third objective is for the participants to articulate a model of teaching, either from their present practice or from their reading and experience as students, composing pedagogic frames through which they can use a performance approach in order to fulfill their own objectives with specific classes of students. As we move through these objectives, the participants will move toward developing not only a model or frame but an array of practices they will employ, test out, experiment with, and refine in their own classrooms.

This triple focus can be made more specific by articulating eight activities the participants will perform. During the term they will:

1. Define the features that constitute the unique form we call drama.
2. Develop an understanding of the basic theatrical structures and conventions that shape a given period of drama, and use this knowledge to sharpen their grasp of performance possibilities.
3. Learn to ask and answer some basic questions that guide a theatrical approach to creating characters and shaping scenes. Here they will work on creating an interpretation in action.
4. Learn to ask and answer some basic questions that guide a literary approach to the patterns of language and patterns of action that are embodied on the page. Here they will work on creating an interpretation in writing.
5. Read *Romeo and Juliet* and *Hamlet* in order to explore the distinctive challenges entailed in reading, performing, and eventually, teaching a play by Shakespeare.
6. Sketch out a pedagogic frame or model in which they can situate a performance approach to drama, and drama itself in a classroom.
7. Explore the dramatic, performative, and pedagogic dimensions of a play of their own choosing.
8. Demonstrate their mastery of both theoretical concepts and practical concepts in conducting a model class, and in a written paper presenting their pedagogic scripts and reflecting on what that script does when performed by a class.

Finally, as a transition to the specific activities I am about to describe, I need to make explicit the two most important premises for all the work in these courses: First, we can say that in learning to *read*—which also means *perform*—a dramatic text in its own language, we must all learn to read as experimenters, asking both "What do these words do?" and "What can these words be made to do?" And second, we can say that a constitutive element for becoming such an experimental reader or experimenter is precisely learning to use one's voice and body as the medium for your experiments.

Realizing the Challenges of Reading Differently

The important thing is not to think about Shakespeare but to think Shakespeare.
—CHARLES H. FREY[3]

I turn to describing two of the opening activities I use to immerse the participants in the performance approach. In both, the participants immediately experience the shift to using their bodies as the medium of experimental action and to asking "What do these words do?" and "What can these words be made to do?" *Romeo and Juliet* is a particularly useful play to start with here because it offers two beginnings: the Chorus's overview and the opening scene on the streets of Verona. Exploring this double beginning, we can see how even an overtly expository opening is also a form of action; even as we can see how an overtly action-packed opening also performs audience-framing functions. In exploring the second beginning, furthermore, participants will be making the necessary move of learning to read the play as performing a double communication—we are asking "What are the characters doing to each other?" and we are asking "What is the dramatist using the performance to do to us?"

What Does the First Beginning of Romeo and Juliet *Do?*

In the literary study of drama, as the teachers and teachers-to-be I work with have been taught, the traditional terms for describing the parts that constitute the plot of a play include exposition, rising action, climax, falling action, and denouement. Exposition, as they all know, defines that part of the play where the dramatist lays out the elements of the story. But I suggest that framing an inquiry in "What is X?" form, as in asking "What is the exposition of *Romeo and Juliet*?" tends to perpetuate a static sense of the play and a passive sense of the audience, for the term "exposition" focuses attention on how the play "transmits information" to the audience. Of course, weak exposition does operate in this manner. But even with an apparently flatly expository opening, as is the case with the Chorus which opens this play, we can see how it works as action in relation to the audience.

I ask one person to read the Chorus's opening speech, with no particular attempt to perform it, while the rest of the class, acting as first-time spectators, raise their hands to stop the Chorus each time we are given some expository information:

> Two households, both alike in dignity,
> In fair Verona, where we lay our scene,
> From ancient grudge break to new mutiny,
> Where civil blood makes civil hands unclean.
> From forth the fatal loins of these two foes
> A pair of star-cross'd lovers take their life;
> Whose misadventur'd piteous overthrows
> Doth with their death bury their parents' strife.
> The fearful passage of their death-mark'd love,
> And the continuance of their parents' rage,
> Which, but their children's end, nought could remove,
> Is now the two hours' traffic of our stage:
> The which if you with patient ears attend,
> What here shall miss, our toil shall strive to mend.
> *(Romeo and Juliet*, Prologue 1–14)

As the raised hands reveal, the expository information is laid out very crisply, with one or, more often, two items in every one of the first eight lines of the sonnet, including, of course, the Chorus's preview of the basic plot from start to finish. At the same time, this activity vividly enacts—indeed, physicalizes—the two-part nature of the prologue, which is revealed when you ask "Why were there no hands raised after ŝtrife'?" "Because the Chorus is just repeating what we now know!"

Next, we have a repeat reading, with each piece of information examined in more detail; with the less-obvious functions of the last six lines explored; and with each class member formulating her or his overview of the play and a set of expectations that a first-time spectator might formulate. It is worth asking, "Why would the dramatist want to give away the ending in this fashion?" And it will be worth it, of course, to come back to the striking phrase "Doth with their death bury their parents' strife" when you examine what the end of the play does. But in terms of introducing the approach, what this activity does is to physicalize the interaction between the Chorus and the spectators, and compel the participants to begin to make the shift to asking "What does this element do?"

What Does the Second Beginning of Romeo and Juliet *Do?*

In this second example, simple as it is, one aim is to have the participants experience, at the most basic level, the core principle that the medium of drama is the actor's body, even as it also enables them to begin to learn the crucial distinction between how a playtext mandates some elements of the action while leaving other elements open for the co-creative energies of the players. More specifically, in this activity we embody two key elements in learning to read in a different language, namely the importance of the flow of bodies on and off the stage and the temporal experience of the play creating a rhythm in part through this varying number and density of bodies. In the course of this activity, I am also modeling the way in which they can learn to move from discerning the dramatist's design to imagining something as fundamental yet elusive for most readers as the rhythm of performance.

This activity can be performed in two ways. You can simply record the number of bodies as the participants trace the entrances and exits of the scene. Or you can make the illustration more vivid if you have the appropriate number of people come to the "on-stage" part of the classroom and place themselves in positions that roughly seem to be demanded by the action. Schematically, the scene builds and ebbs as follows:

Sampson and Gregory	=	2 bodies
+ Abraham and Balthasar	=	4 bodies
+ Benvolio	=	5 bodies
+ Tybalt	=	6 bodies
+ 4 Citizens	=	10 bodies
+ Capulet and Lady Capulet	=	12 bodies
+ Montague and Lady Montague	=	14 bodies
+ Prince and Train	=	20 bodies
Exeunt Prince and others, leaving Montague, Lady Montague, Benvolio	=	3 bodies
+ Romeo	=	4 bodies
Exeunt Lord and Lady Montague leaving Benvolio and Romeo	=	2 bodies

In short, the scene starts with two bodies, increases to four then six as it bursts into violence, then escalates with fearsome rapidity to about twenty bodies. As that violence is quelled, the stage rapidly depopulates until, once again, only two bodies are left. (You might also note the gender ratio in this scene, which accurately foreshadows the ratio of men to women on the streets.) What readers are quite likely to miss will be a central element of the mandated theatrical experience, namely our introduction to Verona as a place where tensions run so high that a person walking on the streets on an errand, or on no errand at all, may suddenly find himself in a potentially lethal brawl. Even more specifically, we discover that to wear a sword and to use it in an attempt to keep the peace may actually have the opposite effect, for the scene's design mandates that Benvolio's act of drawing his sword, which he does to break up the fight and prevent a riot, actually contributes to the riot he is trying to prevent; and, what's more, could easily become a fatal mistake because it offers a pretext for the maniacally aggressive Tybalt to draw his weapon in order to attack Benvolio.

Similar patterns occur in many plays and indeed we must learn to read for the flow of bodies not only within but across scenes. So *Hamlet*, as we see later in the term, moves through a sequence in which there is a small group, fluctuating from two to four to three to four (with the Ghost); then the stage is flooded as the first court scene begins (it too may have about twenty people on stage), only to have the flood wash away, leaving Hamlet alone—the first of many moments during the play when the stage is commanded by a solitary figure whose isolation is created, in part, precisely by the rapid depopulation of a stage that only seconds before was filled with life.

The filling and emptying of the stage is also crucial for how a play ends—and yet here also the complex possibilities are usually ignored by readers, for whom the word "Exeunt" makes all the characters vanish instantly and simultaneously. What such readers miss are the rich potentials latent in something as simple as the sequence in which the characters exit. The flow of bodies at the end also creates meaning by the sequence with which they exit and who, if anyone, remains. Thus I suggest to the class that it is always worth looking to see if they can recreate or imagine such patterns. Looking to grasp rhythm is another example of reading differently, where you are trying to teach people to read what is on the page in ways that come nearer to imagining the experience they would have while witnessing a performance.

I conclude the present example by pointing out that once again there are textually mandated elements and open variables even within this rhythmic flow.

Textually, the design establishes how dangerous the streets of Verona are: You can be walking along at 9:00 A.M., peacefully minding your own business, and suddenly either start or be engulfed in a feud-generated brawl, which may become lethal. In particular, once Benvolio draws his sword, even though he draws it to restore peace, he becomes immediately open to challenge by Tybalt, in what could become a lethal duel. Certainly teachers and students in contemporary America, especially those in large urban areas such as the Los Angeles basin where I work, instantly recognize the principle of "Don't draw your weapon unless you are prepared to use it!" They also know that to put away your weapon leaves you vulnerable to attacks on your manhood, to being called "effeminate." Indeed the Benvolio-Tybalt encounter previews Romeo's dilemma later when he meets Tybalt's challenge, tries to intervene in the Mercutio-Tybalt duel, and then returns to challenge Tybalt.

In terms of performance, however, the point to grasp is that within the mandates of the design there is a crucial open element in which the director and actors choose how lethal the specific Verona of their production will initially seem. This is to say that I.i also establishes the initial balance of comedy and tragedy in its particular Verona, making this violence seem relatively harmless or imminently lethal. If you use film or video you might, for example, contrast the Howard-Shearer version (1936), the Zeffirelli version (1968), and the Baz Luhrmann version (1996) to demonstrate the range of options within the mandates of the text.

Epilogue

I will conclude this essay with an image that encapsulates, in miniature, the core challenges and rewards of this work of inviting teachers to rehearse and adopt a performance approach to Shakespeare. This moment comes from the summer of 1998, when I was working with a group of 25 K-12 teachers. As we completed the exploration of how *Romeo and Juliet* creates its specific Verona and how the flow of bodies in a performance impels the audience to feel the dangers of this world kinesthetically, one of the participants, who teaches not only high school English but also music, paused and, after a moment's reflection, asked me "So you are showing us that Shakespeare *orchestrated* the opening scene to create these specific effects?"

In response to this insight, and following the lead of Prospero, many readers of this book will murmur "'Tis new to thee." And many will recall that one major book on performance is Jean Howard's *Shakespeare's Art of Orchestration*. But for Bruce Jones and the other teachers it was a moment that opened several doors. And for the next ten minutes, as we unpacked this insight, they made a number of discoveries, not the least of which was how Bruce could deploy the set of concepts he uses to teach music to help himself and his students achieve new ways to read and understand a playtext as a score to be performed by actors. The quiet excitement of this moment rippled through the remaining weeks of our work together.

I close with this moment because it brings us back to the third element, the most elusive yet vital element of this work, the art of teaching. This moment reminds us, I think, that so much of what we must do when we work with other teachers is to create conditions in which the teacher-students can teach themselves, discovering what cannot be taught but must be (re)learned if they are to make teaching Shakespeare a core part of their own classes.

Notes

1. Seymour B. Sarason, *Teaching as a Performing Art*. (New York and London: Teachers College, Columbia University, 1999): xi.
2. Harold Clurman, "In a Different Language," *Theatre Arts* 34 (January 1950): 18–20. Reprinted in *Directors on Directing: A Source Book of the Modern Theatre*, ed. Toby Cole and Helen Krich Chinoy (Indianapolis: Bobbs-Merrill, 1976): 272–78.

3. Charles H. Frey, *Making Sense of Shakespeare*. (Madison and Teaneck, NJ: Fairleigh Dickinson University Press, 1999): 162.

Works Cited

Clurman, Harold. "In a Different Language," *Theatre Arts* 34 (January 1950): 18–20. Reprinted in *Directors on Directing: A Source Book of the Modern Theatre*, ed. Toby Cole and Helen Krich Chinoy. Indianapolis: Bobbs-Merrill, 1976. 272–78.

Evans, G. B. et al., eds. *The Riverside Shakespeare*. Boston: Houghton Mifflin, 1997.

Frey, Charles H. *Making Sense of Shakespeare*. Madison and Teaneck, NJ: Fairleigh Dickinson University Press, 1999. 162.

Sarason, Seymour B. *Teaching as a Performing Art*. New York and London: Teachers College, Columbia University, 1999. xi.

Works Consulted

Adams, Richard, ed. *Teaching Shakespeare: Essays on Approaches to Shakespeare in Schools and Colleges*. London: Robert Royce, 1985.

Frey, Charles. "Teaching Shakespeare in America." *Shakespeare Quarterly* 35 (1984): 541–58.

Lusardi, James P. and June Schlueter. *Reading Shakespeare in Performance: "King Lear"*. Associated University Presses, 1991.

McCloskey, Susan. "Teaching Dramatic Literature." *College English* 46 (1984): 385–91.

McDonald, Joseph P. "A Reflective Conversation about Teacher Education." (A review of Schon's *Educating the Reflective Practitioner*.) *Harvard Educational Review* 59 (1989): 251–59.

———. "Raising the Teacher's Voice and the Ironic Role of Theory." *Harvard Educational Review* 56 (1986): 355–78.

Robinson, Randall. *Unlocking Shakespeare's Language: Help for the Teacher and the Student*. Urbana, IL: NCTE, 1988.

Schon, Donald. *The Reflective Practitioner: How Professionals Think in Action*. New York: Basic Books, 1983.

———. *Educating The Reflective Practitioner: Toward a New Design for Teaching and Learning in the Professions*. San Francisco: Jossey-Bass, 1987.

Bibliography

Illustrated Biographies

Aliki. *William Shakespeare and the Globe*. New York: HarperCollins, 1999.
Bender, Michael. *All the World's A Stage: A Pop-up Biography of William Shakespeare*. San Francisco: Chronicle Books, 1999.
Rosen, Michael. *Shakespeare: His Work and His World*. Illus. Robert Ingpen. London: Walker Books, 2001.
Stanley, Diane, and Peter Vennema. *Bard of Avon: The Story of William Shakespeare*. Illus. Diane Stanley. New York: Morrow Junior Books, 1992.

Illustrated Adaptations

Beneduce, Ann Keay. *The Tempest*. Illus. Gennady Spirin. New York: Philomel Books, 1996.
Birch, B. *Shakespeare Stories*. 3 vols. New York: Wing Books, 1993.
Burdett, Lois. *A Child's Portrait of Shakespeare*. Ontario, Canada: Firefly, 1995.
———. *Hamlet for Kids*. Ontario, Canada: Firefly, 2000.
———. *Macbeth for Kids*. Ontario, Canada: Firefly, 1996.
———. *A Midsummer Night's Dream for Kids*. Ontario, Canada: Firefly, 1997.
———. *Romeo and Juliet for Kids*. Ontario, Canada: Firefly, 1998.
———. *The Tempest for Kids*. Ontario, Canada: Black Moss/Firefly, 1999.
———. *Twelfth Night for Kids*. Ontario, Canada: Firefly, 1995.
Chute, Marchette. *Stories from Shakespeare*. New York: Meridian, 1987.
Coville, Bruce. *William Shakespeare's A Midsummer Night's Dream*. Illus. Dennis Nolan. New York: Dial Books, 1996.
———. *William Shakespeare's Macbeth*. Illus. Gary Kelley. New York: Dial Books, 1997.
———. *William Shakespeare's Romeo and Juliet*. Illus. Dennis Nolan. New York: Dial Books, 1999.
———. *William Shakespeare's The Tempest*. Illus. Ruth Sanderson. New York: Bantam Doubleday Dell, 1994.

———. *William Shakespeare's Twelfth Night*. Illus. Tim Raglin. New York: Dial Books, forthcoming 2003.

Deary, Terry. *Top Ten Shakespeare Stories*. Illus. Michael Tickner. New York: Scholastic, 1998.

Early, Margaret. *Romeo and Juliet*. New York: Harry N. Abrams, 1998.

Escott, John. *Macbeth*. Illus. Eric Kincaid. New Market, England: Brimax, 1997.

———. *A Midsummer Night's Dream*. Illus. Eric Kincaid. New Market, England: Brimax, 1996.

———. *The Tempest*. Illus. Eric Kincaid. New Market, England: Brimax, 1996.

Garfield, Leon. *Shakespeare Stories*. Illus. Michael Foreman. Boston: Houghton Mifflin, 1985. [*TN, KL, Tempest, MV, TS, RII, 1HIV, Hamlet, R&J, Othello, MND, Macbeth*]

Garfield, Leon. *Shakespeare Stories II*. Illus. Michael Foreman. Boston: Houghton Mifflin, 1995. [*MAAN, JC, A&C, MM, AYLI, Cymbeline, RIII, CE, WT*]

Lamb, Charles and Mary. *Tales from Shakespeare*. Illus. Arthur Rackham. New York: Crown, 1975. Facsimile of 1909 edition. [*Tempest, MND, WT, MAAN, AYLI, TGV, MV, Cymbeline, KL, Macbeth, AWTEW, TS, CE, MM, TN, R&J, Hamlet, Othello, Pericles*]

Lamb, Charles and Mary. *Tales from Shakespeare* (New York: Signet, 1986).

Lewis, A. and T. Wynne-Jones. *Rosie Backstage*. Illus. B. Slavin. Toronto: Kids Can Press, 1994.

Miles, Bernard. *Well-Loved Tales from Shakespeare*. Illus. Victor G. Ambrus. Twickenham, England: Hamlyn Publishing, 1986.

Mulherin, J. *As You Like It*. Illus. G. Thompson. New York: Peter Bedrick Books, 1989.

Nesbit, E. *The Best of Shakespeare: Retellings of 10 Classic Plays*. Introd. by Iona Opie; afterword by Peter Hunt. Oxford: Oxford University Press, 1997. [*R&J, TN, Hamlet, Tempest, KL, Macbeth, AYLI, WT, Othello*]

Williams, Marcia. *Tales from Shakespeare: Seven Plays*. New York: Scholastic, 1998. [*R&J, Hamlet, MND, Macbeth, WT, JC, Tempest*]

———. *Bravo, Mr. William Shakespeare!* London: Walker Books, 2000. [*AYLI, MAAN, TN, MV, RIII, A&C, KL*].

Shakespeare Series:

Adapted by Diana Stewart, illus. Charles Shaw (Austin, Texas: Steck-Vaughn); Adapted by Leon Garfield, illus. by various artists (London: Heinemann Young Books) [different from *Shakespeare Stories*, cited above]; Complete Text, illus. by various artists (New York: Workman).

Young Adult Novels

Hamlet

Coville, B. *The Skull of Truth*. New York: Pocket Books, 1997.

Duncan, L. *Killing Mr. Griffin*. New York: Bantam Doubleday Dell, 1990.

Fiedler, Lisa. *Dating Hamlet: Ophelia's Story*. New York: Henry Holt and Company, 2002.

Paterson, K. *Bridge to Terabithia*. New York: Harper Trophy, 1977.
Sonnenmark, L. *Something is Rotten in the State of Maryland*. New York: Scholastic, 1990.

Macbeth

Draper, S. M. *Tears of a Tiger*. New York: Aladdin Paperbacks, 1994.
Gilmore, K. *Enter Three Witches*. New York: Scholastic, 1992.
Katz, W. W. *Come Like Shadows*. Toronto: Puffin Books, 1993.
Lively, Penelope. *The House in Norham Gardens*. New York: Dutton Children's Books, 1974.
————. *The Whispering Knights*. London: Mammoth, 1971.
Pratchett, T. *Wyrd Sisters*. London: Corgi Books, 1988.

A Midsummer Night's Dream

Masson, S. *Malkin*. Winona, Minnesota: St. Mary's Press, 2001.
Pratchett, T. *Lords and Ladies*. London: Corgi Books, 1992.
Singer, M. *The Course of True Love Never Did Run Smooth*. New York: Harper & Row, 1992.

Othello

Dhondy, F. *Black Swan*. Boston: Houghton Mifflin, 1993.
Gilmore, K. *Jason and the Bard*. Boston: Houghton Mifflin, 1993.
Lester, J. *Othello: A Novel*. New York: Scholastic, 1995.
Plummer, L. *The Unlikely Romance of Kate Bjorkman*. New York: Bantam Double-day Dell, 1995.

Richard III

Ford, J. *The Dragon Waiting: A Masque of History*. New York: Avon, 1983.
Tolan, S. *The Face in the Mirror*. New York: Morrow Junior Books, 1998.

Romeo and Juliet

Avi. *Romeo and Juliet Together (and Alive!) at Last*. New York: Avon, 1987.
Belbin, D. *Love Lessons*. New York: Scholastic, 1998.
Masson, S. *The Tiger*. Sydney: HarperCollins Australia, 1996.
McCaffrey, A. *The Ship Who Sang*. London: Corgi Books, 1969.
Trease, G. *Cue for Treason*. London: Puffin Books, 1941.

The Tempest

Covington, D. *Lizard*. New York: Bantam Doubleday Dell, 1991.
L'Engle, M. *A Wrinkle in Time*. New York: Farrar Straus Giroux, 1962.
Masson, S. *Hopewell Shakespeare's Tempestuous Voyage*. London: Hodder Children's Books, forthcoming 2003.
ONeal, Z. *In Summer Light*. New York: Bantam Books, 1985.

Siegel, Jan. *Prospero's Children*. New York: Ballantine Publishing Group, 1999.
Williams, T. *Caliban's Hour*. New York: Harper Collins, 1994.

Twelfth Night

Boock, P. *Dare Truth or Promise*. Boston: Houghton Mifflin, 1999.

Poetry

Holdridge, Barbara, ed. *Under the Greenwood Tree: Shakespeare for Young People*. Illus. Robin DeWitt. Owing Mills, MD: Stemmer House, 1994.
Kastan, David Scott and Marina Kastan, eds. *William Shakespeare: Poetry for Young People*. Illus. Glenn Harrington. New York: Sterling, 2000.
Pollinger, Gina, ed. *Something Rich and Strange: A Treasury of Shakespeare's Verse*. Illus. Emma Chichester Clark. New York: Kingfisher, 2000.

Noteworthy Historical Fiction for Readers of Shakespeare

Blackwood, Gary. *Shakespeare's Scribe*. New York: Dutton Children's Book, 2000.
————. *The Shakespeare Stealer*. New York: Dutton Children's Books, 1998.
Cheaney, J. B. *The Playmaker*. New York: Alfred A. Knopf, 2000.
————. *The True Prince*. New York: Alfred A. Knopf, 2002.
Cooper, S. *The King of Shadows*. New York: Margaret K. McElderry Books, 1999.
Coville, Bruce. *Fortune's Journey*. New York: BridgeWater Paperback, 1997.
Graham, H. *A Boy and His Bear*. New York: Simon & Schuster, 1994.
Masson, S. *My Brother Will*. London: Hodder Children's Books, forthcoming 2004.
McCaughrean, G. *A Little Lower Than the Angels*. New York: Oxford University Press, 1987.
Walsh, J. P. *A Parcel of Patterns*. New York: Farrar Straus Giroux, 1983.

Supplementary Materials

Brownfoot, Andrew. *High Fashion in Shakespeare's Time* [*a study of period costume with pull-up scenes*]. Norfolk, England: Tarquin Publications, 1992.
Caselli, Giovanni. *The Renaissance & the New World*. History of Everyday Things. New York: Peter Bedrick Books, 1985.
Claybourne, Anna, and Rebecca Treays. *The World of Shakespeare*. London: Usborne Publishing, 1996.
Davidson, Rebecca Piatt. *All the World's a Stage*. Illus. Anita Lobel. New York: Greenwillow, forthcoming 2003.
Ganeri, Anita. *The Young Person's Guide to Shakespeare* (*with performances on CD by the Royal Shakespeare Company*). San Diego: Harcourt Brace, 1999.
Guy, John. *Elizabeth I & the Armada*. Snapping Turtle Guide. London: Ticktock Publishing, 1997.
————. *Henry VIII & His Six Wives*. Snapping Turtle Guide. London: Ticktock Publishing, 1997.
————. *Tudor and Stuart Life*. Snapping Turtle Guide. London: Ticktock Publishing, 1997.

Herbert, Susan. *Shakespeare Cats*. Boston: Little Brown, 1996.

Kerr, Jessica. *Shakespeare's Flowers*. Illus. Anne Ophelia Dowden. New York: HarperCollins, 1982.

Koscielniak, Bruce. *Hear, Hear, Mr. Shakespeare: Story, Illustrations, & Selections from Shakespeare's Plays*. Boston: Houghton Mifflin, 1998.

Langley, Andrew. *Shakespeare's Theater*. Illus. June Everett. Oxford: Oxford University Press, 1999.

Laroque, Francois. *The Age of Shakespeare*. New York: Harry Abrams, Inc., 1993.

Marsh, Carole. *"Bill S!": Shakespeare for Kids!* Quantum Leap Books. Atlanta: Carole Marsh/Gallopade Publishing, 1995.

Middleton, Haydn. *William ShakespeareThe Master Playwright: What's Their Story?* Oxford: Oxford University Press, 1998.

Morley, Jacqueline, and John James. *Shakespeare's Theater: Inside Story*. New York: Peter Bedrick Books, 1999.

Naylor, Edward W. *Shakespeare Music*. New York: DaCapo Press, 1973.

Ross, Stuart. *Shakespeare and Macbeth: The Story Behind the Play*. Illus. Tony Karpinski. Forward by Kenneth Branagh. New York: Viking, 1994.

Ruby, Jennifer. *Costume in Context: The Stuarts*. London: B.T. Batsford, 1988.

————. *Costume in Context: The Tudors*. London: B.T. Batsford, 1987.

A Shakespearean Coloring Book. New York: Bellerophon, 1998.

St. James, Renwick. *A Shakespeare Sketchbook*. Illus. James C. Christensen. Shelton, CT: Greenwich Workshop Press, 2001.

Stanley, Diane, and Peter Vennema. *Good Queen Bess: The Story of Elizabeth I of England*. Illus. Diane Stanley. New York: Four Winds Press, 1990.

Swope, Martha. *A Midsummer Night's Dream: The Story of the New York City Ballet's Production*. Photos by Martha Swope. New York: Dodd, 1977.

Time-Life Editors. *What Life Was Like in the Realm of Elizabeth: England, AD 1533–1603*. Alexandria, VA: Time-Life Books, 1998.

Games

The Game of Shakespeare. Avalon Hill Game Co., 1966.

The Play's the Thing: A Dramatic Introduction to Shakespeare. Aristoplay, 1993.

Pedagogical Resources

Aagesen, Colleen, and Margie Blumberg. *Shakespeare for Kids: His Life and Times. 21 Activities*. Chicago: Chicago Review Press, 1999.

Adams, Richard, ed. *Teaching Shakespeare: Essays on Approaches to Shakespeare in Schools and Colleges*. London: Robert Royce, 1985.

Foster, Cass, and Lynn G. Johnson. *Shakespeare: To Teach or Not to Teach*. Chandler, AZ: Five-Star Publications, 1996.

Frey, Charles. *Making Sense of Shakespeare*. Madison and Teaneck, NJ: Fairleigh Dickinson University Press, 1999.

Gibson, Rex. *Teaching Shakespeare (Cambridge School Shakespeare)*. Cambridge: Cambridge University Press, 1998.

Gibson, Rex and Janet Field-Pickering. *Discovering Shakespeare's Language*. Cambridge: Cambridge University Press, 1998.

Gilmour, Maurice, ed. *Shakespeare for All: Volume 1: The Primary School.* London: Cassell, 1997.

Herz, S. K. and D. R. Gallo. *From Hinton to Hamlet: Building Bridges Between Young Adult Literature and the Classics.* Westport, CT: Greenwood Press, 1996.

Isaac, Megan. *Heirs to Shakespeare: Reinventing the Bard in Young Adult Literature.* Portsmouth, N.H.: Heinemann, 2000.

Livesey, Robert. *Creating with Shakespeare.* Mississauga, Ontario: Little Brick Schoolhouse, Inc., 1988.

Lusardi, James P. and June Schlueter. *Reading Shakespeare in Performance: "King Lear".* London: Associated University Presses, 1991.

Nelson, Pauline, and Todd Daubert. *Starting with Shakespeare: Successfully Introducing Shakespeare to Children.* Englewood, CO: Teacher Ideas Press, 2000.

Reynolds, Peter. *Practical Approaches to Teaching Shakespeare.* Oxford: Oxford University Press, 1991.

Riggio, Milla Cozzart, ed. *Teaching Shakespeare Through Performance.* New York: MLA, 1999.

Robinson, Randall. *Unlocking Shakespeare's Language: Help for the Teacher and the Student.* Urbana, Illinois: NCTE, 1988.

Sarason, Seymour B. *Teaching as a Performing Art.* New York and London: Teachers College, Columbia University, 1999.

Schultz, Lois V. *The Bard for Beginners.* Middletown, OH: Globe-Three Press, 1985.

Sedgwick, Fred. *Shakespeare and the Young Writer.* New York: Routledge, 1999.

Critical Studies

Allen, B. "A School Perspective on Shakespeare Teaching." In *Shakespeare and the Changing Curriculum,* ed. L. Aers and N. Wheale. London: Routledge, 1991. 40–57.

Austin, Patricia and Carol Woltering. "Such Stuff as Dreams are Made On: Connecting Children with Shakespeare." *Booklinks* April/May 2001: 9–16.

Blake, Ann. "Children and Suffering in Shakespeare's Plays." *Yearbook of English Studies* 23 (1993): 293–304.

Bottoms, J. "Of *Tales* and *Tempests.*" *Children's Literature in Education.* 27 (2), 1996: 73–86.

Frey, Charles. "Teaching Shakespeare in America." *Shakespeare Quarterly* 35 (1984): 541–58.

Hyle, Rebecca. "Teaching Shakespeare to Third Graders." *Shakespeare in the Classroom* 5.1 (1997): 64–66.

Marsden, Jean I. "Shakespeare for Girls: Mary Lamb and Tales from Shakespeare." *Children's Literature* 17 (1989): 47–63.

McCloskey, Susan. "Teaching Dramatic Literature." *College English* 46 (1984): 385–91.

Moore, John Noell. "Intertextualities: *The Tempest* in *Morning Girl, Lizard,* and *In Summer Light.*" In *Adolescent Literature as a Complement to the Classics,* 3rd vol. Ed. Joan F. Kaywell. Norwood, MA: Christopher Gordon Publishers, 1993. 71–92.

Osborne, Laurie E. "Poetry in Motion: Animating Shakespeare." In *Shakespeare, the Movie: Popularizing the Plays on Film, TV, and Video.* Ed. Lynda E. Boose and Richard Burt. New York: Routledge, 1997, 103–120.

Peterson, Sarah Innerst. "Sidewalk Shakespeare." *California English* Fall 1999: 26–27.
Reed, A.J.S. "Using Young Adult Literature to Modernize the Teaching of *Romeo and Juliet.*" In *Adolescent Literature as a Complement to the Classics*, ed. Joan F. Kaywell. Norwood, MA: Christopher Gordon Publishers, 1993. 93–115.
Rocklin, Edward L. "Framing *Macbeth*: How Three Films Create the Play's World." *California English* Spring 2000: 10–11.
———. "How Does One Teach a Play Anyway?" *California English* Fall 1999: 12–13.
Stephens, J. "Not Unadjacent to a Play About a Scottish King: Terry Pratchett Retells *Macbeth.*" *Papers: Explorations into Children's Literature.* 7 (2), 1997: 29–37.
Stewig, J.W. "The Witch Woman: A Recurring Motif in Recent Fantasy Writing for Young Readers." *Children's Literature in Education* 26.2 (1995): 119–33.
Thompson, Neal. "A School Makes Much Ado About Shakespeare." *Christian Science Monitor* May 29, 1997: 1, 12.
Williamson, David. "English Children Are Too Sophisticated for Shakespeare." *The Use of English* 38.2 (Spring 1987): 27–32.
Wood, Robin H. "Shakespeare in an Elementary School Setting." *Phi Delta Kappan* February 1997: 457–59.

Selected Web Sites

http://daphne.palomar.edu/Shakespeare/theater [video clips of Elizabethan dances]
http://www.actwin.com/REDUCED/index.html [Reduced Shakespeare Company comedy troupe]
http://www.english.upenn.edu/~bushnell/english-101/gallery.html [collection of over two dozen images from Renaissance period; created by Prof. Rebecca Bushnell, University of Pennsylvania]
http://www.cup.org/shakespeare/WSBtop.html [World Shakespeare Bibliography info from Cambridge University Press]
http://www.folger.edu [largest collection of Shakespearean printed material in the world: Folger Library]
http://www.folger.edu/education/teaching.htm [Teaching Shakespeare site]
http://www.legends.dm.net/swash/rapier.html [metasite for primary resources on period sword fighting]
http://www.renaissance.dm.net [brief, historical synopses about common, everyday Elizabethan-era life; topics include money and coinage, games, food, education and schooling]
http://www.shakespeares-globe.org [information on original Globe Theatre and newly reconstructed Globe, including close-up photos of stage and play performances]
http://www.shakespeare.org.uk [Shakespeare's birthplace site: Stratford-upon-Avon]
http://www.shakespeare-oxford.com [site debates authorship of Shakespeare's plays]
http://www.springfield.k12.il.us/schools/springfield/eliz/elizabethanengland.html [introduction to Elizabethan period of English history and literature; pictures of Tower of London; created by seniors at Springfield High School]
http://www.stratford.co.uk/hislife/ [life and times of Shakespeare]
http://www-tech.mit.edu/shakespeare/works.html [*The Complete Works of William Shakespeare*; full text of all plays and sonnets; dictionary of archaic terms; sponsored by M.I.T.]

Contributors

Aliki (Liacouras Brandenberg) is a native of Philadelphia, born to Greek parents. She is the author-illustrator of more than 55 fiction and non-fiction books for children, and illustrator of some 200 books for other authors, including her husband Franz Brandenberg. She lives in London, England, and travels regularly to the U.S., Greece, Switzerland, and points unknown.

Jim Andreas served on the faculty of the Bread Loaf School of English after his retirement from Clemson University in 2000. He was founder and director of the Clemson Shakespeare Festival and the South Carolina Shakespeare Collaborative. He was Editor of *The Upstart Crow: A Shakespeare Journal* from 1983 until his death in 2002. He has to his credit more than twenty articles on the subject of teaching Shakespeare.

John Barnes recently left Western State College of Colorado, where he was Associate Professor of Theatre and Communications, to resume a full-time writing career. He is the author of more than twenty novels and of more than fifty articles in the *Oxford Encyclopedia of Theatre and Performance*, 4th edition, plus a variety of scholarly articles, short stories, general journalism, and anything else that paid.

Pamela J. Benson is Professor of English at Rhode Island College, where she teaches courses on Shakespeare and related material. She is the author of *The Invention of the Renaissance Woman*, *Italian Tales from the Age of Shakespeare*, and numerous essays on literature and culture in Renaissance Italy and England.

Gary L. Blackwood has published eight novels and fourteen nonfiction books for young readers. *The Shakespeare Stealer* and its sequel, *Shakespeare's*

Scribe, were on the ALA's list of Best Books for Young Adults and have been translated into several languages. His latest book is an alternate history novel, *The Year of the Hangman*.

Lois Burdett is an elementary school teacher in Canada who has authored the award-winning Shakespeare Can Be Fun series, offering verse adaptations of Shakespeare plays for younger readers. She has presented many seminars at schools and conferences around the world, and served as the creative consultant for the documentary film *The Secret of Will*, that features her classroom work with children.

Jennifer Lee Carrell is a writer living in Tucson, Arizona. A frequent contributor to *Smithsonian Magazine* and a former performing arts critic with the *Arizona Daily Star*, she is working on her first book. She earned a Ph.D. in English Literature at Harvard University, where she taught, primarily in the History and Literature Program, for four years after graduating.

Sheila T. Cavanagh is Masse-Martin/NEH Distinguished Teaching Professor at Emory University. She is the author of *Cherished Torment: The Emotional Geography of Lady Mary Wroth's Urania* (2001), *Wanton Eyes and Chaste Desires: Female Sexuality in The Faerie Queene* (1994), and numerous articles on Renaissance literature and pedagogy. She is also the Director of the Emory Women Writers Resource Project, a Web site devoted to women's writing from the sixteenth to the twentieth centuries.

Janie B. Cheaney was born in Dallas, Texas, and has lived in several places. *The Playmaker* is her first published novel. A sequel, *The True Prince*, is forthcoming.

Tiffany Conroy is a doctoral student at Northeastern University. Her main areas of interest include Shakespeare, film theory and history, and cultural studies. She has taught Shakespeare, literature, and writing to college students and adult learners.

Bruce Coville is a former elementary school teacher who has published over eighty books for young readers of all ages. His best known titles include *My Teacher is an Alien* and *Into the Land of the Unicorns*. A frequent speaker at schools and conferences, Coville recently founded Full Cast Audio, a publishing company that produces unabridged, multi-voiced recordings of books for family listening.

Rebecca Piatt Davidson holds Bachelors and Master of Arts degrees in English from Brigham Young University. She taught composition and British Literature at Orange Coast College in Costa Mesa, California, before moving to Arizona with her family in 1999. Since then, she has been writing books for children. *All The World's A Stage* is her first picture book.

Regine Ebner is the founder and Director of The Montessori Schoolhouse in Tucson, Arizona, and has taught children of all ages. She has developed classroom materials for young people on numerous subjects, from the Middle Ages to Organic Chemistry. She has an M.Ed. in Family Counseling and has written many articles on parenting and child development. Her comedy screenplay, *Understanding Edison*, won an Actors' Choice award at the Santa Fe Conference on Screenwriting.

Janet Field-Pickering, Head of Education at the Folger Shakespeare Library, directs all of the Folger's educational projects, including the Teaching Shakespeare Institute and Web site and the elementary outreach program Shakespeare Steps Out. She has written articles and presented numerous workshops on teaching Shakespeare through performance and is co-author of *Discovering Shakespeare's Language* with Rex Gibson.

Megan Lynn Isaac is the author of *Heirs to Shakespeare: Reinventing the Bard in Young Adult Literature*, a book that explores and discusses how a number of young adult novels use and reinterpret Shakespeare's characters and plots. She was formerly an associate professor at Youngstown State University and now writes and lives in Auburn, Alabama, with her husband and son.

Miranda Johnson-Haddad is currently Visiting Lecturer in the English Department at UCLA. She is a performance editor for *Shakespeare Quarterly* and a regular reviewer for *Shakespeare Bulletin*. She is especially proud of her contribution to this volume, because it represents the ideal convergence of her professional and her domestic/maternal lives that she constantly strives to attain.

Douglas King works as an Assistant Professor of English at Gannon University in Erie, Penn. One of his greatest pleasures is watching, directing, or performing Shakespeare with his three children. He believes that if children are introduced to Shakespeare from—say—birth, there's nothing particularly difficult about him; rather, he is a treat and a friend.

Mark Lawhorn teaches writing courses in the Department of Language Arts at the University of Hawaii-Kapiolani as well as courses in Shakespearean drama at the University of Hawaii-Manoa. He is completing a book on children in the plays of early modern England, the topic of several of his published articles.

Greg Maillet is Assistant Professor of English at Campion College at the University of Regina. He regularly teaches Shakespeare and the history of literary criticism, and is also the founding director of ACTIO, a literature performance group that over the past five years has offered over 25 different presentations to a wide variety of Regina audiences.

Howard Marchitello is Associate Professor of English at Texas A&M University where he is also Director of Graduate Studies. He is the author of *Narrative and Meaning in Early Modern England: Browne's Skull and Other Histories* (1997) and editor of *What Happens to History: The Renewal of Ethics in Contemporary Thought* (Routledge 2001). He is currently working on *Hamlet Machine*, a book-length study of early modern science.

Sophie Masson, born in Indonesia to French parents, came to live in Australia as a child and spent much of her life shuttling back and forth between France and Australia. She has published nearly thirty books, mostly for children and young people, but also for adults. Her Shakespearean novels are *Cold Iron* (1998 and 2001, published as *Malkin* in the United States in 2000); *The Lost Island, or Hopewell Shakespeare's Marvellous Voyage* (2003); and *My Brother Will* (forthcoming). She also writes short stories, essays, reviews, and articles for publications all over the world.

Currently a graduate student at the University of Arizona, **Amy E. Mathur** is pursuing her doctoral degree in Renaissance studies with a concentration in Shakespearean drama.

Caroline McManus, Associate Professor of English at California State University, Los Angeles, is the author of *Spenser's Faerie Queene and the Reading of Women* (2002) and several essays on early modern literature. Her essay on Edith Wharton's adaptation of Shakespearean romantic comedy is forthcoming in *Philological Quarterly*, and she is currently working on a book-length study of women and fools in the drama of Shakespeare and his contemporaries.

Naomi J. Miller is Associate Professor of English Literature and Women's Studies at the University of Arizona. She has published an award-winning collection of essays, co-edited with Naomi Yavneh, *Maternal Measures: Figuring Caregiving in the Early Modern Period* (2000), as well as a book-length study of a woman writer in Shakespeare's time, *Changing the Subject: Mary Wroth and Figurations of Gender in Early Modern England* (1996). In addition to her articles on representations of maternity and Renaissance women writers, her most recent project is a young adult novel based on Shakespeare's *The Tempest*, co-authored with Bruce Coville.

Kristen L. Olson is Assistant Professor of English at The Pennsylvania State University, Beaver Campus, where she also serves as coordinator of the Honors program. From 1998–2000, while completing her Ph.D., she was Program Coordinator in Language, Communication, and Early Childhood Literature at the English Nanny and Governess School in Chagrin Falls, Ohio. Her current research includes book-length projects on Shakespeare's *The Phoenix and the Turtle* and on visuality and mimesis in early modern poetics.

Cynthia Perantoni teaches English and French at Canfield High School, Canfield, Ohio, where, with her students, she celebrates Shakespeare's birthday twice a year, an accommodation necessitated by semester block scheduling. She earned an M.A. in English from Youngstown State University and is a National Board Certified Teacher in Adolescence and Young Adulthood English Language Arts.

Alison H. Prindle is Chair of the English Department at Otterbein College and teaches Shakespeare to a yeasty mix of theater majors, English majors, and future teachers. She has managed an English festival for area high school students, which featured the books and presence of a noteworthy young adult author. Otterbein's liberal arts core curriculum received state and national recognition for excellence in the late 1980s under her leadership.

Edward L. Rocklin, Professor of English at California State Polytechnic University, Pomona, has published articles in *Shakespeare Survey*, *Shakespeare Quarterly*, *Shakespeare Yearbook*, *The Journal of Dramatic Theory and Criticism*, *College English*, and *California English*. Two other pedagogic essays have appeared in *Teaching Shakespeare Through Performance* (1999) and *Approaches to Teaching Hamlet* (2001). He is currently working on a performance history of *Measure for Measure*.

Gregory M. Colón Semenza is Assistant Professor of English at the University of Connecticut, where he teaches Shakespeare, Milton, and Renaissance literature. He is the author of articles on Milton, Shakespeare, Thomas Kyd, and sixteenth-century polemical prose, among other subjects. Several of these articles are early versions of work from his current book-length study in progress, *Sport, Politics, and Literature in the English Renaissance*.

Diane Stanley is the author and illustrator of more than forty books for children. She is most noted for her series of award-winning picture-book biographies, including *Bard of Avon: The Story of William Shakespeare*, and was the winner of the 2000 Washington Post / Children's Book Guild Nonfiction Award for the body of her work.

Marcia Williams has had a lifelong passion for children's literature and Shakespeare. She has written and illustrated over twenty children's books, including two volumes of Shakespeare's plays reimagined for children. Williams has just completed a volume of six Dickens novels entitled *Charles Dickens and Friends*, and is currently working on an illustrated retelling of The Bible for children. She lives in London with her family.

Georgianna Ziegler is Louis B. Thalheimer Head of Reference at the Folger Shakespeare Library. She has published on early modern women and on Shakespearean heroines in art. She is engaged in a larger project on the reception of Shakespeare and his heroines during the Victorian period.

Permissions

The publisher and the editor are grateful for permission to reproduce the following: illustrations from *William Shakespeare and the Globe* by Aliki Brandenberg, copyright 1999 by Aliki Brandenberg. Used by permission of HarperCollins Publishers. Texts and illustrations from *Mr. William Shakespeare's Plays*, copyright 1998 by Marcia Williams; *Bravo, Mr. William Shakespeare!*, copyright 2000 by Marcia Williams. Reproduced by permission of Walker Books Ltd., London. Artist's working sketch for *All the World's a Stage* by Rebecca Piatt Davidson, illustrated by Anita Lobel, to be published by Greenwillow Books. Image appears courtesy of Anita Lobel. Children's illustrations reprinted by permission of Lois Burdett. Cover of *The Skull of Truth*, illustrated by Gary A. Lippincott, Harcourt Brace, 1997. Courtesy Harcourt, Inc. Covers of *William Shakespeare's A Midsummer Night's Dream*, Retold by Bruce Coville, Pictures by Dennis Nolan, Dial Books, 1996, *William Shakespeare's Macbeth*, Retold by Bruce Coville, Pictures by Gary Kelley, Dial Books, 1997, and *William Shakespeare's Romeo and Juliet*, Retold by Bruce Coville, Pictures by Dennis Nolan, Dial Books, 1999. Courtesy of Dial Books for Young Readers. Cover of *William Shakespeare's The Tempest*, Retold by Bruce Coville, Pictures by Ruth Sanderson, Bantam Doubleday Dell, 1994. Image appears courtesy of Ruth Sanderson. Cover of Puffin Edition by Greg Call, copyright 2000 by Greg Call, from *The Shakespeare Stealer* by Gary Blackwood. Used by permission of Dutton Children's Books, an imprint of Penguin Putnam Books for Young Readers, a division of Penguin Putnam Inc. Cover image from *The Playmaker* by J. B. Cheaney. Cover illustration copyright 2000 by David Kramer. Reprinted by permission of Alfred A. Knopf Children's Books, a division of Random House, Inc. Romeo and Juliet Scrapbook. Reproduced by permission of the Folger Shakespeare Library. Alice in *Through the Looking Glass*. Reproduced by permission of the British Library. Illustrations from *Bard of Avon: The Story of William Shakespeare* by Diane Stanley. Reprinted by permission of HarperCollins Children's Books.

Index

Aagesen, C., 241, 243, 244, 245, 246, 248, 249
Aaron the Moor, 104
Aboriginal songlines, 229 n. 5
Abridgement, *see* Condensation/abridgement
Acocella, Joan, 163, 169
ACTIO, 8, 269, 276 n. 6
Action, *see* Plot/story/action
Actors, *see also* Productions and staging
    children's roles, 5, 85–96
    Elizabethan , 27–28
        female roles, 26, 245
        imagining, 81, 83
    in "The Play's the Thing," 271, 274
Adaptation process, *see also specific works*
    politics of, 6–7, 180–188, 224
    role of adaptor, 130
    stages of
        analysis, 63–65
        background, 56–60
        condensing, 65–66
        immersion, 61–63
        re-visioning, 65
        selection, 60–61
Adaptations, 4, 5; *see also specific works*
    for children
        Moss Gown and *Mama Day*, 260–268
        teaching future high school teachers,
          257–258
    for early childhood education, 224
    eighteenth century, 8
    illustrated books, 125–126; *see also* Illus-
        trated and picture books
    novels, *see* Novels
Admiral's Company, 271

Adults, essay collections for, 9
Adventures of Huckleberry Finn, The
    (Twain), 99
Advertising, Shakespearean allusions, 261
African American retellings, *Moss Gown* and
    Mamma Day, 260–268
Agas map of London, 255
Alice (*Henry V*), 247
Alice in Wonderland, 5, 98
Alice's Adventures Under Ground, 111, 113*f*
Aliens and otherness, 5; *see also* Magical and
    supernatural elements
    allusions to in *Mama Day*, 266
    Covington's *Lizard* and, 153–160
    protection of children from, 100–102
    in *Tales from Shakespeare*, 98–106
Alighieri, Dante, 163
Aliki, 4, 6, 13–21, 122–123, 241, 243, 244, 250
Allegory, 154–155
All's Well That Ends Well, 257
All the World's a Stage (Davidson), 39–43
*All the World's a Stage: A Pop-up Biography
    of William Shakespeare* (Bender),
    194
Allusions to films, 283, 285
Allusions
    Harry Potter series, 162–170
    intertextuality, 184–185
    Lizard, 153–160
Almereyda, Michael, 1, 2, 3, 32
Alonso (*The Tempest*), 104, 139, 141, 148,
    149, 150
Alonzo-Antonio-Sebastian plot, *The Tempest*,
    139, 140, 141

American Library Association, 99
Analysis, *see* Literary analysis
Andreas, James, 5, 98–106
And to Think I Saw It on Mulberry Street (Dr. Seuss), 218
Animations
  early childhood education, 197
  The Tempest, 149, 152, 197
Anthologies, 120, 241
Antipholus (*Comedy of Errors*), 41
Antonio (*The Merchant of Venice*), 101
Antonio (*The Tempest*), 139, 140, 141
Antony and Cleopatra, allusions to in *Mama Day*, 264, 265
Architecture, theater, 122, 123
Arico, Diane, 56
Ariel (*The Tempest*), 104, 148, 276 n.5
  All the World's a Stage, 42
  comparison of adaptations, 132, 139–140
  Sallie in Covington's *Lizard*, 156
  Williams's adaptation, 132, 148
Aristoplay: "The Play's the Thing," 8, 270–278
Armado (*Love's Labours Lost*), 90, 91
Armour, Richard, 82
Art, role of in *Lizard*, 155–156, 158–159
Arthur (*King John*), 95
Art of Shakespeare's Sonnets, The (Vendler), 221
As You Like It, 34f, 47, 122, 199 n.2
Atlanta Ballet, 197
Audience
  Elizabethan, 82
  King Lear schoolyard production, 238
Audio, 4
Audiotapes, 63
Authorship, joint, 280

Backyard productions, 82–83
Ballet, 194, 197, 199 n.4
Banned books, 99
Bantam edition, 120
Bard of Avon: The Story of William Shakespeare (Stanley and Vennema), 22–28, 23f, 25f, 26f, 27, 28f, 124, 241, 243, 245
Barnes, John, 7, 231–238
Bartholomew (*The Taming of the Shrew*), 92
Barton, John, 276
Bassanio (*The Merchant of Venice*), 101
Beatrice (*Much Ado About Nothing*), 115

Bedford Companion to Shakespeare, The, 241, 248
Bender, Michael, 194
Beneduce, Ann, *The Tempest* adaptation, 6, 139, 140–141, 147–152
Benson, Pamela J., 8, 252–259
Benvolio (*Romeo and Juliet*), 294
Best of Shakespeare: Retellings of Ten Classic Plays (Nesbit), 129, 182, 186 n.1
Bettelheim, Bruno, 7, 163, 195, 196, 197, 197, 199 n.3, 199 n.5, 199 n.8
Bible—biblical texts, 109–110
Bibliography, 298–304
Biographies of Shakespeare, 4
  nineteenth century, 109
  Shakespeare's life and times course, 242
Birch, Beverley, 208, 209
Blackwood, Gary, 4, 5, 74–80
Blake, Ann, 92
Bloomberg, M, 241, 243, 244, 245, 246, 248, 249
Blyton, Enid, 163
Board game, 8
Boccaccio, G., 257
Books and manuscripts
  First Folio, 18, 172, 270
  Shakespeare's life and times course, 245
Bottom (*A Midsummer Night's Dream*), 131, 197
Bottom's Dream (Updike), 257–258
Boudoir Shakespeare, The (Cundell), 108
Bowdler, Henrietta Maria, 31, 100, 108, 109, 261
Bowdler, Thomas, 100, 108
Bowdlerization, 99, 100
  Dodgson's "Bowdlerizing Bowdler," 107, 108, 11
  modern, 261
Brabantio (*Othello*), 103
Branagh, Kenneth, 83–84, 90, 172, 173, 175, 177, 239, 280, 284
Brandram edition, 108
Brave New World, 99
Bravo, Mr. William Shakespeare, 29–38, 30f, 34f, 35f, 36f, 37f
Brent-Dyer, Elinor M., 163
Brigden, Susan, 89
Bright, *Characterie: An Arte of Short, Swift, and Secret Writing*, 77
Brook, Peter, 91

Brooks, Peter, 187–188, n.8, 224
Brown, Mary, 108
Buckingham (*Richard III*), 167, 168
Burbage, Cuthbert, 24
Burbage, James, 24, 25
Burbage, Richard, 244
Burdett, Lois, 6, 44–55, 132–134, 136, 137 n.
    3, 138, 139, 143–144, 147–152,
    186, 194, 226, 227
Burgess, Anthony, 241, 243

Caliban (*The Tempest*), 5, 104, 139, 148, 285
    Burdett's adaptation, 132, 133
    comparison of adaptations, 141
    Covington's *Lizard* and, 153–160
    Williams's adaptation, 132
Canonical literature, censorship and bowdler-
    ization, 98–107
Canterbury Tales, The, 98
Carrell, Jennifer, 6, 168, 171–179
Carrick, Donald, 263
Carroll, Lewis (Charles Dodgson), 5,
    106–117, 113*f*
Cartoons, Victorian, 111
Cartoons—animations, *The Tempest*, 149, 152
Cassell's Shakespeare, 109, 112, 113*f*
Cassio (*Othello*), 103
Casting, cross-gender
    child roles played by actresses, 91, 94–95
    in Elizabethan theater, 26
    student objections to, 204–205
Catcher in the Rye (Salinger), 99
Catherine (*Henry VIII*), 111
Cavanaugh, Sheila, 7, 193–200
Censorship
    bowdlerization, 99, 100, 101
    elementary student self-censorship, 211
Ceres (*The Tempest*), 133, 141
Césaire, Aimé, 104
Cesario (*Twelfth Night*), 42
Chambers edition, 108
*Characterie: An Arte of Short, Swift, and
    Secret Writing* (Bright), 77
*Characteristics of Women, Moral, Poetical,
    Historical* (Jameson), 110
Character, 84
    children's responses to Shakespeare,
        142–143
    Hopewell Shakespeare, 72
    second grade class writing and role play-
        ing, 48

Shakespeare's life and times course, 243,
    247
staging, analysis for, 178
The Tempest (Burdett adaptation), 150
theory of adaptation, 185
The Play's the Thing, 271, 272, 274
Charlotte's Web (White), 162
Chaucer, Geoffrey, 100
Cheaney, J.B., 5, 81–86
Chiasmus, 226
Child characters and actors, 5, 85–96
Children's Macbeth, The (Johnson), 208, 209,
    209, 210, 215–216
Children's Midsummer Night's Dream, The
    (Edzard), 89
Chocolate War, The (Cormier), 99
Chomsky theory of language, 217–218
Chorus (*Henry V*), 282, 283–284
Chorus (*Romeo and Juliet*), 291–292
Christ Church Cathedral, 115
Chronicles of Narnia, The (Lewis), 163
Chute, Marchette, 6, 130, 138, 139, 140, 183,
    185, 187 n.6, 188 n.10, 208,
    209–210, 211
Cinderella elements in *Moss Gown*, 262, 263
Cinthio, Giraldi, 257
Clarke, Charles, 109, 113
Clarke, Henry Savile, 112
Clarke, Mary Cowden, 109, 110, 113, 116
Claudio (*Much Ado About Nothing*), 51
Claybourne, 241, 243
Cleopatra, 104
Clothing—costume, 74
Coined by Shakespeare, 243
Cold Iron (Sophie Masson), 71–72
Collaborations, Shakespeare's, 246
Collaborative aspects of playwriting, 81–86
Collector, The, 58
College-level teaching
    film, conceptual approach to use of,
        279–287
    at Harvard, 171–180
    performance games ("The Play's the
        Thing"), 270–278
    Nanny School course approach, 227–228
    Shakespeare's life and times, 239–250
    teaching performance to teachers,
        289–297
    training high school teachers, 252–259
Comedies, 27
Comedy, traditional classifications, 281

Comedy of Errors, The, 40, 41, 47

Comic strip, *Bravo, Mr. William Shakespeare*, 29–38, 30*f*, 34*f*, 35*f*, 36f, 37*f*

Community standards, 99

Company of Boys, 242, 243

Composition of plays, 5

Concept productions, 323–322

Condensation/abridgement, 99
   adaptation process, 65–66
   censorship and bowdlerization, 98–107
   decision making, 129–130
   politics of adaptation, 186–187 n.2
   The Tempest adaptations, 139, 142

Conroy, Tiffany A., 239–251

Cooper, Alice, 107

Cooper, Susan, 8, 89, 239–250

Copy editors, foibles of, 79

Cordelia (*King Lear*), 8, 43, 110, 260–261, 262, 266

Cormier, Robert, 99

Cosby Show, 261

Countess of Lincoln's Nursery, The, 256

Coursen, Herbert, 282

Coville, Bruce, 4, 5, 6, 56–66, 126–127, 130, 138, 140, 142, 147–152, 194, 216 n. 2, 203, 225

Covington, Dennis, 6, 153–160

Cowden Clarke, Mary, 109, 110, 113, 116

Crashawe, William, 90

Critics
   on Caliban, 155
   Harry Potter stories, 163
   Oval editions reception, 135–136

Cukor, George, 173–174, 175

Cultural assumptions, race and ethnicity in *Tales from Shakespeare*, 98–106

Cumulative tales, 39–43

Cundell, Henry, 108

Cymbeline, 60, 109

Daisy Chain, The (Yonge), 109

Dance
   ballets, 194, 197, 199 n.4
   second grade class, 49
   Shakespeare Dance Trilogy, 200

Danes, Claire, 177

Davidson, Rebecca Piatt, 5, 39–43

Decameron (Boccaccio), 257

Deller, Alfred, 67, 71

DeLuca, Maria, 96

Dench, Judi, 31

Desdemona (*Othello*), 102, 110, 115, 257, 260

Design for theater as play, 235–236

Devil's Revenge, The, 246

DeVito, Danny, 261

DeWitt, Pat, 208

DeWitt, Robin, 208

Dickens, Charles (*Nicholas Nickleby*), 260

Dialect, rustic, 76–77

Dictionaries
   Oxford English Dictionary, 253, 254, 259
   Shakespeare's life and times course, 243

Dilation-elaboration, in novelizations, 187 n.2

Discovering Shakespeare's Language, 221

Discovery of the Bermudas, A (Jourdain), 285

District of Columbia public schools, *Shakespeare Steps Out* project, 207–216

Divine Comedy, The, 163

Documentary Life, A, 18

Dodgson, Charles (Lewis Carroll), 5, 106–117, 113*f*

Doran, Greg, 94–95

Dover edition, 120

Dramatic conventions, structuring *Bard of Avon*, 26–27, 123

Dramatic function, child characters in original plays, 89–90

Dramatic learning, 1, 3, 7, 8; *see also* Role playing
   backyard productions, 82–83
   child play, 196
   college class, 176
   early childhood education, 204–205, 222–223, 228 n.1
   elementary students, *Shakespeare Steps Out* project, 208, 211, 212
   experimenting with, 86
   games, "The Play's the Thing," 8, 273–274, 275
   poetry and meter, 225
   teaching performance to teachers, 289–290

Dromio (*Comedy of Errors*), 41

Dr. Seuss, 212–213, 217, 218

Duchess (*Alice* books), 115

Duchess of Malfi, The (Webster), 246

Duke Theseus (*A Midsummer Night's Dream*), 270

Dying Sun, The (Blackwood), 75

Earle, Beatrice, 111
Early, Margaret, 6, 125–126, 195
Early childhood education settings, 7
    English Nanny and Governess School
        approaches, 217–229
    Montessori classroom, 201–205
    Reggio Emilia model of, 193–200
Ebner, Regine, 7, 201–206
Edgar (*King Lear*), 8
Editions
    First Folio, 18, 172, 270
    representations of theater in, 120
Editors, 79
Edward (*Richard III*), 167
Edzard, Christine, 89
Egan, Brett, 176
Elementary education settings
    Hamlet School, 44–55, 44*f*, 46*f*, 47*f*, 48*f*,
        49*f*
    Shakespeare Steps Out project, 207–216
    supernatural elements, 129–137
Elizabeth I, Queen
    early childhood education, 202, 205
    Shakespeare's life and times course, 248,
        249
    The Play's the Thing, 271
    Williams' device, 131
Elizabeth I (Somerset), 241
Elizabeth of York, 168
Elizabethan culture, *see* Shakespeare's life
        and times; Theater world of
        Shakespeare
Elizabethan speech, 78–79
Eliot, T. S. (*Four Quartets*), 9
Elliott, Madeleine, 110
Ellis, Sarah Stickney, 109
Emblem literature, 225
Emilia (*Othello*), 103
English Nanny and Governess School, 7,
        217–229
English school story, 162–163
Episodic structure, *Lizard*, 154
Erasmus, instruction method of, 269–270,
        274
Ethics of adaptation, new, 186
Everett, June, 122
Everyman edition, 120
Experimentation, *see* Play and experimentation
Eyre, Richard, 32

fabula, 183, 184, 185, 224
Facets video distributors, 199 n.10

Fairy tales, 196
Fairy Tales and the Uses of Enchantment
        (Bettelheim), 163, 195
Falstaff: Chimes at Midnight (Welles), 92
Family representations, 261
Family Shakespeare, The, 31, 261
Faucit, Helena, 108–109, 114
Ferdinand (*The Tempest*), 139, 140, 142, 144,
        265
Field-Pickering, Janet, 7, 207–216, 221, 225,
        276 n.5
Figurative concepts, 229 n. 13
Figurative language, 226, 255, 259
Film, 1, 2, 4, 8, 9, 239, 279–287
    animated, 149, 152, 197
    "Baby Shakespeare" film, 199–200 n.10
    child actors, 93–94
    conceptual approach to use of
        intertextuality, 284–285
        metatheatricality, 282–284
        textural indeterminacy, 280–282
    early childhood education, 197–198
    Forbidden Planet, The, 173, 175
    Hamlet
        Almereyda, 3, 32
        Branagh, Gibson, Olivier, 175
    Henry V, 83–84, 282, 283–284
        Branagh, 172, 175, 177, 284
        Olivier, 175, 283–284
    high school and college teachers, 279–287
    Macbeth (Kurosawa and Polanski), 173,
        175, 257
    Midsummer Night's Dream, A, 284–285
        Noble, 197
        Reinhardt, 197, 198
    Much Ado About Nothing (Branagh), 173,
        175, 177
    Othello (Parker, Welles, Buchowetzki),
        173, 175
    Prospero's Books (Greenaway), 173,
        175
    Richard III, 282–283, 284
        Loncraine, 170n. 7, 283, 284, 285
        Olivier, 283–284
    Romeo and Juliet, 296
        Cukor, 173, 173–174, 296
        Luhrmann, 3, 32, 173, 175, 177, 281,
            296
        West Side Story, 281
        Zeffirelli, 173, 174, 175, 281, 296
    Shakespeare in Love, 1, 6, 21, 93, 177,
        181, 240, 242, 246

Shakespeare's life and times course, 240, 241, 246, 248
Stratford Festival Shakespeare Collection, 197
Taming of the Shrew, The (Taylor), 197, 282
teaching future high school teachers, 257
Tempest, The, 173, 175, 285
Titus (Taymor), 89, 93, 94, 96. 170 n.7
Twelfth Night, 197
West Side Story, 281
Film allusions, 283, 285
First Folio, The, 18, 172, 270
Fletcher, John, 280
Folger Shakespeare Library, 7
Folger Shakespeare Library *Shakespeare Steps Out* project, 207–216
Folkloric elements, *see also* Magical and supernatural elements
in *Cold Iron* or *Malkin*, 71–72
in *Moss Gown*, 262, 263
Food, 74
Fool (*King Lear*), 51
Fools and clowns, 245
Forbidden Planet, The, 173, 175
Foreman, Michael, 32–33
Formalists, Russian, 183, 184
Fortune's Journey, 57–58
Four Quartets (Eliot), 9
Fowles, John, 58

Game rules
children and, 232, 235
"The Play's the Thing," 272
Games, 8
Shakespeare's life and times course, 242–243
"The Play's the Thing," 270–278
Garber, Marjorie, 174–175, 176
Garfield, Leon, 6, 32, 60 138, 141–142, 147–152, 184
Gender issues, early childhood education, 204–205
Gender representations, 261
Genre-based approach to use of film, 279–287
Genre transformation, 6
Geoffrey of Monmouth, 8, 261
Georgia Renaissance Fair, *Macbeth*, 199 n.7
Georgia Shakespeare Festival, Camp Shakespeare, 197
Gertrude (*Hamlet*), 265

Gertrude and Claudius (Updike), 3
Ghosts, 167, 168; *see also* Magical and supernatural elements
Gibson, Rex, 221
Gilbert, Miriam, 91
Girlhood of Shakespeare's Heroines (Clarke), 110
Girls
Dodgson project, 5, 106–117, 113*f*
protection from offending text, 100–101
roles played by boys, 26
Girl's Own Paper, The, 110
Girl's Shakespeare Project of Charles Dodgson, 108, 111–112, 115–116
Gli Hecatommithi, 257
Globe Theater
Shakespeare's life and times course, 244, 4, 194
ambience, 33–34. 36
Bard of Avon, 25–26, 26*f*
early childhood education, 203
imagining the players, 81
models of, 46, 194
representations of, 6
teaching future high school teachers, 256
The Play's the Thing, 271
William Shakespeare & the Globe, 13–21, 14*f*, 16*f*, 18*f*, 20*f*, 21*f*
Williams's adaptation of *The Tempest*, 144
Globe Theater, new, 122, 123, 250
Gloucester (*King Lear*), 262
Godwin, W., 29, 30
Goneril (*King Lear*), 260
Gonzalo (*The Tempest*), 159
Grant, Ulysses S., 260
Gratiano (*The Merchant of Venice*), 101
Greenaway, Peter, 173, 175
Green Eggs and Ham (Dr. Seuss), 212–213, 218
Gulliver's Travels, 98, 105
Gurr, Andrew, 256
Guthrie, Tyrone, 91

Hal, Prince (*Henry IV*, part 2), 114
"Halfway Down" (Milne), 219–220
Hamlet, 2
All the World's a Stage, 40, 41, 42
Bravo, Mr. William Shakespeare, 36*f*
second grade class, 47
The Skull of Truth, 58
Updike's *Gertrude and Claudius*, 3
Hamlet, 109, 169, 239, 270, 276, 280

adaptation to storybook, selection of story, 60
allusions to in *Mama Day*, 264, 265, 266
Dodgson and, 111
early adaptations, 108
experimenting with, 86
film versions (Branagh, Olivier, Zeffirelli), 173, 175
puppet versions, 195
teaching performance to teachers, 291
Hamlet (Almeryda), 1, 3, 32
Hamlet (Wishbone), 3
Hamlet ballet, 194
Hamlet Public School, Stratford Ontario, 45
"Happiness" (Milne), 218–219
Harrison, G.B., 31
Harry Potter and the Chamber of Secrets, 166
Harry Potter and the Goblet of Fire, 162, 163–164, 168
Harry Potter and the Order of the Phoenix, 169
Harry Potter series, 4, 6, 99, 162–170
Hawaii Homeschool Association Shakespeare Festival, 89
Hawkes, Terence, 90
HBO Animated Tales series, 149, 152
Heirs to Shakespeare: Reinventing the Bard in Young Adult Literature, 127
Helena (*A Midsummer Night's Dream*), 115
Henderson, Monica, 176
Henry III (*King John*), 95
Henry IV, parts 1 and 2, 92, 114
Henry V, 109
  child characters in original plays, 92
  Dodgson and, 111
  films, 83–84
    Branagh, 172, 177, 284
    metatheatricality, 282, 283–284
    Olivier, 283–284
  Shakespeare's life and times course, 241, 247
Henry (VII) Tudor (*Richard III*), 167. 168
Henry VIII, 111
Hermia (*A Midsummer Night's Dream*), 115
Hermione (*The Winter's Tale*), 42, 111, 163
Heroines, 110
High school settings, *see* Secondary education settings
Hippolyta (*A Midsummer Night's Dream*) , 248

Historica Danica, 3, 261
Historical and cultural context, *see* Shakespeare's life and times
Historicism, 224
History of Geoffrey of Monmouth, 3, 261
Hodges, C. Walter, 31
Holinshed, R., 261
Holland, Peter, 89
Homer, 98
Hooks, William, 8, 261–264
Hop on Pop (Dr. Seuss), 218
Howard, Lesley, 173
Howell, Jane, 93
Huckleberry Finn, 98
Hughes, Arthur, 112, 117
Hughes, Thomas, 163
Hull, Agnes, 111
Hundred Languages, 193, 194
Hunt, Peter, 129, 142, 182, 183
Hunter, William, 22, 23
Hussey, Olivia, 173
Huxley, Aldous, 99
Hyperion Theater Company, 171–179

Iago (*Othello*), 103, 135, 184
Iambic pentameter and tetrameter, 212, 225
I Know Why the Caged Bird Sings, 102
Illustrated and picture books, 4–5, 6, 225
  adaptation of text to, 56–66, 57f, 59f, 61f, 62f, 64f
  All the World's a Stage, 39–43, 41f
  Bard of Avon, 29–38, 30f, 34f, 35f, 36f, 37f
  Bravo, Mr. William Shakespeare, 29–38, 30f, 34f, 35f, 36f, 37f
  condensation decisions, 148
  role of illustrator, 130
  Shakespeare Steps Out project, 208, 209, 210, 211
  Shakespeare's Stories (Garfield), 32–33
  supernatural elements, 129–137
  The Tempest, 6, 224; *see also Tempest*, adaptations, comparing
  William Shakespeare & the Globe, 13–21, 14f, 16f, 18f, 20f, 21f
Illustrations
  Moss Gown, 263–264
  Shakespere adaptations, 29–38, 130–136
  Victorian, 111, 113f
  Williams, 29–38
Imogen (*Cymbeline*), 109
Ingpen, Robert, 124–125

Inner-city classrooms, 7, 207–216
Internet Shakespeare, 241, 250, 304
Interpretation of text
   teaching future high school teachers,
      253–255
   The Play's the Thing, 272–273
Intertextuality, 8
   Caliban and Covington's *Lizard*, 153–160
   film examples, 284–285
   Harry Potter series, 162–170
Iris (*The Tempest*), 133, 141
Ironweed, 59
Isaac, Megan Lynn, 6, 120–128

James, John, 241, 243
James I, King, 123, 256
Jameson, Anna, 110, 116
Jannings, Emil, 173
Jessica (*The Merchant of Venice*), 101
Johnson, Meredith, 208, 209, 210, 215–216
Johnson-Haddad, Miranda, 6, 162–170
Jonson, Ben, 18
Jourdain, Sylvester, 285
Judge, Ian, 91, 92
Juliet (*Romeo and Juliet*), 1, 115, 127, 195, 256
   Alice as, 117
   All the World's a Stage, 40
   death scene, 177
   Dodgson's Alice and, 112, 114
Julius Caesar, 109, 239, 260
   backyard production, 82–83
   child characters in original plays, 92
   experimenting with, 86
   imagining the players and theater, 81
   productions, liberties taken with interpre-
      tation, 83
   second grade class, 47
Juno, 133, 140

Kane, John, 91
Karpinski, Toney, 123–124
Kate (*The Taming of the Shrew*), 42
Katherine (*Henry V*), 247
Kelley, Gary, 203
Kemble, Fanny, 111
Kennedy, William, 59
Kent, 43
King, Douglas, 6, 129–137, 227
King Alonso (*The Tempest*), 104, 139, 141,
     148, 149, 150
King John, child actors, 95–96
King Lear, 8, 51, 260–261

   allusions to in *Mama Day*, 264, 265
   children's version, 31
   Dodgson and, 115–116
   early childhood education, 199 n.6
   experimenting with, 86
   Moss Gown, 261–264
   playground performance, 231–238
   second grade class, 47
   Shakespeare: His Work and His World
     (Rosen and Ingpen), 125
   Smiley's *A Thousand Acres*, 3
   sources, 261
   stylistic-thematic link, 42–43
   touring children's version, 7
King Lear (Pollock), 134–135, 136
King of Hearts, 115
King of Shadows (Cooper), 8, 89, 239–250
King's Men, 123
Kitchin, Alexandra, 116
Knowledge bases, *The Play's the Thing*, 272
Kozol, Jonathan, 215
Krausnik, Dennis, 173
Kurosawa, Akira, 173, 175, 257

Lamb, Charles and Mary, 5, 6, 29–30. 31,
     98–106, 107, 108, 183, 187 n.5,
     208, 224
   King Lear adaptation, 261
   Shakespeare Steps Out project, 208
   The Tempest adaptation, 133, 138, 140, 143
Lamb, Mary, 185
Langley, Andrew, 122, 123
Language, 5, 67
   adaptations
     condensation decisions, 129–130
     treatment of poetry, 224
     Shakespeare Stealer, The, 74–80
     storybook process, analysis, 65
     in *The Tempest For Kids* (Burdett),
       132, 133
     theory of, 217–218
   development in children, 7, 217–229
   Dodgson's Girl's Shakespeare Project,
     108, 111–112, 115–116
   early childhood education, 197, 202, 204
   elementary students
     Hamlet School second grade class,
      49, 49f, 52. 53
     Shakespeare Steps Out project, 208,
      209, 210, 211, 212–214, 215. 216
   performance approaches, 176–178
   performance as, 289–290

Shakespeare: His Work and His World
(Rosen and Ingpen), 125
Shakespeare's life and times course, 243
teaching future high school teachers, 253,
254, 258–259
The Tempest adaptations
Beneduce, 140
comparison of, 150–151
The Play's the Thing, 272–273, 275, 276
n. 5
*Under the Greenwood Tree: Shakespeare
for Young People*, 208
Language arts, 3, 7
Lawhorn, Mark, 5, 89–97
Leah (*The Merchant of Venice*), 101
Lear, 51
All the World's a Stage, 42–43
Dodgson and, 115–116
Moss Gown, 262
Leaves of Grass (Whitman), 99
Legal restrictions on children's work, 94
Leontes (*The Winter's Tale*), 51
Lester, Julius, 187 n.7
Levine, Lawrence, 260
Lewis, Amanda, 122
Lewis, C.S., 163
Liddell, Alice, 111
Life of Shakespeare, *see* Shakespeare's life
and times
Lindroth, Mary, 96
Linguistic rules, children's inference of, 228
n.4
Lippincott, Gary A., 59*f*
Literacy, 3
Literary analysis
teaching with film
intertextuality, 284–285
metatheatricality, 282–284
textural indeterminacy, 280–282
teaching future high school teachers,
252–253
Literature
representations of theater, 120–127
teaching approaches, 85
Lizard (Covington), 6, 153–160
Lobel, Anita, 39, 41*f*
Local habitations and names, 3
Logic, dramatic, 2
Loncraine, Richard, 170n. 7, 283, 284, 285,
285
Lord Chamberlain's Men, 83
Lord Chamberlain's Players, 271

Lord of the Revels, 99
Lord of the Rings, The (Tolkien), 163
Lorenzo (*The Merchant of Venice*), 101
Lost Island, The (Masson), 72
Love's Labour's Lost, 5, 239, 270, 276 n.5
child characters, 90, 92
Shakespeare Steps Out project, 209
"Winter's Song," 213
Lucas, George, 283
Lucius (*Julius Caesar*), 92
Lucius (*Titus Andronicus*), 96, 165
Luhrmann, Baz, 1, 2, 3, 32, 173, 177, 281
Luscombe, Christopher, 91, 95

Macbeth, 51–52, 164, 226, 239
adaptation process, 62–63
analysis, 63–64
selection of story, 60
adaptations
Burdett, 51, 52
Chute, 210
Coville, 60, 62–64, 203
Von, 134, 136, 208, 210
Williams, 131
early childhood education, 197, 202,
204–205
elementary students
second grade class, 47, 48, 48*f*
Shakespeare Steps Out project, 208,
209, 210
film versions
Polanski, 173, 175
Throne of Blood (Kurosawa), 173,
175, 279, 257
puppet versions, 195
rap version of sleepwalking scene, 276 n.
6
Rosie Backstage, 122
*Shakespeare and Macbeth: The Story
Behind the Play* (Ross), 123–124
Shakespeare: His Work and His World
(Rosen and Ingpen), 125
teaching future high school teachers, 256,
257
witches speeches, 221–222
"Witches Spell, A," 214
Macbeth (Georgia Renaissance Fair), 199 n.7
Macbeth: The Folio Edition (Von), 134, 136,
208, 210
Magical and supernatural elements, 5, 6,
70–71, 227
Cold Iron or *Malkin*, 71–72

Desdemona's handkerchief, 103
ghosts, 167, 168
illustrated books for young children,
129–137
*Best of Shakespeare: Retellings of Ten
Classic Plays* (Nesbit), 129
King Lear (Pollock), 134–135, 136
Macbeth (Von), 134, 136
Othello (Zarate), 134, 135
Oval Projects editions, 134–136
Tales from Shakespeare (Williams),
130–132, 134, 136
Tempest For Kids, The (Burdett),
132–134, 136
in *Lizard*, 157–158
Nerissa's ring, 101–102
Shakespeare's life and times course,
247–248
The Tempest adaptations, *see also Tempest, The*
Beneduce, 140–141
Burdett, 132–134, 136
Williams, 130–132, 134, 136
Maillet, Gregory, 8, 269–278
Malaguzzi, Loris, 193
Malkin (Masson), 71–72
Malory, Richard (character), 85
Malvolio, (*Twelfth Night*), 40
Malvolio's Revenge (project), 72
Mamillius (*The Winter's Tale*), 5, 94–95
Mama Day (Naylor), 261, 262, 264–267
Map of London, 256
Mapping stage, 48
Marchitello, Howard, 6–7, 180–189, 224
Marcus (*Titus Andronicus*), 165
Martin, Helena Faucit, 110–111, 114
Massey, Daniel, 91
Masson, Sophie, 5, 67–73
Mathur, Amy, 6, 147–152, 224
Mazursky, Paul, 173, 175
McGuire, Joshua, 95
McManus, Caroline, 8, 260–268
Meaning
social constructions, 186
structural patterns to embody, 220–221
The Play's the Thing, 272–273, 276 n. 5
Measure for Measure, textual indeterminacy,
281
Merchant of Venice, The, 108, 111
Mercutio (*Romeo and Juliet*), 126, 127, 295
Merriam-Webster *Coined by Shakespeare
dictionary*, 243

Merry Wives of Windsor, The, 92
Metacinematic vocabulary, 283, 284
Metadramatic language, 284
Metatheatricality, 8, 282–284
Meter, 225
early childhood education, 221
elementary education, 212–214
The Play's the Thing, 273
Middle grade level novel, 5
Middle school level books, recent bowdlerizations, 261
Midsummer Night's Dream, A, 3, 8, 111, 112,
174, 227, 270
adaptations
Burdett, 47, 48–51
Coville and Nolan, 60, 61
Williams, 37, 130–132
adaptation process, selection of story, 60
book adaptations based on
Cold Iron or *Malkin*, 71–72
King of Shadows, 89
Noble, 197
Reinhardt, 197, 198
books featuring
All the World's a Stage, 194
Bravo, Mr. William Shakespeare, 37f
*Shakespeare: His Work and His
World*, 125
early childhood education, 201, 202,
203
elementary education, second grade class,
47, 49, 49f
film versions
Adrian Noble, 197
*Children's Midsummer Night's Dream,
The*, 89
intertextuality, 284–285
Reinhardt, 197
Hyperion Theater Company production,
171–172, 176, 178–179
Shakespeare's life and times course,
239–250
teaching future high school teachers,
257–258
Miles, Bernard, 6, 138, 140, 141
Miller, Gordon, 91
Miller, Naomi J., 1–9, 138
"Miller's Tale, The" (Chaucer), 100
Milne, A. A., 217, 218–220
Mimesis, 220, 224, 225, 270
Miranda (*The Tempest*), 110, 158
Burdett's, 132, 133.

comparison of adaptations, 139, 140, 141, 142

Williams's, 132

Mnemonic strategy, narrative as, 218

Models, Globe Theater, 194

Modes of representation, 225

Montague, 1, 2

Montaigne, 285

Montessori classroom, 7, 201–205

Morley, J., 241, 243

Moshinsky, Elijah, 91

Moss Gown (William Hooks), 8, 261–264

Mother Goose's Melody, 108

Moth (*Love's Labours Lost*), 5, 90–92, 92, 95

Mouthful of Air (Burgess), 241, 243

Movement
    meter, teaching, 212
    teaching performance to teachers, 294–295, 286

Mr. William Shakespeare's Plays, 37, 186

Much Ado About Nothing, 51
    Bravo, Mr. William Shakespeare, 35f
    experimenting with, 86
    Hyperion production, 176
    second grade class, 47

Much Ado About Nothing (Branagh), 173, 177

Mulready, William, 29–30

Multiple productions of film, 282

Music and songs, 276 n.5
    Mother Goose's Melody, 108
    second grade class, 49
    Shakespeare's life and times course, 246
    Shakespeare's Songs and Consort Music, 67
    The Tempest adaptation
        Beneduce, 140
        Lizard, 156
    "Winter's Song," 213, 214, 276 n.5

Musicals, Loves Labour's Lost, 239

My Brother Will (project), 72

Names, 1–2, 3

Name-voice synergy, 2

Narnia Chronicles, The, 67

Narrative
    adaptations, treatment of poetry, 224
    condensation decisions, 129–130
    early childhood education, 218, 221, 228 n.1
    genre transformation, 6

instinctive aspects of language acquisition, 218
    versus poetics, 227
    plot-driven, 224
    reconstruction of, 228 n.1
    second grade class, 47–48
    The Tempest adaptations, comparison of, 138–146

Naylor, Gloria (*Mama Day*), 8, 261, 262, 264–267

Nerissa (*The Merchant of Venice*), 101

Nesbit, E., 6, 58, 60, 129, 138, 139–140, 142, 143, 180, 182–183, 186 n.1, 187 n.4, 224

Nested phases, 226

New American Shakespeare Company, 195

New Criticism, *see* Literary analysis

New Fogler Library edition, 120

New Globe, The, 122, 123, 250

New Globe Web site, 241, 250

New Historicism, 240

Nicholas Nickleby (Dickens), 260

Noble, Adrian, 197

Nokes, David, 136

Nolan, Dennis, 6, 61f, 62f, 126–127

Norman, Marc, 1

Novelization, politics of adaptation, 186–187 n.2

Novels, 4
    nineteenth century, 109
    young adult, 5
    A Thousand Acres (Smiley), 3
    adaptation of text to, 56–66, 57f, 59f, 61f, 62f, 64f
    Cold Iron or *Malkin*, 71–72
    Fortune's Journey (Coville), 57
    Gertrude and Claudius (Updike), 3
    The Lost Island (Masson), 72
    The Playmaker (Cheaney), 84–85
    Sea Changes (Coville and Miller), xiv
    The Shakespeare Stealer, Shakespeare's Scribe (Blackwood), 5, 74–80
    The Skull of Truth (Coville), 58

Nunn, Trevor, 197

Nutcracker ballet, 194, 199 n.4

Oberon (*A Midsummer Night's Dream*), 197
    Hyperion production, 178–179
    second grade class interpretations, 49, 49f, 50, 50f
    Williams' adaptation, 131

O'Brien, David, 91
Odyssey, 98
"Of the Cannibals" (Montaigne), 285
Olivier, Lawrence, 83, 173, 283–284
Olson, Kristen L., 7, 217–230
On Some of Shakespeare's Female Characters (Martin), 110
Opera, 194, 197
Ophelia, 40, 112, 114, 117, 265
Oral presentations, early childhood education, 205
Order of the Garter, 169
Orsino (*Twelfth Night*), 42
Orwell, George, 105
Orwell: The Lost Writings, 105
Othello, 5, 102–103, 104
Othello, 5, 224, 260, 279, 280
  adaptations
    Lamb treatment of, 102–103, 104
    Lester, 185, 187 n.7
    theory of adaptation, 183, 184
    Zarate illustrated book, 134, 135, 208–209, 208, 210
  allusions to in *Mama Day*, 264, 265
  film versions, 173, 175
  source of, 257
Othello: A Novel (Lester), 185, 187 n.7
Othello: The Illustrated Edition (Zarate), 134, 135, 208–209, 208, 210
Oval Projects editions, 134–136
Ovid, 285
Ownership of plays, 82
Oxford Companion to Children's Literature, 31
Oxford English Dictionary, 253, 254, 259
Oxford School Shakespeare, 120

Packer, Tina, 173
Paintings, Victorian, 117
Palmer, Henrietta Lee, 110
Paradise Lost, 163
Paraphrasing text, *see* Text, paraphrasing
Paris (*Romeo and Juliet*), 126, 195
Parker, Oliver, 175
Paton, Joseph Noel, 112
Patriarchal figures, 115
Pattern, language development in children, 217–229
Patterson, Tom, 52–53, 226
Pedagogy, 3
Perantoni, Cynthia, 6, 153–161
Perdita (*The Winter's Tale*), 95, 110

Performance/dramatic enactments/recitations, *see* Dramatic learning
Performance pedagogy, 4, 8–9, 289–297
Performances, attending
  adaptation, personal preparation process, 63
  elementary students
    children's responses to, 142–143
    Hamlet School second grade class, 46–47, 50
  early childhood education, 195, 199 n.2
Performances, staging, *see* Productions and staging
Performance squares, "The Play's the Thing," 273–274, 275
Period, concept productions, 232
Period fiction, 4
Picture books, *see* Illustrated and picture books
Pinker, Steven, 218
Pitman, I.R., 108
Place/locale, setting of concept play, 232–233
Plague, 244
Play and experimentation, 86; *see also* Dramatic learning
  Hyperion Theater at Harvard, 171–179
  The Tempest adaptations, 144–145
  performance approaches, *King Lear*, 231–238
  performance games ("The Play's the Thing"), 270–278
Playground production, enactments, 4, 231–238
"Playing with the Bard," 138
Playmakers, 82
Playmaker, The (Cheaney), 84–86, 85*f*
Playscript, genre transformation, 6
"Play's the Thing, The," 8, 270–278
Plot/story/action, 2
  adaptation
    analysis of action, 64
    condensation decisions, 129–130
    theory of, 180–181, 182, 183–184, 185
  in *Bard of Avon*, 26–27
  cultural prestige of plot, 187–188 n.8
  early childhood education, 203, 224
  poetry as separable from, 188 n.10, 227
  plot-driven narrative, 224
  sources and versions
    King Lear adaptation, 261
    teaching future high school teachers, 256–257, 259

staging, 177–178
teaching performance to teachers, 292–296
The Tempest adaptations, comparison of, 148–150, 152
"The Play's the Thing," 272, 274
Plural formation, 228 n.4
Poetics
    adaptation process, 182
    versus narrative, 227
Poetry
    "Baby Shakespeare" film, 199–200 n.10
    Chute on, 188 n.10
    enactment, 225–226
    English Nanny and Governess School approaches, 221
    "The Play's the Thing," 273
    Under the Greenwood Tree: Shakespeare for Young People, 208
Polansky, Roman, 173
Political cartoons, Victorian, 111
Politics, Elizabethan, 245–246, 247
Politics of adaptation, 6–7, 180–188, 261
Pollack, Richard, 199 n.3
Pollinger, Gina, 227
Pollock, Ian, 134–135, 136
Polyvocality, staged, 186
Popular culture, 1, 261
Portia (*The Merchant of Venice*), 101, 110
Pre-Raphaelites, 112
Preschool children, 193–200
Primary education, 44–55
Prince Edward (*Richard III*), 167
Prince Hal (*Henry IV* part 2), 114 look H"
Prince Henry (*King John*), 95
Prince of Morocco (*The Merchant of Venice*), 102
Prindle, Alison, 6, 138–146, 224, 225
Productions and staging, 4
    child actors and characters, 85–96
    classroom projects
        Globe Theater models, 194
        mapping, second grade class, 48
    Hyperion Theater Company, 171–179
    liberties taken with interpretation, 83
    playground *King Lear*, 7, 231–238
    in Shakespeare's time, *see* Theater world of Shakespeare
    stage directions, 170 n. 4, 174
Project development, Reggio model, 199 n.2
Prose, early childhood education, 224

Prospero (*The Tempest*), 104, 157, 158
    All the World's a Stage, 40, 42
    Burdett's adaptation, 132, 133
    comparison of adaptations, 139, 140, 141, 142, 149
    Garfield adaptation, 150
    Williams's adaptation, 132
Prospero's Books (Greenaway), 173, 175
Puck (*A Midsummer Night's Dream*), 179, 197, 201, 270
Puck's gift, 5, 67–73
Punch cartoons, 111, 112
Puppet versions of plays, 195
"Pyramus and Thisbe," 83, 284–285

Queen Catherine (*Henry VIII*), 111
Queens Men, The, 246
Quotes/quotations
    Shakespeare: His Work and His World (Rosen and Ingpen), 125
    teaching approaches, 85
    The Tempest adaptation (Beneduce), 140
    William Shakespeare & the Globe, 17–18
    "The Play's the Thing," 272, 273, 274

Race/race relationships, 261
    elementary students, *Shakespeare Steps Out* project, 209, 215
    in *Tales from Shakespeare*, 98–106
Rackin, Donald, 114
Rankin, Baji, 194
Reading for the Plot Reading for the Plot: Design and Intention in Narrative (Brooks), 187–188 n.8
Reading and recitations of parts, 67, 274; *see also* Dramatic learning
Realism, children and, 234–236
Regan (*King Lear*), 260
Reggio Emila model of early childhood education, 7, 193–200
Reinhardt, Max, 197, 198
Renaissance period, *see* Shakespeare's life and times
Renaissance emblem literature, 225
Renaissance Man (DeVito), 261
Renaissance period
    Bard of Avon, 22–28, 23f, 25f, 26f, 27, 28f
    early childhood education, 202, 203–204
    representations of, 6
Renaissance period fiction, 4
Rephrasing, *see* Text, paraphrasing

Representation, modes of, 225
Research paper, early childhood education, 205
Rhetorical figure, 226
Rhyme and meter, *see* Meter
Richard II, 124, 169
Richard III, 5
    child actors, 92–93
    film versions
        intertextuality, 285
        metatheatricality, 282–283, 284, 286
    Harry Potter stories, 163, 167–168
    staging, period and place, 232
Richard III (Loncraine), 170n. 6, 283, 284, 285
Richmond (*Richard III*), 167, 168
Rival theater company, in game, 271, 274
Riverside Shakespeare, The, 241
Robbins, Jerome, 281
Robin (*The Merry Wives of Windsor*), 92
Rocklin, Edward, 8–9, 289–297
Role playing, *see also* Dramatic learning
    experimenting with performance and plot, 86
    second grade class, 48, 49
    "The Play's the Thing," 271
Romeo, 1, 21, 127
    All the World's a Stage, 40
    death scene, 177
Romeo and Juliet, 7, 61*f*
    adaptations
        Burdett, 51–52
        Coville and Nolan, 126–127
        Early, 125–126, 195
        Gonoud opera, 194
        Lamb edition, 261
        Nesbit, 182–183, 187 n.4
        storybook, selection of story, 60
    allusions to in *Mama Day*, 264, 265
    college level courses, teacher training literature, 256
    performance, 291, 292–296
    early childhood education, 195–196
    elementary education, second grade class study, 47, 52
    experimenting with, 86
    film versions
        Cukor, 173–174, 175, 296
        Luhrmann, 1, 3, 32, 173, 175, 177, 281, 296
        Shakespeare in Love, 1, 6, 21, 93, 177, 181, 240, 242, 246

West Side Story, 281
    Zeffirelli, 173, 174, 175, 281, 296
    New American Shakespeare Company, 195
    opera, 194
    puppet versions, 195
    in *Shakespeare: His Work and His World* (Rosen and Ingpen), 125
    text, stage directions, 174
    textual indeterminacy, 281
Root, Amanda, 91
Rosalind (*As You Like It*), 115
Rosen, Michael, 124–125
Rose Theatre, 14
Rosie Backstage (Lewis, Wynne-Jones, and Slavin), 122
Ross, Stewart, 6, 123–124
Rowling, J.K., 4, 6, 99, 162–170
Rowse, A.L., 208
Royal Shakespeare Company, child actors, 3, 91, 92, 94–95, 95
Rules of the game, 232, 235
Ruskin, John, 110
Russian Formalists, 183–184

Salinger, J. D., 99
Sanderson, Ruth, 66, 225
Saturninus (*Titus Andronicus*), 165
Savage Inequalities: Children in America's Schools (Kozol), 215
Sayers, Valerie, 263
Schoenbaum, S., 18
School-Shakespeare, The (Pitman), 108
Scoring options, "The Play's the Thing," 275
Script cards, "The Play's the Thing," 274, 275
Scripts, plays as, 174
Sebastian (*The Tempest*), 42, 139, 140, 141
Secondary education settings, 7–8
    film, conceptual approach to use of, 279–287
    future, teaching Shakespeare to, 252–259
    teaching performance to, 289–297
Secondary texts, 8
Second grade, 44–55, 44*f*, 46*f*, 47*f*, 48*f*, 49*f*
Sedgwick, Fred, 228 n.9
Sellwood, Emily, 108–109
Selous, Henry, 111, 113*f*
Semenza, Gregory Colón, 8, 279–288
Sesame and Lilies (Ruskin), 110
Seuss, Dr., 218
Shakespeare, lifeline of, 6

*Shakespeare and Macbeth: The Story Behind
    the Play* (Ross), 123–124
Shakespeare and the Globe (Aliki), 241
"Shakespearean Stage, The" (Gurr), 256
Shakespeare Can Be Fun! series (Burdett),
    45, 48, 186
Shakespeare & Company of Lennox, MA,
    173
Shakespeare for Kids series (Burdett), 5; *see
    also specific plays*
*Shakespeare for Kids: His Life and Times, 21
    Activities* (Aagesen and
    Bloomberg), 241, 243, 244, 245,
    246, 248, 249
Shakespeare: His Work and His World (Rosen
    and Ingpen), 124–125
Shakespeare in Love, 1, 6, 21, 93, 177, 181,
    240, 242, 246
Shakespeare Institute, 89
Shakespeare's Garden of Girls (Elliott), 110
Shakespeare's last will and testament, 46, 46*f*
Shakespeare's life and times, 4, 6
    game contents, "The Play's the Thing," 271
    books about Shakespeare
        *Bard of Avon: The Story of William
            Shakespeare* (Stanley and Ven-
            nema), 22–28, 23*f*, 25*f*, 26*f*, 27,
            28*f*, 124
        Shakespeare: His Work and His World
            (Rosen and Ingpen), 124–125
    books about theater, *see* Theater world of
        Shakespeare
    film, *Shakespeare in Love*, 1, 21, 6, 93,
        177, 181, 240, 242, 246
    teaching
        early childhood education, 202,
            203–204, 205
        future high school teachers, 253, 255
        A Midsummer Night's Dream and
            King of Shadows, 239–250
        second grade class, 46
        syllabus for, 7–8
Shakespeare's Scribe (Blackwood), 5, 77, 78,
    79
Shakespeare's Songs and Consort Music
    (Alfred Deller), 67, 71
Shakespeare's Stories (Garfield), 32
Shakespeare's Stories: Tragedies (Birch),
    208, 209
Shakespeare Stealer, The (Blackwood), 5,
    74–80, 75*f*

Shakespeare Steps Out project, 7, 207–216
    lesson plan, 212–216
    materials, 207–208
    responses of students to, 208–212
Shakespeare's Theater (Morley and James),
    241, 243, 244, 245, 249
Shakespeare's Theatre (Langley), 122, 123
Sharpe, Martha, 109
Sharpe, Molly, 109
Shearer, Norma, 173
Shirreff, Emily, 109
Shorthand, 77–78
Shylock (*The Merchant of Venice*), 5,
    101–102, 104
Signet Classic editions, 120
Sims, Lucius (*Lizard*), 153–160
sjuzet, 183, 184, 185, 224
Skull of Truth, The, 58, 59*f*
Slaughterhouse-Five, 99
Slavin, Bill, 122
Smiley, Jane, 3, 261
Social constructions of meaning, 186
Solanio (*The Merchant of Venice*), 101
Solerio (*The Merchant of Venice*), 101
Somers, Sir George, 104
Somerset, Anne, 241
*Something Rich and Strange: A Treasury of
            Shakespeare's Verse* (Pollinger),
    227
Sonnets, 224, 241
    early childhood education, 221, 222–223
    Shakespeare's life and times course, 248
Sound play
    early childhood education, 221
    rhythm and meter, 212–214
    "The Play's the Thing," 272
Sources
    Shakespeare's manipulation of, 2
    Shakespeare, modern writers' use of, 3
    teaching future high school teachers,
        256–257
Speech, Elizabethan, 78–79
Speedie, Sam, 175–176
Staged polyvocality, 186
Staging, *see* Productions and staging; Theater
            world of Shakespeare
Stanley, Diane, 4, 6, 22–28, 124, 241, 243
Star Wars (Lucas), 163, 283, 285
Stephano (*The Tempest*), 139, 140
Stevenson, Robert Louis, 217, 220
Stoppard, Tom, 1

Stories from Shakespeare (Chute), 130, 138, 183, 187 n.6, 208, 208, 209–210, 211
Story, *see* Plot/story/action
Storybook format, 5
Story cards, early childhood education, 203
Storytelling, 58–60
Stratford, Ontario *Shakespeare for Kids*, 5
Stratford Festival Shakespeare Collection, 197
Stratford Gallery: or the Shakespeare Sisterhood, The (Palmer), 110
Streatfield, Noel, 163
Structure
    language development in children, 217–229
    Lizard, 154
    Macbeth, analysis for adaptation to storybook, 64
    poetry, 226
    The Tempest adaptations, comparison of, 148–150, 152
Stylistic-thematic links, cumulative narration, 42–43
Subjunctive habit of thought, 234
Subplots, *The Tempest*, 149, 150
Supernatural elements, *see* Magical and supernatural elements
Sutton, Nina, 199 n.4
Swift, Jonathan, 105
"Swing, The" (Stevenson), 220
Sword fighting, 196, 245, 295
Sycorax (*The Tempest*), 104, 159
Sylvie and Bruno (Dodgson), 107–108

Tales from Shakespeare (Williams), 130–132, 134, 136, 216 n. 2
Tales from Shakespeare Designed for the Use of Young Persons (Lamb), 5, 29–30, 31, 107, 108, 183, 187 n.5, 224
    elementary students, *Shakespeare Steps Out* project, 208
    race and ethnicity in, 98–106
        Caliban, 104
        Othello, 102–103, 104
        Shylock, 101–102, 104
Taming of the Shrew, The, 2
    adaptation to storybook, selection of story, 60
    child characters in original plays, 92

productions, liberties taken with interpretation, 83
    puppet versions, 195
    second grade class, 47
Taming of the Shrew, The (Taylor), 197, 282
Tamora, 169
Tate, Nahum, 8, 261, 262
Tattercoats, 71
Tauté, Anne, 134
Taylor, Sam, 197, 282
Taymor, Julie, 89, 93, 94, 96
Teacher training, 8
    literature, 252–259
        adaptations for children, 257–258
        film, 257
        historical and cultural context, 253, 255
        interpretations of plays, 253–255
        interpretation worksheet, 258–259
        language, 253, 254
        literary analysis as prerequisite, 252–253
        plot—story sources and versions, 256–257
        theater, 256
    performance, 289–297
Teaching, *see also* Early childhood education settings; Elementary education settings; Secondary education settings
    college-level, *see* College-level teaching
    English Nanny and Governess School approach, 217–229
    experimenting with performance and interpretation, 86
    Shakespeare's life and times course, 239–250
Tempest, The, 56, 104, 176, 224, 276 n.5
    adaptation process, 6
        authenticity and creativity, balancing, 147–152
        condensation, 65
        illustration, 66
        selection of story, 60
    adaptations, comparing
        Beneduce, 140–141, 147–152
        Burdett, 132–134, 136, 138, 139, 143–144, 147–152
        Chute, 130, 138, 139, 140
        Coville, 138, 140, 142, 147–152
        Garfield, 138, 141–142, 147–152

Mazursky, 173
Miles, 138, 140, 141
Nesbit, 138, 139–140, 143
Williams, 132–134, 136, 138, 139,
    144
allusions to in *Mama Day*, 264, 265–266
Caliban and Covington's *Lizard*, 153–160
Dodgson's Girl's Shakespeare Project,
    107
film versions
    animated, 149, 152, 197
    intertextuality, 285
    Mazursky's, 173, 175
    genre transformation, 6
    picture storybook, 56, 57*f*
Rosie Backstage, 122
second grade class, 47
Shakespeare: His Work and His World
    (Rosen and Ingpen), 125
Shakespeare's life and times, course
    materials, 241
source of play, 104
Tempest For Kids, The (Burdett), 132–134,
    136, 138, 139, 143–144, 147–152
Tempête, Le , 104
Tenniel, John, 112
Ten Things I Hate About You, 2
Terry, Ellen, 111–112
Text
    interpretation, *see* Interpretation of text
    paraphrasing
        gameplay, "The Play's the Thing,"
            273, 275
        Hamlet School second grade class,
            49–50
    staging, analysis for, 177–178
    transformation of
        censorship, bowdlerization, expurga-
            tion, 99, 100, 101
        theory of adaptation, 180–188
Text editions, representations of theater in,
    120
Textual indeterminacy, 8, 280–282
Theater productions, *see* Performances,
    attending; Productions and staging
Theater world of Shakespeare, 82, 99, 122
    in game, "The Play's the Thing," 271
    novels and illustrated books representing,
        120–127; *see also specific books*
    *Bard of Avon: The Story of William
        Shakespeare*, 124

Playmaker, The, 84–86, 85*f*
Romeo and Juliet (Coville), 126–127
Romeo and Juliet (Early), 125–126
Rosie Backstage, 122
*Shakespeare and Macbeth: The Story
    Behind the Play*, 123–124
*Shakespeare: His Work and His
    World*, 124–125
Shakespeare Stealer, The, 74–80
Shakespeare's Theatre, 122, 123
William Shakespeare and the Globe,
    122–123
Shakespeare's life and times course, 243,
    244, 246, 247, 248
teaching future high school teachers, 256
Theme, stylistic-thematic link in cumulative
    narration, 42–43
Theory of adaptation, 6–7, 180–188, 224
Theory of language, 217–218
"The Play's the Thing" (Aristoplay),
    270–278
Theseus (*A Midsummer Night's Dream*), 3,
    83, 270
Thidwick, the Big-Hearted Moose (Dr.
    Seuss), 218
Thousand Acres, A (Smiley), 3, 261
Thribbling, 247
Throne of Blood (Kurosawa), 173, 175,
    257
Through the Looking Glass (Dodgson), 114,
    117
Titania (*A Midsummer Night's Dream*), 111,
    131, 197, 201
Titus Andronicus
    Harry Potter stories, 163, 165–166, 168,
        169
    Taymor's *Titus*, 89, 93, 94, 96, 170n. 5
Toby (*Twelfth Night*), 196
Tolkien, J.R.R., 163, 176
Tom Brown's Schooldays, 163
Tom (*King Lear*), 134–135, 199 n.6
Treays, 241, 243
Trinculo (*The Tempest*), 104, 139, 141–142
Troilus and Cressida, 232
Twain, Mark, 99
Twelfth Night, 56, 116
    adaptation to storybook, selection of
        story, 60
    All the World's a Stage, 42
    early childhood education, 196
    film versions, 197

Oval edition cancelled, 137 n. 4
picture storybook, 56
second grade class, 47
text, stage directions, 174
Twisted Tales of Shakespeare (Armour), 82
"Two Noble Kinsmen, The," 280
Tybalt (*Romeo and Juliet*), 126, 195, 196, 295

Under the Greenwood Tree: Shakespeare for Young People, 208, 209, 210
Updike, John (*Gertrude and Claudius*), 3, 257–258
Urban inner city schools, 7
Useful and Instructive Poetry (Dodgson), 114
Uses of Enchantment, The (Bettelheim), 163, 195
Utah Shakespeare Festival, 52

Vendler, Helen, 221
Vennema, Peter, 6, 124, 241, 243
Victoria, Queen, 110–111
Video games, 1
Videos, 2; *see* also Film
    adaptation, personal preparation process, 63
    animated, 149, 152, 197
    early childhood education, 194
    second grade class, 49
Viola (*Twelfth Night*), 42, 116
Violence
    elementary students, *Shakespeare Steps Out* project, 209, 210, 211
    Romeo and Juliet
        in illustrated books, 126–127
        and preschool children, 195, 196, 197
    The Tempest adaptation, 140
Visuality, 225
Vogel, Scott, 89
Voice, 2, 3
Von (artist), 134, 136, 208, 210
Vonnegut, Kurt, 99

Wanamaker, Sam, 13, 14, 122, 123, 250
Web sites, 1, 241, 250, 304
Webster, John, 93, 94, 246
Welles, Orson, 92, 173, 175
Wells, Dr. Stanley, 32
West Side Story, 281
White, E. B. (*Charlotte's Web*), 162

Whiting, Leonard, 173
Whitman, Walt, 99, 260
Wilders, John, 91
Williams, Marcia, 4, 6, 29–38, 130–132, 134, 136, 137 n. 2, 138, 139, 144, 186, 216 n. 2
William Shakespeare & the Globe (Aliki), 13–21, 14*f*, 16*f*, 18*f*, 20*f*, 21*f*, 122–123
Wind in the Willows, The, 68
Winnie the Pooh stories, 68
"Winter Song, A," 213, 214, 276 n.5
Winter's Tale, The, 5, 51, 111, 163
    adaptations
        Burdett, 47
        Davidson, 42
    child roles, 94, 95
    second grade class, 47
Wishbone *Hamlet*, 2
Witches, 104, 159, 256
Witches scene
    second grade treatments of, 48
    Williams's *Macbeth*, 131
"Witches Spell, A," 214
Wordplay
    Dodgson and, 115
    early childhood education, 221
    performance approaches, 176–177
    "The Play's the Thing," 276
Words and story, 177–178; *see also* Language
Wordsworth, Elizabeth, 110
World of Shakespeare, The (Claybourne and Treays), 241, 245
"Wrestling Macbeth," 199 n.9
Writing, Hamlet School second grade class, 48–52, 49*f*, 50*f*, 51*f*
Wynne-Jones, Tim, 122

Yonge, Charlotte, 107, 109, 116
Yorick (*Hamlet*), 58
Yorkshire dialect, 76–77
Young adult novels, adaptation of texts to, 5, 56–66, 57*f*, 59*f*, 61*f*, 62*f*, 64*f*; *see also* Novels, young adult
Young Ladies' Reader, The, 109

Zarate, Oscar, 134, 135, 208, 209, 210
Zeffirelli, Franco, 173, 174, 175, 281, 296
Ziegler, Georgianna, 5, 107–119, 113*f*

Printed in the USA/Agawam, MA
November 2, 2015

625491.194